SECURITY, ARMS CONTROL AND DEFENCE RESTRUCTURING IN EAST ASIA

Security, Arms Control and Defence Restructuring in East Asia

Edited by
BJØRN MØLLER
Copenhagen Peace Research Institute (COPRI)

Routledge
Taylor & Francis Group
LONDON AND NEW YORK

First published 1998 by Ashgate Publishing

Reissued 2018 by Routledge
2 Park Square, Milton Park, Abingdon, Oxon OX14 4RN
711 Third Avenue, New York, NY 10017, USA

Routledge is an imprint of the Taylor & Francis Group, an informa business

Copyright © B. Møller 1998

All rights reserved. No part of this book may be reprinted or reproduced or utilised in any form or by any electronic, mechanical, or other means, now known or hereafter invented, including photocopying and recording, or in any information storage or retrieval system, without permission in writing from the publishers.

Notice:
Product or corporate names may be trademarks or registered trademarks, and are used only for identification and explanation without intent to infringe.

Publisher's Note
The publisher has gone to great lengths to ensure the quality of this reprint but points out that some imperfections in the original copies may be apparent.

Disclaimer
The publisher has made every effort to trace copyright holders and welcomes correspondence from those they have been unable to contact.

A Library of Congress record exists under LC control number : 98006525

ISBN 13: 978-1-138-34645-1 (hbk)
ISBN 13: 978-1-138-34648-2 (pbk)
ISBN 13: 978-0-429-43725-0 (ebk)

Contents

	Preface Bjørn Møller	vii
1	Introduction: Defence Restructuring in Asia Bjørn Møller	1
2	Transparency, Confidence-Building and Security in East Asia Owen Greene	37
3	Arms Control and Disarmament in the Post-Cold War World: A View from India Jasjit Singh	57
4	International Cooperation in Regional Security: 'Non-Interference' and ASEAN Arms Modernization Joon Num Mak	77
5	Regional Security and Nuclear Weapons in North-East Asia: A Japanese Perspective Mitsuru Kurosawa	93
6	Resolving the Arms Control Dilemma on the Korean Peninsula Yong-Sup Han	109
7	Defence Conversion and Conservation: China's Ambivalent Military Reform Yitzhak Shichor	137
8	Unification of Divided States in East Asia Bjørn Møller	157
9	Taiwan's Defence Policy: Threat Assessment and Security Strategies Cheng-yi Lin	199

10	Russia's Security Policy in East Asia *Alexander A. Sergounin*	221
11	The US Role in East Asia *Jonathan Dean*	265
	About the Contributors	273
	Recent Books on Asia	275
	Acronyms	283
	Index	285

Preface

BJØRN MØLLER

The present work is the product of a conference held in Beijing in December 1996. This was a joint venture between three organizations: the Global Non-Offensive Defence Network, founded by the present author, funded by the Ford Foundation, and home-based at the Copenhagen Peace Research Institute (COPRI); the United Nations Institute for Disarmament Research (UNIDIR), based in Geneva; and the Chinese People's Association for Peace and Disarmament (CPAPD), based in Beijing and serving as the local host. The editor is grateful to both UNIDIR and CPAPD for their collaboration; to the Ford Foundation for making the conference possible; to the participants in the conference for their contributions to lively and fruitful discussions; and to those among them whose papers are included in the present volume for their additional work.

In addition to the papers presented at the conference, the present volume features two specially commissioned chapters: one on Russia, written by Professor Alexander Sergounin of the University of Nizhny Novgorod, and one on Taiwan, written by Dr. Cheng-yi Lin of the Institute of European and American Studies, Academia Sinica, Taipei. To both these authors the editor is particularly grateful for their collaboration.

Copenhagen, January 1998

1 Introduction: Defence Restructuring in Asia

BJØRN MØLLER

In this introductory chapter, some of the Western misperceptions of Asia will be criticized, followed by a brief survey of security and defence political trends in 'Asia'. This 'super-region' has been subdivided into the regions of North-East, South-East and South Asia, whereas space constraints have precluded an inclusion of both South-West[1] and Central Asia.

'THE WEST' LOOKS AT ASIA

Asia has been the subject of heated debates in 'the West' for several years, both in Western Europe and the United States (where the general understanding of the region is poor) and in Australia, where the understanding is usually much better. Among the disputed issues have been the following:

- Is 'the West' heading for a confrontation with 'the rest', i.e. an 'unholy alliance' between the Confucian and Islamic civilizations, as argued by Samuel Huntington who foretells such a 'clash of civilizations'[2]—or are the two parts of the world merely different, but entirely capable of peaceful, perhaps even amicable, coexistence?
- Does the lack of international organizations in Asia imply that the region is a 'raw' international anarchy, or are there 'functional substitutes' at work—or are international institutions anyhow of negligible importance?[3]
- Are Asian nations fundamentally bellicose, or at least more inclined to use force than the West—perhaps because of their allegedly lesser respect for human lives?
- Should the West be concerned about the apparent arms build-up in (parts of) Asia, and/or about the risks of a proliferation of nuclear and other weapons of mass destruction, or of ballistic missiles—even though the general level of armaments and means of mass destruction remains inferior to that of the West?
- If so, is the appropriate Western response a compensatory build-up, perhaps accompanied be the adoption of 'counter-proliferation' strategies? Or should 'we' rather adopt a 'carrots-and-stick' approach to the problem (if so it is), for instance in the form of arms control initiatives?

While the present author is strongly inclined to dismiss all of the above myths, some of them need to be taken seriously. If policy-makers in Europe and the United States should share merely some of the concerns voiced by independent analysts, this might well produce a political 'response' by the West to which Asian nations would, in their turn, have to react. The ensuing action-reaction chain might be seen as *ex post facto* validating the original threat perceptions which may thus have an unfortunate propensity to become self-fulfilling prophecies. In the following, I shall therefore take a closer look at each of the above myths.

THE WEST AGAINST THE REST?

The only element worth salvaging from the aforementioned 'clash of civilizations' thesis seems to be the notion that civilizations, i.e. cultures (in the widest sense of the term) matter, also for foreign and security policies[4]—a view that contrasts sharply with that of 'Realism', which simplistically regards all nations as driven by the same concern for 'national interest defined in terms of power'. However, not only is Huntington's concept of 'civilization' ill-defined, it is also profoundly xenophobic and eurocentric, especially as far as his prediction of a clash between 'the West and the rest' is concerned:

First of all, the West is far more heterogenous than he gives 'us' credit for, which is also the case for both the Confucian and the Islamic cultures. Just compare Turkey with Sudan, Malaysia or Indonesia; or China with Singapore. Secondly, the similarities between Confucianism and Islam are much less significant than Huntington seems to think. In fact in many respects Islam resembles Christianity and Judaism much more than it does Confucianism. Thirdly, the empirical evidence of any *rapprochement* between the two non-western civilizations is very weak, to put it mildly: a few arms sales from North Korea to Iran or from China to Saudi Arabia, which are easily explicable in other terms—say, as simple responses to Western embargoes. Furthermore, these arms deals differ little from, say, American arms sales to both Islamic and Confucian civilizations, such as the GCC (Gulf Cooperation Council) countries or Taiwan.

Unless the West thus views Asia as, by its very nature, hostile and responds accordingly there is no reason to expect any clash between the two civilizations. Huntington is simply wrong.

A RAW ANARCHY?

There is no disputing the fact that the network of international organizations is far less dense in Asia (and anywhere else, for that matter) than in Europe. However, this does not necessarily make the Asian regional subsystems into 'raw anarchies'.

First of all, there are actually several sub-regional organizations in Asia: in

South-West Asia there is the GCC (Gulf Cooperation Council), albeit unfortunately with neither Iran nor Iraq as members (yet).[5] In South Asia, there is SAARC (South Asian Association for Regional Cooperation), on which more later. In South-East Asia we have ASEAN with its several 'affiliates' or off-shots such as the PMC (Post-Ministerial Conferences) and ARF (ASEAN Regional Forum) as well as a dense network of 'track two' institutions (*vide infra*). The only sub-region without such organizations is North-East Asia, but even from this region several of the countries meet regularly in other settings, *inter alia* under the auspices of the ARF, or bilaterally.

Secondly, several global organizations comprise most or all of the Asian nations. Nearly all of the latter are thus members of the United Nations (with the exception of Taiwan),[6] and a growing number of them are members of the WTO (World Trade Organization). Also a number of international organizations transcend the traditional boundaries between regions: a large part of Asia, namely Russia, thus belongs to the OSCE, among other European institutions; others belong to APEC (Asia Pacific Economic Cooperation);[7] some belong to the GCC; and others to the Commonwealth, etc.

Thirdly, one should be careful not to confuse 'institutions' in the sense of Hedley Bull ('a set of habits and practices shaped towards the realisation of common goals') with international organizations. It is perfectly conceivable that a region may have 'institutions' that provide a degree of order without, or with only few and weak, organizations.[8] There may thus be functional substitutes, perhaps very informal ones, for international organizations.

Neither is Asia thus a complete institutional vacuum, nor is the relative weakness of international organizations necessarily tantamount to anarchy.

ASIAN BELLICOSITY?

The allegations that Asian countries (or even Asians as such) are fundamentally bellicose, and that the absence of international organizations and formal institutions is therefore a cause of concern, seems to be based on a very ahistorical view of the world as well as on xenophobia bordering on racism.

First of all, it is, of course, undeniable that some of the bloodiest wars since 1945 have taken place in Asia, among which the first Indo-Pak war, the Korean War, the Vietnam War(s) and the Iran-Iraq war—in addition to which there have been a number of 'smaller' wars such as those between India and China, India and Pakistan, China and Vietnam, etc. On the other hand, in terms of wars Asia is rather below than above the world average. In a recent study,[9] for instance, the author listed the following numbers of wars between Asian states (excluding those fought against European states, the USA or Israel): three out of ten 'classic invasions': (Vietnam/Kampuchea 1978-89, Iraq/Iran 1980-88, Iraq/Kuwait 1990-91); three out of eight 'postimperial wars' (India/Pakistan 1947-48, Korean 1950-53,

Indonesia/Malaysia 1963-66); three out of twelve 'continuation wars' (Pakistan/India 1965 and 1971, Cambodia 1970-75); three out of nineteen 'civil wars with international elements' (China/Tibet 1950, China/Taiwan 1958, Laos 1959-75), one out of twelve wars about 'maintenance of spheres of influence' (India/Sri Lanka 1983-90), one out of two 'neocolonial wars' (Indonesia/East Timor 1975-83) and five out of 35 instances of 'limited use of force' (Thailand/Cambodia 1953-62, Afghanistan/Pakistan 1961, China/India 1962, Laos/Thailand 1975-88, China/Vietnam 1979). If we look further back into history (just beyond 1945), European wars have generally been much more frequent as well as more destructive. Just remember the Thirty Years War and the two world wars in this century.

Secondly, this relative absence of war in Asia is not due to an absence of possible *casus belli*, as the continent features a wide range of territorial and other potential causes of war. Perhaps analysts should look at the wars that did *not* take place rather than at those that did. Examples might be the recent non-wars between Russia and China, China and Japan, China and Taiwan, Japan and Korea, etc.

Thirdly, countries such as India and China have a centuries-long history of peaceful relations with their neighbours,[10] and a shared tradition of being at the receiving end of invasions and other forms of aggression. Furthermore, some of the intra-Asian wars have exhibited a remarkable degree of self-restraint on the part of the belligerent sides, hence have produced fairly modest numbers of casualties. This has, for example, been the case of those between India and Pakistan (with the notable exception of the first) as well as of those between India and China, and China and Vietnam).

Fourthly, compared with the great powers of the West, those of the East have generally been far less interventionist. They thus have a much better track record of compliance with international law—notwithstanding the fact that this law has largely been written by 'us'. Both the United States and the former Soviet Union have, for instance, been far more interventionist during the Cold War than China or India have ever been.

Generally and historically speaking, Asia is thus much less, and the West much more inclined towards war than either is usually given credit for.

ARMS RACES?

The Western concerns about the (alleged or actual) arms build-up (or even arms race) in Asia also appear exaggerated and based on an application of double standards:

First of all, the general level of armaments in Asia is far below that of Europe and, even more so, the United States (see Table 1).[11] Each American citizen thus spends sixteen times as much as the average Iranian on 'his' military, twenty times as much as the average Chinese, and a staggering 132 times as much as the average

Indian. Even though Samuel Huntington refers to the non-Europeans as 'weapon states',[12] this label is thus much more appropriately applied to the United States or even to the less militarized countries in Europe.

TABLE 1: 'WEAPON STATES'?	World	USA	China	India	Iran
Milex (Bill. 1995 $)	864.5	277.8	63.5	7.8	4.2
GNP (Bill. 1995 $)	30,960.0	7,247.0	2,759.0	326.2	158.2
Population (Mill.)	5,672	263	1,198	937	65
Armed Forces (Mill.)	22.8	1.6	2.9	1.3	0.4
MILEX pc (1995 $)	152	1,056	53	8	65
MILEX/GNP (Percent)	2.8	3.8	2.3	2.4	2.6
AF/1000 population	4.0	6.2	2.4	1.4	6.8

Secondly, while it is true that most European countries have disarmed somewhat since the end of the Cold War, a few have not (Greece and Turkey, for instance) and those that have have done so from a very high level. On the other hand, several Asian countries (e.g. China and Vietnam) have completed very drastic arms build-downs in recent years (*vide infra*) which have gone largely unnoticed in the West.

Thirdly, even though the arms expenditures of several Asian countries (ASEAN, China, Japan, for instance) have risen in absolute terms, they have generally not done so as a percentage of GDP—as one would have expected from an arms race. Moreover, where military expenditures have risen, there are often very good and perfectly 'innocent' explanations for this, such as a replacement of run-down or obsolete equipment or better renumeration for the soldiers. Generally, there is no solid evidence of arms races (*vide infra*), with that between the two Koreas representing the only possible exception.

A caveat is, however, in order. Even though the West should not be concerned about 'excessive' Asian armaments, several Asian states may have good reasons to take a less sanguine view of the armaments of their respective neighbours. Taiwan or the ASEAN states may thus fear China, Pakistan India, etc.—and often for good reasons. Moreover, precisely because the general level of armaments is relatively low in Asia, even a small increase in a single state's defence spending may produce significant changes in the balance of power.[13]

Finally, it should also be kept in mind that military spending poses other problems than those related to risks of war. Several Asian states face daunting development tasks, the shouldering of which is hampered by military spending.[14]

PROLIFERATION RISKS?

The West's concerns about particular arms acquisitions by Asian countries, and the resultant proliferation risks, also seem vastly overblown.

Even though recent arms acquisitions (e.g. aircraft, ballistic missiles, aircraft carriers) will provide several states with enhanced power projection capabilities,[15] these still remain far inferior to those of the West. Only India thus possesses an (embryonic) blue water navy, including some on-board air power, while most other nations will be hard pressed merely to patrol their EEZs (Exclusive Economic Zones) and remain entirely incapable of seaward attack against anybody.[16]

Besides Russia, Asia only contains one declared nuclear power, namely China, as well as two 'threshold states': India and Pakistan, both of which are assumed to be able to cross the nuclear threshold at short notice, and either of which may possess some assembled nuclear weapons (*vide infra*). The remaining (alleged) proliferation risks (North Korea, Iraq, Iran, Japan) appear small and perfectly manageable.

Even though several countries have ballistic missiles in their inventories, the risks commonly associated with these weapons seem exaggerated, unless the country in question possesses nuclear (or possibly biological) weapons—in which case the warheads are the main problem, not the missiles.[17]

None of the states in Asia thus pose any noteworthy threats to the West, even though several may pose threats to their respective neighbours. As the strategic reach of most military postures is rather short, moreover, even the latter dangers are relatively modest.

That the proliferation risk is exaggerated does not, of course, mean that it can safely be ignored. For all its obvious unfairness, the NPT (Non-Proliferation Treaty) probably serves the national interests of most (if not necessarily all) Asian nations, as would any curtailment of a future proliferation of WMD (Weapons of Mass Destruction) and long-range ballistic missiles. Even though anti- or even 'counter-proliferation' may thus be desirable, in principle, the US counterproliferation initiative seems unwise.[18] To envision, as the United States apparently does, to 'seize, disable, or destroy WMD arsenals and their delivery means prior to their use' is tantamount to threatening unprovoked and unilateral attacks against sovereign states that are presumably seeking to develop or acquire certain categories of weapons that the United States has had in its possession since 1945 (in much larger numbers and with superior performance) and which it has shown no particular eagerness to abolish. Such implicit threats will give the envisioned target states compelling incentives to pre-empt an attack. A much preferable approach to anti-proliferation is arms control, which is also (it must, in all fairness, be said) the USA's preferred means.

We have thus seen that the West's view of Asia is flawed and partly based on an application of double standards. On the other hand, having warned against generalizations, it seems necessary to conclude this article with an assessment of (some of) the most significant recent military trends in Asia, subdivided into the following regions: North-East, South-East and South Asia.

NORTH-EAST ASIA

In the following, North-East Asia is defined as comprising Japan, the two Koreas (the DPRK and the ROK) and Mongolia as well as parts of both China and Russia —both of which also belong to other regions. North-East Asia is of particular importance, as it exhibits by far the highest level of militarization, and includes two nuclear powers. It further features a plethora of conflicts, each of which could conceivably lead to war. Finally, the region is characterized by an almost complete absence of regional institutions that might help avert these dangers.[19]

CHINA

China remains something of an enigma to the West, *inter alia* because of the closed nature of Chinese society and the lack of reliable data on military expenditures, arms production, military planning, etc. Interpretations of prevailing trends therefore differ widely, in several respects.

Noting the unreliability of official Chinese military expenditure data, some observers systematically prefer the highest estimates, while others opt for the lowest. The most 'responsible' analysts assume the truth to be somewhere in-between. However, the only thing that can said with any degree of certainty and scholarly rigour is probably that nobody knows—perhaps not even the Chinese authorities themselves. The price structure may simply be so artificial that real military expenditures are incommensurable both with themselves over time and with those of other countries. A rather safe bet may be that China's MILEX are rising (which nobody seems to dispute), yet from an unknown level and at an unknown rate.[20] The Chinese acquisitions of major weapons systems from abroad are known with some certainty from various sources, despite gaps in the reporting to the UN conventional arms transfer register.[21] Acquisition from domestic sources is more uncertain, yet it appears implausible that any major changes would go undetected.

For all its vagueness, the emerging picture is of a China that has abandoned the Maoist 'people's war doctrine'. This doctrine called for, *inter alia*, large numbers of mobilizable troops of a fairly primitive and 'rugged' nature and with rather basic equipment and weaponry. Such were China's perceived needs in the event of a major war (e.g. a world war between socialism and either capitalism or 'social imperialism'), in which it was envisioned to withdraw to the depth of the country and fight a protracted war of resistance.[22] No major power projection capabilities were required for the implementation of such a strategy, and nuclear weapons would mainly serve to deter the enemy from nuclear strikes against the PRC, as well as perhaps to avert a total defeat. Hence also the no-first-use policy which was probably more than a mere propaganda ploy, as it would seem to reflect China's actual strategy.[23]

The abandonment (or major revision) of this people's war doctrine may also explain the fact that China in the 1980s undertook a large-scale demobilization of more than a million troops and embarked on a programme of conversion of large parts of its arms industry.[24] What has replaced this doctrine, however, remains rather obscure. A new term has been brought forward, i.e. 'active defence' or 'people's war under modern conditions'.[25] Furthermore, elements of the new doctrine may safely be deduced from developments in Chinese posture, e.g. the intention to patrol an extended maritime perimeter. For further details, readers are referred to the paper by Yizthak Shichor.

The underlying political intentions are even harder to fathom as the facts lend themselves to different interpretations:

Leaving aside as implausible the hypothesis that China should be seeking superpower status, many observers believe that China is aiming for a future role as a regional hegemonic power. This would explain its quest for the acquisition of power projection capabilities such as aircraft carriers, long-range aircraft and ballistic missiles. It would also explain the establishment of ties with Myanmar, that could either be directed against India or the rest of ASEAN states, or both.[26] Not only if this is true, but also if it is believed to be so by Tokyo, such a strategy for regional dominance seems predestined to pit China against Japan as the most likely contending candidate for this role.[27]

Others explain the perceived need for such capabilities with reference to China's (significant, but rather modest) territorial claims on other countries: various ASEAN states, India, Russia, etc. Even though Beijing has recently put most of these claims on the back-burner, it may well revive them once it has achieved the strength to get its will. The most important among these is undoubtedly the dispute over the Spratly and Paracel islands in the South China Sea.[28]

Still others regard Chinese arms acquisitions as rather trivial, hence in need of no explanation in doctrinal terms. China may simply be engaged in a 'business as usual' modernization of its armed forces which the impressive economic growth of recent years has made possible. Also, the perception of the Gulf War as a defeat for Soviet-type weaponry (very similar, indeed superior to, what China has in its inventory) may have created a sense of greater urgency about this modernization.[29] No country that can afford 'state of the art' military equipment will be content with the second-best.

One might even take the latter explanation a step further and explain the build-up as strictly defensive. Ever since 1949 China may have felt a 'security deficit' vis-à-vis both Russia, Japan and the United States, *inter alia* because of its history, exposed borders and technological and economic inferiority. While it may thus all along have wanted to, Beijing may well feel that the moment has now finally come to correct this deficit. However, it may not necessarily want to proceed beyond such defensive 'sufficiency' and acquire the ability to threaten others.[30]

Part of the above uncertainty stems from the numerous unanswered questions about non-military matters that impact on the assessment of observed developments in the military domain:

- Will China gradually disintegrate[31] or will it remain unified, perhaps even proceed with the 'reunification' (if so it is) of China? One might regard the return of Hongkong as merely a first instalment, to be followed shortly by Macao. Next may come Taiwan, either peacefully or by means of force. Perhaps China may even harbour further ambitions of incorporating other (parts of) states which have a majority (or merely significant) Chinese population.[32] This is elaborated upon in the papers by the present author and by Cheng-yi Lin in the present volume.
- What will be China's geopolitical orientation? Will it see itself as primarily an Asian power (with or without hegemonic aspirations), or will it give higher priority to a global position? Will the latter lead to a realignment with Russia against a western, especially American, global hegemony? or even with Japan in an anti-western, pan-Asian joint venture? or with other dissatisfied states such as Iran?[33]
- Will the present economic boom continue or will the 'bubble' eventually burst?[34] If it the latter should happen, what will be the political and military implications thereof?
- Will China's economic modernization and liberalization eventually lead to greater respect for human rights and political liberalization, perhaps even to a Western-style democracy? Some argue, for instance, that capitalism and democracy are two sides of the same coin, hence that the apparent introduction of the former will inevitably lead to an introduction of the latter. Others view the matter more instrumentally, in the sense that the West may apply a 'human rights (or even democratic) conditionality' to our export of much desired high technologies, hence that Beijing may be forced to reform in order to succeed with modernization.[35] Still others acknowledge the modernization-reform linkage, but fear that the PLA might seek to avert this danger by wresting the reigns of power from the party?[36]

There are thus many uncertainties surrounding China. Regardless of who is right, however, the fact remains that all of China's neighbours are watching developments with some concern. Indeed, they are forced to respond to these developments in 'the Middle Kingdom', their reluctance to speak openly about any 'Chinese threat' notwithstanding. Hence the widespread desire, in ASEAN and elsewhere, to 'engage' (as opposed to contain) China,[37] implying both expanded economic links and attempts to somehow 'lure' China to the negotiation table. This regional desire is mirrored by a global quest for engagement and involvement that should, among other things, help control China in its alleged role as 'rogue' supplier of armaments to international outcasts.[38] Even though actual multilateral negotiations have yet to take place, what one might view as 'pre-negotiations' have taken place in the form of informal consultations under the auspices of ARF (*vide supra*), just as there have, of course, been bilateral negotiations with nearly all of China's neighbours as well as with the United States.

JAPAN

Even though it is a much more open society, with a free press etc., interpretations of Japan diverge almost as widely as they do concerning China, albeit not so much with regard to capabilities as to intentions.[39]

There is no disputing the fact that Japan remains a constrained military power, inter alia as a result of the peace constitution and the 'one percent rule'. The former prohibits Japan from fielding armed forces (yet permits self-defence, hence the label SDF: Self-Defence Forces), while the latter is a political consensus limiting military expenditures to one percent of GDP.[40] However, one percent of a huge and, until recently, rapidly rising GDP can buy a country very formidable 'self-defence forces'. Depending on the China estimate, Japan is thus either the third or fourth largest military spender in the world. Furthermore, Japan's unique type of dispersed and diversified arms industry provides the country with very formidable force generation potential. Should a decision to mobilize the nation for war be taken, the government could bring Japan on a war footing faster than most other countries would be able to.[41]

Opinions differ when it comes to the future. Some analysts regard the above constraints as purely externally imposed, hence widely resented by the population of Japan and, as a result, fragile and unlikely to last. According to this interpretation, as soon as the opportunity arises, Japan will re-emerge as what it has secretly been all along, namely an inherently expansionist, aggressive and militaristic state.[42] Others regard the constraints as internalized, hence see Japan as a 'post-militaristic' (or even 'post-military') nation that has grasped the horrors of war, discovered the advantages of low military spending—and which has maintained strong civilian control over the military.[43]

These different basic views are reflected in diverging interpretations of concrete phenomena such as the (very modest) reinterpretations in recent years of the constitution to allow Japan to participate in UN operations. While the former are alarmed by this, viewing it as the first step in the direction of renewed military assertiveness, the latter welcome it as reflecting a laudable cosmopolitan attitude, i.e. as personifying 'the Japan that wants to be liked'.[44] Also, while the 'alarmists' are worried about Japan's stockpiling of plutonium that would make it (technically) unproblematic to cross the nuclear threshold, the optimists point to the fact that Japan adheres faithfully to, and complies perfectly with, the NPT, to which constraints should be added the three non-nuclear principles. The plutonium stockpile, according to this interpretation, is merely a safeguard against a future severance of the sea lines of communications that could result in an energy shortage that could cripple Japan's main strength, i.e. its industry.[45]

Many Japanese further believe that whatever guilt Japan may bear for the Second World War must have been redeemed by now, hence that their country is entitled to an international role commensurate with its economic strength—implying, for instance, a permanent seat on the UN Security Council.[46] Others place greater emphasis on Japan's potential role as a regional hegemon, hence the strong 'Asia first' tendency, which critics see as an attempt at recreating the infamous Greater East Asia Co-Prosperity Sphere of the 1930s.[47]

Both views fit nicely with the repeated US admonitions to Japan that it ought to assume a greater part of the burden of upholding the world order from which it benefits so much, as well as of its own national security—thereby producing a more equitable burden-sharing.[48] The revised 1997 US-Japan defence pact thus envisages Japan assuming an expanded role in support of US operations in East Asia, seemingly including the Taiwan Strait—a plan to which China has not responded favourably at all.[49]

The present author belongs to the non-alarmist camp, and strongly believes in the peaceful Japan, if only because it strains the imagination that Japan should abandon a 'post-military' strategy that has worked so eminently well for it.[50] The problem is, however, that most of Japan's neighbours seem to belong to the other camp who watch Japan's every move with deep suspicion. For a further elaboration, readers are referred to the paper by Mitsuru Kurosawa in the present volume.

THE KOREAN PENINSULA

Both the levels of tension and militarization remain high on the Korean peninsula, i.e. between the DPRK (Democratic People's Republic of Korea, better known as North Korea) and the ROK (Republic of Korea, i.e. South Korea) and its US ally. Even though it has abated significantly after the resolution (if so it is) of the nuclear question, tension remains high and hostilities may flare up at short notice.[51] Even in Korea, however, interpretations differ quite widely:

First of all, estimates of North Korean military strength differ, for the same reasons as was the case for China, only even more so. The extremely closed nature of the DPRK make any estimates extremely unreliable, even with regard to material holdings, especially when qualitative factors are taken into account. There is no doubt that the North is numerically superior to the South, but considerable disagreement on how to factor in Seoul's qualitative and economic edge over Pyongyang.[52]

Secondly, North Korea's intensions are more unfathomable than is often assumed. Nearly all South Korean and most foreign analysts appear to regard North Korea as profoundly aggressive, i.e. bent on launching another war of aggression against the South unless adequately deterred.[53] However, 'revisionists' have pointed to certain anomalies that seem to contradict this interpretation, including significant non-events and a noteworthy absence of certain capabilities that would appear indispensable for a new attack against the South.

First of all, the Kim Il Sung regime did *not* jump through what must have seemed to be 'windows of opportunity', namely those occasions when the ROK's military was preoccupied with *coups d'etat*, hence presumably considerably weakened in terms of defensive strength. Secondly, the DPRK has *not* acquired any significant amphibious capability, as would have been natural for a presumably aggressive country, which has even itself been on the receiving end of amphibious assaults not too long ago (the Inchon landing during the Korean War).[54]

While radical revisionists make an utterly unconvincing case for the basic peacefulness of the regime in the North, or even for its inherent superiority over the South,[55] moderately revisionist interpretations seem to make a lot of sense. They depict North Korea as quite aware of its own economic and political weaknesses, hence basically (albeit reluctantly) defensive. Pyongyang merely seeks to attract the world's attention by occasional military incidents, just as it may have done with its nuclear programme. Indeed, the main purpose of the latter may have been to achieve exactly what it did accomplish: a direct diplomatic channel between Pyongyang and Washington that allows the former to bypass Seoul, a modernization of its energy supplies, and some much needed economic assistance.[56]

Even after these accomplishments (if so they were), however, the DPRK regime seems moribund, if only because of its economic debacle and the insecure power basis of the Kim Jong-il regime.[57] Hence a reunification of the two Koreas is likely to happen sooner or later—and probably sooner rather than later, say within the next decade. It can happen in two different ways: either as a swift absorption of the North by the South, i.e. 'German style', only even more complicated than the unification of the two Germanies (if only because of the legacy of the Korean War that is neither easily forgotten nor forgiven);[58] or through a gradual 'growing together'. The latter might pass through a resumption of the DPRK-ROK dialogue of the early 1990s, and a limited detente to unification, implemented in two stages producing, first, a confederation and then a federal stage.[59] In either case, the military postures and strategies will have to be amended.

Should unification happen swiftly, the unified Korea will emerge as a very formidable military power, not only because of the merger of two large armies, but also because the combined armed forces could now be directed towards the outside. This could easily upset the balance of power in the region, e.g. by leading to a Japanese abrogation of the above-mentioned constraints that would provoke a Chinese response, etc. Should unification, on the other hand, proceed gradually and smoothly, the armed forces would, for obvious reasons, have to cease being poised against the respective other half of the country. A first step might be an entry into force of the nuclear-weapons-free zone treaty of 1992, a second might be CFE-type arms limitations, and a third might be a defensive restructuring of the armed forces in both Koreas.[60]

In either case, arms control and disarmament measures would have the added benefit of releasing resources that would be badly needed for unification.[61] For a further elaboration, readers are referred to the paper by Professor Yong-Sup Han in the present volume.

RUSSIA

Russia remains the 'odd man out' in North-East Asia, that is both part of the region and an external power, and the future role of which remains undecided.[62] On the one hand, its military power is close to (material as well as moral) collapse, as illustrated by the decay of the Pacific Fleet, which is no longer really operational.[63] On the other hand, Russia remains in possession of the region's largest and most technologically sophisticated nuclear arsenal.

Furthermore, Moscow's geopolitical position has been far less affected in East Asia by the dissolution of the USSR than has been the case in Europe, and it remains in control of Asia's largest land-mass. Upon successful completion of its present transition from a moribund planned to a functioning market economy, Russia may therefore well re-establish itself as an Asian great power. It is even conceivable (if unlikely) that Russia may opt for a swing position between 'the West and the rest' by placing greater emphasis on its uniqueness as a Eurasian power with an Asian 'half-identity' *sui generis*. Indeed, the heated 1996/97 debate about NATO enlargement was accompanied by Russian overtures to its Asian neighbours, such as Iran and China, and even today the 'Eurasians' (as opposed to the 'Westernizers') remain a political force to be reckoned with.[64] According to official declarations, Russia's new military (or 'security') doctrine that was announced in May 1997 was also intended to provide 'good cover in the East',[65] whatever this may mean.

In any case, it would be very premature and short-sighted to write off Russia as a major power in North-East Asia. Because of space constraints I shall nevertheless bypass Russia in the present context, referring readers to the paper by Alexander Sergounin.

SOUTH-EAST ASIA

In the following, South-East Asia is defined as comprising the ASEAN member states as well as the rest of Indochina, i.e. the 'old' members of ASEAN (Indonesia, Malaysia, Singapore, the Philippines, Thailand and Brunei) and the new members

(Vietnam as well as Laos and Myanmar whose applications for membership were accepted in 1997) plus Cambodia, the admission of which was postponed, but probably not for long. Both mainland China and Taiwan are counted as peripheral states.[66]

Because of the relative openness in military matters that characterizes most of these countries (with the notable exception of Myanmar), it is possible to get a rather clear and reliable picture of the region's arms acquisitions and military expenditures.[67] This emerging picture is one of quite steeply rising military spending and rather massive arms purchases. Not only would this normally be a cause for alarm. What might appear even more worrisome is the fact that a substantial part of the outlays are for major conventional weapons systems (warships and aircraft) that will provide the recipients with enhanced power projection capabilities, pointing towards a situation where states may pose offensive threats against others.[68] Because transparency does not extend to the intentions underlying this arms build-up, however, it lends itself to different interpretations:[69]

Some might interpret the ASEAN arms build-up as an arms race with China. It might be a defensive response to the above-mentioned Chinese build-up, which is seen as calling for a response because of the geographical proximity and the territorial disputes focusing on the Spratlys (*vide supra*).

Others might see the regional states being entrapped in a traditional arms race with each other, each responding to perceived potential threats created by the arms acquisitions of the others. If Greece and Turkey can arms race with each other within a closely-knit alliance such as NATO, it is surely conceivable that members of a much looser structure such as ASEAN might do the same. Alternatively, one might see it as a special (almost 'virtual') arms race, where it is not so much actual military capabilities that matter as the projection of images of great power status. Large warships, for instance, are not only useful for extending one's maritime perimeter, but also for impressing one's neighbours, even if they are only used for friendly port calls. By implication, if what is happening in South-East Asia is an arms race at all, it may not be a 'serious' one, but one of posturing and make-believe.

Even if one takes the arms build-up seriously, it is possible to interpret most arms purchases as reflecting perfectly 'innocent' amendments of military doctrine. The armed forces were formerly used mainly for counter-insurgency warfare, but most of these insurgencies have been 'put to rest' (one way or the other) over the last decade. As a result, the armed forces may now be reassigned to their 'real' mission, namely national defence.[70] For obvious reasons, this necessitates certain arms acquisitions, the more so as it happens to coincide with new developments in the law of the sea that require states to patrol expanded EEZs.[71] A final, and related, interpretation is that the arms build-up represents nothing but business-as-usual, i.e. that it simply reflects the growing purchasing power produced by an extended period of high economic growth.

Even if the 'innocent' interpretations hold true (as seems likely) there may still be grounds for concern. Even if the original impetus for the build-up may have little or nothing to do with arms racing, states may gradually come to regard their neighbours' growing military strength as a threat that calls for countervailing steps. It is also conceivable that some of the ASEAN states may gradually develop ambitions that go beyond their present one of national defence. The appetite may simply grow with the eating, and states may develop ambitions commensurate with their growing military strength, rather than the other way around.

While the above holds true for the old ASEAN nations, the (planned and probable) newcomers are different—not only from the rest but also from each other.

- The most significant military power among them, Vietnam, has been building down militarily for quite some time, under the *doi moi* strategy. The opportunity for this was created by the disappearence of the most important threats to Vietnamese national security (inter alia the signing of an accord with China), while the need for adjustment was created by the collapse of the socialist bloc that had previously supported the country.[72] There is no reason to expect this to change in the foreseeable future.
- Laos is militarily inferior to all its neighbours and has no realistic chance of changing this. It is simply too poor and unlikely to receive any significant foreign support, even from China.[73]
- Cambodia is only gradually recovering from a decades-long sequence of national disasters: American bombardments as part of the Vietnam War, the Khmer Rouge's genocidal rule of terror, a Vietnamese invasion, followed by a protracted civil war that may not even be quite over yet, the massive United Nations involvement notwithstanding.[74] It thus strains the imagination to envision Cambodia playing any more assertive military role in the near or mid-term future.
- Myanmar's military is almost exclusively directed against its own population, and both the military regime and the armed forces are internationally isolated and deeply demoralized. The only threat emanating from this country may thus be that of a spill-over of general instability (e.g. in the form of refugees) as well as the prospect that the Chinese connection may develop further to make Myanmar a passive accessory to a future Chinese aggression, e.g. against India. Not likely at all, but perhaps not entirely inconceivable.[75]

For nearly all of ASEAN the China factor is of decisive importance for future developments.[76] If China should seek to extend its reach to the Spratlys once again, and/or if it should try to 'teach lessons' to any of the ASEAN states (as to Vietnam in the past), then something would have to be done. Either the nations of South-East Asia might close ranks against China, say by transforming the organization into an actual defence alliance. Or they might invite a countervailing great power into the region, which would most likely be the United States, but which might conceivably also be Japan or India. In either case, this would represent a violation or abrogation of ZOPFAN (the Zone of Prosperity, Freedom and Neutrality, *anno* 1971). Finally, ASEAN might disintegrate under the strains of conflicting pressures, say if one or more states should chose to 'bandwagon' with China rather than balance against it.[77]

Fortunately for the stability and security of the region, it is much more institutionalized than North-East Asia. One might even argue that is has been better at adapting to changing circumstances that have more 'established' organizations such as NATO or the European Union. Not only has ASEAN been expanding to take in new members (first Vietnam, then Laos and Myanmar, Cambodia to come later), thereby removing external threats by embracing them rather than containing them by means of countervailing power. ASEAN is also extending cooperation to new fields.

First of all, a free trade agreement (AFTA) is about to enter into effect, which may promote economic integration between member states. Secondly, cooperation has been extended to the security field with the declaration of a nuclear-weapons-free zone,[78] and with an institutionalization of, first, the ASEAN Postministerial Conferences (PMC) and subsequently the ASEAN Regional Forum (ARF). In both fora, security political matters are discussed in a highly formalized setting, even though the participating states guard their sovereignty by avoiding binding decisions and by refraining from all supranationalism. Nevertheless, most observers agree in viewing especially the ARF as a very significant conflict prevention and management mechanism *sui generis*.[79]

In the fullness of time, these developments may transform South-East Asia into a 'security community', defined as a group of states among the members of which war has ceased to be regarded as an option. Even though this is still not the case, it may well become so in the not so distant future.[80] For an elaboration of all of the above trends, readers are referred to the paper by Joon Num Mak in the present volume and to that by Owen Greene for details on transparency-enhancing measures.

SOUTH ASIA

In the following, South Asia is defined as comprising India, Pakistan, Sri Lanka, Bagladesh, Nepal and Buthan, with Afghanistan, Iran, Myanmar and China counted as 'peripheral states'.[81]

Due not least to its colonial past and the resultant weak state structures and ethnic conflict potential, South Asia has more than its fair share of conflicts. Most of these are intra-state,[82] yet with an in-built propensity to become internationalized.[83] Both such internationalized internal conflicts and the region's genuine international conflicts centre on India. Not only is India by far the largest state in the region, indeed much larger than all the others taken together. It is also located in the centre of the region, bordering with all other states.

The direction of India's security and defence policy remains disputed, notwithstanding the almost complete transparency that characterizes military planning in this the world's largest democracy, where the military remains under firm civilian control.[84]

Some analysts view India as aiming for regional hegemony in the Indian Ocean region,[85] an interpretation that is at least compatible with recent arms programmes. They will provide India with a true blue-water navy as well as with longer striking range by means of missiles and aircraft.[86] Others point to India's exceptionally low level of armaments (*vide supra*). In fact it is one of the world's least militarized countries in terms of military expenditure or men under arms per capita. Also, despite its opposition (for political reasons) to the NPT regime, India has not emerged as a declared nuclear power. At most, it is relying on a strategy of 'recessed deterrence'.[87]

The only country in the region that may provide a counterweight to India is Pakistan. Hence international conflicts tend to revolve around these two countries that seem locked into a perennial conflict, also because of their incompatible notions of nation and statehood: Pakistan's sees itself as 'the India of (all) the Muslims', while India has all along claimed to be a secular state that should, ideally, encompass all areas inhabited by ethnic Indians or even the 'historical India'.[88] The present conflict focuses on Jammu and Kashmir, where the two state/nation conceptions are manifested in a seemingly unending struggle between the Indian authorities and the secessionist movement, supported by Pakistan.

It is entirely conceivable, if not likely, that the present low-intensity armed conflict could escalate into full-scale war—for instance initiated by a desperate Pakistani *fuit en avant*, or by an Indian preemptive attack spurred by the prospects thereof.[89] That such a future war might conceivably go nuclear makes the prospects even more frightening. However, opinions differ about the implications of the possible possession by both countries of nuclear weapons.

Some regard the situation as relatively stable, indeed as stabilized by the nuclear stand-off. India would have little incentive to use nuclear weapons against Pakistan, as it could not possibly be defeated by the latter by conventional means; nor would it have anything to gain from a nuclear first-strike that might provoke a Pakistani retaliatory strike. While Pakistan would also find a first-strike unrewarding, Islamabad might conceivably have an incentive to use nuclear weapons to avert complete defeat in a future conventional war.[90] However, the prospects thereof would undoubtedly tend to limit India's ambitions, so that the overall effect of nuclear deterrence would be to prevent and/or limit the intensity of war without causing any intolerable risk of nuclear war.

Others would disagree with this analysis, pointing to the risks of malfunction and accidental or unauthorized launches of, after all relatively primitive, nuclear weapons. Moreover, whatever may be said in favour of opacity, it hampers nuclear arms control, as it is a highly delicate matter to negotiate constraints on, or reductions of, weapons that neither party to a set of negotiations openly admits to having.[91]

The risk of war is not the only problem caused by the high level of armaments, if so it is. Military spending also detracts seriously from a domestic pool of resources that are badly needed for economic development and for the eradication of poverty.[92]

While there is thus plenty of conflict potential in South Asia, especially between India and Pakistan, it should not be forgotten that both sides have shown some restraint in the past, and that a number of confidence-building measures have been negotiated between the two parties (as well as between India and Pakistan's former ally, China)—even though their implementation leaves something to be desired.[93]

One might also hope that the regional organization, SAARC, might gradually develop into a significant war-inhibiting factor, say if it were to promote intra-regional trade and facilitate cross-border contacts of all sorts, pointing towards increasing interdependence. Unfortunately, however, SAARC's growth potential seems limited, inter alia because of the region's asymmetrical structure. Unless the organization allows itself to be dominated by India, it will not really be in India's national interest to transfer political authority to it, considering that bilateralism provides greater leverage over neighbouring states. On the other hand, a SAARC dominated by India is not particularly appealing to the rest, and especially not to Pakistan.[94]

For a further elaboration on the above problems, readers should proceed to the paper by Jasjit Singh below.

THE 'SIGNIFICANT OTHER': THE UNITED STATES

The United States obviously continues to play an important role in Asia, especially in South-West and North-East Asia.[95] It maintains defence treaties with Japan and South Korea, where it is present in quite sizeable numbers. In addition to this, it maintains a treaty of sorts with Taiwan that entails some rather vague security guarantees. That they were not mere hollow rhetoric was demonstrated during the Taiwan Straits crisis in March 1996, when the United States sought to demonstrate its continuing commitment to its former ally by means of declarations and a naval presence.[96]

There has been talk about a gradual and partial withdrawal, but not much has come out of these plans—perhaps because the USA is concerned about the risk of thereby creating a vacuum.[97] Even though the entire notion of *vacui* is ill-defined and theoretically 'fuzzy', it is quite conceivable that either Japan or China (perhaps even India) might try to fill the vacuum—or that either of the three might fear that one of the others should do so, hence do so pre-emptively.

Seen in this perspective, a certain US presence may serve a stabilizing function, even though this will depend on how it is used.[98] To the extent that it is (seen as) impartial, i.e. as protecting all states against attacks by their neighbours (or others) it will undoubtedly be stabilizing, but if it is seen (as may well be the case today) as biased and partisan, it may, under certain conditions, exacerbate already tense and crisis-prone situations. For an American view, please see the paper by Jonathan Dean below.

Conclusion

There are far too many unresolved questions in the preceding analysis to allow for any firm conclusions. At best, the above has shown that the views on Asia that predominate in the West are questionable, if not necessarily wrong. While the allegations of the 'Asia pessimists' are mostly based on insufficient and inherently ambiguous evidence, especially when it comes to intentions, the optimists are not necessarily right.

In fact, the future may still remain open, in the sense that Asia may develop in either of two directions. Either Asian nations may arm to a point where all of them come to see the rest as threats that had better be neutralized before it is too late, and where their new-found wealth is wasted on arms races that, at the end of the day, benefit nobody, except perhaps the American and European arms industries. Or they may go 'the ASEAN way' of peaceful coexistence in respect for each other's national sovereignty and territorial integrity. If so the general level of armaments may gradually decline, reflecting the fact that states increasingly come to see each other as partners in a mutually beneficial collaboration rather than as rivals and potential enemies.

Notes

1. On South-West Asia, see Møller, Bjørn: 'Resolving the Security Dilemma in the Gulf', *Occasional Papers*, no. 9 (Abu Dhabi, UAE: The Emirates Center for Strategic Studies and Research, 1997).
2. Huntington, Samuel: *The Clash of Civilizations and the Remaking of World Order* (New York: Simon & Schuster, 1996). For a critique see Welch, David A.: 'The "Clash of Civilizations" Thesis as an Argument and as a Phenomenon', *Security Studies*, vol. 6, no. 4 (Summer 1997), pp. 197-216. An earlier, and much less xenophobic version of the 'cultural approach' is Wallerstein, Immanuel: *Geopolitics and Geoculture. Essays on the Changing World-System* (Cambridge: Cambridge University Press, 1992), pp. 139-237.
3. Buzan, Barry & Gerald Segal: 'Rethinking East Asian Security', *Survival*, vol. 36, no. 2 (Summer 1994), pp. 3-21. It was criticized by James L. Richardson, *ibid.*, vol. 37, no. 1 (Spring 1995), pp. 185-186, where the two authors also respond, *ibid.*, pp. 186-187.

4. This is the thesis of Katzenstein, Peter J. (ed.): *The Culture of National Security. Norms and Identity in World Politics* (New York: Columbia University Press, 1996). See also Goldstein, Judith & Robert O. Keohane (eds.): *Ideas and Foreign Policy. Beliefs, Institutional, and Political Change* (Ithaca, NY: Cornell University Press, 1993); Kratochwil, Friedrich: 'Is the Ship of Culture at Sea or Returning?', in Yosef Lapid & idem (eds.): *The Return of Culture and Identity in IR Theory* (Boulder: Lynne Rienner, 1995), pp. 201-221.

5. Graz, Liesl: 'The GCC as Model? Sets and Subsets in the Arab Equation', in Charles Davies (ed.): *After the War: Iran, Iraq and the Arab Gulf* (Chichester: Carden Publications, 1990), pp. 2-24; Faour, Muhammad: *The Arab World After Desert Storm* (Washington, DC: United States Institute for Peace, 1993), pp. 55-97; Awad, Ibrahim: 'The Future of Regional and Subregional Organizations in the Arab World', in Dan Tschirgi (ed.): *The Arab World Today* (Boulder: Lynne Rienner, 1994), pp. 147-160; Tow, William T.: *Subregional Security Cooperation in the Third World* (Boulder: Lynne Rienner, 1990), pp. 45-56 & *passim*; Bill, James A.: 'The Geometry of Instability in the Gulf: The Rectangle of Tension', in Jamal S. al-Suwaidi (ed.): *Iran and the Gulf. A Search for Stability* (London: I.B. Tauris, 1996), pp. 99-117.

6. On Taiwan's quest for a seat in the UN see Henckaerts, Jean-Marie (ed.): *The International Status of Taiwan in the New World Order* (London: Kluwer Law International, 1996), *passim*; Yang, Maysing H. (ed.): *Taiwan's Expanding Role in the International Arena* (Armonk, NY: M.E. Sharpe, 1997).

7. Bergsten, C. Fred: 'APEC and World Trade', *Foreign Affairs*, vol. 73, no. 3 (May-June 1994), pp. 20-27; Clark, Jonathan: 'APEC as a Semi-Solution', *Orbis*, vol. 39, no. 1 (Winter 1995), pp. 81-95; Bello, Walden: 'Trouble in Paradise: The Tensions of Economic Integration in the Asia-Pacific', *World Policy Journal*, vol. 10, no. 2 (Summer 1993), pp. 33-40; Cossa, Ralph A. & Jane Khanna: 'East Asia: Economic Interdependence and Regional Security', *International Affairs*, vol. 73, no. 2 (April 1997), pp. 219-234; Harris, Stuart: 'The Economic Aspects of Security in the Asia/Pacific Region', in Desmond Ball (ed.): *The Transformation of Security in the Asia/Pacific Region* (London: Frank Cass, 1996), pp. 32-51.

8. In Bull, Hedley: *The Anarchical Society. A Study of Order in World Politics* (1977, 2nd edition Houndmills, Basingstoke: Macmillan, 1997), p. 71. 'Order' is here defined as 'a pattern of activity that sustains the elementary or primary goals of the society of states, or international society' (p. 8), in its turn defined as 'a group of states, conscious of certain common interests and common values ... [which] conceive themselves to be bound by a common set of rules in their relations with one another, and share in the working of common institutions' (p. 13).

9. Weisburd, A. Mark: *Use of Force. The Practice of States Since World War II* (University Park: Pennsylvania State University Press, 1997).

10. Khanna, B.K.: 'Ancient Military Heritage in India and Current Relevance', *Strategic Analysis* (New Delhi: IDSA), vol. 18, no. 5 (August 1995), pp. 677-692; Singh, Jasjit: 'The Indian Experience', in idem & Vatroslav Vekaric (eds.): *Non-Provocative Defence. The Search for Equal Security* (New Delhi: Lancer, 1989), pp. 215-233; Faust, John R. & Judith F. Kornberg: *China in World Politics* (Boulder, CO: Lynne Rienner Publishers, 1995), pp. 11-15, 31-33.

11. Based on ACDA (U.S. Arms Control and Disarmament Agency): *World Military Expenditures and Arms Transfers 1996* (Washington, DC: U.S. Government Printing Office, 1997), table 1, pp. 49-99.
12. Oral comment made at a seminar in Copenhagen, 30 June 1997.
13. Dibb, Paul: 'Towards a New Balance of Power in Asia', *Adelphi Papers*, no. 295 (1995); Zhao, Suisheng: *Power Competition in East Asia. From the Old Chinese World Order to the Post-Cold War Regional Multipolarity* (New York: St. Martin's Press, 1997).
14. On the general relationship between military expenditures and economic development see Ball, Nicole: *Security and Economy in the Third World* (Princeton, NJ: Princeton University Press, 1988); Graham, Norman A. (ed.): *Seeking Security and Development. The Impact of Military Spending and Arms Transfers* (Boulder: Lynne Rienner, 1994).
15. Ball, Desmond: 'Arms and Affluence: Military Acquisitions in the Asia-Pacific Region', *International Security*, vol. 18, no. 3 (Winter 1993/94), pp. 78-112; Wattanayagorn, Panitan & idem: 'A Regional Arms Race?', in Ball (ed.): *op. cit.* (note 7), pp. 147-174; Gill, Bates: 'Arms Acquisitions in East Asia', *SIPRI Yearbook 1994*, pp. 551-562; Willet, Susan: 'Dragon's Fire and Tiger's Claws: Arms Trade and Production in Far East Asia', in Colin McInnes & Mark C. Rolls (eds.): *Post-Cold War Security Issues in the Asia-Pacific Region* (London: Frank Cass, 1994), pp. 112-135.
16. Roy-Chaudury, Rahul: *Sea Power and Indian Security* (London: Brassey's, 1995); Suri, R.B.: 'Maritime Dimension of India's Security', *AGNI, Studies in International Strategic Issues*, vol. 1, no. 2 (November 1995), pp. 107-115.
17. Fetter, Steve: 'Ballistic Missiles and Weapons of Mass Destruction: What is the Threat? What Should be Done?', *International Security*, vol. 16, no. 1 (Summer 1991), pp. 5-42; Neuneck, Götz & Otfried Ischebeck (eds.): *Missile Proliferation, Missile Defence, and Arms Control* (Baden-Baden: Nomos Verlagsgesellschaft, 1992); Findlay, Trevor (ed.): *Chemical Weapons and Missile Proliferation. With Implications for the Asia/Pacific Region* (Boulder, CO: Lynne Rienner, 1991). On the limited conventional value of missiles see Nolan, Janne E.: *Trappings of Power. Ballistic Missiles in the Third World* (Washington, D.C.: Brookings, 1991), pp. 64-73; Harvey, John R.: 'Regional Ballistic Missiles and Advanced Strike Aircraft: Comparing Military Effectiveness', *International Security*, vol. 17, no. 2 (Fall 1992), pp. 41-83.
18. Spector, Leonard S.: 'Neo-Nonproliferation', *Survival*, vol. 37, no. 1 (Spring 1995), pp. 66-85; Goldring, Nathalie J.: 'Skittish on Counterproliferation', *Bulletin of the Atomic Scientists*, vol. 50, no. 2 (March-April 1994), pp. 12-14. On the new weapons being developed for the purpose of 'taking out' suspected nuclear targets (including converted Minuteman-II ICBMs) see Arkin, William M.: 'What's "New?"', *ibid.*, vol. 53, no. 6 (Nov-Dec 1997), pp. 22-27.
19. Inoguchi, Takashi & Grant B. Stillman (eds.): *North-East Asian Regional Security. The Role of International Institutions* (Tokyo: United Nations University Press, 1997); Gill, Bates: 'North-East Asia and Challenges to Multilateral Security Institutions', in *SIPRI Yearbook 1994*, pp. 149-168; Kwak, Tae-Hwan & Edward A.

Olsen (eds.): *The Major Powers of Northeast Asia: Seeking Peace and Security* (Boulder: Lynne Rienner, 1996); Ross, Robert S. (ed.): *East Asia in Transition: Toward a New Regional Order* (London: M.E. Sharpe, 1995); Dibb: *loc. cit.* (note 13). See also Segal, Gerald: 'North-East Asia: Common Security or à la carte?', *International Affairs*, vol. 67, no. 4 (1991), pp. 755-767; Brown, Michael E., Sean M. Lynn-Jones & Steven E. Miller (eds.): *East Asian Security. An* International Security *Reader* (Cambridge, MA: MIT Press, 1996).

20. For an overview of the methodological problems see IISS: *The Military Balance 1995/96*, pp. 270-275. For 1994, for instance, SIPRI's most recent estimate is $7.5bn, while the IISS's is $28.5bn, and that of ACDA $58.4bn, the differences reflecting, *inter alia*, whether official figures are used or unofficial estimates, and what currency is used. See IISS: *The Military Balance 1996/97*, p. 179; ACDA: *op. cit.* (note 11), p. 65; *SIPRI Yearbook 1997*, p. 197.

21. Gill, Bates & Taeho Kim: *China's Arms Acquisitions from Abroad: A Quest for 'Superb and Secret Weapons'*. SIPRI Research Report, no. 11 (Oxford: Oxford University Press, 1995).

22. Lin Piao (1965): 'Long Live the Victory in the People's War', in Walter Lacqueur (ed.): *The Guerilla Reader. A Historical Anthology* (London: Wildwood House, 1978), pp. 197-202. It is based on the writings of Mao from the 1930s: Mao Tse-Tung (1936): 'Problems of Strategy in China's Revolutionary War', in *Selected Works of Mao Tse-Tung*, vol. 1, (Peking: Foreign Languages Press, 1975), pp. 179-254; idem (1938): 'On Protracted War', *ibid.*, vol. 2, pp. 113-194; idem (1938): 'Problems of Strategy in Guerilla War Against Japan', *ibid.* pp. 79-112; idem (1938): 'Problems of War and Strategy', *ibid.*, pp. 219-235.

23. Segal, Gerald: 'China', in Regina Cowen Karp (ed.): *Security With Nuclear Weapons? Different Perspectives on National Security* (Oxford: Oxford University Press/SIPRI, 1991), pp. 189-205; Pollack, Jonathan: 'The Future of China's Nuclear Weapons Policy', in John C. Hopkins & Weixing Hu (eds.): *Strategic Views from the Second Tier. The Nuclear Weapons Policies of France, Britain and China* (New Brunswick: Transaction Publishers, 1996), pp. 157-166; Xue, Litai: 'Evolution of China's Nuclear Strategy', *ibid.* 167-189; Larkin, Bruce: *Nuclear Designs. Great Britain, France and China in the Global Governance of Nuclear Arms* (New Brunswick: Transaction Publishers, 1995), pp. 41-50 & *passim*; Johnston, Alastair Iain: 'China's New "Old Thinking": The Concept of Limited Deterrence', *International Security*, vol. 20, no. 3 (Winter 1995/96), pp. 5-42.

24. Brömmelhörster, Jörn & John Frankenstein (eds.): *Mixed Motives, Uncertain Outcomes. Defense Conversion in China* (Boulder: Lynne Rienner, 1997); Frankenstein, John & Bates Gill: 'Current and Future Challenges Facing Chinese Defence Industries', *The China Quarterly*, no. 146 (June 1996), pp. 394-427; Shichor, Yitzhak: 'Demobilization: The Dialectics of PLA Troop Reduction', *ibid.*, pp. 336-359; Singh, Swaran: 'China's Military Modernization', *Asian Strategic Review 1993-94* (New Delhi: IDSA, 1994), pp. 274-305; idem: 'China's Defence Production', *Asian Strategic Review 1994-95* (New Delhi: IDSA, 1995), pp. 256-294.

25. Ma Ping: 'The Strategic Thinking of Active Defence and China's Military Strategic Principle', *International Strategic Studies*, no. 1 (Beijing: China Institute for International Strategic Studies, March 1994), pp. 1-6; Xu Xin: 'China's Defence Strategy Under New Circumstances', *ibid.*, no. 3 (September 1993), pp. 1-6; Nan Li: 'The PLA's Evolving Warfighting Doctrine, Strategy and Tactics, 1985-95: a Chinese Perspective', *The China Quarterly*, no. 146 (June 1996), pp. 443-464. See also Godwin, Paul H.B.: 'From Continent to Periphery: PLA Doctrine, Strategy and Capabilities Towards 2000', *ibid.*, pp. 464-487; Kastur, Bhashyam: 'China's Defence Strategy', *Indian Defence Review*, vol. 10, no. 2 (April-June 1995), pp. 35-39.

26. Wortzel, Larry M.: 'China Pursues Traditional Great Power Status', *Orbis*, vol. 38, no. 2 (Spring 1994), pp. 157-175; Shambough, David: 'Growing Strong: China's Challenge to Asian Security', *Survival*, vol. 36, no. 2 (Summer 1994), pp. 43-59; idem: 'China's Military in Transition: Politics, Professionalism Procurement and Power Projection', *The China Quarterly*, no. 146 (June 1996), pp. 265-298; Zhan, Jun: 'China Goes to the Blue Waters: The Navy, Seapower Mentality and the South China Sea', *The Journal of Strategic Studies*, vol. 17, no. 3 (September 1994), pp. 180-208; Lewis, John Wilson & Hua Di: 'China's Ballistic Missile Programs. Technologies, Strategies, Goals', *International Security*, vol. 17, no. 2 (Fall 1992), pp. 5-40. See also Roy, Denny: 'Hegemon on the Horizon? China's Threat to East Asian Security', *International Security*, vol. 19, no. 1 (Summer 1994), pp. 149-168; Harris, Stuart & Gary Klintworth (eds.): *China as a Great Power. Myths, Realities and Challenges in the Asia-Pacific Region* (New York: St. Martin's Press, 1995); Klintworth, Gary: 'China and East Asia', in Ramesh Thakur & Carlyle A. Thayer (eds.): *Reshaping Regional Relations. Asia-Pacific and the Former Soviet Union* (Boulder: Westview Press, 1993), pp. 125-152; Munro, Ross H.: 'China's Waxing Spheres of Influence', *Orbis*, vol. 38, no. 4 (Fall 1994), pp. 585-605. On ties between Myanmar and China see (for Indian perspectives) Singh, Udai Bhanu: 'Recent Trends in Relations Between Myanmar and China', *Strategic Analysis*, vol. 18, no. 1 (April 1995), pp. 61-72; Singh, Swaran: 'Sino-Myanmar Military Ties: Implications for India's Security', *U.S.I. Journal*, vol. 125, no. 521 (July-September 1995), pp. 348-357. For a South-East Asian view see To, Lee Lai: 'East Asian Assessments of China's Security Policy', *International Affairs*, vol. 73, no. 2 (April 1997), pp. 251-262.

27. Segal, Gerald: 'The Coming Confrontation between China and Japan?', *World Policy Journal*, vol. 10, no. 2 (Summer 1993), pp. 27-32; Whiting, Allen S. & Xin Jianfei: 'Sino-Japanese Relations. Pragmatism and Passion', *World Policy Journal*, vol. 8, no. 1 (Winter 1990-91), pp. 107-136.

28. Valencia, Mark J.: 'China and the South China Sea Disputes', *Adelphi Paper*, no. 298 (1995); Chang, Felix: 'Beijing's Reach into the South China Sea', *Orbis*, vol. 40, no. 3 (Summer 1996), pp. 353-374. For a more sanguine view see Gallagher, Michael G.: 'China's Illusory Threat to the South China Sea', *International Security*, vol. 19, no. 1 (Summer 1994), pp. 169-194. On the economic reasons for China's presumed ambitions see Leifer, Michael: 'Chinese Economic Reform and Security Policy: The South China Sea Connection', *Survival*, vol. 37, no. 2 (Summer 1995), pp. 44-59; Salameh, Mamdouh G.: 'China, Oil and the Risk of Regional Conflict', *ibid.*, no. 4

(Winter 1995-96), pp. 133-146.
29. Chong-Pin Lin: 'Chinese Military Modernization: Perceptions, Progress, and Prospects', *Security Studies*, vol. 3, no. 4 (Summer 1994), pp. 718-753; Arquilla, John & Solomon M. Karmell: 'Welcome to the Revolution ...in Chinese Military Affairs', *Defense Analysis*, vol. 13, no. 3 (December 1997), pp. 255-270.
30. For an excellent attempt at empathizing with China see Nathan, Andrew J. & Robert S. Ross: *The Great Wall and the Empty Fortress: China's Search for Security* (New York: W.W. Norton & Co., 1997). See also Munro, Ross H.: 'Eavesdropping on the Chinese Military: Where It Expects War—Where It Doesn't', *Orbis*, vol. 38, no. 3 (Summer 1994), pp. 355-372; Whiting, Allen S.: 'The PLA and China's Threat Perceptions', *The China Quarterly*, no. 146 (June 1996), pp. 596-615.
31. This is the thesis of Gerald Segal. See his 'China Changes Shape: Regionalism and Foreign Policy', *Adelphi Paper*, no. 287 (1994). For qualifications see Goodman, David S.G. & idem (eds.): *China Deconstructs. Politics, Trade and Regionalism* (London: Routledge, 1994).
32. Yu, Peter Kien-Hong: 'Chinese Re-Unification. Opening a Window of Opportunity', *Security Dialogue*, vol. 27, no. 4 (1996), pp. 475-484. On Hong Kong see Horlemann, Bianca: 'Hongkong's Future', *Aussenpolitik*, vol. 48, no. 2 (2nd Quarter 1997), pp. 195-204; Kuan, Hsin-Chi: 'Does Hong Kong Have a Future?', *Security Dialogue*, vol. 28, no. 2 (June 1997), pp. 233-236. On the China-Taiwan dispute see Hughes, Christopher: *Taiwan and Chinese Nationalism. National Identity and Status in International Society* (London: Routledge, 1997); Cheng, Tun-jen, Chi Huang & Samuel S.G. Wu (eds.): *Inherited Rivalry. Conflict Across the Taiwan Straits* (Boulder: Lynne Rienner, 1995); Leng, Tse-Kang: *The Taiwan-China Connection. Democracy and Development across the Taiwan Straits* (Boulder: Westview Press, 1996). On the PRC's present lack of military options see Chang, Felix K.: 'Conventional War across the Taiwan Strait', *Orbis*, vol. 40, no. 4 (Fall 1996), pp. 577-607; Lin, Chong-Pin: 'The Military Balance in the Taiwan Straits', *The China Quarterly*, no. 146 (June 1996), pp. 577-595. On peaceful unification see Huan, Guocang: 'Taipei-Beijing Relations. No Longer a Zero-Sum Game', *World Policy Journal*, vol. 9, no. 3 (Summer 1992), pp. 563-579; Li, Rex: 'The Taiwan Strait Crisis and the Future of China-Taiwan Relations', *Security Dialogue*, vol. 27, no. 4 (1996), pp. 449-458; Jian, Chen: 'Understanding the Logic of Beijing's Taiwan Policy', *ibid.*, pp. 459-462. On overseas Chinese see Smith, Paul J.: 'The Strategic Implications of Chinese Emigration', *Survival*, vol. 36, no. 2 (Summer 1994), pp. 60-77.
33. Menon, Rajan: 'The Strategic Convergence Between Russia and China', *Survival*, vol. 39, no. 2 (Summer 1997), pp. 101-125. For background on US-USSR-PRC relations during the Cold War see Kim, Ilpyong J. (ed.): *The Strategic Triangle. China, the United States and the Soviet Union* (New York: Paragon House, 1987).
34. Hornik, Richard: 'Bursting China's Bubble', *Foreign Affairs*, vol. 73, no. 3 (May-June 1994), pp. 28-42.
35. Baum, Richard: *Burying Mao. Chinese Politics in the Age of Deng Xiaoping* (Princeton, N.J.: Princeton University Press, 1994). See also Ahn, Yinhay: 'Vying Influence: Reform in China', *The Korean Journal of National Unification*, Special

Edition (Seoul: Research Institute for National Unification, 1993), pp. 179-195; Harding, Harry: '"On the Four Great Relationships"': The Prospects for China', *Survival*, vol. 36, no. 2 (Summer 1994), pp. 22-42.

36. On civil-military relations see Joffe, Ellis: 'Party-Army Relations in China: Retrospect and Prospect', *The China Quarterly*, no. 146 (June 1996), pp. 299-314; Dreyer, June Teufel: 'The New Officer Corps: Implications for the Future', *ibid.*, pp. 315-335; Shambough, David: 'China's Military in Transition: Politics, Professionalism, Procurement and Power Projection', *ibid.*, pp. 265-298; Swaine, Michael D.: 'The PLA in China's National Security Policy: Leaderships, Structures, Processes', *ibid.*, pp. 360-393; Godwin, Paul: 'The Chinese People's Liberation Army Under Attack: Party-Military Relations After Tienanmen', in Eberhard Sandschneider & Jürgen Kuhlmann (eds.): 'Armed Forces in the USSR and the PRC', *Forum International*, no. 14 (Munich: Sozialwissenschaftliches Institut der Bundeswehr), pp. 73-114; Barylski, Robert V.: 'Perestroika and Civil-Military Relations in the Soviet Union and the People's Republic of China', *ibid.*, pp. 127-212; Nan Li: 'Political-Military Changes in China, 1978-89', *Security Studies*, vol. 4, no. 2 (Winter 1994-95), pp. 426-458.

37. Segal, Gerald: 'Tying China into the International System', *Survival*, vol. 37, no. 2 (Summer 1995), pp. 60-73; idem: 'East Asia and the "Constrainment" of China', *International Security*, vol. 20, no. 4 (Spring 1996), pp. 107-135; Shambaugh, David: 'Containment or Engagement of China? Calculating Beijing's Responses', *ibid.*, vol. 21, no. 2 (Fall 1996), pp. 180-209; Johnson, Chalmers: 'Containing China: U.S. and Japan Drift Toward Disaster', *Japan Quarterly*, vol. 43, no. 4 (Oct-Dec 1996), pp. 10-18.

38. Bitzinger, Richard A.: 'Arms to Go. Chinese Arms Sales to the Third World', *International Security*, vol. 17, no. 2 (Fall 1992), pp. 84-111; Segal, Gerald: 'China: Arms Transfer Policies and Practices', in McInnes & Rolls (eds.): *op. cit.* (note 15), pp. 156-173; Hua Di: 'China's Case: Ballistic Missile Proliferation', in William C. Potter & Harlan W. Jencks (eds.): *The International Missile Bazaar. The New Suppliers' Network* (Boulder: Westview Press, 1994), pp. 163-180.

39. Arase, David: 'A Militarized Japan?', in Ball (ed.): *op. cit.* (note 7), pp. 84-103.

40. Cronin, Richard P.: 'Japan', in Richard Dean Burns (ed.): *Encyclopedia of Arms Control and Disarmament* (New York: Charles Scribner's Sons, 1993), vol. I, pp. 129-147; Mochizuki, Mike M.: 'The Disarming and Rearming of Japan', *ibid.*, vol. II, pp. 801-807; Watanabe, Wakio: 'Japan's Postwar Constitution and Its Implications for Defence Policy: A Fresh Interpretation', in Ron Matthews & Keisuke Matsuyama (eds.): *Japan's Military Renaissance?* (New York: St. Martin's Press, 1993), pp. 35-49; Ueta, Takato: 'Japan: A Case of a Non-Control Regime', in Fred Tanner (ed.): *From Versailles to Baghdad: Post-War Armament Control of Defeated States* (New York: United Nations/Geneva: UNIDIR, 1992), pp. 101-114. The most recent official formulation of Japan's defence policy is the White Paper *Defense of Japan 1996*, available at http://www.jda.go.jp/pab/8aramasi/defcont.htm.

41. Endicott, John E.: 'Japan', in Douglas J. Murray & Paul R. Viotti (eds.): *The Defense Policies of Nations* (Baltimore: John Hopkins University Press, 1994), pp. 351-377; idem: 'Japan's Military Renaissance? Prognosis into the 1990s and Beyond', in

Matthews & Matsuyama (eds.): *op. cit.* (note 40), pp. 233-248; Samuels, Richard J.: *'Rich Nation, Strong Army'. National Security and the Technological Transformation of Japan* (Ithaca, NY: Cornell University Press, 1994). On the arms industry see Edgar, Alistair D. & David G. Haglund: 'Japanese Defence Industrialisation', *ibid.*, pp. 137-163; Chinworth, Michael W.: *Inside Japan's Defense. Technology, Economics and Strategy* (Washington, D.C.: Brassey's, 1992); Renwick, Neil: *Japan's Alliance Politics and Defence Production* (New York: St. Martin's Press, 1995); Huber, Thomas M.: *Strategic Economy in Japan* (Boulder: Westview Press, 1994).

42. See, for instance, Ienaga, Saburo: 'The Glorification of War in Japanese Education', *International Security*, vol. 18, no. 3 (Winter 1993-94), pp. 113-133; Mochizuki, Michael M.: 'Review Essay: The Past in Japan's Future. Will the Japanese Change?', *Foreign Affairs*, vol. 73, no. 5 (Sept-Oct 1994), pp. 126-134.

43. Barnett, Robert W.: *Beyond War. Japan's Concept of Comprehensive National Security* (Washington: Brassey's, 1984); Katzenstein, Peter J.: *Cultural Norms and National Security. Police and Military in Postwar Japan* (Ithaca: Cornell University Press, 1996); idem & Nobuo Okawara: 'Japan's National Security: Structures, Norms, and Policies', *International Security*, vol. 17, no. 4 (Spring 1993), pp. 84-118; Berger, Thomas U.: 'From Sword to Chrysanthemum. Japan's Culture of Anti-Militarism', *ibid*, pp. 119-150; Hook, Glenn D.: *Militarisation and Demilitarisation in Contemporary Japan* (London: Routledge, 1996). On civil-military relations see Gow, Ian: 'Civilian Control of the Military in Postwar Japan', in Matthews & Matsuyama (eds.): *op. cit.* (note 40), pp. 50-68.

44. Tamamoto, Masaru: 'The Japan That Wants to Be Liked: Society and International Participation', in Danny Unger & Paul Blackburn (eds.): *Japan's Emerging Global Role* (Boulder: Lynne Rienner, 1993), pp. 37-54.

45. Harrison, Selig S. (ed.): *Japan's Nuclear Future. The Plutonium Debate and East Asian Security* (Washington, D.C.: The Carnegie Endowment, 1996); Kaneko, Kumao: 'Japan Needs No Umbrella', *Bulletin of the Atomic Scientists*, vol. 52, no. 2 (March-April 1996), pp. 46-51.

46. Drifte, Reinhard: *Japan's Rise to International Responsibilities. The Case of Arms Control* (London: Athlone, 1990); Lincoln, Edward J.: *Japan's New Global Role* (Washington, D.C.: The Brookings Institution, 1993); Unger & Blackburn (eds.): *op. cit.* (note 44), *passim*; Inogochui, Takashi: 'Japan's Role in International Affairs', *Survival*, vol. 34, no. 2 (Summer 1992), pp. 71-87; Segal, Gerald: 'Adjusting to the New International Order', in Matthews & Matsuyama (eds.): *op. cit.* (note 40), pp. 102-116.

47. Mendl, Wolf: *Japan's Asia Policy. Regional Security and Global Interests* (London: Routledge, 1995); Unger, Danny: 'Japan's Capital Exports: Moulding East Asia', in idem & Blackburn (eds.): *op. cit.* (note 44), pp. 155-170; Gordon, Bernard K.: 'Japan: Searching Once Again', in James C. Hsiung (ed.): *Asia Pacific in the New World Politics* (Boulder: Lynne Rienner, 1993), pp. 49-70; Arase, David: 'Japan in East Asia', in Tsuneo Akaha & Frank Langdon (eds.): *Japan in the Posthegemonic World* (Boulder: Lynne Rienner, 1993), pp. 113-136; Chittiwatanapong, Prasert: 'Japan's Roles in the Posthegemonic World: Perspectives From Southeast Asia', *ibid,*,

pp. 201-232; Bridges, Brian: *Japan and Korea in the 1990s. From Antagonism to Adjustment* (Aldershot: Edward Elgar, 1993). For a critical Chinese assessment see Dalin, Zhang: 'An Analysis of Japan's Strategy of Returning to Asia', *International Studies*, no. 4-5 (Beijing: China Institute of International Studies, 1994), pp. 1-10.

48. Sasae, Kenichiro: 'Rethinking Japan-US Relations', *Adelphi Paper*, no. 292 (1994); Curtis, Gerald L. (ed.): *The United States, Japan, and Asia. Challenges for U.S. Policy* (New York: W.W. Norton & Co., 1994); Asher, David L.: 'A U.S.-Japan Alliance for the Next Century', *Orbis*, vol. 41, no. 3 (Summer 1997), pp. 343-374; Cossa, Ralph A.: 'Avoiding New Myths: US-Japan Security Relations', *Security Dialogue*, vol. 28, no. 2 (June 1997), pp. 219-231; Levin, Norman D.: 'Prospects for U.S.-Japanese Security Cooperation', in Unger & Blackburn (eds.): *op. cit.* (note 44), pp. 71-84; Shikata, Toshiyuki: 'Behind the Redefinition of the Japan-U.S. Security Setup', *Japan Review of International Affairs*, Fall 1996, pp. 291-313.

49. *The Times*, 25 September 1997.

50. Wan, Ming: 'Spending Strategies in World Politics: How Japan Has Used Its Economic Power in the Past Decade', *International Studies Quarterly*, vol. 39, no. 1 (March 1995), pp. 85-108; Ward, Michael D., David R. Davis & Corey L. Lofdahl: 'A Century of Tradeoffs: Defense and Growth in Japan and the United States', *ibid.*, pp. 27-50; Matsuyama, Keisuke, Mitsuhiro Kojina & Yutaka Fukuda: 'Military Expenditure and Economic Growth: The Case of Japan', in Matthews & Matsuyama (eds.): *op. cit.* (note 40), pp. 117-136; See also Bienen, Henry (ed.): *Power, Economics, and Security. The United States and Japan in Focus* (Boulder: Westview Press, 1992); Garby, Craig C. & Mary Brown Bullock (eds.): *Japan. A New Kind of Superpower* (Baltimore: John Hopkins University Press, 1994).

51. The nuclear issue has received an extraordinary amount of attention. See, for instance, Mack, Andrew (ed.): *Nuclear Policies in Northeast Asia* (New York and Geneva: United Nations, UNIDIR/95/16); Mazarr, Michael J.: *North Korea and the Bomb. A Case Study in Nonproliferation* (New York: St. Martin's Press, 1994); Han, Yong-Sup: 'Nuclear Disarmament and Non-Proliferation in Northeast Asia', *Research Paper*, no. 35 (New York and Geneva: United Nations, UNIDIR/95/12); Kihl, Young Whan & Peter Hayes (eds.): *Peace and Security in Northeast Asia. The Nuclear Issue and the Korean Peninsula* (Armonk, NY: M.E. Sharpe, 1997). On the DPRK's motivation see also Bracken, Paul: 'Nuclear Weapons and State Survival in North Korea', *Survival*, vol. 35, no. 3 (Autumn 1993), pp. 137-153; Maull, Hann W.: 'North Korea's Nuclear Weapons Programme: Genesis, Motives, Implications', *Aussenpolitik*, vol. 45, no. 4 (4th Quarter 1994), pp. 354-363.

52. Masaki, Stuart K.: 'The Korean Question: Assessing the Military Balance', *Security Studies*, vol. 4, no. 2 (Winter 1994-95), pp. 365-425.

53. Nearly all South Koreans seem to hold this view. American analyses to the same effect include Bodansky, Yossef: *Crisis in: Korea* (New York: SPI Books, 1994); Dupuy, Trevor N.: *Future Wars. The World's Most Dangerous Flashpoints* (New York: Warner Books, 1992), pp. 235-254 (about 'the Second Korean War').

54. Kang, David C.: 'Preventive War and North Korea', *Security Studies*, vol. 4, no. 2 (Winter 1994-95), pp. 330-364.

55. Simons, Geoff: *Korea. The Search for Sovereignty* (Houndmills, Basingstoke: Macmillan, 1995); Park, Han S.: *North Korea. Ideology, Politics, Economy* (Englewood Cliffs, NJ: Prentice Hall, 1996).
56. Roy, Denny: 'North Korea and the "Madman" Theory', *Security Dialogue*, vol. 25, no. 3 (September 1994), pp. 307-316; idem: 'North Korea as an Alienated State', *Survival*, vol. 38, no. 4 (Winter 1996-97), pp. 22-36. On the implications for US-ROK relations see Kim, Kyu-Ryoon: 'The Future Developments of US-DPRK Relations: Impact on North-South Korean Relations', *The Korean Journal of National Unification*, vol. 3 (Seoul: Research Institute for National Unification, 1994), pp. 111-126; Kwak, Tae-Hwan: 'Korea-US Security Relations in Transition', *ibid.*, pp. 205-235; Park, Sang Hoon: 'North Korea and the Challenge to the US-South Korean Alliance', *Survival*, vol. 36, no. 2 (Summer 1994), pp. 78-91.
57. On the economic crisis see Eberstadt, Nicolas: 'North Korea: A Statistical Glimpse into a Closed Society', *The Korean Journal of National Unification*, Vol. 2 (1993), pp. 31-62; Oh, Seung-Yul: 'Economic Reform in North Korea: Is China's Reform Model Relevant to North Korea?', *ibid.*, pp. 127-153; Park, Young-Ho: 'Will North Korea Survive the Current Crisis? A Political Economy Perspective', *ibid.*, pp. 105-126; Namkoong, Young: 'Assessment of the North Korean Economy: Status and Prospects', *US-Korean Relations at a Time of Change* (Seoul: Research Institute for National Unification, 1994), pp. 7-28. On the power succession and legitimacy crisis of the Pyongyang regime see Ahn, Byung-joon: 'The Man Who Would Be Kim', *Foreign Affairs*, vol. 73, no. 6 (November-December 1994), pp. 94-108; Chon, Hyun-Joon: 'The Basis of Power Succession of Kim Jong-II and Policy Directions', *The Korean Journal of National Unification*, Vol. 1 (1992), pp. 175-194; Ahn, Yinhay: 'Elite Politics and Policy Making in North Korea: A Policy Tendency Analysis', *ibid.*, Vol. 2 (1993), pp. 63-84; Koh, Byung-chul: 'Prospects for Change in North Korea', *ibid.*, Vol. 3 (1994), pp. 237-256; Huh, Moon Young, Kyu Sup Chung & Hyun-Joon Chon: 'The Advent of Kim Jong-il Regime in North Korea and Prospects for Its Policy Direction', *Policy Studies Report*, no. 1 (Seoul: Research Institute for National Unification, 1994); Suh, Jae-Jean & Byoung-Lo P. Kim: 'Prospects for Changes in Kim Jong-Il Regime', *ibid.*, no. 2 (1994); Kim, Hakjoon: 'North Korea after Kim Il-song and the Future of North-South Korean Relations', *Security Dialogue*, vol. 26, no. 1 (March 1995), pp. 73-91.
58. Gong, Gerrit W.: 'Remembering and Forgetting: A Contextual Approach to Korean Peninsula Developments', *The Korean Journal of National Unification*, Vol. 2 (1993), pp. 153-176; idem: *Remembering and Forgetting: The Legacy of War and Peace in East Asia* (Washington, DC: Center for Strategic and International Studies, 1996). Good historical accounts of the war are Whelan, Richard: *Drawing the Line. The Korean War, 1950-1953* (Boston: Little, Brown & Co., 1990); and Stueck, William: *The Korean War. An International History* (Princeton, NJ: Princeton University Press, 1995).
59. On dialogue and detente see Ok, Tae Hwan: 'The Process of South-North Dialogue and Perspectives for Unification of Korea', *The Korean Journal of National Unification*, Vol. 1 (1992), pp. 85-106; Park, Young-Ho: 'Issues and Prospects for Cross-Recognition: A Korean Perspective', *ibid.*, Vol. 3 (1994), pp. 49-62; Suh,

Mark B.M.: 'Normalization and Unification Prospects in Korea', *Aussenpolitik*, vol. 43, no. 3 (Autumn 1992), pp. 256-266; Harrison, Selig S.: 'A Chance for Detente in Korea', *World Policy Journal*, vol. 8, no. 4 (Fall 1991), pp. 599-632. On unification see Kihl, Yong Wan (ed.): *Korea and the World. Beyond the Cold War* (Boulder, CO: Westview Press, 1994), *passim*; Harrison, Selig S.: 'Confederation or Absorption? Key Issues For South Korea and the United States', *The Korean Journal of National Unification*, Special Edition (1993), pp. 97-124; Jhe, Seong Ho: 'How to Build a New Peace Structure on the Korean Peninsula', *ibid.*, vol. 4 (1995), pp. 7-27; Eberstadt, Nicholas: 'Hastening Korean Unification', *Foreign Affairs*, vol. 76, no. 2 (March-April 1997), pp. 77-92. On the applicability of the German models see Schmidt, Helmut: 'Lessons of the German Reunification for Korea', *Security Dialogue*, vol. 24, no. 44 (December 1993), pp. 397-408; Kim, Dae-Jung: 'Korean Reunification. A Rejoinder', *ibid.*, pp. 409-414; Yang, Sung-Chul: 'The Lessons of United Germany for Divided Korea', in Kihl (ed.): *op. cit.*, pp. 261-278; Flassbeck, Heiner & Gustav A. Horn (eds.): *German Unification: an Example for Korea?* (Aldershot: Dartmouth, 1996).

60. On the NWFZ treaty see Cheon, Seong W.: 'Verifying a Denuclearized Korean Peninsula: Current Negotiating Agenda', *The Korean Journal of National Unification*, Vol. 1 (1992), pp. 107-126; Shen, Dingli: 'Securing a Nuclear-Weapon-Free Korean Peninsula', *INESAP Information Bulletin*, no. 3 (Darmstadt: Information Network of Engineers and Scientists Against Proliferation, October 1994), pp. 8-10. On conventional arms control see Lee, Chung Minh: 'The Future of Arms Control in the Korean Peninsula', *Washington Quarterly*, vol. 14, no. 3 (Summer 1991), pp. 181-197; Wendt, James C.: 'Conventional Arms Control for Korea: a Proposed Approach', *Survival*, vol. 34, no. 4 (Winter 1992), pp. 108-124; Han, Yong-Sup: *Designing and Evaluating Conventional Arms Control Measures: The Case of the Korean Peninsula* (Santa Monica, CA: RAND Graduate Institute, 1993); Kwak, Tae-Hwan: 'Current Issues in Inter-Korean Arms Control and Disarmament Talks', *The Korean Journal of National Unification*, Vol. 2 (1993), pp. 177-206; Scholz, Joachim E.: 'Military Options on the Korean Peninsula', *US-Korean Relations at a Time of Change* (Seoul: Research Institute for National Unification, 1994), pp. 131-151; Park, Tong Whan: 'The Korean Arms Control Through Complex Military Balance', *Korea Observer* (Seoul: The Institute of Korean Studies), vol. 25, no. 2 (Summer 1994), pp. 207-227; Park, Tong Whan: 'Improving Military Security Relations', in Kihl (ed.): *op. cit.* (note 59), pp. 217-232. On defensive restructuring see Wiberg, Håkan: 'Nonoffensive Defence and the Korean Peninsula', in UNIDIR (ed.): *Nonoffensive Defense. A Global Perspective* (New York: Taylor & Francis, 1990), pp. 132-142; Møller, Bjørn: 'Non-Offensive Defence and the Korean Peninsula', *Working Papers*, no. 4 (Copenhagen: Centre for Peace and Conflict Research, 1995); idem: 'Common Security and Non-Offensive Defence: Are They Relevant for the Korean Peninsula?', in Hwang, Bypong-Moo & Yong-Sup Han (eds.): *Korean Security Policies Toward Peace and Unification*, KAIS International Conference Series, no. 4 (Seoul: Korean Association of International Studies, 1996), pp. 241-291.

61. Park, Kun Y.: '"Pouring New Wine into Fresh Wineskins": Defence Spending and Economic Growth in LDCs with Application to South Korea', *Journal of Peace Research*, vol. 30, no. 1 (February 1993), pp. 79-93; Heo, Uk: 'The Political Economy of Defense Spending in South Korea', *ibid.*, vol. 33, no. 4 (November 1996), pp. 483-490; Hong, Kyudok: 'Defense Spending vs. Economic Growth: A New Controversy in the Era of Inter-Korean Reconciliation and Cooperation', *The Korean Journal of National Unification*, vol. 1 (1992), pp. 127-150; Graham, Norman A. & Peter M. Lewis: 'Military Regimes, Military Spending, and Development: A Comparison of Brazil, Nigeria, Pakistan, and the Republic of Korea', in Graham (ed.): *op. cit.* (note 14), pp. 209-227.
62. See, for instance, Thakur & Thayer (eds.): *op. cit.* (note 26), *passim*; Harada, Chikahito: 'Russia and North-east Asia', *Adelphi Paper*, no. 310 (1997).
63. By the end of 1996, the Pacific Fleet had thus been cut from 335 ships in 1992 to 140, to say nothing about combat readiness. See *Jane's Defence Weekly*, vol. 26, no. 25 (18 December 1996), p. 10; and *ibid.*, vol. 24, no. 18 (4 November 1995), p. 42.
64. On the Russian vacillation between a European and Eurasian orientation see Richter, James: 'Russian Foreign Policy and the Politics of National Identity', in Celste A. Wallander (ed.): *The Sources of Russian Foreign Policy After the Cold War* (Boulder: Westview, 1996), pp. 69-93; Porter, Bruce D.: 'Russia and Europe After the Cold War: The Interaction of Domestic and Foreign Policy', *ibid.*, pp. 121-145; Buszinski, Leszek: *Russian Foreign Policy after the Cold War* (Westport, Connecticut: Praeger Press, 1996), pp. 49-53; Alexandrova, Olga: 'Divergent Russian Foreign Policy Concepts', *Aussenpolitik*, vol. 44, no. 4 (Fall 1993), pp. 363-372; Buszynski, Leszek: 'Russia and the West: Towards Renewed Geopolitical Rivalry?', *Survival*, vol. 37, no. 3 (Autumn 1995), pp. 104-125; Likhotal, Alexander: 'The New Russia and Eurasia', *Security Dialogue*, vol. 23, no. 3 (September 1992), pp. 9-18; Petrov, Yuri: 'Russia in Geopolitical Space', *Eurobalkans*, no. 19 (Summer 1995), pp. 26-29; Rubinstein, Alvin Z.: 'The Geopolitical Pull on Russia', *Orbis*, vol. 38, no. 4 (Fall 1994), pp. 567-583; Simon, Gerhard: 'La Russia: un hégémonie eurasienne?', *Politique Étrangère*, vol. 59, no. 1 (1st Quarter 1994), pp. 29-48; Stenseth, Dagfinn: 'The New Russia, CIS and the Future', *Security Dialogue*, vol. 23, no. 3 (September 1992), pp. 19-26; Tsipko, Alexander: 'A New Russian Identity or Old Russia's Reintegration?', *ibid.*, vol. 25, no. 4 (December 1994), pp. 443-456.
65. *RFE/RL Newsline*, vol. 1, no. 27 (9 May 1997).
66. Good overviews of the region are the annuals *Southeast Asian Affairs 19xx* and *Regional Outlook. Southeast Asia 19xx-xx*, both published by the Institute of Southeast Asian Studies, Singapore. A valuable source of official information is the ASEANWEB on the internet (http://www.aseansec.org/). See also 'Laos and Myanmar Join ASEAN on 23 July 1997', *ASEAN Update*, vol. 2/97 (May-August 1997). On the region in general see further Acharya, Amitav: 'A New Regional Order in South-East Asia: ASEAN in the Post-Cold War Era', *Adelphi Paper*, no. 279 (1993); Cunha, Derek da (ed.): *The Evolving Pacific Power Structure* (Singapore: Institute of Southeast Asian Studies, 1996); Wurfel, David & Bruce Burton (eds.): *Southeast Asia in the New World Order. The Political Economy of a Dynamic Region* (New York: St. Martin's Press, 1996).

67. Chalmers, Malcolm: *Confidence Building in South-East Asia* (Boulder: Westview, 1996), pp. 61-119; Nayan, Md Hussin: 'Openness and Transparency in the ASEAN Countries', *Disarmament*, vol. 18, no. 2 (1995), pp. 135-144.
68. Singh, Udai Bhanu: 'Growth of Military Power in South-East Asia', *Asian Strategic Review 1994-95* (New Delhi: IDSA, 1995), pp. 311-351; Willet: *loc. cit.* (note 15); idem: 'East Asia's Changing Defence Industry', *Survival*, vol. 39, no. 3 (Autumn 1997), pp. 107-134.
69. For an excellent analysis see Acharya, Amitav: *An Arms Race in Post-Cold War South-East Asia: Prospects for Control* (Singapore: Institute of Southeast Asian Studies, 1994); and Chalmers: *op. cit.* (note 67), pp. 61-119.
70. Cunha, Derek da: 'The Need for Weapons Upgrading in Southeast Asia: Present and Future', *ISEAS Working Papers*, no. 1/96 (Singapore: Institute of Southeast Asian Studies, 1996); Jeshurun, Chandran: 'Malaysian Defence Policy Revisited: Modernization and Rationalization in the Post-Cold War Era', *Southeast Asian Affairs 1994* (Singapore: Institute of Southeast Asian Studies, 1994), pp. 194-206; Mak, J.N. & B.A. Hamzah: 'The External Maritime Dimension of ASEAN Security', in Ball (ed.): *op. cit.* (note 7), pp. 123-146. On the resolution of domestic conflicts see Findlay, Trevor: 'Turning the Corner in Southeast Asia', in Michael E. Brown (ed.): *The International Dimensions of Internal Conflict* (Cambridge, MA: MIT Press, 1996), pp. 173-204.
71. Janssen, Joris: 'ASEAN Navies Extend their Maritime Reach', *Jane's Defence Weekly*, vol. 26, no. 22 (27 Nov 1996), p. 25; Bateman, Sam: 'The Functions of Navies in the Southwest Pacific and Southeast Asia', in Hugh Smith & Anthony Bergin (eds.): *Naval Power in the Pacific. Toward the Year 2000* (Boulder: Lynne Rienner, 1993), pp. 129-143; Bristow, Damon: 'Between the Devil and the Deep Blue Sea: Maritime Disputes between Association of South East Asian Nations (ASEAN) Member States', *RUSI Journal*, vol. 141, no. 4 (August 1996), pp. 31-37.
72. Thayer, Carlyle A.: *The Vietnam People's Army Under Doi Moi* (Singapore: Institute of Southeast Asian Studies, 1994). See also Betts, Richard K.: 'Vietnam's Strategic Predicament', *Survival*, vol. 37, no. 3 (Autumn 1995), pp. 61-81.
73. Carpenter, William M.: 'Laos', in idem & David G. Wiencek: *Asian Security Handbook. An Assessment of Political-Security Issues in the Asia-Pacific Region* (Armonk, NY: M.E. Sharpe, 1997), pp. 174-177.
74. Disarmament and Conflict Resolution Project: 'Managing Arms in Peace Processes: Cambodia', *UNIDIR/96/17* (New York: United Nations and Geneva: UNIDIR, 1996); Findlay, Trevor: *Cambodia. The Legacy and Lessons of UNTAC*. SIPRI Research Report, no. 9 (Oxford: Oxford University Press, 1995); Frost, Frank: 'Cambodia: From UNTAC to Royal Government', *Southeast Asian Affairs 1994* (note 70), pp. 79-101; Heininger, Janet E.: *Peacekeeping in Transition. The United Nations in Cambodia* (New York: Twentieth Century Fund Press, 1994).
75. Kyi, Khin Maung: 'Myanmar: Will Forever Flow the Ayeyarwady?', *Southeast Asian Affairs 1994* (note 70) pp. 209-230. On the Chinese connection, see above, note 27.
76. On the Spratly Islands dispute see above, note 29. See also To, Lee Lai: 'Der China-Faktor in der Sicherheitspolitik Asiens. ASEAN's pragmatische Dialog- und Kooperationspolitik', *Internationale Politik*, vol. 52, no. 6 (June 1997), pp. 17-22.

77. On ZOPFAN see Hänggi, Heiner: *Neutralität in Südostasien. Das Project einer Zone des Friedens, der Freiheit und der Neutralität* (Bern: Verlag Paul Haupt, 1993). On the balance- or-bandwagon dilemma see Walt, Stephen M.: *The Origins of Alliances* (Ithaca: Cornell University Press, 1979), pp. 27-33; idem: 'Alliance Formation and the Balance of World Power", *International Security*, vol. 9, no. 4 (Spring 1985), pp. 3-43; Labs, Eric J.: 'Do Weak States Bandwagon?', *Security Studies*, vol. 1, no. 3 (Spring 1992), pp. 283-416.
78. 'Treaty on the Southeast Asia Nuclear-Weapon-Free Zone', *Strategic Digest*, vol. 26, no. 3 (New Delhi: IDSA, 1996), pp. 320-328. See also Dewitt, David & Brian Bow: 'Proliferation Management in South-east Asia', *Survival*, vol. 38, no. 3 (Autumn 1996), pp. 67-81.
79. On AFTA see Lim, Linda Y.C.: 'ASEAN: New Modes of Economic Cooperation', in Wurfel & Burton (eds.): *op. cit.* (note 66), pp. 19-35; Campos, Jose Edgardo & Hilton L. Root: *The Key to the Asian Miracle. Making Shared Growth Credible* (Washington, D.C.: Brookings, 1996). On ARF see Findlay, Trevor: 'South-East Asia and the New Asia-Pacific Security Dialogue', in *SIPRI Yearbook 1994*, pp. 125-148; Leifer, Michael: 'The ASEAN Regional Forum. Extending ASEAN's Model of Regional Security', *Adelphi Paper*, no. 302 (1996); Acharya, Amitav: 'A New Regional Order in South-East Asia: ASEAN in the Post-Cold War Era', *Adelphi Paper*, no. 279 (1993).
80. Acharya, Amitav: 'A Regional Security Community in Southeast Asia?', in Ball (ed.): *op. cit.* (note 7), pp. 175-200.
81. Buzan, Barry, Rother Rizwi *et al.*: *South Asian Insecurity and the Great Powers* (London: Macmillan, 1986); Bajpai, Kanti P. & Stephen P. Cohen: 'Introduction', in idem & idem (eds.): *South Asia After the Cold War. International Perspectives* (Boulder: Westview Press, 1993), pp. 3-14; Montgomery Jr., Stephen E.: 'South Asia: Security of a Region', in Murray & Viotti (eds.): *op. cit.* (note 41), pp. 447-462; Wriggins, W. Howard: 'South Asian Regional Politics: Asymmetrical Balance or One-State Dominance?', in idem with F. Gregory Gause, III, Terrence P. Lyons & Evelyn Colbert: *Dynamics of Regional Politics: Four Systems on the Indian Ocean Rim* (New York: Columbia University Press, 1992), pp. 89-152; Bajpai, Kanti P.: 'Regions, Regional Politics, and the Security of South Asia', in Murray G. Weinbaum & Chetan Kumar (eds.): *South Asia Approaches the Millennium. Reexamining National Security* (Boulder: Westview Press, 1995), pp. 205-233.
82. Rupesinghe, Kumar & Khawar Mumtaz (eds.): *Internal Conflicts in South Asia* (London: Sage, 1996); Ganguly, Sumit: 'Ethno-Religious Conflict in South Asia', *Survival*, vol. 35, no. 2 (Summer 1993), pp. 88-111; Thomas, Roy: 'Secessionist Movements in South Asia', *ibid.*, vol. 36, no. 2 (Summer 1994), pp. 92-114; Ghashal, Baladas: 'Internal Sources of Conflict in South Asia', in Bajpai & Cohen (eds.): *op. cit.* (note 81), pp. 67-90; Little, David: *Sri Lanka. The Invention of Enmity* (Washington, D.C.: United States Institute of Peace Press, 1994). On the colonial roots of the problems see Silva, Kingsley M.de: 'Conflict Resolution in South Asia', in Luc van de Goor, Kumar Rupesinghe & Paul Sciarone (ed.): *Between Development and Destruction. An Enquiry into the Causes of Conflict in Post-Colonial States* (Houndmills, Basingstoke: Macmillan, 1996), pp. 298-320; Ayoob, Mohammed: *The*

Third World Security Predicament. State Making, Regional Conflict, and the International System (Boulder: Lynne Rienner, 1995).

83. Muni, S.D.: Pangs of Proximity. India and Sri Lanka's Ethnic Crisis (New Delhi and London: Sage, 1993); Midlarsky, Manus I. (ed.): The Internationalization of Communal Strife (London: Routledge, 1992), passim, but especially Johnson, James T.: 'Religion, Ideology, and Ethnic Identity in the Sri Lankan Conflict', ibid., pp. 45-68; Ispahani, Mahnaz: 'India's Role in Sri Lanka's Ethnic Conflict', in Ariel E. Levite, Bruce W. Jentleson & Larry Berman (eds.): Foreign Military Intervention. The Dynamics of Protracted Conflict (New York: Columbia University Press, 1992), pp. 209-239; Ganguly, Sumit: 'Conflict and Crisis in South and Southwest Asia', in Brown (ed.): op. cit. (note 70), pp. 149-172.

84. On the role of the military see Rosen, Stephen Peter: Societies and Military Power: India and Its Armies (Ithaca: Cornell University Press, 1996); Elkin, Jerrold: 'India', in Murray & Viotti (eds.): op. cit. (note 41), pp. 463-481, especially pp. 477-479. On Pakistan see Shafquat, Saeed: Civil-Military Relations in Pakistan (Boulder: Westview Press, 1997).

85. Gill, Veena: 'India as a Regional Great Power: in Pursuit of Shakti', in Iver B. Neumann (ed.): Regional Great Powers in International Politics (New York: St. Martin's Press, 1992), pp. 49-69; Gupta, Shekhar: 'India Redefines Its Role', Adelphi Papers, no. 293 (1995).

86. Smith, Chris: India's Ad Hoc Arsenal. Directions or Drift in Defence Policy? (Oxford: Oxford University Press/SIPRI, 1994); Roy-Chaudury: op. cit. (note 16); McCarthy, Timothy V.: 'India: Emerging Missile Power', in Potter & Jencks (eds.): op. cit. (note 38, pp. 201-234; Arnett, Eric: 'Military Technology: the Case of India', in SIPRI Yearbook 1994, pp. 343-366; Bedi, Rahul: 'India Will Build Aircraft Carrier for New Century', Jane's Defence Weekly, vol. 24, no. 8 (26 August 1995), pp. 3-4. See also Singh, Jasjit: 'Future Directions of India's Defence Policy', Strategic Digest (New Delhi: Institute for Defence Studies and Analyses), vol. 26, no. 5 (May 1996), pp. 605-612; Sharma, V.N.: 'India's Defence Forces: Building the Sinews of a Nation', USI National Security Papers, no. 13 (1994);

87. See the chapter by Jasjit Singh in this volume. See also Mattoo, Amitabh: 'India's Nuclear Status Quo', Survival, vol. 38, no. 3 (Autumn 1996), pp. 41-57; Chellaney, Brahma: 'India', in Mitchell Reiss & Robert S. Litwak: Nuclear Proliferation After the Cold War (Baltimore: John Hopkins University Press, 1994), pp. 165-190; Bidwai, Praful & Achin Vanaik: 'India and Pakistan', in Karp (ed.): op. cit. (note 23), pp. 258-276.

88. Ganguly, Sumit: The Origins of War in South Asia. Indo-Pakistani Conflicts Since 1947 (Boulder, CO: Westview Press, 1994).

89. For a rather plausible scenario see Dupuy: op. cit. (note 53), pp. 58-88. The author envisions an Indian pre-emptive attack against Pakistan via Kashmir, leading to an Indian victory, fortunately without the use of nuclear weapons by either side. On the background Bose, Sumantra: The Challenge in Kashmir. Democracy, Self-Determination and a Just Peace (New Delhi: Sage, 1997); Tremblay, Reeta Chowdhari: 'Nation, Identity and the Intervening Role of the State: A Study of the Secessionist Movement in Kashmir', Security Dialogue, vol. 28, no. 2 (June 1997),

pp. 471-497; Vinod, M.J.: 'Kashmir and India-Pakistan Relations: Problems and Prospects', *Strategic Analysis*, vol. 18, no. 8 (November 1995), pp. 1141-1155. See also Paul, Thaza Varkey: *Asymmetric Conflicts: War Initiation by Weaker Powers*, Cambridge Studies in International Relations, vol. 33 (Cambridge: Cambridge University Press, 1994), pp. 107-125 (on Pakistan's motives in the 1965 war).

90. Sheikh, Ali T.: 'Pakistan', in Reiss & Litwak: *op. cit.* (note 87), pp. 191-206; Pande, Savita: 'Pakistan's Nuclear Strategy', *Asian Strategic Review 1993-94* (New Delhi: IDSA, 1994), pp. 324-347.

91. Hagerty, Devin T.: 'Opaque Proliferation, Existential Deterrence, and the South Asian Nuclear Competition', *Security Studies*, vol. 2, no. 3/4 (Spring/Summer 1993), pp. 256-283; idem: 'Nuclear Deterrence in South Asia: The 1990 Indo-Pakistani Crisis', *International Security*, vol. 20, no. 3 (Winter 1995/96), pp. 79-114; Fetter, Steve & Devin T. Hagerty: 'Correspondence: Nuclear Deterrence and the 1990 Indo-Pakistani Crisis', *ibid.*, vol. 21, no. 1 (Summer 1996), pp. 176-185. On nuclear arms control see Chellaney, Brahma: 'The Challenge of Nuclear Arms Control in South Asia', *Survival*, vol. 35, no. 3 (Autumn 1993), pp. 121-136; Joeck, Neil: 'Maintaining Nuclear Stability in South Asia', *Adelphi Paper*, no. 312 (1997).

92. Maaß, Citha D.: 'Indien', in Veronika Büttner & Joachim Krause (eds.): *Rüstung statt Entwicklung? Sicherheitspolitik, Militärausgaben und Rüstungskontrolle in der Dritten Welt* (Baden-Baden: Nomos Verlag, 1995), pp. 133-159; Zingel, Wolfgang-Peter: 'Pakistan', *ibid.*, pp. 160-183; Ziem, Karlernst: 'Bangladesch', *ibid.*, pp. 184-207. For a contrary assessment, see Looney, Robert E. & David Winterford: *Economic Causes and Consequences of Defense Expenditures in the Middle East and South Asia* (Boulder: Westview Press, 1995), pp. 26-40 *et passim*; Bethélemy, Jean-Claude, Réma Herrera & Somnath Sen: 'Military Expenditure Reduction in India and Pakistan: Analytical Perspectives', *Peace Economics, Peace Science, and Public Policy*, vol. 2, no. 3 (Spring 1995), pp. 21-28.

93. Krepon, Michael & Amit Sevak (eds.): *Crisis Prevention, Confidence Building, and Reconciliation in South Asia* (New York: St. Martin's Press, 1996); Ganguly, Sumit & Ted Greenwood (eds.): *Mending Fences. Confidence- and Security-Building Measures in South Asia* (Boulder: Westview Press, 1996); Dixit, Aabha: 'India-Pakistan: Are Commonly Accepted Confidence-building Structures Relevant?', *Security Dialogue*, vol. 26, no. 2 (June 1995), pp. 191-204.

94. Wagner, Christian: 'Regional Cooperation in South Asia: Review of the SAARC', *Aussenpolitik*, vol. 44, no. 2 (2nd Quarter 1993), pp. 181-190; Wriggins: *loc. cit.* (note 81); Bajpai: *loc. cit.* (note 81); idem & Stephen P. Cohen: 'Cooperative Security and South Asean Insecurity', in Janne Nolan (ed.): *Global Engagement. Cooperation and Security in the 21st Century* (Washington, D.C.: The Brookings Institution, 1994), pp. 447-480; Yadav, S.P.: 'India's Role in the Future of SAARC', *U.S.I. Journal*, vol. 125, no. 520 (April-June 1995), pp. 176-197; Reed, Ananya Mukherjee: 'Regionalization in South Asia: Theory and Praxis', *Pacific Affairs*, vol. 70, no. 2 (Summer 1997), pp. 235-251.

95. Curtis (ed.): *op. cit.* (note 48), *passim*.

96. The US House of Representatives thus passed, by 369-14, a non-binding resolution that the USA 'should defend Taiwan in the event of invasion, missile attack, or blockade' by China. See *Jane's Defence Weekly*, vol. 25, no. 13 (27 March 1996), p. 3. On the background see Garver, John W.: *The Sino-American Alliance. Nationalist China and American Cold War Strategy in Asia* (Armonk, NY: M.E. Sharpe, 1997).
97. See the interview with then US Assistant Secretary of Defense for International Security Affairs, Joseph Nye, in *Jane's Defence Weekly*, vol. 22, no. 24 (17 December 1994), p. 32. See also Boatman, John: 'USA Halts Withdrawal in Policy Shift on Asia', *ibid.*, vol. 23, no. 10 (11 March 1995), p. 4.
98. Betts, Richard K.: 'Wealth, Power, and Instability: East Asia and the United States after the Cold War', *International Security*, vol. 18, no. 3 (Winter 1993/94), pp. 34-77; Ahn, Byung-Joon: 'The United States in Asia: Defining a New Role', in Chan Heng Chee (ed.): *The New Asia-Pacific Order* (Singapore: Institute of Southeast Asian Studies, 1997), pp. 131-156.

2 Transparency, Confidence-Building and Security in East Asia

OWEN GREENE

TRANSPARENCY AND CONFIDENCE-BUILDING MEASURES: A PRIORITY FOR THE REGION

After decades of conflict, the Asia-Pacific region is relatively peaceful. Notwithstanding the economic setbacks in 1997, policies of economic liberalization and integration into the international economy have brought new prosperity and developing patterns of economic interdependence in most of the region. Combined with the end of the Cold War and the resolution or amelioration of some long-standing internal conflicts, this process is creating new opportunities for conflict prevention and confidence-building. Nevertheless, a wide range of potential sources of tension and conflict remain in the Asia-Pacific, including a number of 'live' territorial disputes. Moreover, relations of power and influence are changing, as the consequences of the end of the Cold War and economic restructuring work themselves out, generating new tensions and suspicions as well as new opportunities for cooperation.

The combination of rapid economic growth and continuing insecurity in the region has contributed to substantial arms build-ups by several East Asian countries alongside the relative decline in the military presence of Russia and the USA. For their part, with a few limited exceptions, major arms exporters have generally been unable to resist the considerable economic and strategic pressures to supply arms to all those that seek them.

Such arms build-ups can undermine regional security, waste resources, and increase the destruction and suffering if conflict breaks out. Thus, the right of states to possess arms for self-defence must be accompanied by a responsibility to exercise restraint and to act with regard to the concerns of other countries and peoples. Unfortunately, however, there appears to be little prospect for negotiating 'structural' arms control agreements in all or parts of the region in the near future. Even if the political will for such agreements existed (which is not clear), multipolar power structures and complex and dynamic security concerns would make it difficult to achieve agreement on a balanced set of limits and constraints.

With structural conventional arms control ruled out for the time being, confidence-building measures (CBMs) and transparency and consultation arrangements[1] provide the main means of addressing concerns relating to the accumulation or transfer of conventional arms in the region. One of the major advantages of such measures is that they can be much more negotiable than structural arms control. They make no a priori presumption that the accumulation or transfer of conventional arms is illegitimate or destabilizing. They usually impose identical obligations on all parties, allowing debates about 'balance', relative capabilities and security requirements to become more manageable. Because they do not directly constrain forces, they raise fewer national security concerns and are less threatening to powerful domestic interest groups. Instead, they aim to provide concerned parties with more information on military activities or forces of concern, reducing the risk of misunderstandings, contributing to early warning of potential conflicts, and providing a basis on which concerns can be discussed and, hopefully, resolved. Participation in transparency arrangements can itself be an important symbol of an interest in co-operative security and the avoidance of war.

In the context of crisis or armed confrontation, some types of confidence-building and transparency measures can significantly reduce the threat of surprise attack, narrow the scope for using military exercises to intimidate weaker powers, and improve the prospects for successful crisis management. Of course, these good effects do not automatically flow from any transparency measure. Ill-judged transparency measures could make matters worse. In principle, they could: raise unnecessary concerns without providing a framework for resolving them; increase incentives for pre-emptive or offensive attack; exacerbate worrying asymmetries; or lull people into a false sense of security. Fortunately, experience shows that the design of transparency measures can be very flexible: such risks can be avoided and measures that are appropriate to the region and security situation can be developed.

Some recent *bilateral* transparency and confidence-building measures in East Asia have contributed significantly to reducing military tensions and the risk of unintended conflict, and to confidence-building and security. For example, such arrangements on either side of the 'line of control' in disputed territory between Russia/China and China/India have helped to reduce military and political tensions.

Moreover, the recent development of the ASEAN Regional Forum (ARF) has provided an important framework for the development of *multilateral* conflict-prevention institutions and confidence and security-building mechanisms. The next section of this paper aims briefly to identify some priority areas for the further development of such mechanisms and transparency measures in East Asia.

East Asia is also a key region for the development of further measures to prevent proliferation and promote disarmament of missiles and weapons of mass destruction. Even more than for conventional arms, these need to be considered in a global context. However, the challenges and opportunities have an important regional as well as global dimension. Fortunately, in this context, relevant multilateral disarmament and non-proliferation treaties have been established, and there are prospects for further structural arms control and disarmament. Nevertheless, as discussed in section 3, here too transparency arrangements and confidence-building mechanisms could play a central role in the immediate future.

CONVENTIONAL ARMS TRANSPARENCY AND CONFIDENCE-BUILDING

THE EMERGENCE OF MULTILATERAL SECURITY COOPERATION

In the Asia-Pacific, as in most other regions, it is a priority to develop multilateral confidence and security building measures (CSBMs) alongside appropriate bilateral arrangements. They are perhaps particularly appropriate to promoting security in a complex multipolar situation where there are tensions and potential sources of conflict, but very few acknowledged military adversaries. Whereas they cannot normally be fully customised to deal with a particular localised security problem, multilateral arrangements can provide an important regional or global framework for confidence-building and conflict prevention. Multilateral norms, rules and practices can be developed on the basis of which particular bilateral concerns can be more justly or fruitfully addressed. In such a multilateral framework, weaker countries are less vulnerable to direct, self-interested, coercion by great powers.

The recent development of the ARF is thus important. Although the first meeting of ARF was only in 1994, it has developed with remarkable speed (by the glacial standards of most multilateral arrangements). Working group meetings through 1994-5 developed an agenda for discussions on a range of key issues, including CSBMs, maritime issues (such as search and rescue), and preventive diplomacy and other conflict prevention measures.[2] The second ARF meeting in July 1995 established a framework for regular meetings on such issues.[3] Subsequently there has scarcely been a month without at least one ARF working group meeting, or a meeting through the associated 'track two' CSCAP (Council for Security Cooperation in the Asia-Pacific) process. The results of these meetings are fed through to the ARF-SOM (senior officials meetings), held immediately before the annual ARF meeting.

Importantly, the 1995 ARF meeting also agreed on the following:[4] (i) to encourage all ARF countries to enhance their dialogues and consultations on political and security cooperation, including exchanges on security perceptions on a bilateral, sub-regional and regional basis; (ii) for the ARF countries to submit to the ARF or ARF-SOM, on a voluntary basis, an annual statement of their defence policy; (iii) on the benefits of increased high level contacts and exchanges between military academies, staff colleges and training; (iv) to take note of the increased participation in the UN Conventional Arms Register since the first ARF and encourage those not yet participating to soon do so.

Between 1995 and 1997, progress was made in each of these areas. The 1996

ARF meeting reinforced these areas of activity, clarified guiding principles on new participants in ARF, and also endorsed: the development of regional dialogues based on annual defence white papers; information exchanges, observers, and notification of military exercises; and enhancing military exchanges and high-level defence contacts.[5] This agenda was maintained and developed at the 1997 ARF meeting, which also reinforced the importance of the on-going ARF workshop on managing potential conflicts in the South China Sea, noted progress towards a treaty banning anti-personnel landmines and agreed to support de-mining efforts.[6]

Overall, ARF remains at an early stage of development. The commitments of participants are relatively weak, most of the dialogues remain at a fairly general level, and ARF has tended to postpone dealing directly with specific existing conflicts within its institutional framework. Nevertheless, substantial progress has been made in developing ARF after only four meetings, and it is important to note that it took the CSCE (Conference on Security and Cooperation in Europe) over a decade before it could proceed substantially from agreements on general principles to the development and implementation of the important agreements on CSBMs and human rights. The key task now is to build on the existing agreements within ARF, and particularly those relating to military transparency and dialogues and exchanges on defence and security policy. The following sub-sections consider some of the most promising ways in which this could be done.

BUILDING ON THE UN REGISTER OF CONVENTIONAL ARMS

Most East Asian countries now participate in the UN Register of Conventional Arms, in line with the recommendations of ARF. This means that the Register could provide an important basis for the further development of regional or sub-regional transparency arrangements or security dialogues.

The UN Register first came into operation in 1993, and has rapidly achieved wide participation.[7] By early November 1997, 90 states had provided their reports for the fifth year (covering transfers in 1996). By that date, some 138 states had participated in the Register at least once, and a 'core' group of 70-80 states were regularly participating each year.[8] This core group included almost all major arms exporting countries, and most of the main arms importers.

Thus, from its first year, the Register has covered more than 90 percent of the global trade in major conventional arms. Moreover, the scope and quality of the national submissions to the Register have gradually improved. Most participants reporting arms transfers now go beyond the minimum requirements of the Register and provide qualitative information about the types or roles of the weapons as well as the numbers involved in each transfer. Moreover, about thirty countries provide data on their military holdings or procurement from national production as well as transfers.

Participation rates vary from region to region. Significantly, participation is high in East Asia and continuing to grow (see Appendix). In North-East Asia, China, Japan, Mongolia and South Korea take part on a regular basis, as do other key states relevant to sub-regional security including USA, Russia, and Canada. Only North Korea has failed to submit a report. Also, on China's insistence, Taiwan has not been asked to participate. Nevertheless, the US has reported exports to Taiwan in both 1996 and 1997. This practice brought a fierce riposte from China in 1997, noting that 'arms transfers from the US to Taiwan are neither legitimate nor transfers between sovereign states' and asking that such entries be deleted from future annual reports.

In South-East Asia, the widening participation amongst ASEAN states has been one of the most significant developments in the last five years. In the first year, only half of these countries reported. However, by 1997, all ASEAN states submit reports, although the three candidate members (Laos, Myanmar and Cambodia) do not. Australia and New Zealand consistently provide full reports. Otherwise, participation in Oceania has been mixed, with a relatively high rate of 'turnover' in participation.

When the UN General Assembly established the Register in 1992, it was agreed that its scope should be extended to cover military holdings and national procurement. However, two major attempts in 1994 and 1997 to agree ways to expand and strengthen the global Register achieved only very modest results. This means that the Register remains far from achieving its full potential.

Nevertheless, even in its present form, the new transparency regime has made a significant contribution. Its first, and central, achievement has been to establish, on a global scale, a *de facto* norm of transparency relating to conventional arms. Although participation remains far from universal, most major arms importers and exporters regularly participate. The Register has thus significantly strengthened the principle that states' right to procure arms for their defence must be accompanied by a responsibility to exercise that right with restraint, taking due account of the concerns of others. This is important for most regions of the world, including East and South Asia, where norms of co-operative security remain poorly developed.

Second, over 90 percent of the international trade in major conventional arms has probably been reported to the Register each year, together with further information on weapon types, military holdings and procurement from national production. Against the expectations of some sceptics, the Register has revealed much information that was not previously available in the public domain. For example, in recent years the Register has included over fifty separate transactions each year that were not included in the *SIPRI Yearbooks*.[9] In this context, the UN Register has particularly provided new information on transfers of land-based systems such as tanks, artillery, and armoured personnel carriers, which are less easily monitored than ships or aircraft.

Third, the UN Register provides *official* information on arms transfers. In contrast with unofficial sources, which governments can always contest, it provides politically legitimate information. It thus provides a basis on which intergovernmental security dialogues and regional confidence-building processes can be developed for diplomatic discussions at a bilateral and multilateral level, whereas the status of unofficial information is always contestable. This has already proved useful in East Asia, where participation in the Register has been an important dimension of the development of the ASEAN Regional Forum. Even in its present form, the Register could similarly provide a useful basis for confidence and security building dialogues and further transparency measures in Latin America, the former USSR, South and East Asia, and elsewhere.

Fourth, the requirement to provide international reports to the Register has stimulated many governments to establish proper systems for monitoring their own arms transfers. Before they participated in the Register, many governments (including those of major developed countries) did not have such systems even for their own purposes. The challenge of collecting and reporting reliable information to the Register has been taken seriously by most Asian governments, and has stimulated improvements in national monitoring and control systems. There have also been some instances where discrepancies between the data on arms imports collected by national authorities and reports of arms supplying states, have led to the discovery and correction of weaknesses in national import control systems (e.g., the discovery by Pakistan's national authorities that three armoured personnel carriers had been independently imported by Sind regional government).[10]

Fifth, the data submitted for the Register is publicly available. It can be scrutinised by members of national legislatures, research institutes, journalists and interested members of the public. In this respect, the Register is an important advance on the practice of confidential inter-governmental information exchanges in OSCE confidence-building measures or in the Wassenaar Arrangement. It facilitates public debate and democratic accountability as well as inter-governmental discussions. It has provided leverage in a number of countries for civil authorities and parliamentarians to increase disclosure of military procurement and transfers. Before the Register was established, few countries published quantitative information on their annual arms transfers. In many countries, in East and South Asia as elsewhere, such matters were not even regarded to be a matter for legitimate public questioning. The Register is helping to change this situation. Promoting domestic discussion and accountability could ultimately promote restraint as well as more effective national policies.

Thus, there are important opportunities to build on the UN Register to further develop CSBMs in East and South Asia. The Report of the 1994 UN Group of Experts, endorsed by the UN Secretary-General and General Assembly, encourages the establishment of regional registers to complement and move beyond the global register according to regional needs. However, since China and India have been amongst the main opponents of the rapid development of the global register (for example, to include military holdings and domestic procurement), it is probably more useful to focus on ways in which Asian countries could make more use of the existing global register than on trying to establish new regional arms registers for East Asia.

First, it remains important to further increase participation in the Register in Asia. As Myanmar, Laos and Cambodia join ASEAN, they should be strongly encouraged to participate in the Register, as a key indicator of their intention to be 'good citizens' in the region. Similarly, when (and if) North Korea chooses to signal such intentions, participation in the Register could provide a relatively diplomatically straightforward way of doing so, being as it is a global arrangement which North Korea has itself endorsed in the General Assembly.

Ways should also be found for Taiwan to be able to report to the Register without alienating China. Taiwan is a major importer of arms and an emerging arms supplier, and its absence implies a serious gap in the Register's coverage. In recent years, Taiwan has become a relatively open and democratic society. This, combined with its desire to participate in international affairs, means that sections of the Taiwanese government have indicated that Taiwan would be prepared in principle to consider submitting data for the Register.

Fear that China would include Taiwan's data in its own return (as a region of China), as part the diplomatic war of attrition, presently reinforce Taiwanese government reluctance to provide public data on arms transfers. Some reassurance on this issue from China, combined with an understanding that inclusion in the Register of transfers data from 'political entities' such as Taiwan does not indicate any acceptance of them as sovereign states, would not only strengthen the Register, but also be important confidence-building measures in China-Taiwan relations in its own right.

Moreover, ARF countries that are already participating could take steps to promote greater use of the UN Register. ARF members should agree explicitly to use the UN Register, and any other information governments choose to provide, as a basis for routinely reviewing developments relating to arms transfers, procurement and holdings in the Asia-Pacific and discussing any security concerns that might arise. In 1996 and 1997, the discussion was rather perfunctory. In the future, it could be more extensive, particularly in the meetings of senior officials, supplemented by ad-hoc sub-regional or bilateral meetings as appropriate. To facilitate this, ARF governments could circulate their Register submissions amongst themselves at the same time as they send them to the UN Secretariat, as is now done in the OCSE.

Further, ARF countries should aim to make more use of the Register's existing reporting guidelines to report more qualitative information on the types and roles as well as numbers of reported arms transfers, and to provide more 'background information' on their holdings and procurement wherever they feel this can be done without endangering national security. Decisions on whether to take fuller advantage of the Register's reporting mechanism could be left to each national government. However, as more countries did so, informal norms could develop encouraging others to follow. Several Asia-Pacific countries already provide some qualitative information on weapon types, including, for the first time in 1997, China. Greater transparency by the USA in particular in this area would probably greatly stimulate this trend.

There are also realistic and important opportunities to agree guidelines on greater transparency amongst ARF members, at least for some of the categories of arms covered by the Register. Warships might be a particularly good candidate for developing ARF guidelines for reporting on holdings and procurement as well as transfers. Maritime issues are of particular concern in the Asia-Pacific. Moreover, reliable unofficial information is already available on the types and numbers of warships traded and in each country's possession (see, for example, *Jane's Fighting Ships*). Thus, providing such information officially would reveal little that could remotely damage national security, while it would facilitate regional consultations on this key issue of rumour and concern. Submitted data could then be discussed in ARF meetings and distributed regionally, for example as an annex to the ARF Chairman's annual statement or through CSCAP.

DEVELOPING AND REVIEWING DEFENCE 'WHITE PAPERS'

Within the ARF, there has been much discussion of the benefits of countries regularly publishing a Defence 'White Paper'; that is, a document detailing national security policies, defence doctrine, military holdings, spending and procurement. Such White Papers are primarily produced for domestic purposes, for information, accountability and debate. However, they can also contribute greatly to regional and global transparency, consultation and confidence-building. Perhaps the key questions relating to any country's spending on, and accumulation of, conventional arms are concerned with how the forces are organised, the policies, roles and intentions associated with armed forces, and priorities and trends for the future. It is helpful if each government provides a regular and systematic explanation of these, along with information on arms procurement, holdings and spending. This would not only help to prevent misunderstandings, but also provide a basis for further bilateral and multilateral consultations.

The publication of an annual defence White Paper is a national decision, and reflects both the development of domestic accountability and democracy and also an awareness that the governments and peoples of other countries have a legitimate interest in information on its defence policy, spending and military forces. Recently, most states in the Asia-Pacific (including China) have begun to publish such documents. The priority now is to develop their contents and to use them more systematically as a basis for regional dialogues.

The contents of each country's White Paper could vary somewhat, according to domestic circumstances and security sensitivities, but they should provide substantial information on questions of real regional and domestic concern. At a minimum, they should therefore include: a reasonably full explanation of their understanding of the current security situation, their security and defence concerns, and their defence and military policy; an outline of the country's existing and projected military forces and an explanation of their roles; a statement of annual military spending, including some breakdown into sectors (procurement, R&D, pensions, salaries, maintenance, etc.); an outline of policies relating to the import, export, and domestic production of arms; and an outline of military research and development programmes.

DEVELOPING SUB-REGIONAL MULTILATERAL SECURITY COOPERATION IN NORTH-EAST ASIA

The security situation in North-East Asia is at least as complex and serious as in South-East Asia. Not only are there territorial disputes, but it is a prime focus of potential confrontation and rivalry for world and medium powers. No state has an interest in war, but the confrontations in Korea and across the Taiwan Straits have the potential to develop rapidly into full-blown military crises and to trigger major conflicts. However, progress towards developing multilateral frameworks for confidence-building, conflict avoidance, and conflict resolution in this sub-region has been very limited. Compared to North-East Asia (in which I include Taiwan), South-East Asia has developed a dense and promising set of rules, guidelines, and confidence-building procedures. In this context, it is useful briefly to discuss the distinct characteristics of North-East Asia and the prospects for developing multilateral security dialogues.

The decade started quite promisingly, with talks leading to the December 1991 'Agreement on Reconciliation, Non-Aggression, and Exchanges and Cooperation' between North and South Korea. In principle, this agreement continues to provide a good basis for implementing useful CSBMs on the peninsula. In practice, however, no progress was made in implementing these accords, and the development of bilateral CSBMs stalled.

Nor were there any significant multilateral processes in the sub-region of North-East Asia where security issues could be discussed. The most immediate blockage to the development of multilateral security dialogues in this region through most of the 1990s was the refusal of North Korea to participate in international discussions of regional security issues except bilaterally with the USA. It does not participate in ARF, and so far has not participated in CSCAP working group meetings or almost any other 'track two' multilateral dialogues. This has been widely interpreted as a diplomatic tactic, in order to force the US into bilateral relations that might lead to diplomatic recognition of North Korea, with the side benefit of side-lining its South Korean adversaries and sowing discord in US-South Korean relations.

The establishment of four power talks (North and South Korea, China and USA) in 1997 was an important step in the development of multilateral dialogue to address security issues on the Korean peninsular. However, progress is likely to be slow and entirely focused on Korean issues. Thus, they will not provide a framework for addressing the other security issues in the sub-region.

Thus, alongside the four power talks on Korea, a strong case can be made for proceeding to develop broader multilateral dialogues in the sub-region, even if this has to be done without North Korean participation. There are many issues to be addressed besides the confrontation on the Korean peninsula. In practice, this depends on further strengthening the intensity of security relations between Japan and South Korea, and between these countries and China, so that multilateral CSBMs can be firmly based with 'core' participation of China, Japan, South Korea, and USA (with Russia, Canada and the EU also playing potentially significant roles). In the years immediately following the end of the Cold War, US official policy towards the development of multilateral security dialogues in the region was generally sceptical and unsupportive. Now that the Clinton administration has adopted a more positive position in principle, and that US-China relations are improving, it is important to take advantage of this.

A key question is which existing institutions can be used to do this. KEDO (Korean Peninsula Energy Development Organization), i.e. the multilateral institution established to implement the nuclear accords with North Korea, must focus on securing the implementation of its explicit tasks for the foreseeable future. The Tumen river project, to develop a multilateral economic zone involving China, Russia, North Korea, Japan and South Korea, will similarly be stretched even to achieve its core objectives, and is not well adapted as a framework for security dialogues.

Recent sub-regional discussions on cooperation to tackle transboundary air pollution and regional seas management are promising, but become immediately difficult as soon as they even begin to touch on issues relevant to security. Access and use of fishing grounds is a point of major friction and concern to all parties, but is probably sufficiently politically sensitive that discussions on this topic would not provide a promising basis for broader dialogues. APEC (Asia-Pacific Economic Cooperation) and sub-regional frameworks for economic cooperation are of key importance, but is vital that these do not develop an explicit security agenda, not least in order to ensure continued Taiwanese participation.

Thus, in spite of all of the obstacles, the ARF (and CSCAP) working groups and dialogues re-emerge as the most promising framework for sub-regional multilateral security dialogues and confidence-building. Cooperation on maritime search and sea rescue, addressed by the ARF inter-sessional meeting co-chaired by the USA and Singapore, may be able to achieve most rapid progress in the sub-region. However, attention should be given to specifically military security issues, and here naval CSBMs are a clear priority.

In addition to developing information exchanges on transfers, procurement, and holdings of warships on the basis of the UN Register (discussed above), the most obvious focus for such efforts is the establishment of rules of conduct and consultation procedures to prevent incidents at sea. Bilateral agreements on these issues between NATO naval powers and the USSR on significantly promoted security and restraint during the Cold War.[11] Similar agreements could contribute significantly to maritime security in the Asia-Pacific.

In 1997, the USA and China concluded such an agreement bilaterally. However, in this region such CSBMs should be seen as codes of conduct to reduce friction amongst cooperation partners rather than as ways of avoiding war between acknowledged adversaries. For this reason, it might be better if they were further developed within a multilateral framework, such as the ASEAN Regional Forum (ARF), rather than purely bilaterally. Thus ARF could encourage the establishment of a complex of bilateral agreements within the region according to ARF guidelines, and establish a regional or sub-regional framework for reviewing their implementation and further development.

CHINA-TAIWAN CSBMs

The relationship between China and Taiwan remains a major source of concern for regional security. Taiwan has become a developed, democratic and independent 'entity', with its own legitimate concerns and also subject to the pressures and constraints of a democracy. There can be no security in the region unless this is properly recognised. The question of whether and how Taiwan will be unified with China must remain open for the foreseeable future. In the meantime, some accommodation must be found to reduce tensions and the risk of military conflict, and to allow for Taiwanese participation in some way in regional security discussions. This would involve finding some diplomatic formula for Taiwan's international status that is satisfactory to both China and Taiwan (equivalent to the 'customs area' used for APEC purposes). It also means establishing some 'rules of the road' and bilateral (and maybe informal) CSBMs.

In fact, the need for informal codes of conduct and information-exchange and consultation procedures between Taiwan and China has long been recognised. Since the mid-1980s, informal links between Taiwan and the Chinese mainland on economic and human issues developed rapidly. Chinese policy was 'green light' for economic and social relations; 'red light' on security and political issues. Quasi-official bodies on each side of the Taiwan straits—the Straits Exchange Foundation (Taiwan) and the Association for Relations across the Taiwan Straits (PRC)—were established to discuss issues of common concern such as illegal migrants, harassment of fishers, piracy, and communications.

At the same time, occasional modest tension reduction measures coexisted with regular acts of harassment and continual friction due to lack of agreed guidelines or codes of conduct. Such informal consultations were suspended alongside the series of missile tests and military exercises conducted by China in 1995, after the visit to Cornell University by Taiwan's President Lee. These exercises highlighted the risks of military crisis and confrontation across the Taiwan straits. They also illustrated how counterproductive provocative military exercises can be as instruments of national policy.

With political will, the development of useful if informal bilateral CSBMs may be relatively straightforward, focusing on: understandings and consultative mechanisms on access to natural resources in the Taiwan Straits; restraint and notification of military exercises; and the development of wider economic and social relations. However, sustained progress on these issues probably requires some stable and mutually agreeable formulation of Taiwan's status as a de facto independent political entity.

SOUTH CHINA SEAS

The skirmishes and tensions surrounding competing claims to the Spratly/Nansha Islands are well-known.[12] Bilateral understandings aimed at avoiding and resolving conflicts, for example, clearly have a potentially important role to play in tackling this problem. However, so far the most attractive approach has been to aim to develop a multilateral framework for the development of appropriate dialogues consultations. ASEAN states have mostly successfully diffused and avoided such conflicts amongst themselves through the dialogues and understandings developed within ASEAN. Similarly, avoiding and resolving conflicts involving China appears also to require a multilateral framework.

In 1996, the ARF agreed to hold a Workshop on Managing Potential Conflicts in the South China Sea, providing a framework for continuing dialogue amongst all interested parties. Moreover, both China and the ASEAN states have agreed that the conflicts should be addressed according to the rules of the Law of the Sea Convention, which includes a dispute resolution mechanism and a range of potentially useful precedents from the resolution of disputes over territorial waters and Exclusive Economic Zones elsewhere in the world.

Nevertheless, little progress has been made on the substantial disputes over the Spratly Islands, and there is little sign of the compromises necessary for a legal settlement. Thus, it becomes a priority to establish rules and understandings to prevent the territorial disputes escalating into violence. In principle, the states involved have agreed to avoid provocative actions and to desist from placing further installations on the disputed islands. In practice, states have not fully complied with these guidelines, causing continual friction and tension. In this context, it seems important to establish more precise rules and procedures for multilateral consultations if there are concerns about possible non-compliance. At least this could make non-compliance less contestable and more politically costly.

WEAPONS OF MASS DESTRUCTION: DISARMAMENT, NON-PROLIFERATION, AND TRANSPARENCY

BUILDING ON GLOBAL REGIMES

In contrast with the situation with conventional arms, it has proved possible over the last thirty years to develop globally-accepted norms and rules to limit or ban the accumulation and spread of weapons of mass destruction and their associated delivery systems. A series of bilateral nuclear arms reduction treaties have been agreed between the USA and USSR/Russia, including the INF (Intermediate-Range Nuclear Forces) Treaty, START-I (Strategic Arms Reduction Treaty) and START-II. The outlines of a START-III Treaty have been agreed in principle, for negotiation as soon as START-II is ratified. The development, possession or use of chemical and biological weapons is banned by global international conventions. The Nuclear Non-Proliferation Treaty (NPT), extended indefinitely in 1995, bans the spread of possession of nuclear weapons beyond the five recognised nuclear weapon states, and commits these nuclear weapon states to the objective of complete nuclear disarmament. The 1996 Comprehensive Test Ban Treaty (CTBT) is a further important step forward. Hopefully, the Conference on Disarmament will be able to negotiate a substantial Fissile Material Cut-off Treaty in the near future.

Such global regimes improve the security of states in East Asia, as elsewhere. They address regional as well as global security concerns of East Asian countries, which therefore have a strong interest in promoting full participation and implementation in the region. Moreover, the global regime can be used as a framework for improving regional confidence-building and control. Thus, for example, full implementation of the terms of the Chemical Weapons Convention, including provisions for transparency and verification, and for reporting and disposing of existing or past stocks, can itself increase regional confidence and cooperation.

In relation to nuclear weapons, the establishment of regional nuclear weapon free zones can help to reinforce the NPT as well as contribute to the development of regional security cooperation. In December, 1995, the heads of government of South-East Asian countries signed a South-East Asian Nuclear Weapon Free Zone Treaty (SEANWFZ). By 1997 Mongolia and the Central Asian states had also established themselves as nuclear weapon free zones.

The IAEA's (International Atomic Energy Agency) '93+2' Protocol provides an important further opportunity for strengthening regional as well as global confidence and transparency in the nuclear area. Agreed in May 1997, it aims to reinforce the effectiveness of the IAEA's verification regime through a range of transparency, information-exchange, and inspection measures for nuclear facilities, fissile materials and trade in nuclear-related dual-use technologies. The challenge for the next few years is to achieve full implementation of this far-reaching reform by all IAEA members, including almost all East Asian countries.

Asia-Pacific countries, particularly in North-East Asia, could use this new agreement as an opportunity to begin to address regional concerns about nuclear safety, fissile material management, and nuclear weapon potential of neighbouring states. Full participation and implementation would be a first step, particularly if China, as a nuclear weapon state, agreed to place its civil nuclear facilities and materials under similar safeguards. Beyond this, states in the region could agree to exchange amongst themselves at least some of the information they provide to the IAEA, and make provision for supplementary regional consultations. In this way, they could gradually develop some of the regional systems for cooperation, consultation and transparency called-for in proposals for the establishment of a new 'AsiaAtom' or 'PacAtom' agreement.

MULTILATERALIZING THE NUCLEAR DISARMAMENT PROCESS

Several Asia-Pacific countries, and particularly the states dominantly involved in North-East Asian security affairs, have both a strong interest and responsibility in the nuclear disarmament process. As indicated above, significant progress has been made in this area in the 1990s. The US-Russian nuclear arms reduction agreements are central to this process, and will remain so while the nuclear arsenals are so much larger than the other three nuclear weapon states or so-called threshold states. China, France and the UK have indicated that they do not expect to join the START process until the nuclear holdings of Russia and the USA have been reduced to levels more commensurate with their own.

This is an understandable position, but should not be taken to imply that China, France and the UK do not have to become seriously engaged in the nuclear disarmament process until the USA and Russia have implemented START III reduction targets of about 2,000 warheads or below. This might not be achieved until after 2010, and the smaller nuclear weapon states have a responsibility to take action long before then. It is therefore important to develop early ways to 'multilateralize' the nuclear disarmament process to include at least all five declared nuclear weapon states.

There are several promising ways in which this could be done.[13] China, France and the UK could immediately declare that they will cap and/or reduce their nuclear arsenals below 1990 levels (say), provided that the US-Russia arms reduction process remains underway. Measures and consultations to 'de-alert' nuclear forces should involve all nuclear weapon states. Some existing bilateral agreements, such as the ABM and INF treaty regimes, could be 'multilateralized'. For example, all five nuclear weapon states could adhere to the main terms of the ABM treaty and take part in all future discussions on its implementation or revision by participating in the Special Consultative Committee. A global ban on medium and intermediate-range missile forces could be negotiated, with the effect of extending the bilateral INF treaty to include at least all five nuclear weapon states. Participation could then be expanded to include other countries with missile capabilities, such as key members of the Missile Technology Control Regime and, in the longer term, the threshold states and many other countries.

Transparency, consultation and verification measures could provide a particularly important way of involving China, France and the UK in the nuclear disarmament process at an early stage. They could not only be useful confidence-building measures, but also contribute to the development of institutions, experience and shared data on which future multilateral nuclear disarmament agreements could build. Procedures should be established, for example, for all five nuclear weapon states to engage in confidential exchanges and inspection visits at nuclear-weapon facilities, and to the three 'medium' nuclear weapon states to participate in some START II verification activities to gain experience.

A NUCLEAR WEAPONS REGISTER

While much can be done confidentially amongst the five nuclear weapon states, they also have a responsibility to report to the wider international community. In this context, proposals for a Nuclear Weapons Register should also be pursued. The first proposals by governments for such a Register were made in 1993-4.[14] In December 1993, Germany proposed a Register in which the nuclear weapon states would regularly report their stockpiles of nuclear warheads. However, in the face of objections from the then governments of the USA, UK and France, Germany did not pursue its proposal. In 1994 Argentina suggested a modest first step towards such a Register, requesting the nuclear weapon states to provide the UN with copies of any status reports on nuclear forces or reductions that they produce nationally or as part of existing treaties such as START.

Since 1994, the proposal for a Nuclear Weapons Register has faded into the background. However, the demand for increased nuclear weapons transparency remains, for example amongst many non-nuclear and G77 states, and ways should be found to meet it. Central to the concept of a Nuclear Weapons Register is that the five nuclear weapon states should provide information related to their nuclear forces to it, and that it would be published and openly available. Beyond that, many aspects of the design of the Register, and the degree of transparency it would involve, remain open for debate.

As with other transparency arrangements, a Nuclear Weapon Register could begin relatively modestly and develop over time. For example, it could begin with nuclear weapon states providing aggregate data on their total holdings of nuclear warheads. This could be supplemented with information on the numbers of warheads they had dismantled or withdrawn from service during the previous year. In later years the levels of detail reported could be increased, within the constraints of protecting national security and avoiding releases of information that could undermine non-proliferation efforts. For example, nuclear weapon states could release disaggregated data distinguishing between stored and deployed warheads and, preferably, numbers of each category of warheads. In addition, associated information relating to fissile material holdings, delivery vehicles, or dismantlement techniques or schedules, could also be submitted.

Such a Nuclear Weapons Register would be a valuable early step in developing multilateral mechanisms for nuclear weapons involving all nuclear weapon states. It could both improve transparency and symbolise acceptance of the fact that being one of the five recognised nuclear weapon states now involves duties to the international community, including such obligations to report and render themselves accountable.

CONCLUSIONS

The security situation in East Asia has developed greatly since the end of the cold war and the demise of the USSR. There are still serious disputes and potential flashpoints. But whereas in the early 1990s there were worryingly few bilateral security dialogues amongst several key states, and multilateral frameworks for regional security cooperation were almost non-existent, by 1997 substantial progress had been made in each of these areas. The prospects for successful conflict prevention and management have thus improved. Nevertheless, there is still much cause for concern. Transparency arrangements and confidence-building measures could contribute substantially to regional security. This paper has identified and discussed several ways in which these could established or developed in all or part of East Asia in the near future. It is important to pursue such approaches while the security environment remains relatively benign.

NOTES

1. Transparency measures in this context are 'the systematic provision of information on specific aspects of activities in the military field under informal or formal international arrangements': the definition provided, e.g., by the N Panel of Technical Experts: 'Study on Ways and Means of Promoting Transparency in International Transfers of Conventional Arms', *UN General Assembly Document*, A/46/301 (September 1991), p. 13.
2. Research Institute for Peace and Security: *Asian Security 1995-96* (London: Brassey's, 1995), pp. 15-22.
3. Chairman's Statement of the Second ASEAN Regional Forum (ARF), 1 August 1995. See http://www.aseansec.org/politics/pol_arf1.htm for the text *in extenso*.
4. Chairman's Statement of the Second ASEAN Regional Forum (ARF), 1 August 1995. See http://www.aseansec.org/politics/pol_arf2.htm for the text *in extenso*.
5. Chairman's Statement of the Third ASEAN Regional Forum (ARF), 23 July 1996. See http://www.aseansec.org/politics/pol_arf3.htm for the text *in extenso*.

6. Chairman's Statement, The Fourth Meeting of the ASEAN Regional Forum, Subang Jaya, Malaysia, 27 July 1997. For the text *in extenso* see http://www.aseansec.org/politics/pol_arf4.htm.
7. For a detailed examination of the operation and development of the UN Register, see for example: Chalmers, Malcolm & Owen Greene: 'The Register in Its First Four Years', in Chalmers, Malcolm, Mitsuru Donowaki & Owen Greene (eds): *Developing Arms Transparency: the Future of the UN Register*. Bradford Arms Register Studies (BARS), no. 7 (Bradford: Bradford University/CPDNP, 1997), pp. 9-39; idem & idem: 'The UN Register in Its Fourth Year: Analysing the Fourth Year Replies and Priorities for the 1997 Review', *BARS Working Paper*, no. 2 (Bradford: Bradford University, 1996); and idem & idem: *Taking Stock: the UN Register after Two Years* (London: Westview Press, 1995).
8. For a review of the participation in the Register in its fourth and fifth years, and of the data supplied to it, up to October 1997, see idem & idem: 'Developing the UN Register: Challenges and Setbacks', *Disarmament Diplomacy*, no. 10 (October 1997), pp. 11-17; and idem & idem: *loc. cit.* 1996 (note 7).
9. This is not to imply any criticism of the annual SIPRI register, which has played a key unofficial role in promoting transparency. Some of the omissions in the SIPRI register are a result of caution about including unconfirmed reports of transfers, and SIPRI includes details and transfers that are not found in the UN Register.
10. Chalmers, Malcolm & Owen Greene: *Developments in Official Transparency on Conventional Arms in East and South Asia, Particularly Relating to Procurement, Holdings and Transfers* (Tokyo: Centre for Promotion of Disarmament and Non-Proliferation, Japan Institute for International Affairs, 1997), p. 81.
11. The first such agreement was the 1972 Agreement on the Prevention of Incidents at Sea, agreed by the USSR and USA. For further discussion of such measures, see chapters in Jozef Goldblat (ed.): 'Maritime Security: The Building of Confidence', *Topical Papers*, no. 4 (New York: UN Department of Disarmament Affairs, 1990); and Lynn-Jones, Sean: 'The Incidents at Sea Agreement', in Alexander L. George, Philip J. Farley & Alexander Dallin (eds.): *U.S.-Soviet Security Cooperation. Achievements, Failures, Lessons* (New York: Oxford University Press, 1988), pp. 482-509.
12. See, for example, Valencia, Mark J.: 'China and the South China Sea Disputes', *Adelphi Papers*, no. 298 (1995).
13. I have discussed approaches to multilateralizing the nuclear disarmament process at greater length in Greene, Owen: 'Multilateralizing the Nuclear Disarmament Process', *INESAP Bulletin*, November 1997. See also the Canberra Commission: *Report of the Canberra Commission on the Elimination of Nuclear Weapons* (Canberra: Commonwealth of Australia, August 1996); Chalmers, Malcolm: *British Nuclear Weapons Policy: the Next Steps*. ISIS Report (London: ISIS, 1997).
14. See, for example, Mueller, Harald: 'Transparency in Nuclear Arms: Towards a Nuclear Weapons Register', *Arms Control Today*, vol. 24, no. 8 (October 1994); S. Howard, 'Proposals for a Nuclear Weapons Register', in John Poole & Richard Guthrie (eds.): *Verification 1996: VERTIC Yearbook* (Boulder: Westview, 1996), pp. 77-86.

APPENDIX

Participation in each of the first five years of the Register (* as of November 1997)

TABLE 2: REPLIES TO THE REGISTER FOR THE YEARS	1992	1993	1994	1995	1996
Asia and Oceania (34)	20	23	24	23	19
Afghanistan		*			
Australia	*	*	*	*	*
Bangladesh					
Bhutan		*	*	*	*
Brunei					*
Cambodia					
China	*	*	*	*	*
Cook Islands				*	*
DPRK					
Federated States of Micronesia					
Fiji	*	*	*	*	*
India	*	*	*	*	*
Indonesia	*	*	*	*	*
Japan	*	*	*	*	*
Laos					
Malaysia		*	*	*	*
Maldives	*	*	*	*	*
Marshall Islands			*	*	*
Mongolia	*	*	*	*	*
Myanmar					
Nepal		*		*	
New Zealand	*	*	*	*	*
Pakistan	*	*	*	*	*
Palau					
Papua New Guinea	*	*	*	*	
Philippines	*	*	*	*	
Republic of Korea	*	*	*	*	*
Samoa		*	*	*	
Singapore	*	*	*	*	*
Solomon Islands		*		*	
Sri Lanka	*	*	*	*	
Thailand		*	*	*	*
Vanuatu	*	*	*	*	
Vietnam			*	*	*

187 countries have been asked to provide information for the Register: 185 UN members, plus the Holy See and Switzerland. Of these 138 states have participated at least once during this five year period. However, because several of these countries only participate irregularly, the number participating each year is rather less—around 90. Note that states that have only begun to participate in recent years are encouraged to provide reports for earlier years as well, and a few have done so. Thus, the number of participating states for 1992, 1993 etc. have gradually increased over the years. Table 3 in this Appendix presents the states that have submitted a report for a given year, but provides no indication of when the report was received by the UN Secretariat. Thus, the last row of the table provides a better overall indication of trends than the row of 'totals' immediately above it.

TABLE 3: REPLIES TO THE REGISTER FOR THE YEARS	1992	1993	1994	1995	1996
ASIA AND OCEANIA (34)	20	23	24	23	19
AMERICA (35)	19	18	20	16	18
Canada	*	*	*	*	*
USA	*	*	*	*	*
FORMER SOVIET UNION (15)	6	5	9	13	11
Kazakhstan	*		*	*	*
Kyrgystan				*	
Russian Federation	*	*	*	*	*
Tajikistan			*	*	
Turkmenistan				*	*
Uzbekistan					
SUB-SAHARAN AFRICA (48)	10	13	9	9	7
MIDDLE EAST (18)	8	3	3	2	2
EUROPE (38)	31	31	32	32	33
TOTAL	94	93	97	95	90
TOTAL STATES PARTICIPATING by 15 Nov. of following year	82	84	87	92	90

3 Arms Control and Disarmament in the Post-Cold War World: A View from India

JASJIT SINGH

THE COLD WAR EXPERIENCE

Disarmament and arms control, in the final analysis, cannot be pursued for their own sake, but their objective must be peace, understood in a comprehensive and consistent sense. Security will be a natural consequence of peace, but the reverse is not necessarily true. The Westphalian model of sovereign states, unfortunately, implied a paradigm of competitive inter-state security that entailed a unilateral pursuit of absolute security by each sovereign state, which tended to generate a sense of threat and insecurity in other states. Nuclear weapons, of course, provided the most dangerous and destructive manifestation of such competitive security. Lasting peace and security were thus not achievable in any region without a paradigm shift from competitive to cooperative security. Seen in this context, arms control were either relevant as contributions to strategic stability, or as interim steps along the path to the ultimate goal of complete and general disarmament.

For more than four decades, the Cold War was cited in justification for nuclear weapons, but the Cold War has now been over for more than six years. Unfortunately, rather than abolishing their nuclear weapons as no longer justified, the nuclear weapon states (and their military allies) are claiming that their retention is justified because of the prevalence of "uncertainty and unpredictability". However, as we stand on the threshold of the 21st century, decisive movement toward total elimination of nuclear weapons becomes even more important than ever before.

The international community has concluded treaties to eliminate the other two categories of weapons of mass destruction which stand out as models for abolition of nuclear weapons. The Biological Weapons Treaty has been in force since 1972, and the Chemical Weapons Convention entered into force on 29 April 1997. There is no justifiable reason for tardiness with regard to a total elimination of the third category, and the argument that 'the world will be unsafe without nuclear weapons' is only meant to further the narrow self-interests of the nuclear weapon states and their allies.

The end of Cold War should have led to concerted efforts toward a total prohibition of nuclear weapons. Unfortunately, what we have witnessed instead is a renewed focus of "non-proliferation". This might have been a welcome development if it had been situated as an interim step in a process toward a clearly acknowledged goal of total prohibition of nuclear weapons. What has happened instead is a de-linking of non-proliferation from disarmament. The weapon states made concerted efforts to ensure that the NPT (Non-Proliferation Treaty) was extended permanently, but did not clearly commit themselves to disarmament. This has legitimised nuclear weapons in the possession of five states for an indefinite period, but has offered no fair or reasonable solution to the problem of nuclear asymmetry.

Information management and even manipulation have played key roles in the endeavour to generate support for non-proliferation as opposed to disarmament. The revolution in information and communication technologies has provided powerful tools to shape the minds and attitudes of people across the world. These technologies are essentially only available to the industrialised developed states led by the United States that has, after the Gulf War, depicted 'information warfare' as heralding a new revolution in military affairs,[1] but such information warfare also has a political use.

The indefinite extension of the NPT was thus relentlessly pursued by the nuclear-weapon states by means of manipulation of information and the media. The non-nuclear weapon states were lulled into believing that nuclear disarmament would now receive greater attention. It may be recalled that START-II was signed soon after the collapse of the USSR. By 1994 vague promises were also held out of a sequel (START-III) which was to be initiated in the spring of 1995, but nothing has been heard of this after the extension of the NPT in May 1995.

At the same time, new threat perceptions have been nurtured, based on two alleged sources of threat: the danger of proliferation accompanying Soviet disintegration, and the phenomenon of "rogue states" in the role as new proliferators and threats to international peace and security. Saddam Hussein's misadventure in Kuwait lent some credibility to the second thesis, which has also been combined with conceptions of Islamic fundamentalism as the new threat that might produce a "clash of civilisation".

The influential British journal *The Economist*, for instance, came out with a special report on future threats, which highlighted the danger of 'wars of conscience' and 'wars of interests' and which made a clear distinction between "us" (the industrialised North), and "them", i.e. the developing South.[2] We have also been flooded with media reports about leakage of fissile material from the former Soviet Union to unknown destinations, presumably including rogue states. Interestingly, however, according to the connected reports, nearly all the confiscated fissile material has been on its way westward, i.e. into Western Europe, mostly Germany! Significantly, such reports about fissile material trafficking have almost ceased to appear after the NPT was extended.

Concerted campaigns were mounted that highlighted nuclear proliferation risks in the Middle East, South Asia, and North-East Asia. Wittingly or otherwise, many countries lend their support to these campaigns. Pakistan, for example, seeking legitimacy for its own weapons programme, was only too willing to project the threat of nuclear and missile proliferation in South Asia. Myths were propagated, according to which Pakistan and India came very close to a nuclear exchange in the spring of 1990 which was only averted after Mr. Robert Gates intervened— claims that are not only contradicted by the facts, but also by the statements of people who had been involved in the dialogue with Mr. Gates.[3] The US administration began sending reports to the Congress on "Regional Nonproliferation in South Asia", but discontinued this practice as soon as the NPT had been extended. Highly esoteric and fanciful accounts had by then been published of how nuclear war almost broke out between Pakistan and India, even though neither side has had a single soldier crossing the frontiers at any time during these years. Such accounts and media reports, however, seeming to strengthen the non-proliferation argument made it easier to put political pressure on the countries concerned.

THE DISARMAMENT IMPERATIVE

The nuclear weapon states (with the possible exception of China) have taken advantage of the reduced concerns about the risk of nuclear war after the end of Cold War to abdicate even that nominal commitment to nuclear disarmament that had been produced by public opinion.

The receding likelihood of disarmament makes an examination of the rationale for nuclear disarmament as a policy objective of countries like India. There are several central reasons why nuclear disarmament is so critical, especially now that the Cold War has been over for more than six years:

- First of all, there are the moral and ethical rationales for nuclear disarmament. Nuclear weapons are simply the worst category of weapons of mass destruction. Unfortunately, however, many states are, cynically, prepared to sacrifice morality and fundamental human values for the sake of their narrow national interests. Linked to the moral principle is the issue of legality and legitimacy. The weapon states argue that their own possession of nuclear weapons is both legitimate and warranted for their security, but that such possession by others is not. Symptomatic of this quest for a perpetuation of the five's nuclear monopoly is the shift of emphasis from disarmament to non-proliferation.
- Secondly, a complete abolition of nuclear weapons will greatly enhance international peace and security. The argument that nuclear weapons were the decisive factor in keeping the peace during the Cold War is fatally flawed.

Indeed, taken to its logical conclusion, it would sanction the possession of nuclear weapons by most, if not all, sovereign states in the world. The argument that nuclear weapons should be retained for the indefinite future, if only by the nuclear five, is similarly flawed. Nuclear weapons use would affect not only the warring countries, but also large parts of the rest of the world. The findings of experts in the 1980s regarding the danger of a 'nuclear winter' remain valid, and the risks arising from the possible use are no less than they were during the Cold War. The justification for retaining nuclear weapon arsenals with reference to 'strategic uncertainties' is untenable. If nuclear proliferation continues to be a serious threat to international peace and security, then it has to be acknowledged that the strongest incentive for nuclear proliferation is the continuing possession of nuclear weapons by the five states and the security cover that they offer to nearly two dozen industrially advanced states through their alliance systems.

- Thirdly, nuclear weapons need to be eliminated if we are to move toward a more equitable international order. Democracy at the national level cannot be sustained as a core principle without movement toward a democratisation of the international order. However, nuclear weapons help sustain the inequitable international order by upholding the distinction between haves and have-nots. The fact that the five nuclear weapon states are also the only permanent members of the UN Security Council with veto powers has created an unfortunate nexus between international standing and nuclear weapons possession.

For India, the issue of national security remains central. India's strategic and security interests would be better served if there were no nuclear weapons that could impinge on its security calculus. Peaceful resolution of disputes would be facilitated by a removal of the nuclear weapons factor from the equation. Nuclear disarmament, therefore, is not only a moral or ethical desideratum for India, but also a national security imperative.

The nuclear weapon states, however, have been resisting all attempts at committing them to disarmament, and India's approach has been dismissed as unrealistic without further explanation. Past commitments, like Article VI in the NPT, have been ignored completely, as is apparent from the fact that even negotiations under this article (agreed upon in 1968), have yet to start.

THE EMERGING FOCUS

The American CSIS Nuclear Strategy Study Group in 1993 concluded that "There is no consensus, nor any immediate prospect of one, that total and complete disarmament will under any circumstances be a feasible proposition".[4] The report, however, proceeded to state that "it would be a tragedy if the present momentum toward international cooperation and disarmament passed without some attempt to establish a more robust nuclear end-state whose practical effect is virtually to eliminate the risk that nuclear weapons will be used".

As it was unaccompanied by any unambiguous, leave alone binding, commitment to nuclear disarmament, the indefinite extension of the NPT in May 1995 only reinforced the concerns that nuclear disarmament is unlikely in the foreseeable future to be pursued by the weapon states in any meaningful way. On the other hand, certain new voices have since then been raised in favour of a total elimination of nuclear weapons.

- First of all, China (unlike Russia) continues to advocate the elimination of nuclear weapons, and has been seeking a no-first-use treaty among the weapon states.
- Secondly, competent people like a former US defence secretary and senior military commanders (in the report of the committee chaired by General Andrew Goodpaster) have argued that US security would be enhanced by total elimination of nuclear weapons, and they have recommended a phased programme of disarmament that could be achieved in a couple of decades.[5]
- Thirdly, announcing the setting up of the Canberra Commission of experts tasked with working out a plan for the total elimination of nuclear weapons, Australian Prime Minister Mr. Paul Keating stated that "I believe that a world free of nuclear weapons is now feasible". He went on to say that, "We want the nuclear weapon states to carry out their commitments to the elimination of their nuclear stockpiles by adopting a systematic process to achieve that result".[6]
- Fourthly, the adoption of the resolution on Principles and Objectives during the NPT extension conference itself reaffirmed the commitment of Article VI of NPT to negotiate the complete elimination of nuclear weapons. To remind the international community of this obligation, the World Court on 8 July 1996 unanimously ruled that "There exists an obligation to pursue in good faith *and bring to a conclusion negotiations leading to nuclear disarmament in all aspects* under strict international control". (emphasis added)[7]
- Finally, all the nuclear weapon states, declared and undeclared, have at various times articulated their support for total nuclear disarmament.

India has been charged with lack of realism in demanding disarmament under a time-bound programme. But non-Indian experts also hold a time frame of ten years to be realistic. President Gorbachev of the USSR thus called for a total elimination of nuclear weapons in 10-12 years, at a time when the global arsenals amounted to more than 57,000 warheads. Six years after the end of the Cold War the figure has already come down to half that number. While it is often claimed that great progress has been made with the destruction of nearly 2,000 nuclear warheads every year by the USA and Russia, this merely proves that it would be possible to eliminate all nuclear weapons in about twenty years at this pace—and there is no reason why this could not be expedited.

The President of Pugwash Conference on Science and World Affairs —himself an eminent nuclear scientist and erstwhile member of the Manhattan project—Nobel Peace Prize laureate Professor Joseph Rotblat in his Nobel Speech in December 1995 asserted that, "We have the technical means to create a Nuclear Weapon Free World *in about a decade*". (emphasis added). Other Pugwash scientists also regard it as feasible to dismantle nuclear warheads in about ten years, implying that the goal of global nuclear disarmament could be achieved in less than twenty years. Against this background, it is thus clear that the nuclear weapon states and their allies under the nuclear weapon 'umbrellas' are adamant in retaining nuclear weapon into an undefined future simply in order to perpetuate their nuclear hegemony.

THE WORLD COURT RULING

On a request from the UN General Assembly in 1994, the World Court in July 1996 rendered advisory opinion on nuclear weapon. While this ruling does not go far enough for all those seeking elimination of nuclear weapons, it nevertheless contains far-reaching conclusions.

Firstly, the Court unanimously ruled that "there is in neither customary nor conventional international law any specific authorization of the threat and use of nuclear weapons". This is an important opinion which automatically creates a normative inhibition against the use of nuclear weapons. Secondly, the ruling clearly rejected the claim of nuclear weapon states that their possession and use or threat of use of such weapons is legitimate. Thirdly, however, the World Court concluded that there is no specific law prohibiting the use or threat of use of nuclear weapons.

It is necessary to recall in this context that, since 1978, an overwhelming majority of states have been voting at the UN for a convention to outlaw the threat and use of nuclear weapons. India has consistently been supporting such a resolution, and the logical next step is to conclude a convention based on the UN General Assembly resolutions. The 1925 Geneva Convention provides a useful model for this purpose.

A "no-first-use" commitment and a norm of proportionality would also help remove the ambiguities remaining in the Court's rulings with regard to self-defence under specific circumstances related to the survival of the State. Considering that, in the Court's opinion, there is no specific law either authorizing or prohibiting use and threat of nuclear weapons, this would mean that such use and threat of use would be generally inconsistent with law. This would place an obligation for all countries to adapt their nuclear doctrines to make them consonant with the World

Court ruling. There can be no reasonable situation where threat of use of nuclear weapons would be justified for self-defence; but such a threat is implied by the very possession of the nuclear weapons. By implication, therefore, nuclear weapons will have to be totally eliminated from national arsenals.

As shown by the quotation above, the Court also ruled that the international community in general, but especially the five nuclear weapon states, not only have an obligation to negotiate (in good faith) a treaty for total nuclear disarmament, but also are obliged to conclude such a treaty. It may be recalled that in the run up to the permanent extension of the NPT, many experts and diplomats, in particular British, had been arguing that Article VI of the NPT imposes only an obligation to negotiate, but does not actually require conclusion of such a treaty! We may expect that the nuclear weapon states (and their allies under nuclear umbrellas) will cynically disregard this ruling of the World Court as they have ignored the basic obligation itself in favour of their nuclear hegemony. However, the remaining 150 or so countries also bear a responsibility to keep nudging the recalcitrant states into fulfilling their commitments to disarm.

THE TEST BAN TREATY

The nuclear test ban treaty has been a centrepiece in recent years' arms control agenda, next only to the permanent extension of the NPT. Based on a unanimous resolution adopted by the UN General Assembly (No. 49/70), the CD (Conference on Disarmament), as the primary disarmament and arms control negotiating body of the UN, on 25 January 1994 adopted a mandate to negotiate a treaty which would "effectively contribute" to the twin goals of "nuclear non-proliferation in all its aspects" (that is, vertical and horizontal, qualitative and quantitative), as well as to "the process of (global) nuclear disarmament".

The treaty must be judged against this mandate. The so-called CTBT (Comprehensive Test Ban Treaty), which has been opened for signature at the UN, is not at all what it claims to be, but a violation of the parameters for a comprehensive test ban treaty as mandated by the very same General Assembly earlier. As it stands, the term 'Explosive Test Ban Treaty' (ETBT) would be more appropriate.

The ETBT will neither stop vertical proliferation, nor prevent states from acquiring nuclear weapons, even though it will stand in the way of more advanced designs. Moreover, there is every reason to believe that it will set in motion a new qualitative arms race, as the treaty does not prohibit non-explosive testing. The US has clearly asserted its plans to "maintain the capability to design, fabricate and certify new warheads", even though no production of new warheads may be involved. The latter may change any time, however.[8] While the negotiations for a CTBT were in progress the US, furthermore, finalized an agreement to share data and technology with France in order to help the latter make qualitative improvements and produce new weapons in the future without explosive testing. During the same period, the US also allocated $94 million for super computers that should contribute to the design and testing (without explosion) of new nuclear weapons.[9] The US has similar technology sharing arrangements with the UK, and in 1994 even offered simulation technology to China. China's interest in a provision allowing for peaceful nuclear explosions under the CTBT is, no doubt, related to its intention to use this method to acquire data for future qualitative improvements.

Qualitative improvements by the five nuclear weapon states will continue in the absence of a ban on sub-critical testing and simulation processes and techniques—a major concern expressed by India with regard to the CTBT as formulated. Regrettably, these concerns have been proven well-founded by the US conduct of more than one such test within a year of the treaty's being signed. One of the original rationales of the Indian proposal for a test ban was to stop the nuclear arms race, but the nuclear arms race has instead been pursued vigorously by the five countries. There is a profound irony in the prospect that this race, which appeared to have stopped with the end of the Cold War, may now be both propelled and legitimised by the ETBT.

A partial explanation is that the negotiations were dominated by private negotiations between the five nuclear weapon states, acting in the name of "world community". However, the 180 non-nuclear weapon states that are parties to the NPT are already committed to not even proceed toward testing, hence the issue rests with the five nuclear weapon states and the three so-called threshold states, i.e. India, Israel, and Pakistan. Of these, Israel is not faced with a nuclear environment and is protected by US security guarantees. Pakistan, likewise, does not face a nuclear environment, and the country has always predicated its policy on India's without aiming for any autonomy. It is happy riding piggy-back on India as long as its leaders can castigate India as a way of placating domestic audiences.

The issue, therefore, really revolves around only India and the five nuclear weapon states. The weapon states, unfortunately, either have not grasped this elementary reality, or have believed that India's concerns and interests can be ignored with impunity; but the very nature of the nuclear equation now gives strategic importance to Indian attitudes and policies. If an Indian signature to the treaty was so important, it was obvious that Indians would also be aware of this and that they would seek to redress the asymmetry—at least through a commitment to disarmament and better provisions for non-proliferation. However, these are the very commitments that the weapon states have tried hard to avoid.

The Fissile Material Cut-Off Treaty

The proposal for a fissile material cut-off treaty has been another centrepiece on the post-Cold War arms control agenda which also highlights the limitations of arms control and the critical need for disarmament. Here as well, the fundamental issue is whether this is conceived as a step towards a nuclear weapon-free world or as just another arms control measure for its own sake. In the absence of the broader goal, a cut-off treaty would be nothing but yet another non-proliferation measure reinforcing the others.

India had joined the United States in co-sponsoring the resolution in 1993 at the UN General Assembly in favour of a fissile material cut-off treaty. The US had made a notable adjustment in its position by dropping its earlier insistence of including all plutonium under the scope of such a treaty. The treaty will therefore merely ban any further production of fissile material for weapons purposes, except under international safeguards, while allowing countries in possession of weapon-grade fissile material (in stock or in warheads) to retain it outside any international scrutiny or monitoring. However, non-nuclear weapon states parties to the NPT have already foregone their right to possess such fissile material without full scope safeguards, while the five weapon states retain massive quantities of weapon-grade fissile material, both in stockpiles and in warheads. This provision has been described as rewarding the three threshold states (India, Pakistan, and Israel) that are not parties to the NPT. Muslim states in Middle East as well as Pakistan have therefore pushed for an inclusion of existing stockpiles under the treaty, yet without making it explicit whether this would only be for inventory accounting or whether they would come under some form of control and safeguards.

The formal negotiating mandate adopted at the CD reflected the primary goal as spelled out in the UN General Assembly resolution in 1993, but left the door open for the issue of existing stockpiles to be included. However, the CD was not able to commence negotiations by January 1997 as was visualized earlier. The reason is the fundamental uncertainties surrounding the prospects of the treaty. The Muslim states of the Middle East see it as an opportunity to disarm Israel completely. On the other hand, should a comprehensive peace in the region be achieved, Israel's need for nuclear weapons as an insurance for its future security might actually increase. A further obstacle is that, given the major deviation from the mandate of the CTBT described above, it is unlikely that India will be willing to go along with a cut-off treaty that is not clearly linked to a complete elimination of nuclear weapons at an early defined date.

The fissile material cut-off treaty thus, from an Indian perspective, has to be conceived as an interim step toward the total prohibition of nuclear weapons—a linkage that cannot be wished aside. As the weapon states are unwilling to give up their nuclear monopoly, the cut-off treaty is likely to remain a non-starter.

BALLISTIC MISSILE DEFENCE AND REGIONAL SECURITY

There is another issue that could trigger an arms race in the Asia-Pacific region, namely the proposed deployment of (theatre) ballistic missile defences.

Analysis shows regional stability and security to depend on the degree and nature of asymmetry among groups of such states as are likely to deploy either ballistic missiles or ballistic missile defences, or both. The stability equations of various combinations are shown in table 4.

| TABLE 4: REGIONAL SECURITY AND STABILITY ||||
Scenario	Country A	Country B	Implications
1	Missiles + BMD	Missiles, No BMD	Unstable
2	Missiles + BMD	Missiles + BMD	Stable
3	Missiles + BMD	Missiles + partial BMD	Unstable
4	No Missiles + No BMD	Missiles + BMD	Unstable
5	No Missiles + BMD	Missiles + BMD	Unstable
6	No Missiles + BMD	Missiles, No BMD	Unstable

The table shows that only one possible scenario is stable, namely scenario 2. For the next quarter century or more, only the United States and (with a certain time lag) the Russian Federation are likely to be able to possess equivalent systems, especially as far as the command and control infrastructure is concerned that is so critical to BMD operations. It is highly unlikely that these two states would engage themselves in a direct conflict. In other cases, the requisite infrastructure might be provided by the US or Russia to other states, which would weaken crisis stability.

Among the countries that would be adversely affected in its strategic equations by the development and deployment of ballistic missile defences are China and India. With regard to its strategic capabilities China lags technologically behind the US and Russia, but it possesses strategic nuclear weapons in sufficient quality and quantity for deterrence. The last 10-15 years have seen some fundamental changes in these capabilities, and China's strategic doctrine for the use of its nuclear weapons has shifted from minimum to finite deterrence.[10] This has entailed the development of nuclear war-fighting capabilities, and China has been engaged in modernization of its military capabilities in several ways, capitalizing on its high economic growth rates and the improvement of its security that has resulted from the collapse of the Soviet Union. While it lags technologically behind not only the USA but also other states, its total capabilities outweigh all other countries of Asia with the exception of the Russian Federation.

China has made qualitative changes in its strategic capabilities in recent years, including the development of more accurate mobile ballistic missiles. For instance, it tested the new 8,000-km range mobile ballistic missile in 1995, which is expected to be deployed around the turn of this century. While the other nuclear weapon states observed a moratorium, China (besides France) also continued to test nuclear weapons until late 1996 with the objective of making qualitative improvements.

China's nuclear weapons improvements appear to be directed primarily toward increased yield-to-weight ratios in its nuclear warheads, perfection of its multiple re-entry vehicles, and improvements of the accuracy of its survivable delivery systems. The expressed rationale is to narrow the gap separating it technologically from the other nuclear weapon states, especially the United States.

China in 1993 acquired four batteries of Russian S-300 air defence missile systems and related command technology,[11] which should provide some degree of ballistic missile defence. However, China does not yet have the necessary satellite-based early warning capability, which will impose limitations on the effectiveness of a missile defence system. Hence China may be expected to strengthen its satellite-based early warning systems in the near future. With the BMD programme of the US and its allies progressing steadily, it is inevitable that China also will seek to acquire a capable BMD for itself. In the shorter term, however, it will have to rely on counter-BMD strategies, and an accelerated quantitative and qualitative growth of the Chinese nuclear and missile capabilities may be expected to constitute a major element of this strategy. However, such a significant increase in China's capabilities, spurred on by BMD deployments by the United States, will complicate the strategic situation in Asia.

China has already objected to BMD development and will probably raise serious objections to its deployment, especially in East or South-East Asia. A manifestation thereof may be a Chinese refusal to accept constraints on the development of its nuclear and missile arsenal, which would be detrimental to the arms control process. China perceives itself as involved in a race to become a superpower in which the US is its primary competitor.

Aware of its relative weakness with regard to BMD capabilities, it may choose to transfer ballistic missiles to other countries where they may pose a challenge to the US and its allies, e.g. by extending the requisite range of a BMD system and thereby complicating its functioning. The Soviet supplies to Cuba that led to the 1962 Cuban missile crisis hold many lessons in this regard. In 1988 China transferred CSS-2 missiles to Saudi Arabia (with nuclear ambitions), and in 1991 it transferred nuclear-capable ballistic missiles to Pakistan, which had acquired a nuclear weapon capability in 1987. It is also conceivable that China may seek to build on its existing capabilities and construct longer-range cruise missiles (especially for an anti-ship role) that could prove effective against ship-borne BMD. The overall effect would be a contribution to the proliferation of ballistic missiles and high technology strategic weapons in Asia.

In the final analysis, it seems that negotiations for a global regime to eliminate all ballistic missiles hold the promise of much greater payoffs. This would require the five nuclear states to relinquish some of their strategic capabilities, but it would make the nuclear stand-off both more stable and less costly. Such a regime would not jeopardize the security of any of the nuclear weapon states, since all the others would be giving up similar capabilities. The INF Treaty is a relevant precedent, that enhanced the security of both sides simultaneously.

The establishment of such a "Zero Missile" regime may of course prove difficult, but unless serious attention is given to it, it stands even less of a chance to ever become a reality. In the interim, what is needed is an expansion of the INF Treaty to cover all countries and all ballistic missiles with ranges between 50 and 5,500 kms, including those deployed on submarines. This would enhance regional security and crisis stability, in sharp contrast to a deployment of ballistic missile defences which will only lead to the development and deployment of more missiles in the future.

THE CASE OF SOUTHERN ASIA

Southern Asia presents specific challenges for arms control and disarmament, because the regional situation is multipolar as far as the three nuclear weapon-capable states (China, India and Pakistan) are concerned. Pakistan's nuclear weapon programme is driven by the India factor; and India's security calculus is affected by the nuclear weapons of China. This multipolar situation is also linked to the global equations, not least because of the deployment of US and Russian nuclear weapons in the region's vicinity, even if these deployments are not perceived to directly impinge on the security calculus of any of the region's states.

NUCLEAR SCENARIO

The security environment in Southern Asia has been nuclearized since 1964, when China became a nuclear weapon state. Some movement towards nuclear arms reduction has taken place with the signing of the INF and START-I treaties and the agreements on START-II, but China is not party to any of these; in fact, China is generally unwilling to join any nuclear disarmament processes. The US and (former) Soviet Union have withdrawn their non-strategic nuclear weapons, and most of them are slated for destruction. However, China has shown no inclination to withdraw or eliminate its non-strategic nuclear weapons which have relevance only for China's immediate neighbours.

From the Indian standpoint, this has been, and is likely to remain, the most important conditioning factor of national security. Pakistan's going nuclear in early 1987, and its continued access to nuclear weapons and ballistic missile technology from China, only add to the nuclear asymmetry with which India has to cope. A non-nuclear environment would serve India's strategic interests better, but this is not achievable without global nuclear disarmament, which is the reason for India's consistent quest for universal and global de-legitimization and elimination of nuclear weapons. Arms control measures, even with a regional scope, are acceptable only if they contribute to disarmament and if they allow for maintenance of national security in the interim period. However, because the regional environment has been nuclearized for more than thirty years India, as a minimum, needs to keep its nuclear weapon option open.

Public, intellectual, and official opinion in Pakistan unanimously regard the possession of nuclear weapons to be indispensable for national security. The basic rationale is to rely on nuclear deterrence to offset India's conventional superiority. Renouncing the nuclear option would leave Pakistan with a perceived conventional vulnerability vis-à-vis India. Pakistani leaders claim to have obtained assurances from the US (in 1981) that the latter would not raise any questions about Pakistan's nuclear programme,[12] and subsequent events appear to bear out this claim. Pakistan had acquired nuclear weapons capability by 1987,[13] and seems convinced that this capability has already proved a successful deterrent vis-à-vis India.[14] Demands in Pakistan for the adoption of an overt nuclear status are much stronger than for curtailing the capabilities.

Pakistan does not have the technological base to build a large arsenal, hence fears of an open-ended nuclear 'arms race' are grossly exaggerated. Indeed, according to Pakistani interlocutors, Islamabad has already capped its nuclear capability,[15] which is credible in view of the limited resource base available for sustaining a clandestine weapon programme. Logically, as long as Pakistan's nuclear posture is linked to India's conventional forces, a minimum deterrent should also suffice for countervailing such conventional capabilities and for providing an adequate response option against India's limited nuclear posture.

Pakistan's objective, therefore, has not been to build a large arsenal to match that of India or any other state. What Pakistan has been seeking is, first of all, credibility (since 1987) for its nuclear weapon status, and, secondly, an acceptance of the legitimacy of this arsenal (since 1991). As a means to this end it has adopted an arms control approach with a South Asian scope that links its nuclear programme with both the conventional and nuclear capabilities of India.

However, China clearly does not want its nuclear policies to be constrained by any sub-regional (e.g. South Asian) arms control measures. Beijing now supports total elimination of nuclear weapons from the world, but it is not willing to engage in any arms control dialogue before the US and Russian arsenals come down to the level of the Chinese arsenal. Hence global disarmament remains the key, including arms control measures that contribute to this end. China has consistently committed itself to both no-first-use of nuclear weapons and non-use of nuclear weapons against non-nuclear weapon states, but its definition of the latter remained different from that of NPT parties, at least till 1992. Still, these commitments had an important influence on India, allowing it to adopt a more relaxed approach, yet without abandonment of the nuclear weapon option.

Over the years India has acquired a credible indigenous nuclear capability of significant dimensions, primarily as a reflection of its policy of expanding the infrastructure of nuclear science and technology for peaceful purposes. The latter is a vital element in the energy sector in a country which is energy deficient and where adequate energy supplies hold the key for the human development of its population of 900 million people. The PNE (peaceful nuclear explosion) conducted in 1974 demonstrated India's ability to design, fabricate, and detonate a nuclear device under controlled conditions. Since then nuclear capabilities have expanded, yet not to the point of weaponisation, which could only happen in response to perceived threats.

India's relations with China have been improving since 1987, and resulted, among other things, in an agreement reached in September 1993 on the principle of "mutual and equal security", under which it was agreed to delineate the line of actual control along the disputed frontiers, to undertake force reductions along the frontiers, and to institute a series of supporting mechanisms for implementation and oversight. This was elaborated and reinforced by the 1996 agreement. Trade and economic relations between the two countries have also picked up significantly, and there have been discussions on collaborative projects, even on civil transport aircraft design and development. We have thus seen a significant improvement of political relations which itself reduces the perceptions of threat. India thus can afford to take a more relaxed position with respect to its nuclear deterrence needs, also with regard to delivery systems. Indeed, one might argue that the need for countervailing China's nuclear weapon capability will decline considerably if the present rate of growth of cooperative relations between India and China continues through a sufficiently long period, say for two decades.

However, great uncertainties continue to surround China's future evolution, also as far as its strategic posture is concerned. Hence, there is a need for India to adopt a hedging strategy that provides adequate safeguards against any future reversal of the trend towards improvement of the bilateral relations. Such strategy requires keeping the nuclear option open. This no doubt creates a degree of ambiguity; but it is often ignored that the maintenance of ambiguity is also tantamount to an exercise of restraint that could be lost if ambiguity were to be removed. On the other hand, it is possible to confine this ambiguity to variations within a set of parameters that permit maintenance of the element of restraint at the same time as providing for a more credible deterrent posture. This requires a brief look at deterrence.

DETERRENCE DECAY

The end of the Cold War has started the process of decaying of deterrence which, over time, should make nuclear weapons irrelevant. In the interim, it is necessary to remember that the prevailing perceptions and concepts of nuclear deterrence have relied heavily on the doctrines of the United States and the Soviet Union, both of which relied on the maximum (and aggressive) deterrence paradigm. Other countries, especially China, constructed their nuclear postures according to doctrines of minimum deterrence. This was also the case for France and the UK, even though their belonging to NATO meant that the maximum deterrence paradigm also extended to them. After the Cold War, however, we are now witnessing a shift in both the American and Russian doctrines toward finite, if not minimum deterrence.

It is important to recognize that deterrence may function at levels below that of minimum deterrence, which is, in a way, the deterrence posture adopted by India. This might be described as "recessed deterrence" that relies on credible capabilities, but where actual weaponization is deferred and made conditional on actual threats, on the one hand, and tangible progress towards disarmament on the other. Since a shift to weaponization itself would be a response to a rise in perceived threat levels, the weaponization option should act as a restraining factor on other states, unless such an adversary should actually want to escalate for other reasons, in which case the country would move from a recessed to minimum deterrence posture. A posture of recessed deterrence is thus, by its very nature, intrinsically supportive of better strategic stability at low costs and, ideally, all nuclear weapon states should climb down the deterrence ladder to this rung (see table 5).

TABLE 5: DETERRENCE LADDER

Type of Deterrence	Strategy
Maximum	Massive Retaliation
Aggressive	Mutual Assured Destruction
Finite	Maximum deterrence with the lowest finite arsenal
Minimum	Lowest level of weapons that can cause death and destruction which, if imposed on the adversary, would deter it
Recessed	Non-weaponised, with option to weaponize kept open, and linked to rise in threat levels. Committed to no-first-use
Assurance	No nuclear arsenals under national control

However, given the reluctance of the nuclear weapon states to even implement existing arms reduction agreements, leave alone institute disarmament measures, it is clear that this process would take a long time. Hence the importance of building strategic stability at progressively lower levels of deterrence. Southern Asia is at a certain advantage, in this respect, compared to some other parts of the world because of its already lower levels of deterrence capabilities.

India already possesses a recessed deterrence capability which is adequate for current threat scenarios. Recessed deterrence is, by definition, non-weaponized, but it requires possession of other capabilities such as delivery systems. It also presupposes the ability to convert the capabilities to a level higher than the recessed one at short notice and linked to the threat levels. Recessed deterrence occupies an intermediate position between the classical minimum deterrence and a posture of insurance, bordering on reassurance. There is little need to move from recessed deterrence to a more overt form of nuclear deterrence (i.e. to weaponize the option) unless the threat scenario should demand so, which in itself will help deter any escalation of a dispute to the level of nuclear threats or attempts at coercion or blackmail. It is thus consistent with India's general philosophy of non-offensive defence.

NUCLEAR ARMS CONTROL

Given the historical and current realities, the prospects of nuclear arms control in Southern Asia are bleak. China has been the central factor in India's strategic calculus concerning nuclear weapons, and no arms control measures between India and Pakistan would be able to address India's concerns about China's nuclear and missile capabilities, nor remove the existential risks posed by the nuclear weapons of other states.[16]

The first problem is how to obtain workable and meaningful agreements to manage strategic stability at ever reducing levels of weaponization. The key element, however, is the reliability and durability such of agreements. In India's view, the 1954 Panchsheel agreement was violated within a few years, and a war resulted. Pakistan has rarely honoured the international agreements it has freely entered into, the most significant being the non-implementation of the UN resolutions on Kashmir and repudiation in practice of the 1972 Simla Agreement.

Southern Asia has, on the other hand, witnessed an implicit and informal arms control process, as a result of which China, India and Pakistan have unilaterally observed constraints in their nuclear stance vis-à-vis each other, and additional measures to institutionalize such nuclear restraint are conceivable. India and Pakistan have already instituted a bilateral agreement not to attack each other's nuclear installations. Agreements on no first-use of nuclear capabilities (which intrinsically include actual or potential weapons capabilities) would represent further restraints and help to reduce the significance of nuclear weapons. India has already put forward such a proposal to Pakistan in a 'non-paper' in January 1994.

On the other hand, any move towards making the nuclear arms control process explicit, technical and legal (rather than political and strategic, as presently) would presuppose an overt acceptance and formalization of the nuclear weapon status of the three countries involved. It is also unclear whether Pakistan (or for that matter, China) would be prepared to accept formal constraints that would freeze its capabilities at a significantly lower level than that of India. For example, Pakistan is not known to possess weapon-grade plutonium, and a fissile material cut-off treaty would permanently deny it such capability, thereby posing obvious limitations on the type of arsenal it could possess. This seems to have determined Pakistan's policy on the treaty since 1994, where it has also been able to align itself with the

Islamic states that are keen to disarm Israel. Explicit arms control, therefore, entails the risk of removing most of the current restraints, and could thus prove counter-productive in the long run. The desire for regional arms control should be tempered with this reality, and priority should therefore be given to confidence-building measures.

CONVENTIONAL ARMS CONTROL

In September 1993, China and India signed what was perhaps the first conventional arms control agreement in Asia. It was further elaborated upon and reinforced by a follow-on agreement signed during the Chinese president's visit to India in November 1996. The main elements of these agreements were based on the acceptance by both sides of certain core principles intended to ensure that "peace and tranquillity" are maintained along the frontiers, and on the acknowledgment that relations should be built on the basis of "mutual and equal" security. Adequate mechanisms have also been set up (and have been functioning) to translate the agreement into practice. The final goal is to institute force reductions across the line of actual control, avoid military incidents (like air violations) and risks associated with military activities close to borders. This process should go a long way towards stabilizing the frontiers, improving relations, and paving the way for a final resolution of the outstanding territorial disputes.

Conventional wisdom tends to ignore the large body of what might be termed confidence-building and mutual restraint measures between India and Pakistan that have been instituted in the course of the half-century since India's independence. Particularly significant are the half-dozen measures that were instituted in mid-1990 when the tension between the two countries was at an all time high. Strategic experts have been exploring the potential for conventional force reductions on both sides;[17] India has been cutting back its defence spending from 3.6 percent of the GDP in 1987-88 to 2.33 percent in 1996-97; and Pakistan's allocation of national resources for defence have also been reduced from more than 7 percent of GDP in 1988-89 to an estimated 5.3 percent in 1996-97. Facts, therefore, do not support the myth of an arms race between the two countries.[18] On the other hand, they indicate a potential for additional measures that might institute arms control in the conventional arena.

THE ROAD AHEAD

We are now entering the last stages of what has been human history's most violent century. Technology has been harnessed to devise new and horrendous ways of killing masses of people in a single stroke. The argument is often advanced that such weapons cannot be disinvented. This is true, but they can certainly be made obsolete and redundant through cooperative approaches. Most fundamentally, a new paradigm of inter-state security is needed which shifts the emphasis from the traditional competitive to a more cooperative approach. Such co-operative paradigm is needed among potential adversaries and not merely among allies and friends. Concepts like that of non-offensive defence provide the basis of such reorientation. The post-Cold War opportunities need to be exploited to make doctrinal changes towards non-offensive defence. Arms control and disarmament will need to be situated in harmony with such doctrinal changes.

NOTES

1. For an overview see Singh, Ajay: "Fundamentals of Information Warfare", *Strategic Analysis*, vol. 18, no. 8 (November 1995), pp. 1047-1058.
2. "Defence in 21St Century", Special report in *The Economist*, 5 September, 1992.
3. Bhaskar, C. Uday: "The May 1990 Nuclear "Crisis": an Indian Perspective" in *Studies in Conflict and Terrorism*, vol. 20, no. 4 (1997), pp. 317-332. Also see BG Deshmukh, *India Today*, 28 February 1994, p.63.
4. CSIS Nuclear Strategy Study Group: *Toward A Nuclear Peace: The Future of Nuclear Weapons in US Foreign and Defense Policy* (Washington, D.C.: Centre for Strategic and International Studies, June 1993), p.67.
5. *An Evolving US Nuclear Posture*, Second Report of the Steering Committee, Project on Eliminating Weapons of Mass Destruction, Henry L. Stimson Center, Washington DC, December 1995.
6. P.J. Keating (Prime Minister of Australia): Speech given on the 50th Anniversary of the United Nations, October 24, 1995.
7. 'Legality of the Threat or Use of Nuclear Weapons, Advisory Opinion', *Communiqué*, no. 96/23, 8 July, 1996 (The Hague: International Court of Justice).
8. Smith, Harold (Ass. Secretary of Defense): "Assuring Confidence in the US Nuclear Stockpile", cited in *USIA Wireless File*, 31 May 1996, p. 19.
9. *International Herald Tribune*, 17 June 1996.
10. Alstair Iain Johnston has called it "limited deterrence". See his "China's New "Old Thinking": The Concept of Limited Deterrence", *International Security*, vol. 20, no. 3 (Winter 1995/96), pp. 5-42.
11. Allen, Kenneth, Glenn Krumel, & Jonathan D. Pollack: 'China's Airforce Enters the 21st Century', *RAND*, MR-580-AF (1995), p. 157.
12. General K.M. Arif: *Working with Zia* (Karachi: Oxford University Press, 1995), pp. 341-342.
13. General Mirza Aslam Beg in *Nation*, 13 December 1993.
14. For example, see the statement by Pakistan's former Army Chief, General Aslam Beg, at the Stimson Centre, Washington DC, July, 1995.
15. General Aslam Beg in *The Nation*, 12-13 December, 1993.
16. Dr. William Perry, US Secretary for Defense, accepted this reality in his speech at Foreign Policy Association, New York, January 31, 1995 soon after his visit to Pakistan and India.

17. For Indian perceptions see Singh, Jasjit: "Security for Both at Lower Costs", *Times of India*, 26 September, 1991; and idem: "Defensive Security: The Conceptual Challenge", *Disarmament*, vol. 15, no. 4 (1992), pp. 112-125. For Pakistani perception see Kamal, Nazir: "Defensive Security in Regions Other Than Europe", *ibid.*, pp. 136-152. More recently, former Pakistan Army Chief, General Mirza Aslam Beg argued at a seminar in Islamabad in October 1996 that the force ratios between India and Pakistan have remained constant since 1947 although the size of forces has gone up. He made a strong plea for reduction in conventional force levels as long as the nuclear balance is maintained. See Jasjit Singh: "Pakistan's Nuclear Posturing", *Time of India*, 13 November, 1996.
18. See Singh, Jasjit: "Arms race in the Region: Myths and Realities", in S.M. Rahman (ed.): *Security, Trade and Advanced Technologies in South Asia* (Islamabad: FRIENDS, 1995), pp. 15-32.

4 International Cooperation in Regional Security: 'Non-Interference' and ASEAN Arms Modernization

JOON NUM MAK

Arms control of any sort is pre-eminently a political process. It is pursued as an element of a state's security policy and must essentially be judged by whether it enhances national security first, and international security second.[1]

While this phrase was written in 1987, its validity and applicability remains as relevant in Asia today, if not more so.

INTRODUCTION

This paper attempts to assess the problems, possibilities and dynamics of international cooperation in regional security, using the Association of South-East Asian Nations (ASEAN) as a case study.* The approach is therefore more conceptual than prescriptive. While this paper deals largely with the ASEAN experience, many of the observations here apply to a number of East Asian states as well. ASEAN South-East Asia constitutes a relatively homogenous and coherent political sub-region, and the association has often been cited as the only example of a successful regional security organization in Asia. Moreover, ASEAN constitutes the core of the ASEAN Regional Forum (ARF), which is the only multilateral security forum in the Asia-Pacific with a clear security role. Thus, it would appear that ASEAN would be the one region where further international cooperation in regional security would stand the greatest chance of success.

The paper is divided into two parts. The first section discusses in some detail the ASEAN concept of regional security, which is in a number of ways quite distinct from that of the West. This is because threats to ASEAN states, for much of their history, came largely from within their borders rather than from the outside. As a

---

* The views expressed in this paper are strictly the author's own, and do not in any way reflect the opinion or position of the Maritime Institute of Malaysia.

result, South-East Asian states in general have tended to be inward-looking with regard to security, with defence against external threats generally relegated to second place. Military threats from outside their borders were considered less dangerous than external interference in domestic affairs, such as the support for insurgents, political dissidents and factions out to overthrow the regime in power. As a consequence, ASEAN leaders were acutely conscious of the dangers of externally-supported subversion. Thus by 1967 when ASEAN was set up, regional leaders were convinced that freedom from foreign interference in domestic affairs of states was a perquisite for regional security and stability.

Regional security for ASEAN is equated with national security. If individual ASEAN states are secure, than the region will be secure. In other words, the security of the state is paramount, and until recently, there has been no explicit ASEAN effort to ensure the security of the region as a whole. This obsession with 'outside interference' and the supremacy of state security over regional/international security has significant implications for nearly all international initiatives involving the security of South-East Asia.

However, because of the changed strategic environment after the end of the Cold War, ASEAN began to give more thought and priority to the issue of defence against external threats. As a result, beginning roughly in the 1980s, all the ASEAN countries embarked on arms modernization and upgrade programmes The modernization of ASEAN armed forces is marked by two characteristics: It is largely conventional in orientation, and it has a marked maritime emphasis. Section II of the paper outlines the dynamics of the current ASEAN arms modernisation programmes and raises a number of issues for arms control and confidence-building.

The first point of note is that while the arms purchases have raised much media attention, the truth is that the arms and platforms acquired are relatively few in numbers, seen in the overall context of the Asia-Pacific military balance. However, because of the presence of intra-ASEAN tensions, the dynamics of ASEAN arms acquisitions (which will increase ASEAN defence capability exponentially) will have the greatest potential impact on the intra-ASEAN sub-regional balance.

The second issue of note is that the majority of ASEAN leaders, again because of history and their stand on non-interference by external powers, are convinced that each ASEAN country has the right to bear arms, so to speak, and that no one else has the right to tell them otherwise. The ASEAN conviction that national strength and security is the key to regional stability (i.e., that national resilience will result in regional resilience) also reinforces the belief that ASEAN arms acquisitions will not be potentially destabilizing. However, the notion that national military power will contribute to regional defence resilience is somewhat misplaced given the lack of a common ASEAN defence policy or military structure. In other words, ASEAN defence forces to all intents and purposes are still discrete units lacking a common focus. Thus there is the possibility that these discrete forces might be the cause of greater intra-regional instability rather than resilience.

Given the above constraints, what is the role and contribution of international cooperation in ASEAN regional security? Will it be in the realm of arms control and disarmament? Quite obviously, there will be certain impediments to arms control measures being introduced in the region. The ASEAN phobia with regard to external interference makes the members of the Association extremely wary of any external initiatives imposed from outside the region. Thus, international cooperation in ASEAN regional security, and particularly in arms control and disarmament, would appear to be extremely difficult to achieve despite ASEAN's apparent success as a limited security community. Nevertheless, there are a number of limited possibilities, and the paper suggests 'capacity building' in confidence-building and arms control as one international cooperative effort which may be acceptable to the ASEAN states. The bottom line is that international cooperation in regional security must take into account ASEAN sensitivities with regard to the issue of 'non-interference'.

THE LURE OF INTERNATIONAL COOPERATION

The lure of international cooperation, in particular the international dimension of cooperative security, is hard to resist in the post-Cold War era. For a short while in the 1980s, a number of analysts believed that the age of the Pacific Community had dawned. These neo-Liberals believed that growing economic inter-dependence, and the economic dynamism of the Pacific Rim, would lead to greater peace and security despite the existence of different political systems and inter-state tensions. This view of a Pacific peace was reinforced by events of the 1980s and early 1990s. In the northern rim, three major powers—US, China and Japan—seemed to have successfully put a stop to an apparently expansionist Soviet Union. To the west, the Soviet Union began its withdrawal from Afghanistan in 1988/1989 after realizing that it would be unable to continue supporting a Communist regime in Kabul, despite paying a huge price in blood and money.

Farther south, in South-East Asia, the Soviet-backed Republic of Vietnam had also pulled out the last of its forces in Cambodia in September 1989, paving the way for a Cambodian peace settlement in 1991. This ended the confrontation between the then six ASEAN members of South-East Asia—Indonesia, Brunei, Malaysia, the Philippines, Singapore and Thailand—and Vietnam following the latter's invasion of Cambodia in 1979. With the end of the Cold War and the break-up of the Soviet Union together with the whole-hearted embrace of free market economics in the former Communist countries, it appeared that the Asia-Pacific would enjoy a peace dividend. There were even hopes that a genuine Pacific security community would result. The peace dividend was not realized, however. Ironically, the Asia-Pacific region has become an area of strategic tension and potential conflict. This tension is fundamentally between a power on the ascendant,

China, and the world's most powerful military nation, the US. At the same time, differences between Japan and China, the fear of a nuclearized North Korea, and tensions between China and Taiwan have contributed to a general lack of stability. The paradox is that while the Asia-Pacific has undergone great economic growth, a security architecture to ensure continued peace has not been emplaced.

The situation in South-East Asia, however, is quite different. The success of ASEAN as a regional organization in setting an effective, albeit limited, security agenda, and in playing a leading role in the ASEAN-PMC (Post-Ministerial Conference) and later the ARF, seems to imply that there are lessons to be drawn from the South-East Asian experience with regional collaboration for other regions, such as North-East Asia. At the same time, the success of the Conference on Security and Cooperation in Europe (CSCE) also has tempted analysts to suggest transplanting the European system of multilateral and cooperative security to East Asia.

However, international cooperation on regional security has certain limitations in South-East Asia. International cooperation is certainly important, but the domestic dimension of security is still paramount in South-East Asia. The need for domestic order, stability and growth, and for regime stability are still primary driving forces in many East Asian and South-East Asian countries. Indeed, despite the trend towards increased multilateralism in the West, with borderless economies, the nation state (in a strictly limited sense of the term, as opposed to the nation state system) is still alive and well in East Asia. Thus, many Asian states feared, and many of them still do fear, interference in their domestic affairs by outsiders. Unwelcome meddling is considered potentially destabilizing and is deeply resented. Thus, any initiative involving international cooperation must emanate from individual states first, the region second, before finally becoming a true international cooperative effort.

'REGIONAL SECURITY' REDEFINED

The term 'regional security' is often taken to include a general environment of peace, stability and predictability resulting from a process of understanding or compromise between states in a defined geographic area. In another sense, regional security can also be equated with regional order, i.e. the essential requirements of order in inter-state as well as domestic relations.[2] In the context of South-East Asia at least, post-World War II regional security has historically, either explicitly or implicitly, involved the element of non-interference. Mohammed Ayoob for instance defines regional security as comprising three elements. The first assumes that

> external powers with interests in the region...would either willingly desist from interfering in regional issues and problems or would be effectively deterred from doing so....[3]

The notion of non-interference is central to the argument of this paper. South-East Asian states have over the last thirty years consistently sought the goal of non-interference so that they may pursue their domestic agenda unfettered. Young fragile states have always seen external interference in domestic affairs as being very dangerous. In a situation where states were already facing very serious problems of national integration, with domestic threats such as insurgencies and irredentism, external interference by third countries was seen as highly destabilizing.

The underlying reason for the differences between the Western approach to international cooperation, regional security and multilateralism and the South-East Asian approach can be traced to the process of state formation which differ markedly between the European and South-East Asian models. The Western notion of security applies to immunity from outside threats. This notion assumes a strong, cohesive state. A logical extension of the Western concept of state-centric security has been to view security in terms of the world order, i.e. international security is regarded as the maintenance of a world system of law and order, with individual states expected to subjugate their individual, narrow interests to that of the collective or common interest. Thus the Western approach to international/regional security and cooperation tend to be systemic in character.[4] Any threat to an individual developed state is seen as inimical to the entire system, thus a collective response can be expected.[5] The declaratory aim of American security policy, for instance, is to seek prosperity and survival not only for itself, but ostensibly for all of mankind.

The Cold War also reinforced the systemic approach as the world was divided into two blocs or alliances, with the individual state regarded as the smallest security unit. Thus the 'security of units below the level of the state has rarely, if ever, been an important point at issue in most western discussions and analyses of the concept of security'.[6] The systemic approach has great implications for South-East Asian countries. In terms of the world order, it does not greatly matter if regimes come or go, so long as the state itself survives and the new regime does not threaten the world order. In the eyes of many South-East Asian leaders however, regime changes can be extremely dangerous.

UNCONDITIONAL LEGITIMACY VERSUS REGIME LEGITIMACY

At the same time, virtually all Western states have achieved, in the words of Mohammed Ayoob, a state of 'unconditional legitimacy'.[7] In contrast, all South-East Asian ruling elites were still striving for political legitimacy in the 1960s and 1970s. Even today, many of these states are still uncertain that they have achieved 'unconditional legitimacy'.[8] South-East Asian ruling elites are very conscious, therefore, that in the absence of truly democratic structures and institutions, political legitimacy must be 'earned' in other ways, principally through 'performance legitimacy'. The emphasis which ASEAN members have consistently placed on economic performance and on delivering economic goods to the people is a good indicator of the importance of performance legitimacy in winning the moral authority to govern and stay in power for South-East Asian governments.[9]

Because South-East Asia generally still lacks institutional structures for achieving unconditional legitimacy, for power-sharing and to ensure an orderly succession or handover of power, a number of elites have clung on to power, in the process creating quasi-dynasties or charismatic governments based largely on a few key personalities. Given the absence of general legitimacy, South-East Asian governments are therefore very conscious of their vulnerability. In the 1950s and 1960s, internal insurrection was seen as the greatest threat to governments. In the 1980s and 1990s, nearly all South-East Asian governments had earned a measure of political legitimacy, largely through economic performance. The threats to these governments today are therefore not only military in nature. Any initiative which would jeopardise a country's economic performance and its domestic economic distributive system, or ideas and concepts which would challenge and delegitimise the political elites, such as accusations of human rights abuses, are today regarded as very grave threats.

As it is, many of the East Asian countries have become victims of their own economic successes. While many Western analysts like to think that greater interdependence and rapid social change resulting from economic success would lead to more democracy and greater peace and stability ('trade promotes peace'),[10] the truth is that democracy tends to diffuse rather than concentrate power in the hands of ruling elites. Similarly, economic reforms can be destabilizing because they tend to distribute wealth away from the centre and into the hands of the masses, thus threatening the important patronage systems of a number of South-East Asian and East Asian countries. For China, the threat of subversion of central authority has even greater significance, since China's political culture is based on the assumption that the stronger the central authority, the more secure the individual, and there is therefore no question as to the 'primacy of the political order and the importance of the central government as the locus of power'.[11] It is therefore argued that South-East Asian leaders are today still as prickly as ever over any interference by outside powers, although the focus of interference/ intervention has shifted to economics, human rights and non-Asian values which will undermine established notions of hierarchy and authoritarianism. Very striking similarities can be seen in China's fear of external interference as well, which amounts to almost paranoia.

> It has been a widely accepted interpretation in China that foreign invasions, exploitation and influences [emphasis added] were the principal cause of the nation's poverty, social ills, demoralization and loss of greatness.[12]

One must also be conscious of the fact that, unlike in Western countries, the level of consensus on political and social issues in South-East Asia is still quite low, with ruling elites often treating opposition parties as enemies of the state. Very often, there was also little in the way of shared values between the various segments of society and the ruling elites. South-East Asian ruling elites in the 1960s and 1970s therefore tended to define security not so much in terms of national security as in terms of regime security. This explains the *leitmotif* of 'non-interference' which constituted a principal core value of ASEAN in the 1960s and 1970s.

In this sense, while many South-East Asian states, and even China, may command significant military and economic power, they are still relatively weak states, easily subject to subversion. Thus one can understand why the states of South-East Asia, and even China, have regarded security in terms very different from that of the West. The greatest threats were seen as emanating from within. Post-War South-East Asia has usually delegated the burden of dealing with serious external threats to the existing hegemon, be it *Pax Britannica* or *Pax Americana*.[13] As a consequence, the principle of non-interference runs deep in the minds of the ruling elite of South-East Asia even today.

NON-INTERFERENCE: ASEAN'S CREDO

Indeed, one of the key founding principles of ASEAN is that of non-interference in domestic affairs by outside powers, including even (or especially) close neighbours. This fear of external interference reflects a very deep concern over regime stability in states beset with the problems of nation-building. Thus the grouping developed the concept of national and regional resilience to deal specifically with the problem of maintaining domestic and, moving outward, regional stability. One key tool for ensuring internal stability was the concept of non-interference by outside powers. These fragile regimes felt that their states could be easily undermined and their authority challenged by outsiders, hence they worked at a *modus vivendi* to ensure that they would be left alone to manage - or mismanage - their own states.

The history of the ASEAN non-interference principle in practice is marked more by *realpolitik* rather than any notion of morality. When it comes to choosing between non-interference and morality and justice, the choice has invariably been in favour of upholding the principle of non-interference. For instance, when Indonesia forcibly annexed East Timor in 1975, the issue was put before the United Nations General Assembly as a hostile resolution. All the ASEAN members except one, supported Indonesia. Singapore's representative, however, abstained, perhaps reflecting Singapore's fear of large regional states swallowing up smaller ones. However, Singapore subsequently changed its position and supported Indonesia's annexation. The fear of a potential regional hegemony in this instance, was outbalanced by the perceived need to ensure that non-intervention, both direct and indirect, would remain an ASEAN core value. Thus the need to ensure that ASEAN remained cohesive more than outweighed the fear of annexation by Indonesia. It was clear that Singapore was unlike East Timor in that it was a truly sovereign state, had external alliance linkages, and that Indonesia would find Singapore to be a distasteful 'poison shrimp'.

When the Pol Pot regime embarked on a bloody pogrom in the mid 1970s, ASEAN did not condemn Cambodia. However, when Vietnam invaded Cambodia in December 1978, the ASEAN leaders were quick to condemn Vietnamese aggression. The invasion of Cambodia by Vietnam brought into sharp focus the vulnerabilities of weak states to external intervention. The concerted opposition of ASEAN to the invasion was the result of the collective fear that such a precedent in the region should not be allowed at all. Apart from the security implications of the balance of power in mainland South-East Asia shifting in favour of Vietnam, and the threat it posed to Thailand, the Vietnamese invasion of its neighbour was seen as setting a dangerous precedent. Similarly, ASEAN willingness to accept Myanmar into the association, despite Yangon's poor human rights record, reflects its *realpolitik* approach. Yangon's human rights abuses are, after all, part of an attempt to ensure the survival of the State Law and Order Committee (SLORC), and therefore purely an internal affair. This ASEAN stand is understandable if one accepts the assertion that 'the sanctity of national sovereignty is the most sacred [ASEAN] corporate value'.[14]

This fear of non-interference means that ASEAN leaders can be very suspicious of international initiatives, especially if these are initiated by big powers with a penchant for proselytizing liberal ideals. Arms control and disarmament by its very nature involves either regional or international actors, or both. Arms control, at its most basic, can be defined as 'restraint internationally exercised upon armaments, whether in respect of the levels of armaments, their character, deployment or use'.[15] Thus, international arms control initiatives are unlikely to be well accepted in ASEAN. Nevertheless, despite ASEAN being an organization originally designed mainly for 'collective internal security', the changing strategic environment in the Asia-Pacific after the early 1980s has forced the Association's members to pay increasing attention to external defence. This defence re-orientation has been well documented.[16] One strategy was to set up a multilateral organization, the ARF, to 'create the conditions for a stable distribution of power among the three major Asia-Pacific states—China, Japan and the United States'.[17] The other prong of the strategy of the member states was to beef up their external defences individually. ASEAN security had hitherto had been based on non-military means. The post-Cold War situation forced the individual members to address the military dimension of external defence, with all its attendant implications.

ASEAN ARMS ACQUISITIONS

As pointed out earlier, ASEAN has been forced to pay more attention to external defence over the last two decades as a result of the changes in the regional security architecture. The result has been that the ASEAN members have become the big arms spenders of South-East Asia, and indeed, the Asia-Pacific (in relative terms) since the end of the Cold War. This latest round of ASEAN arms acquisitions, which began approximately in 1986-1987, is marked by two characteristics.

- It is essentially conventional in character.
- There is also a marked maritime emphasis. This is reflected in Thailand's contract for a helicopter carrier, Malaysia's contracts for two *Yarrow* frigates, four Italian corvettes originally built for Iraq's Saddam Hussein, and eight *F/A-18 Hornet* maritime strike aircraft, Indonesia's purchase of 39 ex-East German Navy ships, and Singapore's orders for MCMVs, Maritime Patrol Craft (*Fokker Enforcer*) and two Swedish submarines.

NEO-REALIST & NEO-LIBERAL APPROACHES

Many articles have been written on the phenomenon of South-East Asian arms acquisitions. The process has been variously described as an intra-regional arms race, defence modernization and upgrades, or replacement of worn-out, obsolete equipment.[18]

There are two schools of thought that argue that ASEAN arms acquisitions are not inherently destabilizing. The neo-realists say that ASEAN arsenals are so weak, i.e. so few in numbers, that improving military capability can only enhance the feeling of security. Moreover, the new purchases will contribute to 'regional resilience'.[19] The reasoning behind this is that ASEAN's military capability, if combined, can be enough to be a significant counterweight to balance those powers external to the ASEAN region. This combined capability would therefore result in greater ASEAN self-reliance, leading to a greater sense of security in the region. This line of thinking is quite obviously the concept of the national resilience leading to regional resilience, expounded first by President Suharto of Indonesia. In essence, this is a neo-realist balance-of-power approach. It assumes that ASEAN military strength would be required to deal with, or balance, potential extra-regional threats. Paradoxically, however, ASEAN has consistently reiterated that there are really no major external threats it can foresee.

The neo-liberals, on the other hand, argue that political and economic interdependence have led to a situation where war between the ASEAN neighbours would be unthinkable. In their estimation, ASEAN has already become what Karl Deutsch described as a 'security community'. In their assessment, the ASEAN Treaty of Amity and Cooperation is not merely an empty treaty, but has helped to ensure that no ASEAN member has fought a war with another member since 1967. This is really quite a remarkable record in view of the fact that inter-state tensions and mutual suspicions have always existed. Adherents of the neo-liberal school therefore argue that ASEAN arms acquisitions would not be destabilizing.

Unlike the arms buildup by a number of major Asia Pacific powers, the defence modernization now taking place within ASEAN does not seem to create undue anxiety among the members of the association. This is clearly due to the existence of ASEAN cooperation.[20]

There are however, two important considerations when discussing ASEAN's success as a security community. The first is that ASEAN has never resolved conflicts. The ASEAN process is all about conflict management rather than conflict resolution. The second concerns the argument that national arms acquisitions will contribute to regional defence resilience. Why does ASEAN need the capability to defend against or balance an external power? If so, which power will that be? It also assumes that ASEAN is cohesive, which is still somewhat open to debate. Lingering intra-ASEAN tensions and dichotomies, and the grouping's lack of a common security focus and shared threat perceptions are responsible for the absence of internal cohesion.[21] This is compounded by the lack of an imminent external threat.

Cohesion is a pre-requisite for collective, concerted action in the strategic arena. In the absence of a common ASEAN defence policy, doctrine and military structure, ASEAN armed forces will continue to be discrete organizations. Any increase in the military strength of member states is likely to contribute only marginally to regional strength. Instead, there is the possibility that these discrete forces might be the cause of greater intra-regional instability rather than resilience. Given the fact that ASEAN lacks internal cohesion and a common security focus, it is not too presumptuous to say that the build-up in ASEAN is somewhat non-cooperative in nature even though ASEAN officials have always insisted that prior consultations do take place before any ASEAN member embarks on a major arms programme.

THE IMPACT OF NEW TECHNOLOGIES & CAPABILITIES: THE REVOLUTION IN MILITARY AFFAIRS

Although the numbers of platforms acquired by ASEAN countries are not overly impressive, what ultimately should be of concern is that numbers and capabilities are increasing overall. Intentions in the short and medium term are less important than the fact that there is this upward trend in military capability taking place in the ASEAN region. It can be argued that the greatest impact of the acquisitions will be on the ASEAN region itself. This is because the number of new platforms on order and the enhanced capabilities it will give ASEAN armed forces will be very significant for the ASEAN balance, but insignificant in terms of its potential impact on the order of battle or arms balance in the wider Asia-Pacific.[22]

For instance, Malaysia's purchase of 18 *Mig-29s* and 8 *F/A-18 Hornets* might pale in comparison with the 5,000 combat aircraft supposedly in China's inventory. But the 27 new Malaysian aircraft has caused consternation among some of Malaysia's neighbours. Indonesia has only a squadron of *F-16s* with another on order (a squadron of *F-16s* represents something like a 100 percent increase in the number of frontline combat aircraft for Indonesia). Thailand's acquisition of a helicopter carrier introduces a totally new military dimension into the ASEAN region, while Singapore's order for two conventional submarines has left other ASEAN members wondering what Singapore is really up to. As such, ASEAN arms acquisitions could be potentially destabilizing unless monitored or moderated, since all these new purchases represent an exponential increase and a new dimension in ASEAN military power.

While current arms acquisitions may not be perceived as seriously destabilizing for the moment, the fact that ASEAN members are beginning to acquire more sophisticated Command, Control, Communications, Computer and Intelligence (C^4I) capability could well change the entire future regional balance. The theory behind the Revolution in Military Affairs (RMA) is that advances in technology, both in the civilian and military fields, particularly in information gathering and processing, and in targeting, will lead to a new way of conducting war.[23]

The RMA depends on having a society immersed in Information Technology (IT). Singapore is not only high industrialised, but it is the leading IT nation in South-East Asia. Singapore's reliance on technology to overcome its geo-strategic disadvantages and its small population of 2.8 million people seem to set it on a path towards a RMA. Singapore appears to regard a RMA not only as inevitable but essential, and such a development would most certainly be destabilizing.[24] In the absence of more structured confidence-building measures, a RMA would be a negative development. This is because of the very high degree of surveillance and targeting capability which will result from a RMA. Given the fact that suspicions between Singapore and its Malay neighbours are still high, the next round of arms acquisitions which will involve acquiring C^4I capability rather than platforms, would be highly destabilizing indeed.

If Malaysia and Indonesia were to achieve a level of technological sophistication that would result in a RMA, Singapore would be extremely worried. A RMA capability on the part of one member would not contribute to regional confidence-building, since it involves intensive surveillance and targeting even in times of peace. Moreover, the whole notion of a RMA is that it makes wars more winnable, and less expensive in terms of human lives, i.e. that wars can be fought at minimum cost in terms of lives and collateral damage. This might tempt states to go over the brink and attempt to seek a military decision instead of pursuing non-military options. At the same time, a regional RMA which networks all ASEAN military resources is completely out of the question given ASEAN's limited defence cooperation, and its avowed aversion against any kind of multilateral defence arrangement. In fact, any RMA in Malaysia and Singapore would lead to an arms race (or a 'RMA race') in the region.

There is thus a real need for confidence-building mechanisms, and dialogue to promote intra-ASEAN transparency. Optimists have argued that ASEAN is responding to the changed strategic scenario positively. The ASEAN-PMC and the ARF are cited as examples of the widening of ASEAN security cooperation to include confidence-building measures. The ARF, however, is still very much a process of dialogue and consultation. The ASEAN Way or process of conflict management needs to be reinforced by data-sharing and monitoring mechanisms. At the moment, however, ASEAN appears to find transparency to be a dirty word. Transparency, especially military transparency, is still far from being an ASEAN norm.

THE RIGHT TO BEAR ARMS

On balance, however, it would appear that the ASEAN neo-realists seem to have the upper hand at the moment. ASEAN governments today consider it their right to purchase arms and to modernise their armed forces not only because it is necessary in a more unpredictable strategic environment, but because it is their right as independent states to do so. Modern armaments in many ASEAN states in fact serve as symbols of national sovereignty and national virility. This 'right to bear arms' is reinforced by the fact that ASEAN conventional arms arsenals are still relatively small. Thus ASEAN leaders are not convinced that they should cut back on current defence spending levels, much less embark on arms control ventures, given the huge gaps in arms holdings and level of sophistication between the ASEAN members, on the one hand, and the United States and Europe on the other.[25]

Any attempt to introduce an arms control regime is thus likely to be rejected outright by regional leaders. Indeed, South-East Asians are also notably touchy even with regard to transparency, and even less enthusiastic about verification. For instance, when former Prime Minister of Singapore Lee Kuan Yew proposed that Singapore bases be opened to Malaysia for inspection, and vice versa, he was rebuffed by Kuala Lumpur. Given the general ASEAN antipathy to arms control and disarmament, what are the prospects for international cooperation?

It is in the sphere of analysis, and in helping ASEAN decision-makers and academics to delve more deeply and seriously into issues of confidence-building with direct bearing on arms control that the greatest contribution can be made at the international level. While the ASEAN Regional Forum already has confidence-building and defence white papers on its agenda, more effort is still needed to make the study of arms control more rigorous. For instance, most analysts have depended on arms race theories to analyze ASEAN arms acquisitions. While arms race theories can give insights into the phenomenon, it can be argued that the use of an arms race analytical framework has limitations. Most arms race theories usually only explain why and if nations are involved in arms races. In this respect, it is more conceptually challenging to try and assess whether South-East Asia's arms acquisitions is increasing or decreasing tension. In other words, is the latest round of arms acquisitions stabilizing or destabilizing? And if it is stabilizing, at which point will it become destabilizing? This approach at least addresses the problem of whether and when regional arms acquisitions can become stabilizing/destabilizing.

This approach is, however, extremely challenging. Arms control experts have attempted to devise various 'early warning' models, but without too much success.[26] This is because it is virtually impossible to arrive at any consensus as to if, when and at what levels arms acquisitions begin to create tensions between countries and regions. In short, it is almost impossible at this point in time to devise a system of indicators to gauge when arms acquisitions will contribute to stability, destabilize the region, or make no difference.

In the absence of such a consensus on indicators, it is my contention that a theoretical model to monitor arms acquisitions should be devised for South-East Asia, even though it might appear to be totally unnecessary and redundant at the moment because of the ASEAN process of multilateral security. In fact, if one takes the point of view that ASEAN arms acquisitions have the greatest potential to destabilize the intra-ASEAN military balance, and has virtually little or no impact on the wider Asia-Pacific military balance, then confidence-building mechanisms beyond the present informal conflict management process are needed. The other development of consequence is the fixation with high-technology by the industrially advanced countries, which some analysts argue, will eventually culminate in a RMA.[27] As increasingly sophisticated equipment is sold, or co-produced in South-East Asia, the situation will become less stable. This is because new weapons and their associated systems demand increased surveillance and targeting of potential enemies virtually round the clock. ASEAN's current defence planning, in the absence of any clear external threat, is largely based on contingency planning.[28] Thus, in view of present tensions and potential developments, it is necessary to at least emplace a system to monitor arms acquisitions, while at the same time working on a consensus model of indicators. There is a strong argument for a monitoring mechanism. The South-East Asian sub-region is becoming more complex, future arms acquisitions represent a new dimension in military capability and orientation, the number of players are increasing, and as a consequence, the range of interests and intentions has also become broader with less commonality. New approaches of assessing arms acquisitions and build-ups will be less abrasive than the usual structured, rules-based, and imposed form of arms control. Methodologies can be evolved in-country, taking into account the sensitivities of each nation. Since the monitoring mechanism would be consensus-based, and would be seen as an agenda adopted by ASEAN itself, it would hopefully, not be resisted by the ASEAN members.

CONCLUSION

At least one state in North-East Asia, namely China, shares the ASEAN fear of interference by outsiders. One could argue that the fear of outside interference is so deeply ingrained in China as a result of what Chinese scholars have referred to as 'one hundred years of shame', that it has become a part of the national psyche. The question before us is whether this fear of outside interference will continue to hold true for ASEAN and China in the years to come. Given the fact that most governments of these countries are still greatly concerned with regime stability and regime legitimacy, any initiative which is perceived as capable of undermining their authority will continue to be viewed with great distrust.

The importance of the non-interference principle has not diminished with time, and its relevance remain central. The difference is that the central focus has moved away from the fear of physical intervention by outside powers, to a fear of more insidious forms of meddling and subversion, for example attempts at agenda-setting in domestic issues, human rights, and indirect interference in domestic distributive and social systems by outside powers. In other words, the concern now is to maintain domestic political and regime security against external subversion. Hence the debate over Asian values in Singapore and Malaysia has great salience. What this means for arms control and disarmament in East Asia is that any international initiative in the field can be easily construed as meddling in internal decision-making by outside powers. International cooperation in regional security must thus take into account this very real fear (justified or not) of interference by outside powers. Any process involving international cooperation must therefore fit into the domestic agenda of these very sensitive Asian states. More importantly, they must not be misconstrued as potentially destabilizing because they have the potential to undermine or challenge the authority of ruling elites.

This is a real dilemma for arms controllers. Any mechanism introduced from the outside, even by the United Nations, is likely to be deeply resented. Thus, international efforts must be aimed at building up indigenous expertise, and at sensitizing ruling elites to the importance of confidence-building measures, and to efforts at persuading them that arms control is not necessarily prejudicial to the national interest. 'Capacity-building' in this area of expertise is therefore necessary. In addition, the term 'arms control and disarmament' should perhaps be dropped entirely in favour of a more neutral term such as 'arms legitimacy' or 'legitimate defence parity'.

NOTES

1. Segal, Gerald (ed.): *Arms Control in Asia* (London: Macmillan, 1987), p. 3.
2. Acharya, Amitav: 'A Regional Security Community in Southeast Asia?', *Journal of Strategic Studies*, vol. 18, no. 3 (Sept. 1995), p. 175.

3. Ayoob, Mohammed: 'Regional Security and the Third World', in idem (ed): *Regional Security and the Third World* (London: Croom Helm, 1986), p. 3. The second assumption is that regional states would have successfully managed intra-state tensions and dissension, and the final assumption is that inter-state tensions within the specific region would also be manageable. The hypothesis in this paper was developed independently of Ayoob's study. However, I owe an intellectual debt to Ayoob for his conceptual framework and analysis of the differences between Western approaches to security and the approaches adopted by developing countries.
4. This system-oriented approach to security has helped spawn the 'interdependence' school of analysis in international relations.
5. For instance, Iraq's attack on Kuwait was seen as a threat to one vital source of oil supply for the West, and hence to the entire system.
6. Ayoob, *loc. cit.* (note 3), p. 7.
7. *ibid.*, p. 9.
8. See Alagappa, Muthiah (ed.): *Political Legitimacy in Southeast Asia: The Quest for Moral Authority* (Stanford, CA: Stanford University Press, 1995).
9. On performance legitimacy in South-East Asia, see *ibid.*, pp. 41-43.
10. Friedberg, Aaron: 'Warring States: Theoretical Models of Asia Pacific Security', *Harvard International Review*, vol. 18, no. 2 (Spring 1996), p. 13.
11. Wang Jisi: 'Comparing Chinese and American Conceptions of Security', *North Pacific Cooperative Security Dialogue Working Paper*, no. 17 (Toronto: York University, 1992), p. 6.
12. *ibid.*, p. 2.
13. Moeller, Kay: 'East Asian Security: Lessons from Europe?', *Contemporary Southeast Asia*, vol. 17, no. 4 (March 1996), p. 363.
14. Leifer, Michael: *ASEAN and the Security of South-East Asia* (London: Routledge, 1989), p. 14.
15. Bull, Hedley: *The Control of the Arms Race* (London: Weidenfeld, 1961), p. ix.
16. See Mak, Joon Num: 'ASEAN Defence Re-Orientation 1975-1992: The Dynamics of Modernisation and Structural Change', *Canberra Papers on Strategy and Defence*, no. 13 (Canberra: Strategic and Defence Studies Centre, ANU, 1994); Leifer, Michael: 'The ASEAN Regional Forum: Extending ASEAN's Model of Regional Security', *Adelphi Papers*, no. 302 (1996), pp. 5-9.
17. *ibid.*, p. 19.
18. Malaysia's Defence Minister Syed Hamid Albar said at a recent defence exhibition in Kuala Lumpur that 'Malaysia's modernisation efforts and procurement of major capital equipment should not be looked upon as an arms race among the regional states as it was merely intended to meet its defence needs. The high economic growth has enabled regional states to replace and upgrade ageing equipment'. See 'Six Firms Shortlisted for Project', *Business Times*, 24 March, 1996.
19. Singapore Defence Minister Dr Yeo Ning Hong referred to the arms purchases by Indonesia and Malaysia, announced in 1993, as having the potential to strengthen regional resilience and 'help keep the peace and stability in the Asean region'. See 'Singapore Lauds Arms Purchases', *New Straits Times*, 2 July 1993.

20. Anwar, Dewi Fortuna: 'Changing Modalities of Southeast Asian Security', paper presented at the DSA Conference on *Changing Conceptions of Security in a Changing Pacific Asia*, Kuala Lumpur, 25-26 April 1996, p. 4.
21. The analyst who has probably written the most on intra-ASEAN tensions is Tim Huxley. See his 'Insecurity in the ASEAN Region', *Whitehall Paper Series* (London: RUSI, 1993); idem: 'Singapore And Malaysia: A Precarious Balance?', *The Pacific Review*, vol. 4, no. 3 (1991).
22. Probably the most comprehensive and consistent source of data on ASEAN arms acquisitions is Gill, Bates, Joon Num Mak & Siemon Wezeman: *ASEAN Arms Acquisitions: Developing Transparency* (Kuala Lumpur: Malaysian Institute of Maritime Affairs & SIPRI, 1995).
23. Fitzsimonds, James R.: 'The Coming Military Revolution: Opportunities and Risks', *Parameters*, vol. 15, no. 2 (Summer 1995), pp. 30-36. See also Cohen, Eliot A.: 'Come the Revolution', *Defense & Technology*, 31 July 1995, pp. 26-30.
24. Singapore needs technology to offset its strategic handicaps, which are its lack of strategic depth, its small population of 2.8 million people, and the fact that it has all its resources concentrated within a tiny area totalling only 632.6 square kilometres. Two other factors pushed Singapore to use technology to offset its strategic disadvantages. The first was the perception that it is an island state under siege, a Chinese 'nut' caught between the jaws of a Malay nutcracker. The second is the presence of a relatively advanced technocratic/technological population, which Singapore has inducted or co-opted into its armed forces via national service. The absence of any insurgency also allowed Singapore to concentrate on conventional warfare doctrine since its separation from the Federation of Malaysia in 1965. It has pursued this conventional warfare doctrine in a single-minded, systematic manner. It developed first, the army, then developed the air force for strategic strike, and finally built up the navy for the protection of Sea Lines of Communications (SLOCs). Singapore is a good example of a military problem looking for a solution, and technology offered one.
25. Ming, Wan: 'Wealth and Power: The Economic Transformation of Security', *Harvard International Review*, vol. 18, no. 2 (Spring 1966), p. 20.
26. Bates Gill for example, has acknowledged that the debate on defining the 'legitimate needs versus unwarranted development of national military capabilities' in the Asia-Pacific is still very much in its nascent states. See his 'Enhancing National Military Capabilities in the Asia-Pacific Region: Debating Legitimate Needs versus Unwarranted Development', *10th Asia-Pacific Roundtable*, Kuala Lumpur, 8-9 June, 1996.
27. The implications, technologies and theories of RMA were discussed at some length at the *Revolution in Military Affairs Conference* organised by the Australian Defence Studies Centre in Canberra, 27-28 February 1996.
28. See Mak, Joon Num: 'The ASEAN Maritime Re-Orientation: Contingency Planning in an Uncertain World', *International Defense Review Yearbook, Defense 1995* (Coulsdon, Surrey: Jane's Information Group, 1995).

5 Regional Security and Nuclear Weapons in North-East Asia: A Japanese Perspective

MITSURU KUROSAWA

With the end of the Cold War, the military and political value of nuclear weapons has gradually decreased. This has been due to the dissolution of the military and ideological confrontation between the East and the West.

The strategic nuclear forces of the two superpowers have been reduced and the Comprehensive Nuclear Test Ban Treaty was adopted and signed by more than 140 states including the five nuclear-weapon states. Recently nuclear-weapon-free zones have been established in Africa and Southeast Asia, where there had been nuclear weapons during the Cold War era. In Europe, conventional weapons were radically reduced by the CFE (Conventional Forces in Europe) Treaty, and the CSCE/OSCE (Conference/ Organization for Security and Cooperation in Europe) process helped reduce tension, increase transparency, and build confidence among states.

In spite of the end of the Cold War, North-East Asia has not seen much progress in its security environment compared to what has been seen in Europe, Africa, or Southeast Asia. With the dismantlement of the Soviet Union, the threat from that source has been significantly reduced, but the same Cold-War-era kind of thinking still seems to remain, however, in the minds of decision-makers in Japan and the United States.

In this article, I will first take up Japan's security policy in the post-Cold War era to see how Japan is dealing with possible security problems. Then, I will historically review Japan's policy on nuclear weapons and examine recent suspicions regarding Japan's nuclear weapons development. Third, I will emphasize the necessity of increased security cooperation among states in this region in order to build more confidence. Fourth, as an indirect way to prevent nuclear proliferation, I will urge for regional cooperation in the peaceful uses of nuclear energy. Lastly, I will recommend efforts to establish a nuclear-weapon-free zone in North-East Asia, which will contribute to making this region more secure and to dispelling nuclear suspicions about Japan.

JAPAN'S SECURITY POLICY

During the Cold War era, Japan's security policy was strictly framed in the context of the East-West confrontation, and focused on how to deal with the threat from the Soviet Union in the region of North-East Asia. Japan played a very passive role in security matters, shielded by the strong nuclear umbrella of the United States, in its turn based on the US-Japan Security Treaty (The Treaty of Mutual Cooperation and Security between Japan and the United States of America).

Despite the significant reduction of the Soviet threat, the end of the Cold War did not significantly change the security perception of many security experts in Japan. As Seizaburo Sato said, 'Yet, in spite of the recent termination of the East-West confrontation and the ensuing disintegration of the Soviet Union, the continued usefulness of NATO and the US-Japan alliance is still manifest....In the Asia-Pacific region...ensuring that the US maintains its forward deployment intact is an almost absolute necessity for the stability of the region.'[1]

In August 1994, an Advisory Group on Defence Issues, composed of non-governmental experts, was established by the Prime Minister to develop principles of guidance for defence policy in the new post-Cold-War era. This group submitted its report, titled *The Modality of the Security and Defence Capability of Japan*, in which it mainly recommended the following three policies: strengthening of UN peacekeeping operations and the role of the Japan Self-Defence Forces in it; enhancement of the Japan-US Security Cooperation relationship; and the maintenance and qualitative improvement of Japan's self-defence capability.

In February 1995, the US Department of Defense published the document on *United States Security Strategy for the East Asia-Pacific Region*, which stated that, 'Our forward deployed and forward stationed forces in Asia ensured broad regional stability, helped to deter aggression against our allies,...The United States must remain engaged in Asia, committed to peace in the region, and dedicated to strengthening alliances and friendship.' The Department of Defence concluded by promising to continue stationing 100,000 United States personnel.[2]

In November 1995, as a result of the drastic change of international circumstances after the end of the Cold War, a new National Defence Program Outline of Japan was adopted in place of the old Outline of 1976. It stated that, 'In the area surrounding our country, elements of opaqueness and uncertainty still remain, and stable security circumstances have not yet been established...The close cooperation between Japan and the United States based on the Japan-US Security Treaty will promote the establishment of stable security circumstances ...and will play an important role for the security of Japan and stability of international society.'

The Japan-US Joint Declaration on Security, which was signed in Tokyo by Prime Minister Ryutaro Hashimoto and President William Clinton on 17 April 1996, reiterated the significant value of the alliance between the two countries and reaffirmed that the Japan-US security relationship, based on the Security Treaty, remains the cornerstone for achieving common security objectives, and for maintaining a stable and prosperous environment for the Asia-Pacific region as it enters the twenty-first century. It confirmed, once again, that US deterrence under the Security Treaty remains the guarantee for Japan's security.[3] On regional cooperation, it stated as follows:

> The Prime Minister and the President agreed that their two governments will jointly and individually strive to achieve a more peaceful and stable security environment in the Asia-Pacific region. In this regard, the two leaders recognized that the engagement of the United States in the region, supported by the Japan-US security relationship, constitutes the foundation for such efforts.

Recently Japan's security policy, clearly expressed in the above-mentioned documents, has shown a tendency to reemphasize the significance of the Japan-US alliance and nuclear deterrence based on it, even though the severe confrontation between the East and the West in the Cold War era has ended. Indeed, there still remains a degree of uncertainty in North-East Asia, including the Korean Peninsula and Taiwan. However, with the end of the Cold War we should work to establish a regional security framework through regional cooperation. The exclusive emphasis on the bilateral alliance shown in the documents does not contribute to regional security in the longer term, which requires a pursuit of both bilateral and multilateral security cooperation.

JAPAN'S NUCLEAR WEAPONS POLICY

In the last few years, suspicions that Japan would go nuclear have reappeared, based on three observations:[4] Japan plans to use plutonium as nuclear energy and is accumulating large amounts of plutonium; suspicion regarding North Korea's nuclear programme may motivate Japan to go nuclear; and Japan was reluctant to support an indefinite extension of the Nuclear Non-Proliferation Treaty (NPT) in 1993.[5]

From a technical aspect, Xia Liping states that, 'It is reported that Japan will store from five to ten tons of plutonium within the next five years. Although this plutonium is not weapons-grade, it would not be difficult for Japan to make it weapons-grade. Japanese media have reported that, if necessary, Japan could have nuclear weapons within a year. Japan already has strongly powered rockets capable of launching satellites into orbit around the earth and of being transformed into ballistic missiles'.[6]

The Japanese plutonium program is a source of suspicion, but Motoya Kitamura emphasizes the irrelevance of the civilian plutonium program to any potential weapon program, saying, 'with or without the plutonium program, Tokyo could acquire nuclear weapons, if it developed the political will'. Instead, he argues that political motivation is more important than technology, concluding that, 'Tokyo's political will holds the key to preventing nuclear proliferation in Japan, but the nuclear umbrella provided by the United States will have the strongest influence on Tokyo's decision-making'.[7]

In order to allay concerns, Japan has maintained the policy of having no excess plutonium. Recent accidents at the Monju fast breeder reactor and at a reprocessing plant at Tokai-mura, however, will make it difficult for Japan to vigorously pursue plutonium-recycling.

If North Korea gets nuclear weapons it is generally believed that South Korea and Japan will follow suit. A Japanese foreign minister once confessed to the possibility of Japan's withdrawal from the NPT if North Korea were to get a bomb. North Korea's nuclear program, now being frozen through the Agreed Framework between the US and North Korea, should be resolved peacefully with special inspections by the IAEA. It is quite important to settle North Korea's case, both from the viewpoint of regional peace and stability and because of its impact on Japan's future course of action.[8]

At the Tokyo G7 Summit in June 1993, Japan could not join all other nations to support the indefinite extension of the NPT, which caused suspicion about Japan's intentions. The main reason for this indecision derived from the fact that Prime Minister Miyazawa could not get consensus for the extension within the ruling party. He had been a Minister for Foreign Affairs while the treaty was being hotly debated in Japan and therefore knew how difficult it would be to get the treaty approved. Two months later, however, the new Hosokawa administration made it clear that Japan should support the indefinite extension, emphasizing that world peace will be achieved through world disarmament by completely eliminating nuclear weapons.

David Arase explained that a nuclear option for Japan was not out of the question.

> From a legal standpoint, if nuclear weapons are defined as a defensive deterrent, they could be consistent with Article 9. From a political standpoint, the collapse of the left and the new moderate-conservative centre of gravity in Japanese politics—coupled with the threat of a nuclear-armed Korea—makes this legal interpretation sustainable. The technical issues are not difficult for Japan. Japan imported 1.7 tons of weapons grade plutonium from France in late 1992 and additional shipments of this size to schedule...In terms of delivery systems, the new Japanese H-2 rocket will be comparable to advanced US ICBMs in everything but guidance technologies.[9]

It is true that Japan was reluctant to join the treaty, being the 97th party to the NPT seven years after its entry into force, and in domestic debates some politicians and security experts argued for keeping the nuclear option open. However, the Japanese people, who have been victims of atomic bombings in Hiroshima and Nagasaki, have a strong nuclear allergy and public opinion against nuclear weapons remains as strong as ever.

One expression of this sentiment is the policy of the so-called three non-nuclear principles, according to which Japan will neither possess, produce nor permit the introduction of nuclear weapons. The policy was first proclaimed by Prime Minister Eisaku Sato in 1967 and has been reconfirmed in resolutions of the Diet many times. Adherence to the third principle was somewhat ambiguous during the Cold War era, especially as far as port calls and navigation in territorial seas were concerned, which were included in the non-introduction principle, according to the Japanese Government. However, after President Bush's statement on withdrawal of tactical nuclear weapons in 1991, most of the ambiguity has disappeared.

The Basic Law of Atomic Energy of 1955 stipulates that research, development and use of atomic energy shall be limited to peaceful uses only under the principles of democratic and autonomous management and openness of its results. Under this law, any military use of nuclear energy, including nuclear weapons, is completely prohibited.

The merit of the possible acquisition of nuclear weapons by Japan has been analyzed by defence experts as extremely low or almost non-existent from a military point of view, and negative from a political point of view. With this background, the possibility of a nuclear Japan is extremely remote. Japan should make positive efforts, however, to dispel any suspicion by making nuclear activities more transparent and making its political will not to have nuclear weapons as clear as possible by any available means.

REGIONAL SECURITY COOPERATION

The Helsinki process, which started in the early 1970s, produced many documents for security cooperation in Europe, increasing transparency in military activities and building confidence among states. The process also lead to the end of the confrontation between the East and the West in Europe. In sharp contrast to this situation, East Asia, in particular North-East Asia, still suffers from antagonism. As the security setting in East Asia is rather different from Europe, we cannot transplant the CSCE process directly into a 'CSCA' (Conference for Security and Cooperation in Asia), but we can learn from the European experience. In South-East Asia, security cooperation has been developed under the ASEAN framework.[10] In North-East Asia, however, there is no multilateral body or forum to discuss security issues, and a military confrontation on the Korean Peninsula or across the Taiwan strait remains conceivable. Many territorial disputes still remain in this area. For example, Japan has territorial disputes with Russia, China, and the Republic of Korea.

The ASEAN Regional Forum (ARF) is a useful framework to promote security cooperation in East Asia, and it is necessary to exploit this framework to improve the security situation in North-East Asia. A conference on confidence-building measures was held in Tokyo in January 1996 under the auspices of the ARF. In parallel with this multilateral route, countries in North-East Asia should pursue confidence-building measures (CBMs) bilaterally.

CBMs between Japan and Russia have been promoted with an agreement between the two countries in April 1996, and the first concrete measure was taken in the form of the visit to Vladivostok by Japan's Marine Self-Defence supporting ship in July 1996. Furthermore, Russia and China agreed to a joint statement in April 1996 in Beijing, establishing a partnership for strategic cooperation, including some CBMs. This was later reaffirmed at a summit in April 1997 in Moscow. However, there is no similar agreement between Japan and China, in spite of the fact that the relationship between the two countries is an essential element in peace and stability in North-East Asia. Japan and China should work for this purpose as soon as possible.[11]

In North-East Asia where the security situation is complicated, it is necessary to establish a multilateral mechanism for security dialogue and coordination, and one of the focuses should be the establishment of various confidence and security-building measures.[12]

REGIONAL COOPERATION FOR PEACEFUL USES OF NUCLEAR ENERGY

In the East Asia region, the prospect of the use of nuclear energy for power generation is quite high. Japan and the Republic of Korea have been using nuclear energy for many years, and China has also utilized nuclear power generation. With the high rate of economic development in China and South-East Asian countries, nuclear energy will increasingly be used to support their energy needs.

For the safety and security of the use of nuclear energy and for the purpose of non-proliferation, regional nuclear cooperation should be pursued, for the purpose of which EURATOM could be a model. It includes both nuclear-weapon states and non-nuclear-weapon states and promotes peaceful uses of nuclear energy with its own safeguards system. However, East Asian countries do not have the homogeneity of the EURATOM countries culturally, ethically, politically, religiously or technologically. As a first step, the nuclear cooperation will be modest and start from consultation on nuclear safety and security. Next, they should consult on the possibility of a regional framework for multilateral reprocessing and disposal of spent fuel.

According to Hiroyoshi Kurihara, 'In order to increase transparency, and to further peaceful nuclear energy development and non-proliferation, Asian regional cooperation should be enhanced, perhaps in the form of ASIATOM'. ASIATOM (Asia Atomic Energy Community) is needed as an organization to promote regional cooperation and coordination in the research and development of peaceful uses of nuclear energy. It should resolve the issue of sensitive technology, such as enrichment or reprocessing, through the development of a regional fuel-cycle centre. It could be a centre for clearing information on nuclear activities, thereby enhancing transparency. It could help upgrade the level of nuclear safety, radiological protection, nuclear material control, and physical protection, and it could create a regional safeguards system to alleviate the burden on the IAEA. Kurihara's main concern is close cooperation and an information exchange on nuclear material control, domestic safeguards and physical protection of nuclear material among three states in the Far East, i.e. Japan, the Republic of Korea and China.[13]

John Simpson has argued that:

> Regional nuclear energy arrangements covering Korea, Japan, and possibly also China, seem to offer more possibilities, however. Given apparent North Korean concern over stockpiles of plutonium in Japan, the creation of a NEAATOM or ASIATOM along similar lines to EURATOM appear to have attractions to both North and South Korea. In particular, the creation of a regional safeguards system similar to the EURATOM one, in which the regional organization formally owned all the region's fissile materials that were not in military programs, would enhance the transparency of all the region's nuclear activities, and provide additional assurances over nuclear energy activities in North Korea and the stockpiling of plutonium in Japan. It would also be a regional vehicle for providing financial and technical assistance to the nuclear energy programs in North Korea and China, and possibly also in Eastern Russia.[14]

In June 1996, the Council on Nuclear Energy and Disarmament in Tokyo published a report *ASIATOM: A New Framework for Nuclear Cooperation in the Asia-Pacific Region*. The main purposes of ASIATOM are to contribute to the expansion of the peaceful uses of nuclear energy for meeting the increasing needs for electricity, while ensuring that all nuclear energy activities in the region will be carried out in a manner strictly compatible with internationally agreed non-proliferation requirements. The members of ASIATOM will be Australia, Canada, China, Indonesia, Japan, South Korea, Malaysia, Philippines, Taiwan, Thailand, the United States, and Vietnam. Within the framework of ASIATOM, regional centre(s) for nuclear safety and plant operation, regional centre(s) for nuclear fuel cycle services, including waste storage/management, reprocessing, enrichment, and regional safeguards/inspection systems will be created.[15]

Robert A. Manning has proposed PACATOM (Pacific Atomic Energy Community) as a nuclear cooperation regime. PACATOM's goals and functions would be as follows: to serve as a regional safeguards regime and to strengthen physical protection and safety of nuclear materials, cooperation in the monitoring of radiation levels, improvement of safeguards standards and practices, cooperation in research and development, cooperation on the storage and management of spent fuel, establishment of a regional plutonium bank, and the disposal of fissile material from dismantled weapons.[16]

Regarding the name of a cooperative community, that is, ASIATOM or PACATOM, the former emphasized that the centre of the community should be in

Asia and sometimes restricts its membership in Asia, while the latter emphasized that other states might join and that, in particular, the United States should be one of the members. William J. Dirks pointed out, 'A possible way to get China in and broaden the mix of membership would be to include other Pacific Rim states such as Australia, Canada, and even the United States, creating not ASIATOM but a Pacific Atomic Energy Community (PACATOM)'.[17]

With these proposals and ideas, we should proceed to increase our cooperation in the peaceful uses of nuclear energy in the Far East, North-East Asia, East Asia and Asia-Pacific Area step by step with the ultimate goal of establishing the EURATOM-type organization.

TOWARDS A NORTH-EAST ASIAN NUCLEAR-WEAPON-FREE ZONE

THE SITUATION IN SOUTH-EAST ASIA

In December 1995, ten nations in South-East Asia signed the Treaty on the South-East Asia Nuclear Weapon-Free Zone. In April 1996, the African continent was turned into a nuclear-weapon-free zone by signing a treaty. States in Latin America and the South Pacific have signed treaties for nuclear-weapon-free-zones three and one decades ago, respectively. In the post-Cold War era, where many tactical nuclear weapons deployed by the US and the Soviet Union have been withdrawn to their homeland, the establishment of nuclear-weapon-free zones should now be encouraged for international and regional peace.

Five states in South-East Asia agreed to establish ASEAN (Association of the South-East Asian Nations) in 1967, and adopted at its special meeting in November 1971 a declaration on a 'Zone of Peace, Freedom and Neutrality (ZOPFAN)'. Their desire, stated in this declaration, was to make South-East Asia a zone of peace, freedom and neutrality, free from intervention by other nations. The establishment of a nuclear-weapon-free zone has been pursued as one element of the ZOPFAN, but it proved impossible during the Cold War era because the area was involved in the East-West confrontation and because nuclear weapons of the superpowers were deployed within its area of application.

With the end of the Cold War, the United States and the Soviet Union began withdrawing their troops and nuclear weapons, South-East Asia saw 'peace through reconciliation' in Cambodia, and the East-West confrontation has largely disappeared. On the other hand, as China has become a big power in the region, the states in South-East Asia have increasingly felt the need for measures to prevent China's military expansion.

The South-East Asia Nuclear Weapon-Free Zone Treaty entered into force with the ratification of eight states on 27 March 1997. However, the Treaty has not been supported by the five nuclear-weapon states, in particular, the United States and China, because the zone not only includes the territory of the signatory states, but also their continental shelves and exclusive economic zones, which are not included in the NWFZs in Latin America, the South Pacific and Africa. Consultation and negotiation will therefore be necessary between the zonal states and the nuclear-weapon states.

THE KOREAN PENINSULA

On the Korean Peninsula, the tactical nuclear weapons deployed in South Korea were withdrawn to the United States in 1991, and a Joint Declaration on Denuclearization of the Korean Peninsula was initialled by South and North Korea on 31 December 1991 which entered into force on 19 February 1992. The two parties agreed:

1. The South and the North shall not test, manufacture, produce, receive, possess, store, deploy, or use nuclear weapons.
2. The South and the North shall use nuclear energy solely for peaceful purposes.
3. The South and the North shall not possess nuclear reprocessing and uranium enrichment facilities.
4. The South and the North, in order to verify the denuclearization of the Korean peninsula, shall conduct inspection of the objects selected by the other side and agreed upon between the two sides, in accordance with procedures and methods to be determined by the South-North Joint Nuclear Control Commission.
5. The South and the North, in order to implement this joint declaration, shall establish and operate a South-North Joint Nuclear Control Commission within one month of the effectuation of this joint declaration.

First of all, the declaration thus amounted to an agreement by both parties to ban any and all activities associated with nuclear weapons, and thus, to maintain nuclear-weapon-free status there. Secondly, notwithstanding North Korea's insistence that South Korea remove itself from the US nuclear umbrella, this point was not included. Thirdly, the documents also omitted the ban sought by North Korea on the passage through territorial waters or air space, or port calls by ships or aircraft carrying nuclear weapons. Fourthly, it did not incorporate any guarantees, as sought by North Korea, that the United States, the Soviet Union, or China would honour the principle of denuclearization, as it was purely a bilateral agreement. Fifthly, the denuclearization provision banned not only nuclear weapons, but also the possession of facilities for uranium enrichment or spent fuel reprocessing. Sixthly, the scope of inspection was extremely limited, as it had to be agreed among the two parties. Finally, the procedures and methods for inspection were left up to the Joint Nuclear Commission, a body to be established at a later date.

The Joint Nuclear Commission was set up one month later, on 19 March, but the views of the commission delegates from the two Koreas were wide apart regarding the joint bilateral inspection framework. In the expressed interest of removing mutual suspicions about covert nuclear weapons development or possession, North Korea insisted that it be allowed to inspect all US military installations in the South, in return for granting the South access to its nuclear facilities in Yongbyong.

However, South Korea, citing the principle of reciprocity, asserted that the North, too, should open its military installations to inspection and further insisted that both sides be allowed to conduct the same number of inspections on an annual basis. Additionally, the South stressed that it should have the right to conduct special inspections, which should be compulsory and require only 24 hours' advance notice. The North rejected these procedures, however, declaring them outside the scope of the agreement.

Seong W. Cheon cites the following reasons for the breakdown in negotiations on these issues: the first major stumbling block will be North Korea's traditional resistance to openness, which has spawned a hostile attitude toward verification. The second major hurdle is that virtually no trust exists between the two sides. The third obstacle is that the two sides possess virtually no monitoring capabilities except some short-range sensors.[18]

The October 1994 'Agreed Framework' worked out with the US appears to have brought the issue of nuclear development by North Korea closer to a solution. However, many murky points remain. The following is an excerpt detailing the points agreed to on the denuclearization of the Korean Peninsula.

> III Both sides will work together for peace and security on a nuclear-free Korean Peninsula.
> 1) The United States will provide formal assurance to the DPRK against the threat or use of nuclear weapons by the United States.
> 2) The DPRK will consistently take steps to implement the North-South joint declaration on the denuclearization of the Korean Peninsula.
> 3) The DPRK will engage in North-South dialogue, as this agreed framework will help create an atmosphere that promotes such dialogue.

The declaration of denuclearization has not been implemented completely, although it was reaffirmed in the agreed framework. With the general progress regarding nuclear issues in the Korean peninsula, the declaration should be implemented thoroughly and turned into a clearly legally binding undertaking.

William Epstein has pointed out that

> I believe that it would be much better for North and South Korea, as well as for Asia and the Pacific region, if the Koreans would seek to achieve, at the earliest possible date, a psychologically, politically and legally more impressive formal Nuclear-Free-Zone Treaty.[19]

NORTH-EAST ASIA

Establishing a nuclear-weapon-free zone in North-East Asia is an idea that comes up whenever the focus of discussion is on security issues in North-East Asia, including Japan. Though the chances for such a zone seem rather poor compared with other parts of the globe,[20] the idea deserves serious consideration in the post-Cold War era, at least from a medium and longer-range perspective.

While the Korean Peninsula is always a focal point of the idea, Japan and other countries are also given attention. One proposal calls for the establishment of a zone comprising the Koreas and Japan; another would add Mongolia and Taiwan; and yet another has advocated bringing some of the nuclear powers, e.g., China, Russia, or the US into the arrangement. This third proposal calls for the creation of a limited nuclear-free zone in North-East Asia, in one of the following three forms: (i) a circular zone with the centre placed at the centre of the demilitarized zone on the Korean Peninsula, with a radius stretching 1200 nautical miles (thus including China, Taiwan, Japan, Mongolia, the two Koreas and the US); (ii) an elliptical zone with its western border located in North-East China and its eastern in Alaska; or (iii) a Northern-Pacific zone including a portion of North-East China, eastern Russia, the Alaskan US, Japan, the Korean Peninsula and Mongolia. This proposal has several interesting features. For one, it would include territories in the possession of some of the nuclear powers. In addition, rather than banning the deployment of all nuclear weapons, it would first be aimed at non-strategic nuclear forces.[21]

Extending the reach of the declaration for a nuclear-free Korean Peninsula would be one way of bringing Japan and other countries into an arrangement for a nuclear-weapon-free zone. However, as noted earlier, the Korean Peninsula declaration contains a provision banning the possession of facilities for nuclear fuel reprocessing and uranium enrichment. Hence, Japan could not be included within that particular framework in its current form. In general, the concept of a nuclear-weapon-free zone does not include these obligations.

Japan's Security Treaty with the US is perhaps the biggest issue for any proposal that would conceivably hope to include Japan in a nuclear-weapon-free zone. The US has set seven conditions that nuclear-weapon-free zones must meet if they are to win its support. Of those, three have particular relevance here, namely the condition that such zones do not (i) disturb existing security arrangements; or (ii) seek to impose restrictions on the exercise of rights based on the principle of freedom of navigation; or (iii) affect the existing rights to grant transit privileges, including port calls and overflights.

With regard to (iii), it should be noted that the treaties for the four nuclear-weapon-free zones established so far have essentially left decisions on whether or not to grant transit privileges to the independent discretion of each signatory state. The question would not be regulated by treaty. On (ii), there should be no restrictions as long as passage is in accordance with the laws of the sea in general and the provisions of the UN Convention in particular. Innocent passage is guaranteed through territorial waters of other states, and transit passage (which is freer) is permitted when going through straits. When Japan extended its territorial waters from three to twelve nautical miles from land, it kept the three-mile limit in force for five sea straits. This approach was apparently taken in connection with Japan's three non-nuclear principles, to avoid any contradictions with the government's stated policy of refusing passage to nuclear-armed vessels through Japanese territorial waters. If any problem was to arise with Japan's inclusion in a nuclear-weapon-free zone, it would probably be a reverse contradiction: that is, between the country's three non-nuclear principles, which ban port calls or passage through territorial waters by nuclear-armed vessels, and the nuclear-free framework, which might not necessarily impose such bans at all.

As far as the US condition is concerned that such a zone should not disturb existing security arrangements, it may be necessary to explore the potential impact of a nuclear-weapon-free zone in terms of the position taken by the Japanese government, that is, to firmly uphold its security treaty with the US. Though the US currently has military installations in Japan, it also has air and naval installations in Australia and Singapore, as well as bases in Panama and Honduras. Each of those other states is located within a nuclear-weapon-free zone. The implication is that the establishment of those zones has not been compromised by the presence of US military bases, or by security alliances with the US.

The question whether it is possible to be part of a nuclear-weapon-free zone while remaining under the US 'nuclear umbrella' would not present much of a problem, provided that Japan stuck firmly to its three non-nuclear principles, and that the terms for participation in the nuclear-weapon-free zone were less stringent than those three principles. However, it should be noted that the three principles are not legal mandates, but merely expressions of national policy that have been accorded at least verbal support by successive Japanese administrations. Moreover, particularly during the Cold War years, they were applied in a rather permissive manner; indeed, it would be hard to claim they have ever been enforced in the strict sense. After the Cold War, however, the US amended its policies by vowing not to arm its surface naval vessels or submarines with nuclear weapons. With that policy shift, it seems safe to say that Japan is actually observing its three principles now, even though it seems questionable whether comparable conditions can be mandated through a treaty establishing a nuclear-weapon-free zone.

The US pulled its nuclear weapons out of South Korea prior to the declaration on the denuclearization of the Korean Peninsula. Despite that fact, there is no reason to doubt that South Korea remains under the US nuclear umbrella. By implication, nuclear weapons deployment and a nuclear umbrella need not be lumped together as one issue. Should North and South Korea eventually be reunified, one way or the other, it is quite conceivable that the reunified state might possess nuclear weapons. While both countries are parties to the NPT and likely to remain so, their nuclear-free declaration is a bilateral agreement rather than a legally binding international document. As such, it will lose force the moment the two Koreas are reunited. Hence, it might be desirable to establish a treaty for a new nuclear-weapon-free zone that includes the two Koreas with Japan in a trilateral arrangement, and to enact that treaty prior to Korean reunification in order to ensure that its terms and conditions are observed even after reunification.

The concept of a nuclear-weapon-free zone in North-East Asia including the Korean Peninsula and Japan should be examined among government officials and academics, while we have to wait and see how North Korea behaves with regard to the Agreed Framework. In order to make a nuclear-weapon-free zone effective, however, the three nuclear-weapon-states (the United States, Russia and China) must be cooperative not only by giving negative security assurances but also by changing their nuclear posture and deployment.

CONCLUSION

We all should endeavour to make North-East Asia safer and more secure through regional cooperation rather than confrontation in any field. The US-Japan alliance should not be overemphasized, even though it is indispensable for peace and stability in North-East Asia. Rather, in parallel with this, multilateral efforts should be pursued in cooperation with other regional states in respect to confidence-building, peaceful uses of nuclear energy and establishment of a North-East Asia nuclear-weapon free zone.

NOTES

1. Sato, Seizaburo: 'Japanese Perception of the New Security Situation', in Trevor Taylor (ed.): *The Collapse of the Soviet Empire: Managing the Regional Fallout* (London: Royal Institute of International Affairs, 1992), p. 184.
2. See, Nye, Joseph S. Jr.: 'The Case for Deep Engagement', *Foreign Affairs*, vol. 74, no.4 (July/August 1995), pp. 90-102; Johnson, Chalmers & E. B. Keehn: 'The Pentagon's Ossified Strategy', *ibid.*, pp. 103-114.
3. The Joint Declaration was criticized mainly by China, as it represented the 'Cold War thinking'. See, for example, Zhao Jieqi, '"Redefinition" of Japan-U.S. Security Arrangements and Its Repercussions', *Foreign Affairs Journal*, no. 41 (Beijing: The Chinese People's Institute of Foreign Affairs, September 1996), pp. 34-44.
4. On Japan's nuclear weapons policy in comparison with Canada's, see Kurosawa, Mitsuru: 'Nuclear Disarmament and Non-Proliferation: Japanese and Canadian Perspectives', *Osaka University Law Review*, no. 44 (February 1997), pp. 9-25.
5. See, e.g., Harrison, Selig: 'A Yen for the Bomb? Nervous Japan Rethinks the Nuclear Option', *Washington Post*, 31 October 1993, p. C1.

6. Xia Liping: 'Maintaining Stability in the Presence of Nuclear Proliferation in the Asia-Pacific Region', *Comparative Strategy*, vol. 14 (1994), pp. 279-280.
7. Kitamura, Motoya: 'Japan's Plutonium Program: A Proliferation Threat?', *The Nonproliferation Review*, vol. 3, no. 2 (Winter 1996), pp. 1, 10-11.
8. Howlett, Darryl: 'Nuclearization or Denuclearization on the Korean Peninsula?', *Contemporary Security Policy*, vol. 15, no. 2 (August 1994), pp. 174-193; Hughes, Christopher W.: 'The North Korean Nuclear Crisis and Japanese Security', *Survival*, vol. 38, no. 2 (Summer 1996), pp. 79-103.
9. Arase, David: 'New Directions in Japanese Security Policy', *Contemporary Security Policy*, vol. 15, no. 2 (August 1994), pp. 55-56. For a similarly comprehensive analysis of Japan's nuclear capabilities and policy, see also Han, Yong-Sup: 'Nuclear Disarmament and Non-Proliferation in Northeast Asia', *Research Paper*, no. 33 (Geneva & New York: UNIDIR, 1995).
10. Rolls, Mark G.: 'Security Co-operation in Southeast Asia: An Evolving Process', *Contemporary Security Policy*, vol. 15, no. 2 (August 1994), pp. 94-111.
11. Green, Michael J. & Benjamin L. Self: 'Japan's Changing China Policy: From Commercial Liberalism to Reluctant Realism', *Survival*, vol. 38, no. 2 (Summer 1996), pp. 35-58.
12. Xia Liping: *loc. cit.* (note 6), p. 285. On the concept of comprehensive security which was developed in Japan during the Cold War era and received attention after the Cold War, see Yamamoto, Yoshinobu: 'A Framework for a Comprehensive-Cooperative Security System for the Asia-Pacific,' in Jim Rolfe (ed.): *Unresolved Futures: Comprehensive Security in the Asia-Pacific* (Wellington: Centre for Strategic Studies, Victoria University of Wellington, 1995), pp. 17-44; Clements, Kevin (ed.): *Peace and Security in the Asia Pacific Region* (Tokyo: United Nations University Press, 1992).
13. Kurihara, Hiroyoshi: 'Regional Approaches to Increase Nuclear Transparency', *Disarmament*, vol. 18, no. 2 (1995), pp. 36-39.
14. Simpson, John: 'Nuclear Capabilities, Military Security and the Korean Peninsula: A Three-Tiered Perspective from Europe', *The Korean Journal of Defense Analysis*, vol. 4, no. 2 (Winter 1992), p. 26.
15. The Council on Nuclear Energy and Disarmament (CNED): 'ASIATOM: A New Framework for Nuclear Cooperation in the Asia-Pacific Region' (Tokyo, June 1996).
16. Manning, Robert A.: 'PACATOM: Nuclear Cooperation in Asia', *Washington Quarterly*, vol. 20, no. 2 (Spring 1997), pp. 224-225. On the analysis whether the regional approaches adopted in the European Community and Latin America are relevant, see Howlett, Darryl: 'Regional Nuclear Co-operation and Non-Proliferation Arrangements: Models from Other Regions', in idem & John Simpson (eds.): *East Asia and Nuclear Non-Proliferation* (Mountbatten Centre for International Studies, University of Southampton, 1993), pp. 63-71.
17. Dirks, William J.: 'ASIATOM: How Soon, What Role, and Who Should Participate?', in William Clark, Jr. & Ryukichi Imai (eds.): *Next Steps in Arms Control and Non-Proliferation* (Washington, D.C.: Carnegie Endowment for International Peace, 1996), p. 98.

18. Cheon, Seong W.: 'National Security and Stability in East Asia: The Korean Peninsula', in Howlett & Simpson (eds.): *op. cit.* (note 16), p. 42.
19. Epstein, William: 'Nuclear Security for the Korean Peninsula', *The Korean Journal of Defense Analysis*, vol. 4, no. 2 (Winter 1992), p. 64.
20. According to John Simpson, '... the creation of such a regional zone does not appear a viable option ...'. See *loc. cit.* (note 14), p. 25. Andrew Mack agrees, acknowledging that '... negotiating a Northeast Asian zonal agreement will be far more difficult than was the case with the South Pacific or Southeast Asian agreement...'. See his 'Proliferation in Northeast Asia', *Occasional Paper*, no. 28 (The Henry L. Stimson Centre, 1996), p. 55.
21. Endicott, John: 'The Limited Nuclear Free Zone for Northeast Asia', Senior Panel's Deliberations Draft Initial Agreement, 24 February 1995.

6 Resolving the Arms Control Dilemma on the Korean Peninsula

YONG-SUP HAN

INTRODUCTION

As we approach the turn of the millennium, the countries in the world are about to enter a new age of cooperation and prosperity, leaving behind them the harsh military confrontation of the 20th century. The military confrontation and rivalry which shaped the world order during the Cold War period have disappeared completely in Europe, thus leaving the Korean Peninsula as the last relict of the world of the Cold War.

Recently, international efforts and, in particular, coordinated efforts among South Korea, the United States, and Japan have been made to prevent North Korea's venture to develop nuclear weapons. The success in halting North Korea's nuclear program is, of course, a kind of arms control approach, albeit not exactly of the traditional kind. Concerned countries were able to resolve the North Korean nuclear issue by linking political, economic, and security issues to the nuclear issue.

However, despite an initial success in resolving the North Korea's nuclear issue, the situation between the two Koreas remains tense. In particular, the North Korean defence policy and strategy remains unchanged, as demonstrated by the recent submarine incursion into South Korean territorial waters in September 1996. The Korean peninsula remains the most heavily armed region in the world and exhibits no sign of tension reduction. The two Korean governments are not pursuing arms control policy in a systematic and consistent manner, but rather continue adding advanced and lethal weapons to their arsenals.

However, because changes in the security environment in the post-Cold War era compelled the two Koreas to seek a certain modification of their respective security policies, some efforts were made in the late 1980s and early 1990s between the two Koreas with a view to moving away from the forty year-old military confrontation toward peaceful coexistence. South Korea pursued its so-called 'Nordpolitik' in order to create conditions favourable to the peaceful coexistence with Pyongyang, inter alia by establishing friendly diplomatic ties with North Korea's traditional allies, the former Soviet Union and China. However, North Korea pursued its nuclear ambitions at an accelerated pace as a hedge against a future situation of strategic isolation. It thus sought to undercut South Korea's success in Nordpolitik on the one hand, while, on the other hand, seeking inter-Korean dialogue, motivated by a fear of a collapse similar to that of Communism in Europe.

Those efforts produced two major agreements at the end of 1991: an Agreements on Reconciliation, Non-Aggression, and Exchanges and Cooperation between the South and the North and a Joint Declaration of the Denuclearization of the Korean Peninsula. In the subsequent inter-Korean talks on nuclear inspection agreements, however, neither sides got what it wanted. The stalemate in the nuclear talks blocked the inter-Korean talks in their totality, and the two sides went on their separate ways. South Korea resumed the Team Spirit military exercises, and North Korea announced its intention to withdraw from the NPT (Non-Proliferation Treaty) in 1993.

As a consequence, talks between the United States and North Korea replaced the inter-Korean dialogue, producing the Geneva Agreed Framework between the United States and North Korea in October 1994. During the nuclear impasse, however, it became clear, once again, how fragile peace was on the peninsula and how high the possibility of war was. North Korea threatened to go to war if sanctions against Pyongyang were to be imposed. The United States dispatched the Aircraft Carrier to the Eastern Sea in a show of force directed against Pyongyang.

As of today, approximately the same number of forces are deployed on both sides of the Korean Demilitarized Zones (DMZ) as were deployed along the inter-German border during the Cold War, even though the front line is merely one third of that in Central Europe. Pyongyang's military goals and doctrines remain unchanged in spite of its dismal economic predicament. This situation is further exacerbated by the fact that no countries in the North-East Asian region have any explicitly declared constraints on their conventional arms build-up, even though the magnitude of arms build-up has diminished somewhat compared with the Cold War period.

This all shows that it is necessary for the two Koreas, and particularly for North Korea, to change their security concept and philosophy—preferably by learning from the European experience with resolving the security dilemma. With this proposition in mind, the present paper will take a closer look at the new security concepts which were developed in Europe and the United States in the 1980s and 1990s, with a view to illuminating the security problems on the Korean peninsula. This is followed by a comparison and examination of the arms control policies and proposals put forward by the two Koreas and, finally, by proposals for how to constructively resolve the recent security problems on the peninsula.

NEW PHILOSOPHICAL FOUNDATION FOR KOREAN ARMS CONTROL

During the Cold War, the prevailing security concepts were based on notions of absolute security implying that one side's security was to be achieved at the expense of the respective other's security. Deterrence and arms racing characterized mainstream security policies throughout this period, and the arms race became so all-pervasive that no nations were able to stand aloof from it, yet without net gains in security.

Only belatedly did nations arrive at an understanding of the 'security dilemma' phenomenon,[1] on the basis of which security experts proposed alternatives to absolute security that would contribute to a world of peaceful coexistence, including concepts of mutual security, common security, and cooperative security.[2]

MUTUAL SECURITY

In the modern age, security cannot be obtained unilaterally, and the security of one nation cannot be bought at the expense of others. The danger of nuclear war alone assures the validity of this proposition.[3] According to this school of thought, the world is confronted with common dangers, hence must also promote security in common. Mutual security policies thus aim at improving the security of both sides under conditions of some mutual insecurity—a precept that is valid not only for two nations, but also for two alliances or two militant organizations threatening each other.

Mutual security proponents recommend efforts to make the interaction among nations as full of positive-sum games as possible. Under such conditions, where the actors involved see opportunities for positive-sum interactions, substantial improvement in inter-state relations are actually feasible. Thus, one party should create conditions under which the other party becomes aware of the possibility of long-term gains to be derived for engagement. Furthermore, each side should endeavour to demonstrate that its chief goal is nothing but security, because the other side is often liable to misperceive this objective as victory rather than security.[4] The concept of 'the shadow of the future' is very relevant in this connection, implying that it is important for two opposing nations to resist the temptation to seek short-term gains from cheating and defecting and rather cultivate cooperative behaviour to obtain long-term gains.[5]

COMMON SECURITY

Nations seeking to enhance their own security by means of increased threats against others inevitably find themselves facing a security dilemma, as they achieve a loss of security as a paradoxical result of their quest for security.[6] The more defence measures one nation adopts in order to increase its sense of security, the more insecure the other feels. As a consequence thereof, the latter nation responds with further defence measures that render the former nation less secure, etc. The national security of both sides is thus reduced.

Common security advocates the view that international peace must rest on a commitment by each nation to joint survival rather than on threats of mutual destruction. The security of the world becomes increasingly interdependent as interdependence grows among nations in the political, diplomatic and economic domains. Hence, one nation's pursuit of its national security may endanger global security in a world devoid of authority that might control the pursuit of security by individual nations by adopting a global perspective.

As a means to resolve the security dilemma, this school of thought advocates disarmament. Their goal is to prevent nuclear war, hence they urge a cut-down of nuclear arsenals. As a means to alleviate the security dilemma, nations are to be made aware of the irrationality in their arms competition. As a means towards disarmament, nations are urged to adopt a non-offensive defence posture.

Non-offensive defence (NOD) implies that nations change their military postures structurally, including the size, weapons, training, doctrine, logistics, and operational manuals, so as to remain capable of a credible defence, yet become incapable of offence. NOD is a strategy, materialized in a posture, intended to maximize defensive while minimizing offensive capabilities.[7] The NOD approach is the key to tackling otherwise intractable arms race problems, as it targets military capabilities rather than intentions that are, by their very nature, subject to quick changes.

A good example of a unilateral NOD-type measure is South Korea's unilateral abandonment of nuclear enrichment and plutonium reprocessing in November 1991. The United States, likewise, unilaterally announced a withdrawal of all tactical nuclear weapons from South Korea. Those two initiatives exerted pressure on North Korea to respond positively to the request for IAEA's inspections. However, the limitations of unilateral measures in relations with nations such as North Korea became apparent, as the latter came to take such unilateral measures for granted and calling for no reciprocation.

COOPERATIVE SECURITY

The concept of cooperative security implies that nations seek to achieve national security by pursuing only such objectives as are compatible with the security of other nations and that they seek collaborative rather than confrontational military relations.[8] Cooperative security is thus very similar to common security in that nations should recognize the security concerns of other nations, respect each other's security interests as legitimate, and pursue peaceful coexistence. The main difference between the two concepts is that cooperative security places greater emphasis on institutionalized consent and agreed-upon measures for war prevention as well as means to prevent successful aggression so as to ensure security of nations.

Cooperative security has come to the fore in the post-Cold War period. The end of the Cold War and the demise of the former Soviet Union automatically changed traditional security concepts and removed the foundations for previous strategies. Furthermore, the Gulf War showed the world how multinational forces could be effectively mobilized and equipped with the most advanced defence technology to defeat an aggressor's forces—thereby providing cooperative security advocates with insights into effective means of dealing with future aggressors. Moreover, the demonstration that aggression by force is self-destructive and entails enormous costs will also motivate nations to prefer cooperative security.

The main issues facing defence planners under the new circumstances are neither large-scale land attacks nor nuclear war. Deterrence, nuclear stability and containment are no longer the organizing principles of international security. Instead, the main issues have become security based on cooperation and conflict prevention.

Cooperative security cannot be accomplished by means of physical threats, but require that nations show mutual restraints, provide reassurances against a resort to force, and enhance transparency with regard to defence policies and military postures, arms transfers, etc. On the other hand, cooperative security is entirely compatible with those existing arrangements and regimes that have contributed to war prevention, prohibited the proliferation of nuclear, chemical, and biological weapons and long-range missiles, and which have promoted arms control in general. Mutual restraint should be observable and verifiable, and the reassurances that are sought through amendments of military postures, doctrines, weapons production, arms sales and acquisitions presuppose transparency.

COMPREHENSIVE SECURITY

In Asia, the ASEAN member states have vigorously pursued a multilateral security dialogue with a view to facilitating cooperation among the Asia-Pacific states in both the economic and security field—which Andrew Mack has aptly termed a policy of comprehensive security.[9] This is best understood as a commitment by states to resolve interstate problems by peaceful means, to pursue economic cooperation and regional dialogue, also as contributions to enhanced military security. In contrast to Europe, the ASEAN states have thus taken an indirect approach to their security, also as a reflection of the fact that interstate military problems were difficult to raise from the beginning.

The ASEAN Regional Forum(ARF), which started in 1994, numbers 23 member states; and even North Korea submitted its application for ARF membership in 1997. Thanks to the efforts of ARF, China in 1995 for the first time ever in history published a defence white paper; and similar transparency-enhancing measures have been taken by most other Asian states. In South-East Asia, a Nuclear Weapon-Free Zone was established and ratified in May 1997; and through the Conference on Security Cooperation in Asia and the Pacific (CSCAP), the Asian countries are pursuing Track I and Track II dialogues on confidence-building measures and regional security. In South-East Asia, countries have already adopted the concept of comprehensive security and taken steps to modify member states' security policies and doctrines accordingly.

THE REALITY OF THE KOREAN MILITARY CONFRONTATION

As pointed out earlier, the two Koreas are still living with the legacy of the Cold War. Each Korea feels threatened by the other and thus seeks to enhance its national security by means of additional defence measures. The two sides, however, end up with exacerbated insecurity because of the security dilemma phenomenon. However, as a preliminary to examining policies that might resolve the security dilemma on the peninsula, we need to address the two big questions: what are main military threats that the two Koreas perceive? and is any inter-Korean security regime in place that might resolve the security dilemma?

SOUTH KOREA'S THREAT PERCEPTIONS

There are four main factors that affect South Korea's threat perceptions:

- the fact that North Korea launched the Korean war and is prepared to do the same again;
- the fact that North Korea has maintained its offensive strategy envisaging a surprise attack with the objective of a communization of the entire peninsula;
- the military advantage maintained by North Korea;
- the North Korean quest for long-range missiles combined with a clandestine nuclear weapons program.

The Korean War

The memory of the devastating losses incurred in the course of the Korean war and the prospects that Pyongyang might launch another war is one of the most important security concerns of the South Koreans. South Korea was shattered by the North Korean surprise attack in 1950 as they lacked a prepared defence and had inadequate combat capabilities. Without US and UN intervention, the ROK would not have been in existence today. Considering that the losses from another war could be more than twice those of the Korean war, its prevention is the most important security issue for all Koreans.[10]

The Korean war cemented the division of the peninsula into two irreconcilable halves, each holding strong enemy images of the other. As the split within the domestic political spectrum was followed by massive purges of the opposition, repression came to prevail in both parts of Korea, in turn producing a strong bureaucratic inertia and deepening the political and military confrontation. As a result of the war, for instance, the South transferred its right of operational control to the Commander of the UNC that was later given to the US Commander of the Combined Forces Command (CFC), which made a restoration of Seoul's operational control of the South Korean forces difficult.

North Korea's policy of communization of the entire peninsula has been maintained for the past four decades, even though its prospects of prevailing have become increasingly doubtful. The suspicions and misperceptions are so strong that South Korea is reluctant to rely on negotiations with the North as a means of strengthening its security. Bureaucratic and political rigidity continue to stand in the way of the launching of policies that might improve South-North relations. The predominant sentiment is that there can be no compromise with Communists and that superiority is the only safeguard. These patterns of thought rationalize the reliance on the United States for national security and blocks the way for any strategy of self-reliance.

North Korea's Military Doctrine and Strategy

North Korea's military threat to the South derives not only from the asymmetries with regard to capabilities, but also from the manner in which the forces would be used. In the Korean war, the North relied on a doctrine of surprise attack, which was reinforced by the Chinese victories in their first and second campaigns in October and December 1950.[11] The basis of this doctrine is traditional Communist strategy which was reinforced by the experience with guerrilla warfare against the Japanese invasion forces. It has subsequently been refined by drawing on the lessons from the Korean war. The late Kim Il-sung thus promulgated his Four-Point Military Guidelines in 1962, which envisioned arming the entire population, transforming the whole country into an impregnable fortress, converting the whole army into an army of cadres, and modernizing the military establishment. As a result, present-day North Korea is seen as the most dangerous garrison state in the world.

North Korean strategy has also placed greater emphasis on breakthrough and manoeuvre warfare which was to be implemented by a massing of numerically superior ground forces at selected points. This variety of manoeuvre warfare strategy was adopted from Soviet military strategy. Applied to Korea, it envisages breakthroughs and manoeuvres intended to defeat the South Korean forces by first fracturing their defence lines at selected places, and then advancing rapidly into the rear areas where encircling operations are to be undertaken. The defence lines are thus to be broken by means of massed, highly concentrated assaults against known weak points, undertaken by successive waves of attacking forces arrayed in echeloned formations.

North Korea continues to place great emphasis on such manoeuvre warfare which is viewed as preferable to attritional warfare in which the North's inferiority with regard to economic and technological capabilities would be decisive. Defence experts thus reckon with the possibility that North Korea may occupy Seoul within thirty days of battle following Pyongyang launching its breakthrough campaign.[12] These central features of the North Korean military doctrine are reflected in their organizational structure that features an Army Command, Air Force Command, Navy Command, Mechanized Command, Artillery Command, Missile Command, and a Special 8th Corps—all of which are organized for a war combining regular with guerrilla forces as well as manoeuvre with massive firepower.

Military Imbalance

North Korea has been continuously increasing its military manpower, surpassing that of South Korea in 1978 and exceeding 1.1 million in the 1990s, whereas the size of South Korea's armed forces has remained constant at some 600,000 since the 1960s. There are two main reasons for this rapid increase of North Korean military personnel. First of all, North Korea is seeking to compensate with military manpower for its inferiority with regard to other defence resources, as shall be demonstrated later with a comparison of military expenditures. Secondly, the strategic environment is becoming increasingly unfavourable to Pyongyang, both with regard to domestic and external security.

The other main threat is the North's superiority with regard to offensive weapons. As of 1997, its numerical superiority in the main categories of offensive weapons was 1.9:1 for tanks, 2.3:1 for artillery pieces, 1.2:1 for armoured personnel carriers, 2.4:1 for warships and 1.6:1 for tactical aircraft.[13] North Korea has thus clearly been continuously augmenting its offensive capabilities, its simultaneous peace offensive notwithstanding. Furthermore, North Korea has deployed 65-70 percent of its forces forward, which represents a serious threat to the South, especially because it is related to Pyongyang's strategy of breakthrough warfare.

North Korea's Nuclear Weapons Program and Long-range Missiles

After the United States withdrew its nuclear weapons from South Korea, North Korea's nuclear weapons development program came to represent a major threat. Despite the Geneva Accord, Seoul remains suspicious about Pyongyang's nuclear ambitions, because of Pyongyang's track record of unreliable behaviour.

Besides the nuclear weapons program, the North's continuing development of long-range missiles, biological and chemical weapons also pose serious threats to South Korean and regional security. The threat will grow further when North Korea succeeds in developing the *Taepodong-I* and *II* missiles with ranges of 1500-5000 kms. In view of this, Seoul's long-term goal will definitely be to acquire long-range missiles and air defence missiles.[14]

NORTH KOREA'S THREAT PERCEPTIONS

To the extent that North Korea feels 'threatened' there are three main reasons for such perceptions:

- North Korea may collapse and subsequently be absorbed by South Korea as happened to East Germany;
- the US-ROK alliance may be too strong and the combined strength of the two states may inflict devastating damage on North Korea;
- South Korea has stronger economic capabilities and may thus, in the long-run, build combat capabilities superior to those of the North.

Possibility of Collapse

North Korea responded nervously to the international pressure exerted against it over the nuclear issue with claims that the United States intended to strangle its socialist system. The North Korean representatives repeatedly told their interlocutors from South Korean in the inter-Korean dialogue that there could be no true dialogue without the South's abandonment of its secret desire to absorb the North. North Korea's desperate present economic situation has resulted both from failed economic policies over the past five years and a substantial reduction or suspension of economic aid from Russia and China. The political insecurity following Kim Il-sung's death and Pyongyang's growing diplomatic isolation present further elements of uncertainty for the already moribund regime.

Continuing the US-ROK Alliance

The presence of US troops in Korea is a main source of North Korea's threat perception. Pyongyang has consistently criticized the United States for blocking North Korea's revolutionary efforts and, according to their propaganda, peace on the peninsula is only possible after an American force withdrawal from the South.

North Korea has condemned the 'Team Spirit' and similar joint military exercises as evidence of a US strategy of invading North Korea.[15] They have been particularly critical of the massive scale of these exercises and their inherent nuclear elements, and they claim that the US air-land battle doctrine has further added to the threat because of its offensive nature. North Korea has habitually used 'Team Spirit' as a pretext for postponing or boycotting the on-going inter-Korean contacts.

In 1992, for the first time in history, the exercises were therefore cancelled in return for a North Korean acceptance of IAEA nuclear inspections of their nuclear sites. In 1993, the inter-Korean dialogue was suspended and the 'Team Spirit' exercises resumed, when North Korea announced its intention to withdraw from the NPT. From 1994 onwards, however, the exercises were cancelled in order to support North Korea's implementation of the Geneva Agreed Framework. In short, the 'Team Spirit' exercises have been traded and used as incentives to induce North Korea to abandon its nuclear program. As a result, one of the biggest alleged threats to the North has been removed.

South Korea's Economic Superiority

Both economic and long-term military trends are highly unfavourable to the North. As of 1997, the South Korean economy is over twenty times larger than that of North Korea in terms of GNP,[16] and the gap in economic capabilities is expected to widen throughout the 1990s, judging from a comparison of estimated growth. While the North outspent the South with regard to defence until 1975-1976, it has since then been surpassed by the South by a wide margin. This military spending gap reflects the general gap with regard to economic and technological capabilities, which is expected to grow, both in absolute and relative terms.

Up to 1975-76, the reason why North Korea outspent the South was that its economy was superior, because it had maintained most of the industrial bases in the Northern parts and had been quite successful with its early economic development, thereby providing enough resources for the defence sector.

Since then, however, South Korea's remarkable economic growth throughout the 1970s to 1990s has enabled Seoul to surpass Pyongyang in aggregate defence spending. South Korean defence spending in 1996 thus amounted to $15 billion, i.e. more than twice that of North Korea. The gap is expected to reach a ratio of 2.5:1 in the year 2000, and South Korea's cumulative real investments in defence were already estimated to surpass those of North Korea in the mid-1990s.[17]

These long-term trends for economic capabilities and defence resources will clearly add to the threat perceptions of the North Korean government. Furthermore, the improved relations between both China and Russia with South Korea is seen as exacerbating the security of North Korea, inter alia by hampering the provision of offensive weapons.[18] When North Korea has difficulties with access to advanced weaponry, its inferiority to South Korea with regard to military technology is bound to grow.

In a nutshell, Seoul's far superior socioeconomic capabilities are likely to put increasing pressure on Pyongyang. Moreover, there is an imminent danger that the real picture of the South's domestic capabilities may become disclosed to the North's population, once South-North exchanges start, which places Pyongyang under dual pressure: partly stemming from the direct threat from South Korea's ongoing military build-up, and partly from the danger of domestic instability produced by the North's defeat in the economic and technological competition with the South.

SECURITY REGIMES

As of today, there exists no inter-Korean security regime where the two Koreas can address their common security problems. As noted earlier, there have been efforts to establish an inter-Korean security regime through Prime Ministerial talks which were held in 1990-91. Although the two Koreas agreed to establish the South-North Joint Military Commission (JMC), no follow-on talks were held to discuss arms control measures between the two Koreas. The nuclear issue, finally, completely spoiled the prospects of an inter-Korean security dialogue.

The Military Armistice Commission (MAC) is thus the only authority on the peninsula tasked with monitoring the implementation of the Armistice Agreement which was signed by the United Nations Command, China and North Korea in 1953. However, the Armistice regime has recently been rendered obsolete, when China and North Korea withdrew their representatives in 1994, reflecting Pyongyang's attempts to establish a direct channel of communications with the United States. Pyongyang has totally disregarded the MAC, and in April 1996 even sent troops into the Panmunjom area in order to put pressure on the United States to establish direct military talks with North Korea.

Since a South Korean general replaced the US general as head of the MAC in 1991, North Korea has refused to open the MAC meeting. The armistice regime is thus outdated as today's military situation is quite different from that during the war. Both South and North Korea are in agreement with the United States that a new security regime should be established to manage the present security problems; but they hold different opinions on how to transform the armistice regime into the peace regime.

South Korea

The South Korean Government has no channels whatsoever to directly resolve military problems with North Korea. Until 1992, it was only through the US Chairman of the UNC that South Korea could raise questions of North Korea's violations of the Armistice. However, as South Korea plays a major role in defending the armistice, it needs a direct channel to North Korea that would also contribute to improving inter-Korean relations, including such security and stability measures as the two Koreas can agree on.

In 1991 the two Koreas agreed to endeavour to transform the present state of armistice into a solid state of peace, and pledged to abide by the Armistice Agreement of 1953 until such a state of peace had been realized. In May 1992, they agreed to establish a South-North Joint Military Commission to discuss such matters as non-aggression provisions and arms control measures, but to no avail, as the severe confrontation between the South and the North blocked any progress regarding inter-Korean military channels.

After North Korea's repeated refusals to hold direct military talks with the South, South Korea and the United States proposed four party talks to build a peace regime by extending invitations to join the talks to China and North Korea. After three preliminary rounds of such four party talks had been held in New York, the first-ever four party talks convened in Geneva, Switzerland, on 9 December 1997.

North Korea

North Korea has also proposed a change of the armistice regime. However, Pyongyang insists that the United States should be a signatory to a peace treaty, replacing the armistice agreement, because the United States is a legal partner to the latter. Recently, as a result of strong US opposition to any peace treaty with North Korea, Pyongyang has proposed various interim arrangements leading towards a peace treaty. However, even though North Korea is thus very eager to discuss a peace regime, it strongly disagrees with regard to the modalities of the peace regime.

During the 1970s, Pyongyang insisted that tripartite talks with South Korea and the United States would be the appropriate forum for any resolution of security issues. However, both the United States and South Korea opposed this framework, because of the apparent North Korean underlying intention to deny South Korean role as a legitimate negotiating partner. Now, Pyongyang has returned to its original position in favour of a peace treaty signed only with the United States. Nevertheless, North Korea did attend the preliminary meetings of the four-party talks, probably mainly with a view to food provisions from abroad.

The United States

The United States holds the view that the role of the MAC in developing and enforcing measures to reduce military tension along the DMZ should be maintained until the two Koreas reach agreement on its replacement.[19] This view is reflected in the statement of the US Department of Defence as well as in the Joint Communique of the US Secretary of Defence and the South Korean Minister of Defence to the effect that the armistice agreement and the UNC must be maintained essentially in their current form.[20] However, the United States recently expressed strong support for direct negotiations between the South and North Korean governments on a replacement for the armistice regime, just as it has come out in favour of four-party talks on the establishment of a peace regime on the peninsula.[21]

SUMMARY

As noted above, the threat perceptions fuelled by (and fuelling) the mutual arms race and the continuing Cold War-type confrontation still affect security policies, military strategies and postures on the Korean peninsula. The alignments that came into being during the Cold War period remain, even though North Korea's allies are amending their policies. Above all, no security regime exists, under the auspices of which all concerned parties might voice their concerns, except for the 1953 armistice agreement.

With respect to the need for a new peace regime, South Korea and the United States are in agreement, while North Korea strongly disagrees. Most recently, proposals for four party talks (the two Koreas, the United States, and China) had been put forward by South Korea and the United States, but it remains to be seen whether North Korea will participate in a constructive spirit.

ARMS CONTROL OBJECTIVES AND PROPOSALS IN THE PENINSULA

In the following, I shall compare and analyze the arms control objectives and specific proposals of the two Koreas.

SOUTH KOREA'S OBJECTIVES

South Korea's arms control objectives have not been articulated well. A variety of objectives drawn from the European experience with conventional arms control are often cited as applying to the Korean situation. This is, for instance, the case for measures to enhance confidence, reduce the potential for misunderstanding and miscalculation, prevent surprise attack, and facilitate the unification process.

The ultimate arms control objectives of South Korea are thus to enhance security and stability, maintain a peaceful coexistence, and promote unification. These ultimate arms control objectives of South Korea can be inferred from its government proposals. They are to be achieved through a foreign and security policy, the latter including a defence and arms control policy.[22]

To attain those ultimate goals, there are four key operational objectives that particularly pertain to arms control:

- build trust and confidence between the two Koreas;
- lessen misunderstanding and miscalculation;
- prevent surprise attack and large-scale attack possibilities;
- promote further arms reduction with a view to reducing the North Korean numerical superiority.[23]

The South Korean government regards building trust and confidence between the two Koreas as a preliminary step intended to promote further progress in arms control. Trust and confidence are to be built by means of increasing contacts and exchanges of information that will also pave the way for peaceful coexistence and unification, as suggested both by the South Korean Government and by 'functionalists'. However, Pyongyang views this as a South Korean strategy of planting capitalist elements within the North Korean society in the hope of promoting a North Korean collapse under the external influences.[24]

With regard to the second operational objective, misunderstanding and miscalculation are used interchangeably here to denote a cycle of military action and reaction that produces unintended escalation. This is a purposefully narrow interpretation which focuses on situations where benign intent is liable to be misinterpreted and lead to overreaction. The objective is sometimes referred to as reducing the likelihood of a false positive warning of war, where 'positive' denotes offensive intent.[25]

This aspect will become very critical if North Korea should experience political turmoil during the transition period after Kim Il-sung's death. For South Korea, it will be important to avoid a North Korean overreaction to its own responses to such turmoil. Aside from political turmoil, it is important to prevent North Korea's miscalculation to the effect that it could win a war under certain circumstances, for instance based on the misunderstanding that the ROK-US bonds are weakened.

The third operational objective, to prevent a surprise and large-scale attack is rather self-explanatory, considering that the main threat to the South is North Korea's ability to launch a massive surprise attack with its forward-based forces. Coupled with the experience of the Korean War, the DPRK's offensive military doctrine and posture add to this threat perception. North Korea is capable of launching a surprise attack from a standing start, off the march, after mobilization, and even during the apparent de-escalation of a crisis. This objective is often referred to as that of reducing the likelihood of a false negative warning, where 'negative' signifies the belief that nothing hostile is afoot.

In the Korean case, the consequences of false negative warning are more serious than those of a false positive warning, and the possibility of use of force for political intimidation is less relevant here than it was in Europe.[26] The prevention of a North Korean surprise and all-out attack are therefore the most important arms control objectives of the South Korean Government.

The fourth operational objective of reducing North Korea's military superiority through further arms reduction is seen as the last step that will only become relevant after significant progress in the three former objectives. The reason is that its position of numerical inferiority does not leave South Korea with many arms reduction options. Hence, the ROK insists that the DPRK should first reduce its forces to the level of South Korea. However, if there should be solid evidence of a build-down by the North, South Korea could offer certain arms reduction, yet only such as would take into due consideration that the massive size of the armed forces on both sides entail persistent risks of conflict.

NORTH KOREA'S OBJECTIVES

The arms control objectives of North Korea are difficult to identify. However, the DPRK Government Daily (*Nodongshinmun*) and other public statements provide some insights into Pyongyang's official positions on arms control. Official South Korean statements criticizing North Korean policy positions provide some additional information.

The ultimate objectives underlying the DPRK's arms control policies thus seem to be to achieve unification on its own terms and to preserve North Korean regime survival. In the post-Cold War period, it seems that North Korea assigns the highest priority to the survival of their own system, because unification on Pyongyang's terms is severely hampered by their economic and political difficulties. The operational objectives derived from this seem to be to

- remove US influence from the Korean political and military realms;[27]
- accelerate US troop withdrawal and reduction of forces while undermining the South Korean security;
- to weaken or limit a US nuclear deterrence; and to
- maintain a military advantage over the South.

The elimination of the US influence on Korean political and military affairs is presumed to bring about changes in the status quo in North Korea's favour. Pyongyang's approach to confidence-building differs from that of South Korea in its assigning of first priority to arms reduction including a US troop withdrawal from the peninsula, regarding the main threat to be the US deterrence and defence strategy. Pyongyang would therefore regard a removal of the foreign military presence from the South as the most credible indication that the ROK intended to ease tensions and build confidence between the two Koreas.[28]

An accelerated US troop withdrawal is also sought as a means to undermine South Korean security. The DPRK claims to be threatened by the US-South Korean joint military exercises, the US nuclear capabilities, and the US-ROK security alliance itself. These surely represent a major obstacle to North Korea's quest for bringing the entire Peninsula under its control. Hence, the issue of a withdrawal of US troops has been raised continuously since the day of truce negotiations, but the underlying rationale has changed with the changing security environment.

Today, the North Korean propaganda seeks to exploit the global trend in favour of arms control to further its own political goals by contrasting South Korea's dependence on foreign troops with its own policy of self-reliance. North Korea thus seeks to create uncertainties that might grow in the case of a US pull-out, expecting these uncertainties to work in its favour. As a minimum, it attempts to promote anti-Americanism in the South as a means of destabilization. On the other hand, it is to be expected that North Korea will change this position when it realizes that it has no alternative to accepting the status quo.

The elimination of the US nuclear 'umbrella' is a central goal for the DPRK, that has repeatedly alleged that the United States threatens nuclear war on the Korean peninsula. An official justification for their nuclear development has thus been that it was aimed at removing any US nuclear weapons from South Korea.[29] Throughout the nuclear talks, North Korea also argued in favour of a nuclear-free zone on the peninsula, yet ended up with achieving a non-nuclear peninsula as opposed to a nuclear weapons-free zone. By agreeing to the creation of non-nuclear Korean Peninsula, North Korea finally reached its goal of having US nuclear weapons withdrawn from South Korea, proceeding from there to work for a withdrawal from South Korea of the nuclear umbrella as such.

The objective of maintaining a military advantage over the South is a central element in its revolutionary strategy.[30] The North therefore seeks to prevent the South from achieving a decisive qualitative superiority on the basis of its economic and technological strength. Pyongyang has therefore proposed that the South should abandon its policy of building a technologically advanced indigenous weapons industry and of purchasing advanced weapons from abroad. North Korea thus wants to regulate South Korean defence spending as a way of curtailing its procurement of advanced weapons.

ARMS CONTROL PROPOSALS

Arms control proposals were put forward during the high-level talks between the two Koreas in 1991 and 1992. While Seoul proposed traditional confidence-building measures, Pyongyang's proposals included security-building measures as contained in the 1986 Stockholm Documents. North Korea thus wanted to prohibit such military exercises as the 'Team Spirit' and other joint US-South Korean exercises, i.e. all exercises involving foreign forces and military exercises of division size and larger, as well as a suspension of exercises in the proximity of the DMZ. Such constraining measures were obviously intended by Pyongyang to produce a complete suspension of large-scale joint exercises, thus putting strains on the US-ROK alliance and military cooperation as a whole.

Seoul, however, was more interested in CBMs similar to those agreed upon in 1975 in Helsinki: disclosure and exchange of military information, mutual visits and exchanges of military personnel, bans on division-size and larger military exercises, at least 45 days advance notification of and invitation of observers to smaller military exercises as well as prior notification of the movement and manoeuvres of brigade-size and larger military units.[31] The rationale for this preference was that, in South Korea's view, it is critical to build a modicum of confidence between the two Koreas, thus ameliorating the hostile relationship somewhat, before any constraint measures are put in place. South Korea has further proposed that North Korea transform its offensive military structure into a defensive one.

With regard to arms reduction measures, South Korea has underlined the importance of unilateral North Korean reductions that should produce parity in each category of weaponry. Pyongyang, on the other hand, has placed the main emphasis on a phased US troop withdrawal to proceed in parallel with arms reductions pertaining to the two Koreas aiming towards ceilings of 100,000 troops. Underlying such proposals, however, is, almost certainly, a North Korean attempt at maintaining their numerical advantage with regard to weapons and equipment.

There is thus a huge gap separating the arms control proposals of the two sides, reflecting their diverging security interests. Whereas the North seeks to accelerate the US withdrawal from the South by means of arms control, the South wants, as a first step, to enhance trust and confidence between the two Koreas. The prospects for arms control are thus far from promising.

RESOLVING SECURITY PROBLEMS OF THE PENINSULA

As argued above, inter-Korean relations represent a text-book case of the security dilemma. It is manifested in five major security agendas that have to be addressed: the prevention of war; the prevention of North Korea's acquisition of nuclear weapons; policies addressing North Korea's fear of collapse; conventional arms control; and multilateral arms control and security cooperation. In the following, a set of policy measures relating to each security agenda will be considered, based on an application of the new concepts of security that were elaborated above.

PREVENTION OF WAR

There remains a significant danger that the density of forces along the DMZ may produce either an inadvertent or a premeditated war between the two Koreas.

During the nuclear crisis in mid-1994, a war might thus have erupted, if only because North Korea used the threat of war against Seoul by claiming that it would retaliate with war against any imposition of sanctions. In part, these threats were used as a means to squeeze more concessions out of the United States and South Korea. Because neither the United States nor South Korea took any punitive action against this threat of war, Pyongyang may feel free to resort to similar behaviour whenever its regime is on the defensive. The prevention of another war on the peninsula is thus not a trivial matter, but a very serious and urgent security problem.

Deterrence remains in effect on the peninsula, but nuclear deterrence may be losing its relevance with the US promise, according to the Geneva Accord, to provide assurances to Pyongyang against the threat or use of nuclear weapons. As a consequence, conventional deterrence is becoming more relevant, making it all the more worrisome that the conventional arms race on the peninsula seems to be 'heating up'.

While it was agreed in 1991 that the ROK and DPRK would neither use force against each other nor undertake armed aggression,[32] North Korea has done nothing to implement this non-aggression pact. Instead, it has repeatedly violated and abrogated the Armistice Agreements, which, in itself, poses serious problems for the maintenance of peace and stability in the peninsula. Even more disturbing is the fact that North Korea has resorted to threat of war in violation of the non-aggression treaty, as mentioned above. Furthermore, the North Korean submarine intrusion into South Korean waters on 18 September 1997 constituted a clear-cut violation of both this treaty and the Basic Agreements signed by the two Koreas in 1992, not to mention the United Nations Charter. Hence, agreements about abstentions from the use of force need to be accompanied by measures to guarantee their implementation. The most effective such measure will be a North Korean commitment to withdraw excess forces from the forward area and to replace its offensive doctrine and posture with defensive ones, a point to which I shall return below.

The North Korean leaders might be induced to change their minds, if they could come to view their interaction with other nations in a long-term perspective. In that case they might find it to be in their long-term interest to cooperate with others rather than 'defecting' by arms racing or threatening to use force for the sake of short-term gains.

As far as unilateral measures are concerned, South Korea has already foregone its nuclear option and maintained a defensive doctrine with regard to its alliance with the United States. Hence, Seoul's scope for unilateral measures in the conventional field has been exhausted, and it is up to North Korea to admit its policy failures and amend its military policy first. In the course of doing so, however, North Korea may well feel a need for arms control underpinnings. South Korea could thus help by creating conditions under which North Korea would accept tension-reduction measures and actual arms reductions. In this connection, four party talks are timely and useful as they may generate 'positive sum games' in which the North may hope for gains from a linkage of arms reduction with economic benefits.

PREVENTION OF NORTH KOREAN NUCLEAR AND BIO-CHEMICAL PROLIFERATION

Even though it took more than two years to bring the North Korean nuclear programme to a halt, major breakthroughs were achieved with two agreements: the Denuclearization Agreement between the South and the North and the Geneva Accord between the United States and North Korea.

The background for the successful signing of the Denuclearization Agreements in 1991 was the following: first of all, the end of the Cold War and the resultant cooperation among the four powers on the Korean Peninsula served as a catalyst for bilateral nuclear negotiations. Secondly, there was a strong international pressure on the United States to unilaterally withdraw its nuclear weapons from South Korea. Thirdly, the new powers apparently enjoyed by the UN Security Council (illustrated by Resolution 687 on Iraq) may have persuaded North Korea that it had to accept certain external demands. Former US Secretary of State, James Baker, summarized these factors by arguing that the US victory in the Gulf War and its subsequent initiative to withdraw all tactical nuclear weapons from abroad had removed whatever rationale North Korea's may have had for nuclear weapons.[33]

However, South Korea and the United States failed to influence North Korea to work out any bilateral nuclear inspection agreements for three main reasons. First of all, the rigidity of the North Korean bureaucracy and the significant 'sunk costs' related to the programme precluded full disclosure without compensatory measures from the external world. Secondly, North Korea's intended linkage between conventional arms control and the nuclear issue hampered progress with regard to the latter, because Pyongyang was seeking an effective dissolution of the US-South Korean alliance via a suspension of the 'Team Spirit' military exercises and an accelerated US withdrawal of forces from South Korea.[34] Thirdly, neither South Korea's strong emphasis on the need for special inspections nor the resumption of 'Team Spirit' were conducive to the progress of negotiations.

In recognition of the failure to achieve an implementation of the Denuclearization Agreements, and of North Korea's announced intention to withdraw from the NPT regime, negotiations were held between the DPRK and the United States to resolve the nuclear impasse. These negotiations produced the Geneva Accord thanks to the following: first of all, Washington accepted Pyongyang's proposals to resolve the nuclear issue within a broader framework, under which the two sides would improve political and economic relations, while North Korea would freeze its nuclear program. Secondly, Washington provided a security guarantee to the North Korean regime with its assurance against threat or use of force, including nuclear weapons, and it subsequently cancelled the 1994 and 1995 'Team Spirit' exercises. Thirdly, North Korea agreed to suspend all nuclear activities and to replace its entire nuclear program with less nuclear weapon-prone light-water reactors, while the US promised to provide energy substitutes, including crude oil. Fourthly, the United States showed flexibility concerning the timing and modalities of the special inspections requested by the IAEA in February 1993.

Two valuable lessons can be drawn from these recent US and South Korean experiences with dealing with North Korea's nuclear matter, which are perfectly applicable to conventional arms control: arms control has to be pursued in such a way as to enhance the security of both Koreas at the same time; and it should be designed to induce North Korea to see long-term political, economic and security gains from a comprehensive solution.

PRUDENT POLICY TO DEAL WITH NORTH KOREA'S FEAR OF COLLAPSE

Following Kim Il-sung's death, North Korea has taken a vigilant stand against the risk of an impending 'collapse of Communism'. The high level of military mobilization is partly motivated by the risks of political and social turmoil, as was apparent from Kim Jong-il's New Year Address of 1995.

There are good reasons for such vigilance: North Korea's economy is in shambles; trade is experiencing severe problems because of a shortage of hard currency; the recorded grain harvests are steadily deteriorating every year; Pyongyang is unable to provide its people with even two meals a day; the food shortage has reached unprecedented proportions; social stability is in jeopardy; and the energy problem is serious. Oil supplies from Russia have long been suspended and Chinese supplies are at an all-time low, hence North Korea has no alternative to begging the United States for oil supplies.

A policy for revitalizing the economy and establishing good relations with the United States could be identified in the above New Year Address, which placed the emphasis on four points: improving relations with the United States according to the Geneva Accord; reducing threats to North Korean security via a peace treaty with the United States that would, in turn, resolve the military confrontation between the two Koreas; undermining the US alliance with South Korea; and taking advantage of the year of 1995, i.e. the fiftieth anniversary of Korean liberation, to seek contacts with South Korean civic organizations, with a view to arousing anti-government sentiments in the people.

North Korea's intentions are thus obviously to circumvent the South Korean government. While seeking benefits such as crude oil, light-water reactors, US liaison offices and Japanese reparations, intended to contribute to a revitalization of its economy, Pyongyang has been trying to isolate South Korea in the process. Moreover, it has endeavoured to establish direct military channels with the United States (as shown in the 'helicopter case' of December 1994), and it has worked hard to attain a peace treaty.

Pyongyang is thus trying to create divisions between the United States and South Korea, knowing well that South Korea is neither fully satisfied with the provisions of the Geneva Accord nor with the US style of negotiations. By claiming the Geneva Accord to be a political victory for Pyongyang's independent diplomacy, they are contrasting it with the alleged failure of South Korea's 'US-dependent' diplomacy, hoping that such propaganda will fuel anti-American sentiments in Seoul. By splitting the South Korean government from its people, they hope to gain time for their own economic development, at the same time as South Korea will be struggling with political and social instability caused by the North. As long as North Korea remains opposed to inter-Korean talks, this will continue to pose potential problems for South Korea's relationship with the United States.

Dealing with a North Korea fearing impending collapse requires a prudent balancing act. If they judge there is no hope of revitalizing economy, it is conceivable that North Korea may opt for war as a suicidal attack, regardless of how small their chances of victory may be. In consideration of this risk of war, the ROK cannot give North Korea whatever they request for free, as they might spend the money and resources gained on strengthening their war-fighting capabilities. On the other hand, prudence militates against any repetition of the Cold War-type confrontation such as an increase in offensive capabilities that might provoke the North Korean leadership.

While it is thus not the time for the ROK to take unilateral measures to alleviate North Korea's concerns about collapse, it is time to engage North Korea on the basis of conditionality. If North Korea responds constructively to South Korean requests, the ROK should provide economic and massive food assistance and promote economic cooperation and generally improved relations with Pyongyang, which takes us to the next point.

CONVENTIONAL ARMS CONTROL

As argued above, the Korean peninsula is not only militarily unstable, but also is engaged in an arms race. In the absence of a resolution of the conventional arms race problem, it is less meaningful from South Korean perspective to resolve the nuclear issue. The arms race drains resources from the economic sector, thereby adversely affecting the economy of both Koreas, even though the consequences are more serious to the North Korean economy. It is therefore necessary to address the conventional asymmetries on the peninsula as well as the problems presented by North Korea's offensive posture and doctrine.

In the course of the Geneva talks between the United States and the DPRK, US ambassador Gallucci argued that North Korea's excess forces deployed along the DMZ undermined peace and stability on the peninsula. As he testified to the US Congress, the US Government intended to pursue the matters of North Korea's ballistic missile activities and its threatening conventional force deployments in subsequent talks on a diplomatic normalization.[35] The United States thus held the first-ever missile talks with North Korea on 21 April 1996, yet without producing any tangible results. Conventional arms control issues may be raised naturally in the four-party peace talks if North Korea agrees to this; if not, the conventional arms control issues will not be resolved anywhere. A more comprehensive approach may thus be called for, which will allow for a combination of the issues of conventional arms control and economic matters in the same set of negotiations.

The ROK only has little scope for conventional arms control, as it is outnumbered by the DPRK, especially as far as the forward areas are concerned, let alone those of missiles and bio-chemical weapons. In fact, South Korea and the United States made a significant concession by suspending 'Team Spirit' exercises to help resolve the nuclear issue. If the Geneva Accord is implemented satisfactorily, it will be difficult to resume the exercises, which will leave Seoul largely without any scope for other concessions in any future conventional arms control negotiations. Considering that South Korea is conventionally inferior to the North, and the fact that its military doctrine and posture are intrinsically defensive, it becomes obvious North Korea has to take action to reduce its offensive capabilities, change its posture, and pull back its forward-deployed forces before any further progress can be made.

However, no matter how desirable unilateral measures would be on the part of North Korea, they are hardly feasible. Hence, the need for linking the demand for arms control to other issue areas, where North Korea might gain, will add to their negotiability, as well illustrated in the Geneva Accord. Applying this model to conventional arms control, implies an eight-year plan. Until North Korea accepts special inspections (say, in 1999-2000), the ROK should not consider reduction measures unless North Korea is willing to reduce forces in excess of those of South Korea.

Prior to that, the establishment of a depletion or non-deployment zone along the DMZ would be a good first step, as would transparency-enhancing and other confidence-building measures, which might be pursued at the same time. Each side might thus reduce (i.e. pull out completely) forward-deployed forces, with North Korea reducing more than the South in recognition of the existing asymmetry of forces, thereby creating a depletion zone, whereas a non-deployment zone would be tantamount to an extension of the existing DMZ. If one party should enter the zone with forces exceeding one division, it would be regarded as a military attack against the other party, leaving the other party and its allies at liberty to respond immediately, also in the form of offensive action. Such an arrangement would contribute to war prevention and enhance stability on the peninsula. Once a depletion or non-deployment zone has been successfully established, it will become possible to proceed to a reduction of offensive weaponry to a level below what South Korea now possesses. In the process of such reductions, the possibilities should be discussed for a progressive withdrawal of American military units from the peninsula.[36]

While measures such as the above could only be implemented at some time in the future, it is important for the United States and South Korea to develop a strategy for their realization now in order to draw North Korea to the arms negotiation table.

MULTILATERAL ARMS CONTROL AND SECURITY COOPERATION

North-East Asia lacks a multilateral security cooperation regime under the auspices of which concerned nations are able to address security issues or take collective actions against any aggression or other breaches of regional peace and security. Because mutual animosities between states in the region remain, no cooperative approaches to dealing with regional or international conflicts has been taken seriously yet. Hence, the actual risks of regional conflicts remain high and the perceived risks even higher. The absence of fora for arms control and regional security problem is likely to allow the confrontational relationship among the countries in the region to further deteriorate. A closer look at the individual states uncovers several instances of conventional arms build-up.

China has long-standing ambitions of establishing a hegemony over Asia. When China achieves its economic goal of equality with the United States and Japan in absolute terms, it will possess a formidable military strength, if it continues to arm itself at today's pace. China's traditional strategy of using military superiority to advance its national interests over neighbouring countries will most likely persist, in which case any future military superiority will be converted into political influence and supremacy. In the short run, however, China is likely to continue down-sizing its military manpower while improving its naval and air forces both quantitatively and qualitatively.

Japan has already amended its defence strategy from a territorial to a regional defence, and independent strategic thinkers are frequently urging Japan to play a more independent role in determining its security policy. Judging by recent domestic debates over rearmament it is to be expected, at least in the long term, that Japan will increasingly seek defence capabilities commensurate with its economic power.

There is thus a need for building trust and confidence in North-East Asia by institutionalizing the on-going bilateral and multilateral security dialogue, either through regular and active participation in the ASEAN Regional Forum (ARF) or through the creation of a North-East Asian Security Forum, involving the two Koreas and the four powers, i.e. the United States, Russia, Japan, and China. Such an initiative could compensate for the non-participation by Japan and Russia in the four-party talks. The same issues that are discussed in the ARF might be discussed in the North-East Asia Security Forum. If such a forum were firmly in place, it could be of immense help in resolving the security problems on the Korean peninsula, but also in replicating the successful management of the North Korean nuclear problem by addressing other regional nuclear issues. It might, for instance, contribute to reducing China's nuclear arsenals and controlling Japan's stockpiling of plutonium. Such a forum would further help dealing constructively with the historical enmities among states in the region; and it would provide a framework for negotiating mutual restraints on defence build-up and for talks about changes in offensive military postures, doctrines, and weaponry.

CONCLUSION

In this paper, I have compared diverging views on arms control between the two Koreas as well as examined the relevance of arms control for the peninsula.

Considering that North Korea's propensity for war has not diminished, and that their offensive military strategy and posture, their conventional military superiority, and their recent nuclear ambitions and missile programme constitute serious threats to South Korea, the ROK is eager to talk directly with North Korea about these issues.

On the other hand, the North Korean regime fears an impending collapse under the strains of the severe famine and generally dire economic situation. Their main perceived threats concern the strong US-Korean alliance as well as the unfavourable long-term economic trends. However, North Korea prefers to resolve these problems with the United States alone, and tries to drive a wedge between the United States and South Korea, inter alia by working for a US withdrawal.

Those conflicting views allow the security dilemma to steadily deteriorate. Its resolution requires, first of all, that the two Koreas (but particularly North Korea) revise their security concepts, especially with regard to five important policy agendas: war prevention, the prevention of nuclear proliferation; policies for dealing with North Korea's fear of collapse, conventional arms control, and regional arms control and security cooperation. Appropriate revisions in these fields would significantly alleviate tension on the peninsula, thus promoting peaceful coexistence.

Just as the US approach to handling the North Korean nuclear issue was successful, a linkage of the DPRK's vulnerabilities to the ROK's strengths holds the promise of a negotiated settlement to build down military tensions on the peninsula. Arms control endeavours should be combined with non-military measures within a broader framework that would make Pyongyang aware of the prospects for long-term gains to be achieved from negotiations with South Korea and other countries such as the United States and China. A precondition for such gains would be for North Korea to abandon its policy of excluding South Korea in favour of a recognition of the ROK as a legitimate interlocutor.

Furthermore, Seoul needs a long-term and comprehensive plan for conventional arms control to proceed in parallel with the implementation of the Geneva Accord. The first step would be a depletion or non-deployment zone along the DMZ, to be followed by reduction measures as soon as North Korea has accepted special inspections of their nuclear sites. Finally, the establishment of a North-East Asian Security Forum is proposed that could address the security concerns of all six North-East Asian nations. Such a multilateral approach would also facilitate Pyongyang's gradual adjustment to the changed global situations and promote their understanding of the need for arms control negotiations and appropriate implementation measures.

NOTES

1. Jervis, Robert: 'Cooperation under the Security Dilemma', *World Politics*, vol. 30, no. 2 (January 1978), pp. 169-170.

2. Mutual security and common security were used synonymously, but mutual security refers exclusively to East-West security whereas common security refers to the security of all nations.
3. Smoke, Richard & Andrei Kortunov (eds.): *Mutual Security* (New York: St. Martin's Press, 1991), p. 61.
4. *Ibid.*, p. 72.
5. George, Alexander L., Philip J. Farley & Alexander Dallin (eds.): *U.S.-Soviet Security Cooperation: Achievements, Failures and Lessons* (New York: Oxford University Press, 1988), p. 9.
6. Møller, Bjørn: *Common Security and Nonoffensive Defense: A Neorealist Perspective* (Boulder: Lynne Rienner, 1992), p. 26.
7. Idem: 'Small States, Non-Offensive Defence and Collective Security', in Efraim Inbar & Gabriel Sheffer (eds.): *The National Security of Small States in a Changing World* (London: Frank Cass, 1997), p. 131.
8. Nolan, Janne E.: *Global Engagement: Cooperation and Security in the 21st Century* (Washington, D.C: The Brookings Institution, 1994), p. 5.
9. Mack, Andrew & Pauline Kerr: 'The Evolving Security Discourse in the Asia-Pacific', *The Washington Quarterly*, vol. 18, no. 1 (1995), pp. 391-408.
10. The South Korean Ministry of National Defense has estimated the losses within the first ten days to be twice the losses incurred during the first three years of the Korean War.
11. Chinese Academy of Military Science: *Kangmei Yuanchao Zhanshi* (Beijing: Military Science Publishing Co., 1988), pp. 17-71.
12. Bowie, Christopher, Fred Frostic *et al.*: *The New Calculus* (Santa Monica: RAND, 1993).
13. According to the Korean Ministry of National Defense, since 1993 North Korea has deployed forward 170mm self-propelled artillery pieces and 240mm multiple rocket launchers. See The Korean Ministry of National Defense: *Defense White Paper 1996-1997*.
14. South Korea's ballistic missile program remains below a maximum range of 180 miles and a payload of 300 kg. See *Jane's Defense Weekly*, vol. 21, no. 17 (30 April 1994), p. 25.
15. *Nodongshinmun*, 3 February 1991.
16. Economic indicators recently released by the Bank of Korea.
17. According to the Korean Ministry of National Defense, the cumulative total real investments in defense (1953-today) are expected to be the same as those of North Korea in the year 1996. See *Hankuk Ilbo*, 3 February 1990. RAND estimates on cumulative total defense expenditures of South and North Korea between 1968 and 1983 show that South Korea has spent 1.06 times as much as the North in 1979 constant dollars. If we add later spending gap to this differential, we will get a larger ratio. See Wolf, Charles Jr. *et al.*: 'The Changing Balance: South and North Korean Capabilities for Long-Term Military Competition', R-3305 (Santa Monica: The RAND Corporation, December 1985), p. 43.
18. See *Hankuk Ilbo*, 30 October 1990 for an interview with the Soviet Deputy Foreign Minister.

19. Sneider, Richard L.: 'Prospects for Korean Security,' in Richard H. Solomon (ed.): *Asian Security in the 1980s: Problems and Policies for a Time of Transition* (Cambridge, MA: Oelgeschlager, Gunn & Hain, 1979), p. 138.
20. U.S. Department of Defense: *A Strategic Framework for the Asian Pacific Rim: Looking Toward the 21st Century* (Washington, DC: Government Printing Office, 1990), p. 15.
21. Ministry of National Defense: *Defense White Paper 1994-95* (Seoul: Ministry of National Defense, 1995), p. 261.
22. President Rho Tae Woo's speech in the United Nations, *Hankuk Ilbo*, 19 October 1988.
23. Other objectives could be a suspension of the arms race between the South and the North, and non-use of force.
24. North Korean Prime Minister's speech at the South-North Prime Ministerial Talks, 18 October 1990, Pyongyang, *FBIS-EAS-90*203*.
25. Ben-Horin, Y., Richard Darilek *et al.*: 'Building Confidence and Security in Europe: The Potential Role of Confidence and Security Building Measures', *R-3431-USDP* (Santa Monica: The RAND Corporation, December 1986), p. 10.
26. In Europe, the Soviet Union used forces to suppress the political crisis in Poland in 1981 after the CBM agreed in 1975 in Helsinki. Such use of forces for political purposes could be interpreted as Soviet preparations for an invasion of Western Europe. Thus, preventing misperception and miscalculation through arms control was a main objective in Europe, as was clearly stated in U.S. policy statement for the Stockholm Conference.
27. North Korea has traditionally insisted on a non-intervention principle and on the exclusion of foreign troops from Korea. This is the so-called self-reliance (*Chuche*, also known as *Juche*) strategy.
28. Most of North Korea's arms control proposals are related to removal of foreign troops and military exercises.
29. North Korean statement by Foreign Minister, 20 April 1991, *Hankuk Ilbo*.
30. Zycher, Benjamin & Tad Daley: 'Military Dimensions of Communist Systems', *R-3593* (Santa Monica: The RAND Corporation, July 1988), p. viii.
31. See the South-North Prime Ministers' Talks on 5 September 1990 and *FBIS-EAS-90-172*, 6 September 1990. Other arms control proposals come from the same sources.
32. Article 9 of the South-North Nonaggression Pact ratified by the two Koreas in February 1992.
33. Baker, James III: *Politics of Diplomacy* (New York: G.P. Putnam's Sons, 1995), p. 597.
34. On 27 January 1993, the North Korean Ministry of Foreign Affairs announced that it would suspend all South-North dialogue, including the bilateral nuclear negotiations, because South Korea had announced its intention to resume 'Team Spirit'.
35. Testimony of Robert L. Gallucci, Ambassador at Large on the Agreed Framework with North Korea before the U.S. Senate Foreign Relations Committee: Subcommittee on East Asian and Pacific Affairs, 1 December 1994.

36. Bogaturov, Aleksis, Mikhail Nossov & Konstantine Plehakov, 'The Korean Problem and Possible Forms of Soviet-American Interaction,' in Smoke & Kortunov: *op. cit.* (note 3), pp., p. 230.

7 Defence Conversion and Conservation: China's Ambivalent Military Reform

YITZHAK SHICHOR

INTRODUCTION: DEFENCE CONVERSION OR A 'CHINA THREAT'?

Since the late 1970s post-Mao leaders in Beijing have invested much energy, efforts and money in converting various components of China's military system to civilian use. Most of this drive has obviously been concentrated on defence industrial conversion. According to Wu Chou, vice president of the China Association for the Peaceful Use of Military Industrial Technology (CAPUMIT), by mid-1996 China's defence industrial complex had been capable of manufacturing more than 15,000 civilian products. Accounting for about 80 percent of China's total defence industrial output value, civilian production by defence industries plays the predominant and most advertised, though by no means exclusive, role in China's conversion policy.

In addition to defence industrial conversion, about one million troops, or one quarter of the 4.3 million People's Liberation Army (PLA), have been cut down and allegedly 'converted' to civilian life. A considerable part of those 3.2 million left, perhaps one third, are constantly and regularly engaged in only partly military, often purely civilian, activities. Also, since the early 1980s many military facilities such as roads, railroads, mines, harbours, airfields, lands, missile launching pads and laboratories, as well as many military technologies, have been used for civilian purposes or handed over to civilian authorities, thus being 'converted'. Many outdated military production lines, particularly those located in remote inland areas (built in the 1960s and 1970s as part of the so-called Third Line, or *sanxian*) have occasionally been closed down, abandoned, or transferred to better locations near the big cities or the coast. Finally, Beijing had drastically reduced its official defence expenditures in the 1980s; while military appropriation has considerably increased since the early 1990s, it still fails to catch up with inflation meaning that, in real terms, large amounts of potential military capital has supposedly been converted to civilian uses.

These apparently remarkable achievements imply that, in view of the existing domestic and international circumstances, China's peacetime defence conversion is without precedent in its motivations, dimensions, and consequences. Frequently reiterated by Chinese spokesmen,[1] this conclusion is confirmed, and often acclaimed, also by outside observers including the United States that in late 1994 established a Sino-American joint commission on conversion, and the OECD Development Centre that in 1995 prepared and published a detailed and extremely sympathetic report on China's military-to-civilian conversion policy.[2] Far from being a temporary expediency this policy, which has been consistently implemented for nearly twenty years, is still listed as a crucial aspect of the country's development strategy in the Ninth Five-Year Plan (1996-2000), and beyond.[3]

Most of this comprehensive and multi-dimensional policy had been motivated by domestic considerations, primarily economic and social. At the same time, military-to-civilian conversion had inevitably also reflected Beijing's reduced threat perception and its interpretation that the international situation had become more relaxed. Moreover, ostensibly leading to a lower Chinese military profile, this policy had also been intended, among other things, to promote regional stability and international relaxation (considered essential by Beijing to carry out its modernization program) as well as to project an image of a peace-loving and non-militant China. To be sure, such extensive conversion experience—regarded by many as outstanding compared to the conversion agonies of other countries—must have been welcomed as good news by the international community in general, and particularly by China's neighbours. Yet, although winning widespread appreciation in themselves, China's defence conversion policies have so far failed to alleviate global and regional concerns with regard to Beijing's military intentions and capabilities.

On the contrary, it is precisely when China has assumed a more 'moderate' image; shed the cloak of its Maoist militant revolutionary ideology; become more integrated in the global market; embarked on the course of economic growth and development; and apparently converted a wide variety of military hardware and software resources to civilian use, that the issue of the 'China threat' has emerged, more explicitly in the West and rather implicitly in the East. How to reconcile China's reportedly successful conversion, on the one hand, with the 'China threat', on the other? The purpose of this paper is to discuss and analyse the theory and practice of these contradictory dimensions, and perceptions, of China's defence reform and to evaluate their regional and international impact.

THEORY: THE DIALECTICAL FOUNDATIONS OF CHINA'S DEFENCE CONVERSION

Like so many other policies and attitudes, China's defence conversion reflects the traditional dialectical nature of Chinese thought, behaviour patterns, and historical experience. The tension between the terms *wen* (civilian) and *wu* (military) goes back to pre-imperial China. Chinese rulers and philosophers tried throughout history to strike the correct balance between these two concepts which, while representing contradictory aspects, should also complement each other in creating a preconceived harmony. Underscoring their Confucian civilian and cultural (both *wen*) identity, China's imperial dynasties never renounced the use of military power and violence, without which they could have never been established nor survive, let alone expand. At the same time the military, and even more so the militia, were closely integrated with society, performing a variety of economic and social duties in addition to defence. Thus, in pre-modern China the borderline between *wen* and *wu*, civilian and military, peace and war, offensive and defensive, internal and external, formal and informal, was often vague. Modern China, not to mention Chinese Communism, is no exception.

Military power had been a crucial factor in the Chinese Communist Party's (CCP) rise to power, overcoming first the Japanese and then the Guomindang. One of the main reasons for its victory is precisely this military-civilian (*junmin*) combination or the integration of the army with society. This is clearly implied by the term 'people's war' (*renmin zhanzheng*) which could also be interpreted as a 'civilian war', or a non-military war. While the military has continued to play an indispensable role in the consolidation of the People's Republic of China (PRC) in the face of real or perceived external (as well as domestic) threats, integration with the society and the economy persisted, though the balance between the two has changed over time.

Throughout Mao's time, for example, there was no clearcut distinction between civilian and military production and both were often combined under one and the same ministry. To be sure, *wu* was usually more important than *wen*. Mao's Cultural Revolution, for instance, was supposed to lead to a civilian transformation— *wenhua dageming*—but ended up in military predominance. From the early 1950s to the early 1970s countless civilian resources, both human and material, had been 'converted' to satisfy military needs considered more urgent and important. Consequently, this kind of 'civilian-to-military' conversion could go along with and, moreover, provide the basis for, 'military-to-civilian' conversion.[4]

As early as May 1952, every military factory was instructed to select at least one civilian good for production, and Mao Zedong legitimized this policy in the third part of his well known April 1956 speech 'On the Ten Major Relationships' ('The Relations between Economic Construction and Defence Construction'). He then urged defence industries to adopt two sets of technologies for the production of both military and civilian goods.[5] His views were summarized in March 1957 as the 'sixteen characters policy' which, undergoing several revisions throughout the years, was to guide military production in peacetime to this very day. It called for 'military and civilian integration, peace and war integration, giving precedence to the military, and containing the military in the civilian' (*Junmin jiehe, pingzhan jiehe, yijun weizhu, yujun yumin*).[6] Based on this policy, the defence industry was ordered to implement the policy of 'Dual Duty, Dual Skill, Combination of Peace and War Production' namely the 'production of both military and civilian products simultaneously on the basis of ensuring the fulfilment of military production and gradually raising the level of technology'.[7]

The outcome was outstanding and swift. The share of civilian products in China's defence industry's total output value jumped to 52 percent in 1959, and then to 74.5 percent in 1960—a record broken only in the mid-1990s which reflects the industry's enormous surplus civilian production capacity in the 1950s.[8] Also in those years, a large number of PLA troops were mobilized, and demobilized, to undertake economic projects in agriculture, forestry, oil fields, road and rail construction, not to mention welfare and rescue operations, and official military expenditures were reduced both absolutely and, even more so, in proportion to the overall state budget.

Shortly afterwards, however, the implementation of these military-to-civilian conversion policies slowed down and soon stopped altogether. This must have been a combined outcome of interconnected developments that included economic difficulties; an increased threat perception; the withdrawal of Soviet assistance which called for an exceptional effort in military production; and, primarily, revolutionary upheavals and the growing political radicalization during the Great Leap Forward. Under these circumstances, continued civilian production by defence industries was criticized as 'unprofessional' by 'leftists' who blamed military enterprises for 'not attending to their proper duties' and urged them to mind their own business (namely to engage in purely military production), thereby causing a sharp decline in civilian output. By 1962 the share of civilian production in the defence industry total output value plunged to 14.8 percent.[9] Also reflecting these attitudes, official defence expenditures doubled by the mid-1960s and tripled by the early 1970s, compared to the early 1960s, and the size of the PLA began to increase.

An attempt by Premier Zhou Enlai to revive China's conversion policy (as a part of the original version of China's Four Modernizations) at the Third National People's Congress (NPC) held in late 1964, failed. Before long the Cultural Revolution erupted and civilian production by military enterprises practically came to a standstill. By the end of China's Fourth Five-Year Plan (1971-1975) a second attempt to launch the Four Modernizations had failed and the share of civilian production fell to around 10 percent of the total defence industrial output value, reportedly sliding to slightly over 8 percent in 1978, on the eve of post-Mao China's reforms. In July, 1978, shortly after his second rehabilitation and shortly before he successfully launched the third version of the Four Modernizations, Deng Xiaoping reaffirmed the late Zhou Enlai's military-civilian integration policy, saying that at least half of the defence industry output should consist of civilian products.[10]

As mentioned above, non-military social and economic considerations had undoubtedly provided a major incentive for undertaking military-to-civilian conversion in China. To begin with, shielded and protected by the state—its only client—China's defence industrial complex had little interest in reducing costs and efficient production, or in understanding of market mechanisms and the role of profits—unlike other state-owned enterprises. Also unlike other state-owned enterprises, China's defence industries had accumulated an enormous surplus of under-utilized production capacity including manpower, assets, equipment and technology.[11] Determined by perceived threats and the self-reliance predicament caused by the withdrawal of Soviet support, this surplus had been created over the years by waves of expansion and duplication, through endless mobilization of civilian resources. In view of the restored emphasis on rational economic growth, related to the presumably increasing international relaxation, these surplus resources could now be shifted, or reconverted, to civilian production, and subjected to the market forces.

Forsaken since the early 1960s, military-to-civilian conversion policy, 'was once more put on the agenda for discussion' (though not yet as an official policy) following the crucial Third Plenum of the Eleventh CCP Central Committee held in December 1978, that triggered China's overall reform drive. Initiated (or, to be more precise, revived) by Deng Xiaoping, the fundamental assumption of this reform has been that—in order not only to overcome China's inherited backwardness but, even more so, to restore its traditional greatness—civilian needs and economic growth have become more important than military needs and, moreover, a precondition for a thorough defence reform. Military power was no longer China's exclusive yardstick for greatness but rather one component, albeit the predominant, in the so-called 'comprehensive national strength'.[12] Indeed, among China's Four Modernizations, the guiding framework for post-Mao reform, defence has been officially accorded the lowest priority. Thus, the balance between *wen* and *wu* has apparently changed once again, in favour of the former and at the expense of the latter, yet not as drastically as Beijing would want us to believe. Downgraded for a while, military considerations have by no means been written off.

This became evident at a Central Work Conference held in April 1979 when Li Xiannian revised the fourth part of the old 'sixteen characters' (*yujun yumin*, namely to contain the military in the civilian) into *yimin yangjun* (namely using the civilian to provide for the military).[13] This change was needed to underline that while conversion was to go on the military would in no way be neglected, and perhaps also to reassure some concerned and resentful PLA generals that civilian goods would not be produced at the expense of military goods but, on the contrary, would generate more income to finance defence modernization. It is on this general understanding that the trial integration of military and civilian production was launched in 1980.

This drive was endorsed by Deng Xiaoping, now chairman of the CCP Central Military Commission (CMC) and China's uncrowned leader. To remove any doubt (not only external but also internal) that ultimate authority resides in the civilian leadership rather than the military (despite its crucial role in the post-Mao takeover), in January 1982 Deng put forward his own revised version of the 'sixteen characters' policy. Its third part (*yijun weizhu*, namely give precedence to the army, which could imply military predominance in general) was changed into *junpin youxian* (namely give precedence to military products, a more specific and concrete statement which still implied that whatever the scale of civilian production, military needs should never be overlooked and should be guaranteed at all times).

Like Mao's 'instructions' and imitating his style, Deng's version of the 'sixteen characters' has since been enshrined as the guideline for China's military-to-civilian industrial conversion policy: 'combine military with civilian, peace[time] and war[time], give priority to military products, and use the civilian to provide for the military' (*junmin jiehe, pingzhan jiehe, junpin youxian, yimin yangjun*). He then often reiterated the latter part: 'National defence industries should combine military and civilian work, and *make civilian products to finance the military*' (emphasis added). He urged these industries to research, develop and produce civilian goods, *in addition* to fulfilling their assignments for weapons and military equipment.[14]

By that time, spontaneous, experimental, or unofficial conversion had already begun (to be discussed later). Some military leaders must have still betrayed their concern about the harmful effects of converting China's defence industrial capability to civilian use, because in 1984 Deng had to tell the CMC, reiterating his earlier assurances, that using defence industry facilities, manpower, and technology to civilian ends would support not only national economic construction but also national defence: 'This kind of act has one hundred benefits and not one harm' (*zheyangzuo you baili er wu yihai*).[15] It was his insistence that has finally mollified the suspicious military elite and paved the way for a strategic transition gradually yet consistently undertaken by China's military industry.

Turning experimental conversion into official policy, this transition was based on a consensus reached in Beijing in the mid-1980s which reflected the remarkable achievements of the economic reform, the domestic social and political stability, and the considerably reduced threat perception which made defence modernization rather less urgent. Self-confident and enjoying more international respect and prestige than ever before, China's post-Mao leaders could accelerate the transformation of military resources (human as well as material) to civilian needs while undertaking a slower, gradual and selective military reform. Accordingly, one quarter of the PLA manpower was demobilized, military expenditure was mercilessly slashed, and civilian production by defence enterprises was given a boost. In the 1980s *wen* clearly prevailed, though not for long.

Since the early 1990s, however, the situation has changed. Following ten years of accelerated growth, especially in the latter half of the 1980s, the process of military industrial conversion began to slow down. To some extent, this slow-down has been determined by problems within the industry. After overcoming their initial enthusiasm many military enterprises have encountered serious difficulties with quality production, costs, marketing, technology and investment and some have reached saturation in their civilian output. Obviously affected by these difficulties, the revised balance of China's military-civilian integration (and defence policy in general) has been determined much more by other problems.

Emerging since the late 1980s both at home and abroad, these included economic, social and political problems such as accelerating inflation, growing regional gaps and social inequalities, widespread corruption, religious and ethnic unrest, rural dislocations, and political friction. All these problems converged in 1989 during the Tiananmen demonstrations and the subsequent massacre which exposed Beijing's weaknesses and anxieties to the outside world. Indeed, the hostile Western reaction and its consequent political, economic, and military sanctions have revived bitter Chinese memories of earlier years, decades, and centuries, supposed to have been forgotten by then. All these problems began to erode the leadership's self-confidence, on the one hand, and to increase its militancy, on the other.

Concerned about growing domestic instability, suspicious about the intimidating external messages, and aware of their edge over the civilian leadership, a few Chinese military leaders must have begun to argue (probably in private at that stage) that, following ten years of relative neglect, it was about time that China's military system should be given a higher priority. Nothing much was done about it for over a year. In fact, because of the PLA's initial and instinctive reluctance to suppress the Tiananmen demonstrators by force, Beijing muffled any mention of professional military modernization, and concentrated instead on an extensive political and ideological indoctrination campaign among the servicemen. Lasting for about fourteen months this campaign faded, and military modernization resurrected, against the background of the Gulf War. It has taught Beijing three crucial lessons:

- that although the prospects of a global conflict had indeed diminished, the prospects of regional and local conflicts have increased;
- that a militarily-weak state would remain vulnerable to pressure, intimidation, and ultimately to aggression;
- that military power, conventional as well as non-conventional, is still the predominant component of the so-called 'comprehensive national strength' which, in the emerging New World Order, is a function of superior technology.[16]

An additional incentive for a military build-up has, paradoxically, emerged by the disintegration of the Soviet Union. Apparently it has removed the immediate and most serious threat to China's security, thus justifying Beijing's downgraded defence reform and its military-to-civilian conversion policy. At the same time, however, the Soviet collapse and Moscow's shrinking presence in Central, South-East, and North-East Asia, has stimulated greater Chinese military vigilance for two reasons. Negatively, because it has created new potential risks to Chinese security which had to be dealt with; and positively, because it created new potential opportunities for Beijing to restore its long abandoned traditional role as the central and most important regional power in East Asia.[17]

Finally, China's brisk economic growth (an annual average of nearly 10 percent from 1979 to 1996) has affected its military theory (and practice) in several respects. For one, it has induced Beijing to reinforce its military monopoly while the phenomenal economic growth of its southeastern provinces has increased their political leverage to the extent that some people, both in and out of China, anticipate a future breakup. For another, it has made the Chinese leadership aware of the long-term need to protect its ambitious modernization and development drive on land, in the air, and at sea. Finally, for the first time this impressive economic growth has raised (and, if sustained, would continue to raise) enough resources for the reactivation and upgrading of arms R&D and production by defence industries and for an advanced military build-up in the future. In sum, domestic developments (a weakening centre, a problematic periphery, a more prominent PLA, socio-political instability, and impressive economic results) as well as increased threat perceptions and new opportunities abroad, have begun to change the balance between civilian and military modernization, tipping the scale in favour of the latter. *Wu* began to prevail.

Indeed, since the early 1990s there are indications that China's military doctrine and strategic ideology are undergoing a subtle, yet very significant, change. Whereas in the 1980s the Chinese decided to downplay and, in fact, delay, defence modernization as dependent on, and a function of, economic growth, now some high-ranking PLA leaders suggest (still indirectly and unofficially) that it is the other way around: continued economic growth is dependent on, and a function of, defence modernization. This argument, that 'without a strong national defence, there will be neither security nor development to speak of,' emerged as early as January 1991, in the wake of the Western offensive in the Gulf,[18] and has been later reiterated by China's military leadership. Now out of favour but then vice-chairman of the CMC and director of the PLA General Political Department, Yang Baibing indicated that China's modernization drive should be guaranteed by a powerful army: 'Only when we have boosted the economy *and built a powerful army and a firm national defence* can we acquire the proper position of a big country in the international community.'[19] (Emphasis added)

Liu Huaqing, his successor as the senior CMC vice-chairman and, furthermore, a member of the Politburo Standing Committee, has reinforced these views as a part of his efforts to promote defence modernization. Indirectly disapproving Deng's doctrine and timetable, he said: 'It takes a long period to carry out research on weapons and equipment and to manufacture them. Therefore, the thinking that the Army should be modernized only after the economy becomes rich is one-sided. If we do that, the gap between us and the advanced standard in the world will become bigger and bigger.' Therefore, military equipment and weapons should be developed as much and as soon as possible.[20] To overcome the irresolute PLA support in his leadership, Jiang Zemin had to point out: 'The modernization of national defence is a major component of China's socialist modernization, and strengthening national defence building is a basic guarantee for national security and economic development.'[21] And Chi Haotian, PRC national defence minister and a strong supporter of military modernization, summed up in a typically traditional Chinese way: 'The building of national defence and economic construction are mutually complementary. Without the foundation of a considerable economic strength, it is impossible to carry on the building of national defence, and without a stable internal and external environment, it is impossible to develop the economy.'[22]

Defence conversion policy usually implies a one-way flow of military resources to civilian use within the context of a deliberate lowering of military profile.[23] The case of China's defence conversion policy, however, is different. Motivated by the past (e.g. long-standing cultural norms, dialectical thinking, patterns of behaviour, theoretical framework, and historical precedents); the present (e.g. the unanticipated growth of economic resources, inflated sense of nationalism, an influential military, domestic instability, regional and international risks and opportunities); and the future (e.g. restoration of China's greatness and the implicit pursuit of a superpower status), it implies a two-way flow of converting military resources to civilian use as well as diverting civilian resources to military use within the context of maintaining the existing military profile, if not raising it. These conceptually contradictory yet supplementary elements of China's defence conversion policy have shaped its implementation.

PRAXIS: THE DIALECTICAL IMPLEMENTATION OF CHINA'S DEFENCE CONVERSION

Forecasting an imminent change in political winds, some defence enterprises resumed civilian production as early as 1977, immediately after Mao's death and the downfall of the Gang-of-Four. Most Chinese spokesmen claim that during this experimental or 'spontaneous' conversion stage (which lasted until the mid-1980s) defence enterprises were practically forced to produce civilian goods by the 'sharp' or 'drastic' reduction in military orders, 'due to demobilization'.[24] Although demobilization was officially announced only in the mid-1980s, there is some evidence that since the late 1970s and early 1980s some on-going or planned military production projects have been aborted, cut down, or postponed, not so much because of demobilization but much more because their low and outdated technology could no longer satisfy PLA demands, let alone those of foreign customers. Other military production lines, however, must have been reactivated and even expanded and modernized in order to replenish hardware lost during the invasion of Vietnam as well as to provide more hardware for arms sales which gathered unprecedented momentum precisely at that time.

Apparently, arms sales contradict the policy, and logic, of military-to-civilian conversion since they reinforce the *raison d'être* of defence industries, provide an excuse to continue military production, and delay the transfer of military resources to civilian use. Yet many countries engaged in defence conversion still proceed with arms sales, and China is no exception. In fact, as a late-comer to the international power play, China has more incentives to play a growing role in the global arms market. For one, and unlike its previous policy, since the late 1970s Beijing has regarded arms sales as a legitimate commercial transaction whose economic benefits (and perhaps indirect contribution to defence modernization) should not be given up. For another, and perhaps even more important, neither would China like to give up the political benefits of arms trade which is considered an essential symbol of belonging to the great-power league.

To be sure, while promoting its military-to-civilian conversion policy China has managed to become one of the top arms supplier to the Third World, evidently selling conventional weapons but also suspected of selling semi-conventional delivery systems and even dual-use non-conventional technology and know-how.[25] Most, if not all, of these arms transfers have been carried out by corporations created in the early 1980s to replace the old (military) ministries of machine-building and to provide them with a civilian image and outlets.[26] These ostensibly civilian corporations are still controlled and coordinated by the military-oriented Commission of Science, Technology, and Industry for National Defence (COSTIND, created in 1982). Moreover, domestic and primarily international defence conversion conferences and exhibitions officially organized by CAPUMIT (the Chinese Association for the Peaceful Use of Military Industrial Technology, in itself a COSTIND organization), such as the one held in Hong Kong in July 1993, have been regularly used not only for civilian purposes but also for promoting military (both export and import) transactions. Using these avenues for military purposes has been justified in unequivocal terms: 'The existing facts proved that developing export trade of military products is an efficient way for up-keeping defence R&D and production capabilities, stabilizing and training defence science and technical forces, accumulating development capital, and realizing the nurturing of [military] import by [military] export in peace time.'[27]

Generating additional funds for military use, these arms transfers testify that, despite its conversion, China's defence industrial complex still has enough military production capacity to cater for arms transfers, not to mention domestic needs. This by no means implies that China's defence conversion is false. It definitely is not, but it involved huge investments. Governmental conversion loans totalled nearly RMB 4 billion during the Seventh Five-Year Plan (1986-1990) and RMB 6.3 billion during the Eighth Five-Year Plan (1991-1995). Hundreds of civilian production lines have been constructed or imported so that, by the mid-1990s, all military enterprises could produce civilian goods. New management, appropriation, and contractual systems have been introduced, military enterprises (especially inland) were encouraged not only to open 'windows' in the prosperous coastal Special Economic Zones or to move their premises to newly established industrial parks near the big cities, but also to seek joint ventures and sign cooperation agreements with foreign companies. As mentioned above, the value of civilian production by defence industries has increased gradually yet consistently, reaching 80 percent of their total output value by the mid-1990s.[28]

Most of this increase, however, has been achieved not necessarily at the expense of essential military production, but in addition to it. Non-essential military production has indeed been cut down. Already in the early stages of China's defence conversion drive, Deng Xiaoping reiterated that in the period of national economic construction, it would be 'impossible to increase greatly' allocations for producing military equipment and investment in defence industries. Therefore, he added, major projects should be undertaken very carefully and selectively, or not at all. Instead, the development of modern weapons and military equipment should 'concentrate on R&D by every possible means, including reducing weapon system production.'[29] Following his guidelines, China's defence industries have indeed stopped or considerably slowed down the production of outdated weapons and military equipment, mostly based on obsolete Soviet military technology of the 1950s, which in itself derived from German military technology of the 1930s.

At the same time, however, much effort has been exerted not only in upgrading existing systems (primarily for export) but, moreover, in the research, design and development of modern and advanced state-of-the-art weapons. It is impossible within the limits of this paper to provide a comprehensive list of China's hardware and software defence modernization achievements since the late 1970s, when conversion policy had been launched. These achievements include conventional weapons (aircraft, vessels, tanks, armoured personnel carriers, guns and a variety of tactical missiles), semi-conventional weapons (such as strategic missiles), and non-conventional weapons (tactical nuclear weapons and improved warheads, as well as nuclear tests).[30] To be sure, some civilian technologies acquired by China from abroad through conversion cooperation could be and are being used for weapon production (the main reason why the Joint Sino-American Conversion Commission was aborted in early 1996). Mass production of some of these weapons has already begun, though others have only been trial-produced thus laying the groundwork for the long-term transformation of China's military system.

This transformation is based primarily, but by no means only, on China's own efforts, according to the time-honoured principle of self-reliance. Minimizing China's reliance on external sources of military supply was particularly emphasized in the 1980s, either rationalizing or reflecting the lack of funds, technological incompatibility, fear of renewed dependence, and China's reduced threat perception. Consequently, in the early 1980s Beijing decided that, rather than consisting of large-scale acquisitions of weapons, military imports would be limited to 'a few critical technologies'. Yet already in the 1980s—and much more so since the early 1990s, when additional funds and compatible Russian equipment have become available and threat perception increased somewhat—China began to import not only military technologies but also military hardware. This quite extensive and well-documented military import drive,[31] hardly conforms to the peaceful image China has been trying to project as a part of its defence conversion policy. It also raises the issue of funds: while conversion implies a reduction of defence expenditures, where does procurement money come from?

As mentioned above, in the 1980s China's defence expenditures were indeed reduced considerably, both in absolute and in relative terms. In late 1977, soon after Mao's death, the arrest of the Gang-of-Four, and his second rehabilitation, Deng Xiaoping told the CMC: 'The state budget is limited and, moreover, the amount of our military expenditures has to be decided with a view to the overall balance. Our national defence can be modernized only on the basis of the industrial and agricultural development of the country as a whole.'[32] Echoing Mao's words a quarter of a century earlier he added in 1980: 'Our current military expenditures are rather high, to the detriment of national construction.'[33]

In 1979, at the beginning of reform and following the miscarried invasion of Vietnam, China's official defence expenditures were raised by more than 20 percent, reaching over RMB 20 (or even 22) billion, the highest till then in nominal terms. They were subsequently reduced, fluctuating in the next ten years (1979 to 1988) between around RMB 18 and 22 billion, going down slightly in 1980-1984, and up slightly in 1985-1988, with an annual average of RMB 19.3 billion. In *nominal* terms, therefore, the cuts in China's defence expenditures were not only modest, but also inconsistent.[34] Yet they were more significant in two respects. For one, due to China's accelerating inflation in those years, the real value of its defence appropriation declined steadily to RMB 12.7 billion, with an annual average of nearly RMB 16 billion, about 17 percent below their annual nominal value average. For another, due to the considerable increase in China's total fiscal outlays (135 percent from 1979 to 1988, in nominal terms), the share of defence expenditures in the total government budget declined steadily and steeply from slightly over 18 percent in 1979 to slightly over 8 percent in 1988, less than half their earlier share.

The fact that official defence expenditures decreased in the 1980s and lagged far behind the increase in China's total fiscal outlays and its high inflation rates implies that a great deal of potential military funds were indeed converted to civilian use in those years.[35] Since 1989, however, China's defence expenditures began to grow by leaps and bounds. With an average annual growth rate of nearly 16 percent in 1989-1997 (compared to no more than 0.85 percent in 1980-1988), in 1997 China's defence expenditures reached an all-time high of RMB 80.57 billion, nearly four times as much as its 1987 defence budget. It is primarily this increase that triggered the above-mentioned warnings against the so-called 'China threat'. While there is no doubt that more and more funds have become available for China's defence modernization drive, the significance of this increase should still be somewhat qualified.

To begin with, although the ratio of defence expenditures to total fiscal outlays, kept at around 8.5 percent in the early 1990s, has increased to 9.5 percent in 1994 and 9.9 percent in 1995 (still much lower than many countries), its proportion to China's rapidly growing GDP has continued to decline steadily and consistently. From an annual average of 2.76 percent in the 1980s (3.66 in the first half and 1.86 in the second half), the ratio of defence expenditures to the GDP declined to 1.63 percent in 1991, 1.38 in 1992, 1.36 in 1993, and 1.26 in 1994. Among 92 major countries, the PRC ranks 83rd in terms of defence spending ratio to GDP.[36] Moreover, Beijing claims that China's defence expenditures are not only much lower in absolute terms when compared to those of other countries, but among the world's lowest on a per capita, per soldier, per territory and per border-length basis.

Impressively summed up in the official and well-advertised *White Paper on Arms Control and Disarmament in China*, published by the State Council Information Office for the first time in November 1995,[37] all these arguments try to convey and underline China's claimed peaceful image. Yet the inevitable bottom line is that China's defence system and military modernization program have more funds at the present, and will have much more funds in the future. Even if the ratio of defence expenditures to the state budget and to the GDP remains basically unchanged, the continued fast growth of both would create additional sources for *official* defence spending. Known to exist since the PRC establishment, if not before, *unofficial* defence spending is believed to double or even triple China's official military funds.[38]

Various defence-related allocations, such as military R&D; defence industries and corporations; the People's Armed Police Force, the militia and reserve units; conscription and demobilization; military academies, etc. are regularly hidden under various and obscure budgetary items such as 'administrative expenditures' (under 'expenses for building up the national strength'). Some defence expenditures are not included in the state budget at all but are covered by local authorities or by income from PLA commercial enterprises, military facilities handed over to civilian authorities, or PLA non-military activities. Reportedly, Beijing has also provided occasional special extra-budgetary appropriations (sometimes as high as 20 percent of the official defence budget) for military equipment and technology procurement from abroad. Some of these military transactions (for example with Russia and Iran) have been done by barter trade which is not reflected in the regular defence budget.

Finally, it should be emphasized that in terms of purchasing power parity the local value of China's defence (as well as civilian) expenditures by far exceeds their very modest and implausibly stagnant US dollar-converted value. Also, we should not forget (what the Chinese consistently and conveniently do) that relatively more military funds have become available simply because the considerable increase in nominal defence expenditures has been accompanied by a considerable reduction of PLA servicemen. Put differently, while China's official defence spending in 1997 was 4.8 times its 1978 size, the allocation per soldier has grown 7.18 times, from RMB 3,900 in 1978 to nearly RMB 28,000 in 1997. Nonetheless, though leading to increased military outlays per soldier, demobilization can definitely be considered an important aspect of defence conversion in itself.[39]

In late 1977, soon after his second rehabilitation, Deng Xiaoping resumed his effort (begun in the mid-1970s) to streamline what he regarded as an overstaffed PLA. At that time he was more concerned by the military aspects of demobilization, aimed at ridding the PLA of 'unnecessary non-combatants', improving efficient command and control, reforming training, and expediting defence modernization: 'Our policy is to reduce manpower and use the money thus saved to renew equipment. If some savings can be used for economic construction, so much the better.'[40] Overcoming possible PLA opposition, Beijing began demobilizing troops in 1982. By 1984, 650-750,000 troops were swiftly and easily cut down followed by at least 455,000 officers and cadres, demobilized since 1985.

Though considered an integral part of military-to-civilian conversion, this demobilization, however, has hardly eroded China's defence capabilities. For one reason, most of the earlier demobilization consisted of entire para-military or even non-military units such as the Production and Construction Corps, the Capital Construction Corps, and the Railway Corps, as well as public security units, border patrols, teachers, medical staff, etc. Most of the second demobilization consisted of aged and unskilled officers and cadres who, in Deng's words, 'bloated' headquarters and whose contribution to China's defence capabilities had been marginal at best and worthless at worst. In fact, while as a result of this demobilization China's military system may have become smaller, it has undoubtedly become better and fitter in terms of training, control, equipment and mobility.

For another reason, while many of China's demobilized servicemen have been integrated—reportedly with a good deal of difficulties—into civilian life and economic occupations (assigned to departments of industry, commerce, taxation, finance, education, science and research, public health, and 'key construction projects'), others were transferred to judicial, procuratorial, and public security departments. Some 'demobilized' PLA servicemen have continued to perform their traditional 'military' duties as PLA-employed civilians or, moreover, remained in their old units which continue to exist under new and more 'civilian' names and which have even been considerably expanded. Notable examples are the Production-Construction Corps and even more so the People's Armed Police Force which, consistently expanded and relying primarily on 'demobilized' servicemen, has become an efficient para-military organization that could be used not only in peacetime but in wartime as well.[41] Similarly, while regular PLA troops have been reduced, 'demobilized' servicemen, officers, and cadres have been 'remobilized' into the militia and especially into the Reserve Officers Corps which have been reorganized and upgraded both quantitatively and qualitatively so that they can cope with threats not necessarily or exclusively related to domestic unrest and instability.

As we have seen, this kind of vague distinction between internal and external, offensive and defensive, regular and irregular, peacetime and wartime, formal and informal, etc. is typical of China's dialectical cultural outlook. This is true also with regard to other aspects of China's defence conversion. Though PLA units have been encouraged, and tempted, to engage in non-military commercial activities far beyond the limits permissible by time-honoured revolutionary traditions, the damage to China's military capabilities is rather limited not only because of the reduced threat perception which enables the PLA to slow down war preparedness, but primarily because first-line fighting divisions and crack troops have been forbidden, as a rule, to engage in such activities, and also because at least some of the funds generated by these non-military activities have been used to supplement official military expenditures.[42] This is also true of military facilities, assets, technologies, R&D achievements, etc. handed over to civilian authorities. While undoubtedly contributing to economic growth and better administration this transfer which also generates funds for military use, is by no means an irreversible process.

CONCLUSION: DEFENCE CONVERSION AND A 'CHINA THREAT'

Obviously, countries that undergo military-to-civilian conversion have no intention whatsoever of giving up their offensive, let alone defensive, capabilities nor of forsaking their defence modernization. In these respects, China is no exception. It is, however, an exception in terms of its explicitly large scale defence conversion, on the one hand, and its implicitly large scale defence modernization, on the other.

These two confusing and contradictory processes can be easily reconciled by China's actual and modern way of thinking (theory) and way of acting (praxis) which follow its cultural and historical traditions. Accordingly, rather than being irreconcilably antagonistic contradictions (to use Mao's concepts), militarization and demilitarization are two aspects of the same phenomenon that should be kept not at the expense of each other but at a certain balance, depending on the circumstances. Put differently, keeping all options open China's defence conversion has been driven and motivated not so much by idealism as by historical materialism and materialistic determinism and pragmatism in Deng's style of 'seeking truth from facts'.

This kind of 'conversion with Chinese characteristics' makes certain Western and even more so regional governments uncomfortable, suspicious and concerned—the former because of a cultural distance and the latter because of geographical proximity. To be sure, the 'China threat' theory has occasionally been politically manipulated and inflated, as often elaborated by Chinese spokesmen and leaders. Compared to other countries, primarily the United States and those led by and associated with it, the PRC record of using force to promote foreign policy goals or seeking presence far away from its borders is extremely poor.

Its limited intentions have only been matched by similarly limited capabilites. Many components of China's defence system (primarily its air force and the navy) are still technologically backward and relatively small for such a big country whose expanding economic interests and relations may require better protection in the future. Moreover, as mentioned above, since the early 1990s Beijing agreed (though sometimes under duress) to join a number of international disarmament conventions.

All these steps and considerations should, could, and were meant to contribute to greater regional and global relaxation and stability. Yet, whereas the likelihood of a global China threat is rather small (also bearing in mind China's history and enormous distance from Western civilization), the potential for a regional China threat is higher. Such a threat has also been exacerbated by China's stated sovereignty claims to the South China Sea; its occasional (often military) measures taken in order to underline its presence, proclaim its superiority, and to accomplish this sovereignty; and the frequent military exercises conducted by Beijing on land, in the air and, significantly, at sea. While most of these actions can hardly be termed 'aggressive' they have certainly been intimidating, first and foremost for China's neighbours.

In conclusion, while military-to-civilian conversion policy may have produced some far-reaching and positive implications in relation to China's domestic socio-economic conditions, it has so far failed to produce similarly positive implications in relation to its external military-strategic situation. Those who explicitly or implicitly raise the issue of the 'China threat' have not been thoroughly convinced that China's defence conversion would lower China's military profile. To be sure, the 'China threat' does not necessarily reflect an active, aggressive, or offensive policy. So far it has been a passive and defensive threat which has been fed, however, by China's traditional role in East Asia, and by the new international constellation created following the collapse of the Soviet Union which offers the Chinese new opportunities but also involves new risks. To cope with both, Beijing has been simultaneously undertaking defence conversion and defence conservation.

NOTES

1. For example, Huang Shaohui, Zhang Yongning, Wu Shaojie, and Xu Saisheng: 'A Successful Practice of Converting Military-Oriented Industries to Civilian Production', *Renmin Ribao* [People's daily] (Beijing), 14 December 1995, p. 11, in Foreign Broadcast Information Service, *Daily Report: China* (Washington), 5 January 1996, pp. 21-25 (hereafter: *FBIS-CHI*).

2. Berthelemy, Jean-Claude & Saadet Deger: 'Conversion of Military Industries to Civilian Production in China: Prospects, Problems and Policies', *OECD Development Centre Report* (May, 1995). By Spring 1995, for reasons to be discussed below, US Congress funds for the Sino-American Joint Defence Conversion Commission had been cut down and by early 1996 it had practically choked before having been really born.
3. See 'Outline of the Ninth Five-Year Plan for National Economic and Social Development and the Long-Term Target for the Year 2010 of the PRC', *Xinhua*, 18 March 1996, in *FBIS-CHI*, 10 April 1996, p. 44; Deng Ying: 'China Fixes Development Plan for Converting National Defence Industry to Civilian Production in the Ninth Five-Year Plan Period', *Xinhua*, 7 February 1996, in *FBIS-CHI*, 20 February 1996, pp. 32-33; Yin Tan: 'China Quickens Pace of Defence Production Conversion Into Civilian Production', *Wen Wei Po* (Hong Kong), 16 April 1996, p. 5, in *FBIS-CHI*, 6 May 1996, pp. 48-50.
4. Much of this and the following information is based on *China Today: Defence Science and Technology* (Beijing: National Defence Industry Press, 1993), 2 vols (hereafter: *CTDST*), and the various volumes on China's defence industries in the *Dangdai Zhongguo* [China Today] series.
5. Kau, Michael Y.M. & John K. Leung (eds.): *The Writings of Mao Zedong 1949-1976*, vol. 1 (Armonk, NY: M.E.Sharpe, 1986), pp. 49-50; *CTDST*-I, p. 159; and Peng Jian: *Zhongguo Gongye de Pingzhan Jiehe yu Junmin Jiehe* [The Peace and War, Military and Civilian Integration of China's Industry] (Beijing: Bingqi Chubanshe, 1989), p. 1. See also Cao Shixin (ed.): *Zhongguo Junzhuanmin* [China's Military-to-Civilian Conversion] (Beijing: Zhongguo Jingji Chubanshe, 1994), p. 11, translated in *FBIS-CHI* (Supplement), 27 July 1995.
6. Peng Jian: *op. cit.* (note 5), p. 1.
7. Duan Zijun (ed.): *China Today: Aviation Industry* (Beijing: The China Aviation Industry Press, 1989), p. 42.
8. Peng Jian: *op. cit.* (note 5), p. 4.
9. *Ibid.*
10. Huang Shaohui *et al.*: *loc. cit.* (note 1), p. 21.
11. On China's defence industries, see Blaker, James R.: 'The Production of Conventional Weapons', in William W. Whitson (ed.): *The Military and Political Power in China in the 1970s* (New York: Praeger, 1972), pp. 215-227; Parris H. Chang: 'China's Military-Industrial Complex: Its Influence on National Security Policy', *Asian Affairs*, vol. 2, no. 3 (Jan-Feb 1975), pp. 145-154; Jencks, Harlan W.: 'The Chinese "Military-Industrial Complex" and Defense Modernization', *Asian Survey*, vol. 20, no. 10 (October 1980), pp. 965-989; idem: *From Muskets to Missiles: Politics and Professionalism in the Chinese Army, 1945-1981* (Boulder: Westview, 1982), pp. 189-221; Jammes, Sydney : 'China', in Nicole Ball & Milton Leitenberg (eds.): *The Structure of the Defence Industry* (London: Croom Helm, 1983), pp. 257-277; idem: 'Military Industry', in Gerald Segal and William T. Tow (eds.): *Chinese Defence Policy* (London: Macmillan, 1984), pp. 117-132; Gallagher, Joseph P.: 'China's Military Industrial Complex: Its Approach to the Acquisition of Modern Military Technology', *Asian Survey*, vol. 27, no. 9 (September 1987), pp.

991-1002; Frankenstein, John: 'People's Republic of China: Defense Industry, Diplomacy, and Trade', in James Everett Katz (ed.): *Arms Production in Developing Countries: An Analysis of Decision Making* (Lexington: Lexington Press, 1984), pp. 89-122.

12. On the concept of 'comprehensive national strength', see Shichor, Yitzhak: 'Defence Policy Reform', in Gerald Segal (ed.): *Chinese Politics and Foreign Policy Reform* (London: Kegan Paul, 1990), pp. 77-99.
13. Peng Jian: *loc. cit.* (note 5), p. 2.
14. Cao Shixin: *loc. cit.* (note 5), pp. 11-12; and *Beijing Review*, no. 13 (1994), pp. 8-11.
15. Cao: *loc. cit.* (note 5), p. 12.
16. Shichor, Yitzhak: 'China and the Gulf Crisis: Escape from Predicaments', *Problems of Communism*, vol. 40, no. 6 (Nov-Dec 1991), pp. 80-90.
17. Shichor, Yitzhak: 'China's Defence in a Changing World', in Kevin P. Clements (ed.): *Peace and Security in the Asia-Pacific Region: Post Cold War Problems and Prospects* (Tokyo: United Nations University Press, 1992), pp. 183-203.
18. For example, Sa Benwang, in *Jiefangjun Bao* [Liberation Army Daily, hereafter *JFJB*], in *FBIS-CHI*, 11 January 1991, pp. 1-2; Luo Xiaobing, 'Strengthening National Defence Building Is Important Guarantee for Economic Development', *JFJB*, 6 February 1991, in *FBIS-CHI*, March 1, 1991, pp. 33-35.
19. Yang Baibing: 'Shouldering the Lofty Mission of Escorting and Protecting China's Reform and Construction', *Renmin Ribao*, 19 July 1992, pp. 1, 3, in *FBIS-CHI*, 5 August 1992, pp. 29-35.
20. Liu Huaqing: 'Unswervingly Advance Along the Road of Building a Modern Army with Chinese Characteristics', *Qiushi* [Seeking Truth], no. 15 (1993), and *JFJB*, 6 August 1993, pp. 1,2, in *FBIS-CHI*, 18 August, 1993, p. 18. See also Wu Fangming and Wu Xishi: 'Correctly Handle Relationship Between National Defence and Economic Construction', *Guofang* [National Defence], no. 2 (15 February 1996), pp. 4-6, in *FBIS-CHI*, 27 June 1996, pp. 13-17.
21. Li Weixing: 'Strengthening National Defence Building Is a Basic Guarantee for National Security and Economic Development', *Renmin Ribao*, 6 March 1996, p. 9, in *FBIS-CHI*, 8 April 1996, p. 10.
22. Chi Haotian, 'Taking the Road of National Defence Modernization Which Conforms to China's Conditions and Reflects the Characteristics of the Times', *Qiushi*, no. 8 (16 April 1996), pp. 8-14, in *FBIS-CHI*, 20 June 1996, pp. 27-35.
23. There is by now a considerable amount of literature on various aspects of conversion. See, for example, Dumas, Lloyd J. (ed.): *The Socio-Economics of Conversion from War to Peace* (Armonk, NY: M.E. Sharpe, 1995); Gansler, Jacques S.: *Defense Conversion: Transforming the Arsenal of Democracy* (Cambridge, MA: The MIT Press, 1995); United Nations, Department of Disarmament Affairs: 'Conversion: Economic Adjustments in an Era of Arms Reduction', *Disarmament Topical Papers*, no. 5 (New York: United Nations, 1991), vols. 1-2. For an extensive bibliography, see vol. 2, pp. 285-305.
24. For example, Chai Benliang: 'Development and Conversion Issues in China', in Bjørn Møller & Lev Voronkov (eds.): *Defence Doctrines and Conversion* (Aldershot: Dartmouth, 1996), p. 54; and idem: 'Conversion in China', in Manas Chatterji, Henk

Jager and Annemarie Rima (eds.): *The Economics of International Security* (New York: St. Martin's Press, 1994), p. 223. In fact, many military enterprises that launched and later expanded civilian production have been motivated primarily by the prospects of greater profits.

25. There is a good deal of literature on this subject. For the best summary and analysis, see Gill, Bates: *Chinese Arms Transfers: Purposes, Patterns, and Prospects in the New World Order* (Westport: Praeger, 1992). See also Shichor, Yitzhak: 'Unfolded Arms: Beijing's Recent Military Sales Offensive', *The Pacific Review*, vol. 1, no. 3 (October 1988), pp. 320-330; Eikenberry, Karl W.: 'Explaining and Influencing Chinese Arms Transfers', *McNair Paper*, no. 36 (Washington: Institute for National Strategic Studies, National Defense University, 1995).

26. The most comprehensive study of Chinese conversion is Brömmelhörster, Jörn & John Frankenstein (eds.): *Mixed Motives, Uncertain Outcomes: Defense Industry Conversion in China* (Boulder: Lynne Rienner, 1997). See also Frankenstein, John: 'The People's Republic of China: Arms Production, Industrial Strategy and Problems of History', in Herbert Wulf (ed.): *Arms Industry Limited* (Oxford: Oxford University Press, 1993), pp. 271-319; idem & Bates Gill: 'Current and Future Challenges Facing Chinese Defence Industries', *The China Quarterly*, no. 146 (June 1996), pp. 394-427.

27. *CTDST*-I, p. 157.

28. More details in Shichor, Yitzhak: 'China's Defence Capability: The Implications of Military-to-Civilian Conversion', *CAPS Papers*, no. 8 (Taipei: Chinese Council of Advanced Policy Studies, 1995).

29. *CTDST*-I, p. 120.

30. *CTDST*-I, pp. 167-176.

31. Gill, Bates & Taeho Kim: *China's Arms Acquisitions from Abroad: A Quest for 'Superb and Secret Weapons'*, SIPRI Research Report, no. 11 (Oxford: Oxford University Press, 1995); see also Kim Taeho: 'The Dynamics of Sino-Russian Military Relations: An Asian Perspective', *CAPS Papers*, no. 6 (Taipei: Chinese Council of Advanced Policy Studies, 1994); and Jencks, Harlan W.: 'Some Political and Military Implications of Soviet Warplanes Sales to the PRC', *SCPS Papers*, no. 6 (Kaohsiung: Sun Yat-sen Centre for Policy Studies, 1991).

32. 'Speech at a Plenary Meeting of the Military Commission of the Central Committee of the CCP (December 28, 1977)', *Selected Works of Deng Xiaoping (1975-1982)* (Beijing: Foreign Languages Press, 1984), p. 94 (hereafter: *SWDXP*-I).

33. 'Streamline the Army and Raise Its Combat Effectiveness (12 March 1980)', *SWDXP*-I, p. 270.

34. The main aggregate sources for China's military expenditures are Folta, Paul Humes: *From Swords to Plowshares? Defense Industry Reform in the PRC* (Boulder: Westview, 1992), pp. 18-23, 216-219; the *SIPRI Yearbooks*; Saito, Tsutomu (Chief, Second Intelligence Division, Bureau of Defense Policy, Japan Defense Agency): 'On China's FY93 Defense Expenditures', *Securitarian* (Tokyo, 1 June 1993), pp. 18-21, in FBIS, *Daily Report Annex: East Asia*, 28 October 1993, pp. 13-16; and Xu Guangyi (ed.): *Dangdai Zhongguo Jundui de Houqin Gongzuo* [China Today: Armed Forces Logistics] (Beijing: Zhongguo Shehui Kexue Chubanshe, 1990), pp. 302-325.

35. 'Reductions of the (official) military budget have probably saved money theoretically as much as 26 billion *yuan*.' See Gurtov, Mel: 'Swords into Market Shares: China's Conversion of Military Industry to Civilian Production', *The China Quarterly*, no. 134 (June 1993), p. 236. However, if the 1980-1985 15 percent military to civilian expenditures ratio is applied to 1986-1990 (an 8.5 percent ratio) the actual 'saving' could be at least three times as high.
36. These and the following data are based on: Hu Ping (research fellow at the China International Strategic Studies Society): 'There Is No Hidden Defense Spending in China—Refuting the "Theory of China As a Military Threat"', *Wen Wei Po* (Hong Kong), Part I, 7 May 1995, p. A2; Part II, 8 May 1995, p. A2; Part III, 9 May 1995, p. A5; Part IV, 10 May 1995, p. A3, in *FBIS-CHI*, 20 June 1995, pp. 23-28. There are numerous detailed statements of this kind.
37. Full text in *FBIS-CHI*, 16 November 1995.
38. For example, Harris, James *et al.*: 'Interpreting Trends in Chinese Defense Spending', in Joint Economic Committee, US Congress (ed.): *China's Economic Dilemmas in the 1990s: the Problems of Reforms, Modernization, and Interdependence* (Armonk, NY: M.E. Sharpe, 1992), pp. 676-684. See also Starr, Barbara: 'China Spends Treble the Official Defence Budget', *Jane's Defence Weekly*, vol. 23, no. 27 (8 July 1995), p. 14.
39. The following section is based on Shichor, Yitzhak: 'Demobilization: the Dialectics of China's PLA Troop Reduction', *The China Quarterly*, no. 146 (June 1996), pp. 336-359. See also Dreyer, June Teufel: 'The Demobilization of PLA Servicemen and Their Integration into Civilian Life', in idem (ed.): *Chinese Defense and Foreign Policy* (New York: Paragon House, 1989), pp. 296-330.
40. 'Streamline the Army', *loc. cit.* (note 33), pp. 269-270.
41. See Tai Ming Cheung: 'The People's Armed Police: First Line of Defence', *The China Quarterly*, no. 146 (June 1996), pp. 525-547.
42. Bickford, Thomas J.: 'The Chinese Military and Its Business Operations', *Asian Survey*, vol. 34, no. 5 (May 1994), pp. 461-474; Joffe, Ellis: 'The PLA and the Chinese Economy: The Effects of Involvement', *Survival*, vol. 37, no. 2 (Summer 1995), pp. 24-43; Valdecanas, Maria Christina: 'From Machine Guns to Motorcycles', *The China Business Review* (Nov-Dec 1995), pp. 14-18.

8 Unification of Divided States in East Asia

BJØRN MØLLER

The world has in recent years seen serious international trouble involving two of its divided states, both of them in East Asia. First came, in the spring of 1996, the intentionally provocative Chinese military manoeuvres in the Strait of Taiwan.[1] Then came the North Korean violations of the cease-fire agreement in the form of a dispatch of troops into the DMZ (Demilitarized Zone), which were, likewise, deliberately provocative, even though they were probably not (as alleged) parts of the preparations for a full-scale attack on the South.[2]

Such events raise several questions that the following paper shall address, albeit only in a sketchy and tentative manner: What do we understand by a 'divided state'? Is a divided state necessarily a problem, i.e. should such states always be (re)united? What mode of (re)unification should be chosen? What are the implications thereof for security and defence policies, and might a defensive restructuring of the armed forces help?

In addressing these pertinent questions, I shall draw on the experience from other states that are either permanently divided or which have been (re)unified, while focusing especially on China.

DIVIDED STATES

In this part I shall analyze at some length the concept of 'divided states', by looking critically at prevalent views on the matter: that states have a historically defined 'appropriate' territory; and/or that criteria of nationality, religion or geopolitics 'objectively' determine their 'proper' borders. None of these claims stand up to a critical analysis, which leads to the inescapable conclusion that it is all rather arbitrary. What can or cannot be regarded as 'divided' is a matter of political choice, since there are neither any 'objective' criteria for what states should look like, nor whether they should be unified or remain divided. Even though this may smack of 'deconstructivism',[3] the author is neither a 'closet deconstructivist' (perish the thought!) nor a partisan of any of the other fashionable approaches to the study of international relations that are sometimes lumped together as 'post-modernist theory'—but rather a diehard supporter of the 'classical approach'.[4]

For the analysis of divided states, however, deconstructivism has some merits, as it focuses attention on the implications of attaching a label such as 'divided' to a political entity. To speak of a 'divided state' is implicitly normative, i.e. it implies that something is wrong with the actual separation into disparate entities and that these ought to be merged into a unified whole. Such claims for unification are neither objectively true nor always obvious. They fall into two different categories: historically based claims for 'righting wrongs', i.e. for reuniting what has been wrongfully divided, and 'ideologically based' claims for uniting what has never actually been united, but is nevertheless alleged to have a legitimate right to be so.

HISTORICAL CLAIMS

The historical claim to unification is the simpler of the two, but it also raises several questions.

First of all, how far back into history should one go? Many territories have successively belonged to different states, implying that more than one could make a historical claim to it.[5] Moreover, the one with the most recent claim is not necessarily in the right, since the acquisition giving rise to the claim may have been wrongful in the first place. This raises the second question, namely what 'wrongful' is supposed to mean when referring to the division of a state. States may be 'cut into pieces', i.e. divided, in at least three ways: by conquest, secession and disintegration.

Armed conquest by means of aggressive wars is now regarded as wrongful, but this view is of a fairly recent vintage. Most of the European states actually acquired their present shape and size via conquest, and territorial aggrandizement through war was regarded as a perfectly legitimate endeavour for states. Perhaps it even represented their very *raison d'être*, in the sense that a state should expand until it reached the limits of its growth potential, i.e. acquired its 'proper size'. War was regarded as the natural means of this perpetual 'force comparison', either in the sense that states fought actual wars to see who won, or in the sense of 'virtual wars' in the form of arms races, competitive alliance-building, etc. Some have even argued that one might understand the expansion of states according to neoclassical economic principles, i.e. that states expand until the 'marginal utility' of further expansion equals the marginal costs thereof, in its turn a function of the 'loss of strength gradient'.[6]

By implication, most of the present borders are the product of (actual or virtual) wars that would today be regarded as impermissible. Logically, most states might thus claim to be 'divided' in the sense of having lost parts previously belonging to them by means that are today regarded as wrongful. Fortunately for international stability, most states do not press such claims, the results of which would be a plethora of border disputes that might either overtask the international legal machinery, or lead to wars. Most states in the 'old world' are saturated, i.e. comfortable with their present size, hence do not regard themselves as divided. Moreover, in Europe a host of institutions (above all the OSCE) are available for settling whatever border disputes may arise.

Not so in large parts of the Third World, where borders were also drawn by conquest, *in casu* by the establishment of colonial rule by various European powers in accordance with their relative strength. Until the middle of the present century, imperialism was regarded (by the colonial powers) as entirely legitimate, with the partial exception of isolated cases of blatant mismanagement (Belgian Congo, for instance). Gradually, however (beginning with the 'Wilsonian principles' after WWI), anti-colonialism became the predominant international norm, which provided the rationale for struggles for national independence.[7] The process of liberation, however, produced new states within borders that had been drawn up according to procedures now held to have been illegitimate, but which were not unlawful at the time. Furthermore, the borders had been drawn according to criteria having little to do with the realities of the new states: who (of the European powers) got there first, and who had the staying power (militarily and otherwise) to keep other European powers out. These borders certainly produced a multitude of what one might regard as 'divided states' and other 'wrongfully divided' political structures with perfectly legitimate historical claims for reunification.[8] Fortunately, however, the OAU (Organization for African Unity) at its 1963 inaugural summit chose to 'put a lid on' the entire matter, i.e. to rule out border alterations by other than peaceful means.[9]

Secession is another common mode of division, which has traditionally been regarded as illegitimate, at least until recently. The international system is heavily skewed in favour of existing states (regardless of how they came into being in the first place), thus placing the burden of proof on the party wanting to secede. However, secession is surely not always wrongful—in which case we would have to speak of Yugoslavia as a wrongfully divided state and deny recognition to Slovenia, Croatia, Bosnia, and Macedonia.[10]

Sometimes secession occurs by mutual consent, in which case the international community simply has to recognize the secession *de jure*—as it happened with the dissolution of the USSR or the 'velvet divorce' of Czechoslovakia. Paradoxically, the label 'divided state' does not seem to apply to such instances of peaceful and amicable division. In other cases, however, it may be applicable, namely when the secession is contested, and the international community thus forced to take sides, as in the break-up of the Yugoslav Federation. The most precise formulation may thus be that secession is sometimes legitimate, sometimes not, but that international law has yet to lay down clear and universally acknowledged criteria of lawful secession.[11]

Disintegration is a third mode of division, yet one to which it is difficult to apply the term 'wrong', as there is no identifiable wrong-doer. 'Deplorable' or 'tragic' may thus be more appropriate characterizations. Disintegration implies that a state simply falls apart as a result of irresistible centrifugal pressures, as has been the case with 'collapsed' or 'failed states'. The pieces resulting from the division-by-disintegration usually do not form viable states any more than the formerly unified entity did. It is thus neither a matter of a state being entirely or partly engulfed by another, nor of one state's being subdivided into several states, but rather of a regress to an antediluvian pre-state stage of a Hobbesian *bellum omnium contra omnes*.¹² If and when the pieces are ever reunited it is through a process of state-building (or re-building) rather than of reunification.

IDEOLOGICAL CLAIMS

Normative (i.e. 'moral' or ideological) claims to unity are even 'fuzzier' than historical ones. They are based on views about how states ought to be, regardless of whether they have ever been so. If states do not conform with these criteria, they are either argued to be 'divided' (entailing a claim to unification), or the contrary claim is raised that they should be so, i.e. carved up according to certain criteria in order to be legitimate.

In modern times, the main source of legitimacy for states has been the ideology of nationalism, implying that states should be nationally homogeneous as well as exhaustive, i.e. all-inclusive. There should thus be an overlap between 'the sentimental nation [and] the functional state', as aptly put by Charles Kupchan.¹³ In the real world, such overlap is often missing, either because nations are subdivided among several states, or because they form part of multinational states. The former case usually gives rise to claims for a merger of previously disparate political entities, such as the small German of Italian principalities in the 19th century. The latter case of 'entrapped' nations tends to produce claims for secession, as happened in the course of the 1848-49 European revolutions, e.g. within the multinational Austro-Hungarian empire.¹⁴ Finally, the two claims may be combined, in the case of entrapped parts of nations wanting to secede in order to become reunited with their 'mother country', as was the case of the Sudeten Germans in the thirties and is today the case of the Bosnian Serbs.

This nationalist ideology, however, begs the question of the appropriate criteria of nationhood: may any group call itself a nation and invoke a right to statehood, or are there objective criteria of nationhood? Are nations, for instance, to be defined by a common language? Or a shared religion? Or a long common history? Or culture? Or by belonging to the same race or other ethnic subset? Or by any combination of some or all of these features?¹⁵ The choice thus seems to be between 'exclusive' and 'inclusive' definitions, the former combining all criteria, thereby producing very small 'nations' and pointing towards a definition of 'nation states' that practically no existing states would meet. Divided states according to this definition would be a very rare phenomenon, even though Korea might still come close to qualifying as such. According to inclusive definitions, on the other hand, individuals are reckoned as belonging to the nation if only they meet one criterion (language, for instance); hence such definitions tend to produce very large (but often very heterogeneous) nations. As a corollary, they allow many states to count as both nation states and as incomplete and divided ones.

In view of the above complexities, it probably has to be acknowledged that there are no objective criteria 'out there', but that nationhood is a matter of perceptions, attitudes and emotional ties, i.e. that nations are 'imagined communities'.[16] However, for this to qualify as a workable definition, it needs also to stipulate a requirement for recognition by others as such a community. For all its merits, however, a definition of nations in such (inter-)subjective terms is not without problems: to allow for too large 'imagined communities' may, for instance, be conflict-prone, at least if the issue is politicized, in which case the 'mother state' may be hard to saturate. There will always be some pressure to bring nationals abroad 'back home', or the 'mother state' may include its 'nationals abroad' in the category of what to defend.

Subsuming religion under the concept of nationality rarely simplifies matters, but even when kept conceptually distinct, the religious factor may complicate already complex problems. If a nation believes its territorial claims to be founded on divine authority, it tends to regard them as unnegotiable. Any state that believes it has received or been promised a piece of territory 'from above' may thus regard itself as 'divided' until it has actually taken possession of all of the promised land. Hence, for instance, the aversion of orthodox jews and the Likud party to any 'land for peace' settlement,[17] which also explains the doubts held by Israel's neighbours about the territorial saturation of the Jewish state.

Even when religious identity is not linked to any particular piece of (promised) land, problems may arise when states see themselves as the natural home of all members of a particular creed, either universally or within a particular region. This is, for instance, the case of the Islamic Republic of Pakistan, the very *raison d'être* of which is to be a (or even *the*) state of all Indian muslims. However, the entire population of Pakistan is dwarfed by the number of muslims living in India, which sees itself as a secular state (even though some want to emphasize political hinduism). As certain regions on the fringes of India are predominantly muslim, the incompatible Indian and Pakistani conceptions of statehood easily produce territorial disputes—as in the case with Jammu and Kashmir that has already triggered two wars. One explanation of this conflict-proneness is that both states see themselves as divided: Pakistan because it does not encompass all the muslim parts of the sub-continent, and India because of the unwarranted, perhaps even 'illegitimate', secession of Pakistan.[18]

The fact that statehood is always defined in territorial terms, i.e. in the form of recognized sovereignty within certain spatial coordinates, implies that geopolitical considerations often enter into the picture. According to (some varieties of) geopolitical reasoning, certain pieces of territory 'naturally' belong together, hence if they are disjoined the state is 'divided'. There does, indeed, seem to be an implicit international norm pertaining to the territoriality of states, namely that states should have what one might call, 'a neat shape and appropriate size'. This is really a pragmatic consideration, based on the view that states should be able to actually control their territory, which may be impossible for states with very 'odd shapes' and/or 'wrong sizes'. For all its pragmatic merits, however, this territorial norm may be deconstructed in the same way as were the above norms.[19]

In actual fact, many of the states that emerged in Africa and Asia as a product of decolonization were born with 'odd shapes and wrong sizes'. The reason was that they inherited the colonial borders, which reflected the European distribution of power in the late 19th century (*vide supra*). Hence, the newly sovereign states were frequently not viable, because they were either too large (compared to their governing capacity), or too ill-defined territorially, or too heterogeneous with regard to nations and ethnics, or all of the above.

The implicit territorial norm further rules out certain territorial arrangements that might otherwise fit the pattern of nationality, i.e. which might allow for the emergence of nation states that might not otherwise be regarded as feasible. For instance, one might come to accept 'patchwork states' in those cases where nations happen to be intermingled—even though such states could surely be reckoned as divided, albeit usually into more than two pieces; or the international community might come to accept (to a greater extent than today) the notion of *terrae nullius*, i.e. territories that are not under the sovereignty of any state.[20]

In favour of loosening the 'neat shape and appropriate size' norm speaks the fact that the world contains a number of territorial anomalies such as enclaves and exclaves—some of which might be regarded as 'divided states', but some of which are perfectly viable—indeed, so much so that it strains the imagination to envision any problems with them. Table 6 sketches some such anomalies, all of which have real-life manifestations.

An exclave (1) is a part of a state which is physically separated from the rest by (part of) another country. Examples thereof are Alaska and the Russian exclave Kaliningrad. An exclave (2) is a variation on the former, where the exclave forms part of an island, the rest of which forms a separate state. Examples are Malaysia and the UK (with Northern Ireland). An exclave (3) is something as common as an island belonging to a mother country. An example is Sicily—or (as China sees it, at least) Taiwan, more about which in due course. Exclaves of type 4 are, likewise, islands, yet with the added twist that one state's island exclaves are intermingled with those of another state (or other states). An example is the intermingling of Greek and Turkish islands in the Aegean Sea—or the competing, intermingled and overlapping claims to the Spratly Islands in the South China Sea[21] (*vide infra*).

An enclave is an entire country which is completely surrounded by another state. Examples include Lesotho (surrounded by South Africa) and the Holy See (surrounded by Italy). A semi-enclave is a country surrounded on three sides by another state, i.e. whose only outlet is to the sea, as is the case of Gambia, for instance. Most problematic of all is the situation of an enclaved exclave, i.e. an

Unification of Divided States in East Asia 163

exclave belonging to one country but completely surrounded by another, as was West Berlin during the Cold War.

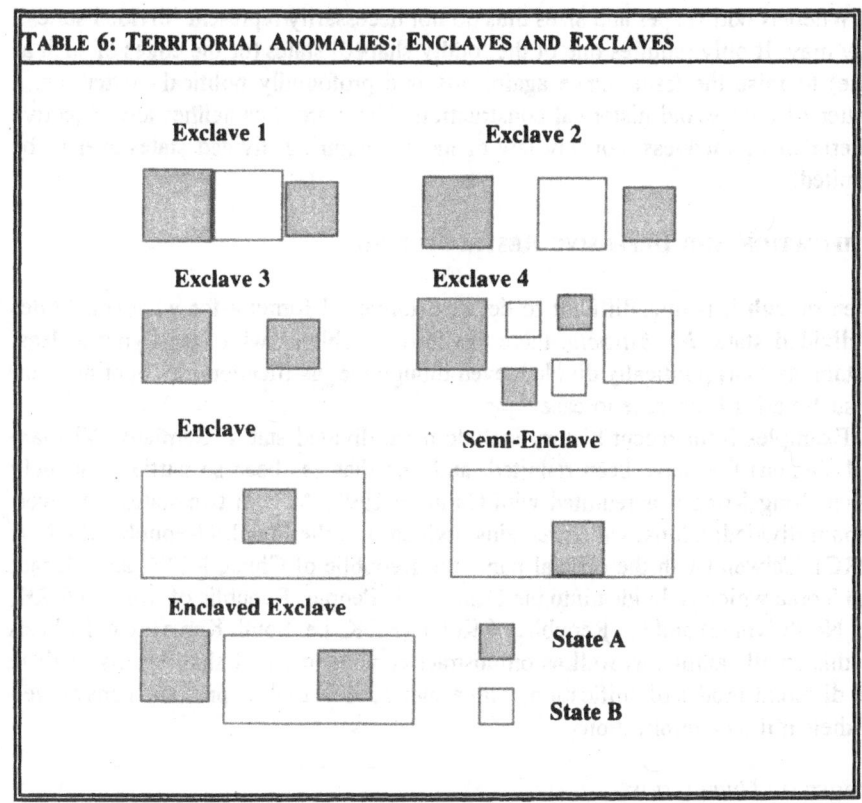

TABLE 6: TERRITORIAL ANOMALIES: ENCLAVES AND EXCLAVES

Some of the above states with exclaves or enclaves are 'divided states' ' in the sense of being physically disunited, but in some cases (Alaska, for instance) this is obviously no problem at all. In other cases, however, it may be a serious problem. It may, for instance, be so for the possible future state of Palestine which will, at best, be divided into two approximate halves (Gaza and all or part of the West Bank). Alternatively, it would obviously be a problem for Israel to be intersected by a 'Palestinian corridor' that might unite the two parts of Palestine. It may also be a problem for Republika Srpska that emerged from the Dayton Agreement to be separated from its 'mother country' (Serbia) as well as having a very far from neat shape.[22]

Solutions to such problems have historically involved the breaking up of 'oddly shaped' states, as it happened to Pakistan with the secession of (what is now) Bangladesh; or the forming of a larger political entity including all three (or more) pieces of the puzzle (as it happened with German unification); or the absorption of the exclave by the surrounding state. In other cases, however, the states involved have learned to live with the anomaly.

Whereas odd shapes and sizes thus do not necessarily represent 'divided states', they may. It only requires one of the 'oddly shaped' states (or the edges of such as state) to raise the issue. Once again, this is a profoundly political matter, i.e. a matter of choice and historical construction. There are thus neither any objective criteria of dividedness, nor any law of nature requiring divided states ever to be reunited.

UNIFICATION AND DEFENSIVE RESTRUCTURING

Even though it is thus difficult to devise a universal formula for what constitutes a 'divided state' *in abstracto*, there are fewer problems with identifying at least certain states as politically divided, even though the justification for counting them as such varies from case to case.

Examples from recent history include three divided states (Germany, Vietnam and Yemen) that have been reunited, and one that has been so partially, namely when Hong Kong was reunited with China in 1997. At least two states, however, remain divided: China, which remains divided into the Peoples Republic of China (PRC), Taiwan (with the official name the Republic of China, ROC), and Macao; and Korea which is divided into the Democratic Peoples Republic of Korea (DPRK, i.e. North Korea) and the Republic of Korea (ROK, i.e. South Korea). On the basis of this small sample, as well as on abstract considerations, I shall briefly analyze the different modes of unification, with a special view to their pros and cons as well as their military implications.

MODES OF UNIFICATION

Accepting, for the sake of the argument, that division is an anomaly that should be corrected, we are left with a choice between several modes of unification, some of which may, of course, be combined.

First of all, there are two modes of unification by military means. Either a state may seek unification simply by conquering the 'missing part', as it was attempted by both sides during the Korean War (1950-53), and as it happened in Vietnam in 1975. Or a state may attempt unification under threat of force, i.e. via intimidation. The means employed for this purpose may resemble those required for deterrence, *in casu* of a would-be secessionist province—as is the case of the mainland Chinese attempts at deterring Taiwan from declaring its independence, more about which in due course.

Secondly, there are (at least) three modes of unification by political means. Peaceful unification may occur by political *fiat*, as it happened on the Arabian

Peninsula in 1990, when North and South Yemen formed a voluntary federation. A slightly more baroque example was the creation of the United Arab Republic in 1958 as a federation of Syria and Egypt, which lasted only until 1961.[23]

It may make sense to subdivide this category into two: voluntary and enforced unification by political *fiat*. In some cases, popular demands may force the government of a part-state to voluntarily negotiate unification, but one can easily image instances of not-quite-voluntary unification treaties. The stronger party (militarily, economically or otherwise) may, for instance, squeeze concessions out of the weaker side by threatening a cut-off of economic support, or by an economic blockade. In such cases, the decision to unify may be a voluntary one in the technical sense, but it is almost indistinguishable from the aforementioned unification by compellence.

Peaceful unification may also take the form of one part-state's absorption of the other, as it happened in Germany in 1990, when East Germany simply ceased to be and was included as several new federal states in the Federal Republic of Germany. Finally, peaceful unification may proceed in the form of a gradual merger that produces a new state structure, as was proposed by Chancellor Kohl and his East German counterpart Modrow during the interregnum period from 1989 to 1990.[24]

In some cases, unification has been the doing of the two part-states alone, while external actors have played an important role in others. Either their acceptance has been a prerequisite for unification (say, if they enjoyed a formal or actual veto over unification, as the USSR did with regard to Germany), or they have served as mediators and facilitators of the process. In Germany, the '2+4' format proved suitable, involving both German states and the four occupying powers, i.e. the Soviet Union, Britain, France and the United States. In Korea, there has long been talk of a 2+2 setting, where the two Koreas would negotiate alongside their respective allies from the Korean War, i.e. China and the United States,[25] and such negotiations finally commenced in December 1997 (see the chapter by Yong Sup-Han in the present volume).

There is also in important difference with regard to the pace of unification. Whereas unification by conquest, compellence, fiat or absorption may be swift, that by gradual merger is, almost be definition, protracted. However, even what is originally conceived, and may start off, as a slow process may accelerate beyond control, as illustrated by the German case. Hence, there may be less to the distinction than meets the eye—also because a seemingly swift unification may merely postpone the problems with 'real' unification, i.e. the 'organic' growing together of the two parts to form an actually cohesive whole.

There are several modes of gradual merger. The difference between them may be one of different end states, or it may be one of sequencing. The different stages of unification may thus be seen either as possible final stations, or as successive steps in the creation of a unified state, i.e. as rungs on an integration ladder.

A special problem is presented by such cases where the two parts, as a matter of principle, do not recognize each other diplomatically, and/or where the level of tension precludes normal relations. This was, e.g., the case of the two Germanies during the coldest of the Cold War, and it remains the case between the two Koreas as well as between two of the three Chinas, i.e. the PRC and Taiwan (*vide infra*). Paradoxically, however, a formal acknowledgment of the actual separation may be a necessary prelude to (re)unification, with the possible exception of the absorption mode. In such cases there may be a need for several preliminary stages, for instance:

- Mutual *de facto* recognition between the two sides, facilitating family reunifications, trade, travel, etc. This was the gist of both the West German *Ostpolitik* of the 1970s and the North Policy pursued by the ROK in the 1990s.[26]
- *De jure* recognition, manifested in the establishment of diplomatic representation. This also implies that inter-state relations will be treated as foreign rather than domestic politics. It also allows for the signing of treaties, say on non-aggression.[27]
- Cross recognition by (significant parts of) the international community, manifested, *inter alia*, in membership of international organizations.[28]

The result will be 'normal' international relations, which may be characterized by amity or enmity, or (more often) a blend thereof. The two states may be each other's competitors, occasionally even enemies, and they may even go to war against each other—but at least they acknowledge each other's existence. It may not be much, but it is something. In such a 'Westphalian setting', states may gradually come to appreciate the need for empathy, if only because the working of such an anarchical system is governed by the security dilemma and the powerful reciprocity principle.[29] States thus respond to each other's every move in a manner that may leave both sides worse off after than before each interactive cycle. Hence the advisability of pursuing only such policies as are acceptable to the respective other side, i.e. which do not provoke a hostile response.

As a reflection of such a maturation of their relationship states may develop what Robert Jervis called a 'security regime', where both sides show restraint in anticipation of reciprocal restraint by their adversaries.[30] Elements of collaboration may thus develop among states that remain adversaries, implying that shared interests are upgraded, even beyond the elementary one of avoiding mutual annihilation. This philosophy has become associated with the notion of 'common security', that was promulgated by the Palme Commission in 1982, and which has recently experienced a renaissance under the term 'cooperative security'.[31]

At some stage in such a process, what Karl Deutsch called a 'security community' will have become a reality, i.e. the states in question will have ceased to regard war as conceivable.³² However, they remain sovereign actors on the international stage, hence the security community remains pluralistic. This will be a very favourable point of departure for a piecemeal amalgamation, i.e. integration. States may either deliberately embark upon this path, as prescribed by federalists, or they may inadvertently find themselves set on such a trajectory as envisaged by functionalists and neo-functionalists. In the latter case, integration will result from functional (e.g. technical and economic) collaboration which gradually 'spills over' into the political field, albeit not automatically.³³ Also the trend toward centralization may be tempered by an application of the principle of subsidiarity.³⁴

The first stage of political amalgamation may be the formation of a confederation, implying a retention of sovereign rights by the merging political units, including the right of secession.³⁵ Typically, certain issue areas are placed under the authority of supranational organs (foreign and defence policy, for instance), while others remain the exclusive domain of the states parties to the confederation. The second stage may be a federation, where the time for secession has passed, but where the constituent parts retain various rights, even though none of them amount to sovereignty.³⁶

At the federation stage, a 'point of no return' has thus legally been passed, but in the rough and tumble of the real world even federations sometimes break up, either by mutual consent or violently, as the Yugoslav example illustrates. Also, there is no guarantee that political integration will ever proceed beyond the federal stage, as illustrated by the United States and the Federal Republic of Germany—neither of which seem likely to ever be transformed into 'ordinary' unitary states. Some do, however, proceed to the third stage of a unified statehood, but some states retain vestiges of their federal past, e.g. in the form of extensive rights for minorities, regardless of their origin. This feature is captured in the term 'consociation', implying a certain division of power among groups, however defined—each with something approaching veto powers over decisions of vital importance.³⁷ The fourth and 'final' stage of statehood is the creation of a unified and centralized state, where everybody is supposed to see themselves primarily as citizens of the state, rather than as belonging to sub-groupings. This may, of course, be combined with extensive protection of minorities, only not in the shape of special political rights.

MILITARY IMPLICATIONS

Whereas unification by conquest and/or intimidation ('compellence') obviously requires substantial offensive capabilities, unification by other means requires the exact opposite, namely a confidence-inspiring and defensive military posture, where neither side is capable of attacking the respective other. Such defensive restructuring of the armed forces, with the aim-point of a non-offensive defence (NOD) is best understood as an application to the military sphere of the aforementioned philosophy of common or cooperative security.[38] To actually abolish offensive capabilities allows a (part-)state to make its defensive intentions perfectly clear to the respective other side, thereby removing the basis for enemy images and creating such mutual confidence as is a precondition for gradual and peaceful unification. What this may mean in concrete terms will differ from setting to setting, but in any case it would have to rule out both invasion and 'compellance' capabilities. Neither should any part-state be in a position to conquer the other, nor should they be able to enforce a unification by threats of air strikes or naval blockades.

Not only will such defensive restructuring facilitate the process of gradual unification, for instance in the form of a confederation leading towards national unity; it will also make the product of this process, i.e. the formation of a unified state, less problematic for the neighbours. In several cases, the armed forces of both parts of a divided country have been directed against the respective other half-state—something that is obviously incompatible with confederation. The military of the GDR was thus directed against the FRG, and vice versa, albeit in both cases embedded within their respective alliances. Had unification proceeded along the confederation-to-federation path (*vide supra*) such offensive schemes would obviously have made no sense whatsoever, whereas strictly defensive plans for territorial defence of the two Germanies would have made eminent sense.

The armed forces of the two Koreas are obviously directed, almost exclusively, against each other. Indeed, the two armies have actually fought a bloody and horribly destructive war against each other, and the post-war period has been characterized by continuous harassment of the South by the armed forces of North Korea—perhaps (but probably not) also by serious preparations for another full-scale war.[39] Should the two Koreas embark upon unification, a defensive restructuring of their armed forces would be absolutely essential, regardless of which version of gradual unification they should adopt. Military measures thus also accompanied the North Policy of the ROK government, starting as early as 1972 with a 'South-North Joint Communique', in which the two sides, 'in order to ease tensions and foster an atmosphere of mutual trust', committed themselves 'not to undertake armed provocations against one another whether on a large or a small scale, and to take positive measures to prevent inadvertent military incidents'. This was followed in 1991/92 by an 'Agrement on Reconciliation, Nonaggression, and Exchanges of Cooperation' and by a treaty establishing a nuclear-weapons-free zone covering the entire peninsula.[40] Furthermore, independent researchers from the ROK and abroad (including the present author and professor Yong Sup-Han) have made proposals for a defensive restructuring (in the form of arms control) that might accompany a resumed North Policy and facilitate unification.[41] Unfortunately, however, the DPRK did not reciprocate, but proceeded with the nuclear programme that was rightly seen as threatening. What might have been the start of a process of gradual unification thus 'went sour'.

The successful unification of two states inevitably implies the merger of two armed forces. Unless accompanied by a substantial disarmament and/or a defensive restructuring, such a merger may well upset a delicate balance-of-power within a region, especially if the two merging states and armies are of comparable strength and if both are significant in comparison with their neighbours.

It is important to get the 'algebra' of unification force comparison right. It is not a question of a simple addition of two armies, but of a much more substantial increase in outwardly directed military strength, often by orders of magnitude, as illustrated in Table 7, where the numbers may represent any measure of military strength. Under certain circumstances, unification might thus upset a regional balance-of-power, either directly or by setting in motions chain reactions: the joining together of A and B would produce a unified state (AB), the military strength of which would represent a latent threat to C, D, E, etc. C might feel especially threatened and decide on an arms build-up that would inadvertently represent a threat to D, who might respond in a manner neither AB, C, E or anybody else could leave unanswered, etc.

TABLE 7: THE ALGEBRA OF UNIFICATION

Military strength			'Domestic' Needs	For 'External Use'
Before unification	A	100	100	0
	B	100	100	0
After unification		200	0	200

In the German case, the rearmament that took place in the 1950s was seen by many observers as precluding reunification, for the simple reason that a unification would produce a military power with which nobody would be comfortable, especially in view of Germany's past.[42] Hence the interest in somehow circumventing the unification-or-rearmament dilemma of the FRG that produced some of the first proposals for defensive restructuring, i.e. NOD.[43] It so happened, of course, that these warnings were not taken seriously, hence Germany remained divided until 1990, and both Germanies became heavily militarized.

By the time of unification in 1989/90, however, some lessons had been learned and it was immediately understood by everybody that Soviet acquiescence with German unification presupposed various accompanying measures to minimize the latent military threat to the Soviet Union that a unified Germany within the Western alliance would represent. Neutralization was debated, yet nobody (perhaps not even the Soviet leaders, their rhetoric notwithstanding) wanted a united and militarily strong Germany in a 'swing position' between East and West. NOD-type restructuring was also recommended by some observers, and the final agreement of the '2+4' negotiations included measures intended to produce the same result by different means: a temporary prohibition on the stationing of NATO forces on former East German soil, a build-down of the combined armed forces to a level below that of West Germany's prior to unification, etc.[44] The subsequent modifications of NATO strategy also helped 'sweeten the pill', since they, among other things, ensured that the 'embedment' of German military power took place in an alliance that was apparently becoming more defensive.[45]

As far as Korea is concerned, the problems posed by a possible unification may be even graver, at least in some respects. While not having anything like the German 'image problem', both Koreas are even more militarized than the two Germanies, hence the simple merger of their two armies would produce a very formidable military power: with close to two million men under arms and a large inventory of heavy and eminently offensive-capable armaments. The only mitigating factor may be the fact that Korea's neighbours (the PRC, Russia and Japan) are all even larger, hence may not be all that concerned. On the other hand, there are no regional institutions that might provide a framework in which to 'embed' Korean unification, not are any likely to appear in the foreseeable future.

LESSONS TO BE LEARNED?

It may be overshooting the mark to argue that there are lessons to be derived from the above. The sample of divided states is simply too small to allow for generalizations, and the countries in the sample too different from each other as well as from the Chinese case to warrant simple extrapolations. What did work for Germany may do so for neither Korea nor China, while what did not work in Europe may do so in Asia. For all its limitations, the comparative perspective may nevertheless have some heuristic value, i.e. it may provide a 'pool of ideas' from which might be drawn some that are applicable to the Chinese case, to which I shall turn in the next section. These ideas include the following:

- Mutual recognition (*de jure* or at least *de facto*) is a precondition of reunification.
- Peaceful unification requires empathy with the respective other's security concerns.
- Threats do not always produce the desired results, whereas conciliatory steps sometimes do.
- Actual reunification is likely to be a protracted process, especially when it is tantamount to a growing together of two different economic, social and political systems.
- External powers may play important roles in unification.
- Even though it is primarily a political process, (re)unification may require

accompanying military steps producing a lowering of tension.
- Defensive restructuring and/or arms control may be relevant for the process of reunification.
- Defensive restructuring and/or military build-down is a prerequisite for avoiding malign external repercussion of unification.

THE CHINESE CASE

China is special in more than one respect: not only is it the world's largest country in terms of population (1.2 billion inhabitants) and one of the very largest with regard to territory (9,561,000 square kilometres). It is also one of the world's great powers in military terms (*vide infra*), one of the five declared nuclear powers, and a permanent member of the UN Security Council.

Finally, but perhaps most importantly, China is a great country with a culture and history stretching back though centuries and millennia. It has traditionally seen itself as 'the Kingdom in the Middle' that was governed by a special 'mandate from heaven'. Culturally as well as politically, China has traditionally felt (and through long periods of history actually been) superior to its neighbours as well as to Europe. Hence the tradition of 'exceptionalism' and isolationism, based on the view that the (Han) Chinese are superior, and non-Chinese are 'barbarians'.[46]

THE DIVISION OF CHINA

Its greatness notwithstanding, China has been divided for long periods of her history, both *de jure* and *de facto*. In the following I shall look briefly at the historical division of the Middle Kingdom, as well as at what might also (but need not) count, for various reasons, as 'division'.

Historical Division

There are two historical sources of the present division:[47] First of all colonialism. Apart from the Portuguese colonial micro-enclave Macao, the last remnants of this was the British crown colony Hong Kong that was returned to China in 1997. It was acquired from the Ch'ing dynasty with the Treaty of Nanking (1842) following one of the most ignoble campaigns in the history of colonialism: the Opium War.

In a certain sense, Taiwan could also be seen as a relict of colonialism, since it (then known as Formosa) was invaded in 1874 by, and in 1895 formally ceded to, Japan in the Treaty of Shimonoseki—after the inhabitants of the island had put up strong resistance and established a short-lived Republic of Taiwan. The island remained under Japanese suzerainty until 1945, when it was returned to the Republic of China which was by that time a rather 'metaphysical' entity. It was represented by the Kuomintang (KMT) government under Chiang Kai-shek which claimed to be the legitimate government of China as a whole, but only controlled Taiwan.

Generally, however, the colonization of China was significantly different from that of Africa, where direct colonial rule was established by the European powers over (largely pre-state) territory. Not so in China, where a state existed (indeed had existed long before the European ones) and where it formally remained in existence throughout the colonial period. From the mid-19th century onwards, however, European powers as well as Japan and the United States established *de facto* rule over various parts of China (enjoying extra-territorial status), yet without depriving the emperor of his *de jure* sovereign power. China was thus in a certain sense divided, i.e. almost 'cantonized'.

Neither the Taiping rebellion (1850-1864) nor the Boxer Uprising (1900) were able to reverse this enforced division. Hence the main goal of the KMT of Sun Yat-sen was not only to liberate but also to unify China, as happened (at least formally) with the 1911/12 revolution. The subsequent 'warlord period' (1916-1927, or even longer), however, represented another of the aforementioned forms of division brought about by *prima facie* internal causes, namely disintegration. The 1930s saw not only attempts by both the communists and the KMT to unify China, but also a return to 'colonial mode' division, when Japan invaded northern China and established the puppet regime of Manchukuo.

The second main source of division was the civil war, which started in 1926/7 with the crushing of the communist-led Canton and Shanghai insurrections,[48] followed by the establishment of communist enclaves in rural China by Mao Zedong and his followers, and the subsequent Long March of 1935.[49] It was interrupted by a period of fragile national unity in the face of a fully-fledged Japanese invasion in 1937, but was resumed in 1945. It only ended in 1949 when the KMT government fled into exile on Taiwan (Formosa), while the Chinese Communist Party (CCP) proclaimed the People's Republic of China (PRC) on the mainland. The superficial resemblance notwithstanding, this division was by no means a secession. On the contrary, both sides have ever since upheld the principle of Chinese unity, each of them claiming to be the true heir to, hence the only legitimate representative of, the 'real' China (*vide infra*).

Metaphysical Division: The 'Real China'

There is virtually no disputing the views that the separation from mainland China of Hong Kong and Macao should count as 'division', and only little controversy over the claim that Taiwan's separation from the rest was somehow wrongful. It is less clear whether this also pertains to other territories that have, at some point in history, been part of the 'Middle Kingdom'—or which should have been. There is further a dispute about the legitimacy of some of what is today *de facto* part of the PRC. Hence there are claims for secession as well as possible claims for expansion.

Unification of Divided States in East Asia 173

- In the former category fall the PRC's territorial claims, some of which have been tabled formally (to the Spratly Islands, for instance), while others are only implicit. In 1992 a very controversial map of China's territorial waters was thus published by the PRC authorities, which seemed to imply future territorial claims against several neighbouring countries. Ever since the 1930s, furthermore, there has been recurrent talk about 'Great China', which would imply a reunification of Inner and Outer Mongolia (under Chinese suzerainty).[50]
- In the latter category falls the question of Tibet, the incorporation of which into the PRC is challenged by most of the rest of the world, but, significantly, not by Taiwan.[51]

Were one to apply criteria of ethnicity, religion or culture, other territories than Tibet might, at some point in the future, also claim their right to secede.[52] Conversely, following the same logic, one might also fear that China might raise the question of 'overseas Chinese', of which there are several millions all over the world, but especially in East Asia: 7.2 million in Indonesia, 5.8 in Thailand, 5.2 in Malaysia, 2.0 in Singapore, 1.3 in Myanmar and 0.8 million in both Vietnam and the Philippines. As these groups tend to 'cluster', thereby sometimes forming local majorities, they might conceivably raise the question of secession, either in the form of a simple claim for national self-determination or with reference to being discriminated against. In such instances, China might possibly want to bring them 'back home'.[53] This has not happened yet, and probably never will, but it might.

DIVIDED CHINA

China could thus be regarded as 'divided' in more than one sense, but I shall focus especially on the historically defined division. The development of the divided China has been determined by several factors, external as well as domestic. In the following, I shall provide a brief, and inevitably superficial, account of the development in the two 'main' Chinas, the PRC and Taiwan, with a special view to the prospects of, obstacles to, and actual policies for unification.

The Cold War

The bipolar conflict of the Cold War set the rules of the game for the two Chinas:[54]

First of all, the US containment policy implied a view of 'Red China' as a Soviet marionette that had to be contained and isolated internationally. This view was reinforced by the experience of the Korean War, where the PRC sent more than 200,000 'people's volunteers' to reinforce North Korea in its war against the UN coalition assembled and led by the USA in support of the ROK. The US saw this as a grand 'puppet show', where Kim Il-sung was a puppet for the red Chinese, in their turn Soviet puppets. Hence the American non-recognition of mainland China, which also implied that the PRC was debarred from the UN, where its seat, including the permanent one in the Security Council, was occupied by Taiwan.

Another consequence was the US support for Taiwan. It was seen as a bulwark against international communism, deserving of all sorts of economic and military support, including an almost unconditional security guarantee entailed by the 1954 mutual defence treaty. As a consequence of bipolarity, most US allies followed their leader in denying recognition to the PRC.

Secondly, notwithstanding its somewhat lukewarm attitude to the CCP of Mao Zedong, the USSR supported the PRC in much the same way the US supported Taiwan. Indeed, Stalin almost went to the point of offering the PRC nuclear weapons. When he went back on his word, however, relations quickly soured, also because of disagreements on the appropriate economic strategy. Gradually (and especially during the Cultural Revolution) the CCP came round full circle to seeing the USSR as the main threat.

This split between the two main communist powers gradually affected the China policy of the United States, yet without fundamentally breaking with the bipolar logic. Having reached the conclusion that the PRC was no subservient puppet to the USSR, the US played the 'China card' as part of a triangular 'linkage' game. It was intended, *inter alia*, to provide an honourable exit from the Vietnam quagmire, as well as to serve as a counterweight to the USSR. Hence the famous 'ping-pong diplomacy' initiated by Nixon and Kissinger, which led to the signing of the Shanghai Communique of 27 February 1972.

This was tantamount to a US recognition of the PRC accompanied by a 'de-recognition' of Taiwan as representing the 'real China' (formalized in 1979), implying that the PRC took over the Chinese seat in the UN (including the Security Council), from both which Taiwan has been debarred ever since.

The PRC

The People's Republic adapted rather flexibly to both isolation and the subsequent international recognition.

Mainland China countered the attempted isolation by cultivating, first, the friendship of the other communist powers (the USSR and Eastern Europe, Cuba, the DPRK and North Vietnam) and, secondly, the new states of what became the Non-Aligned Movement.[55] They apparently sought a leading role in the latter by a combination of communism with *tiermondism*, ideologically underpinned by the theory of the encirclement of the global cities by the global village—in analogy with Mao Zedong's strategy for the Chinese revolution.[56] Hence the establishment of amicable relations with several Third World countries and liberation movements, especially those with a radical quasi-communist ideology.

After the break with the Soviet Union, the PRC took advantage of the bipolar logic by allowing herself to be 'courted' by a United States eager to drive a wedge between the two main communist powers. China also made sure that its subsequent international recognition was accompanied by an ostracism of Taiwan, as implied by the Chinese counterpart of the West German Hallstein doctrine, according to which the PRC was the only legitimate representative of China.

Taiwan

Unsurprisingly, most allies of the United States followed their leader in severing formal ties with Taiwan in the course of the 1970s, as was necessitated by the 'one-China policy' of the PRC (and Taiwan itself). It was either one or the other, but not both. Even though many states maintained good informal ties, and the US continued to support Taiwan (as in the Taiwan Relations Act of 1979), it became increasingly isolated—also because the PRC took a rather rigid view of what types of relations were permissible (*vide infra*).

The only countries left to provide a network were other international 'pariahs', i.e. countries that were, for whatever reason, excluded from the community of states and subjected to embargoes and other sanctions. This 'pariah network' included South Africa, Israel and Chile, who were able to support each other in terms of weapons programmes, etc.[57] However, not only was this a poor substitute for the kind of network to which a 'normal' state has access; it has also been crumbling in recent years with Chile's return to democracy, the fall of apartheid and the Middle Eastern peace process.

While Taiwan initially assigned higher priority to the one-China principle than to international recognition, hence did not seek parallel representation, it has recently shifted priorities. Today Taipei seeks representation, in the UN and other international contexts (e.g. the Olympic Games), as well as bilaterally, in parallel with the PRC, even in a formally subordinate position, i.e. as 'Chinese Taipei' and the like. Taiwan has thus launched a concerted campaign for UN membership, in support of which it has even made generous 'anonymous' donations to various UN and UN-related agencies in the hope of thus opening a 'back door' into the world organization—thus far, however, without success.[58]

Growing Apart or Converging?

Important though these external and legal aspects of division certainly are, the decisive factor is undoubtedly whether the two Chinas are on diverging or converging trajectories, i.e. whether they may be converging inadvertently and almost 'organically'. The answer to this question is less simple than might be expected.

The PRC quickly developed into a totalitarian communist dictatorship with a planned economy. This development was, however, rather 'bumpy', *inter alia* because of the changing relationship with the USSR, both as a role model and as a source of aid. The 'Great Leap Forward' of 1956-58 thus became a leap into an abyss of poverty and starvation—also because the Soviets withdrew their assistance, including blueprints for recently provided technology.

The subsequent 'Great Proletarian Cultural Revolution' of 1967-69, in its turn, became a nightmare for the intelligensia and urban workers, as well as another major backlash for the peasantry. The immediate interregnum period after the death of Mao Zedong was not much of an improvement, dominated by the power struggle between Hua Guofeng and the infamous 'Gang of Four' (Jiang Qing, Wang Hongwen, Yao Wenyuan and Zhang Chunqiao).

In comparison, the subsequent reign of Deng Xiaoping became an era of relative calm and growing prosperity. The 'Four Great Modernizations' were successful in invigorating the economy by means of elements of market mechanisms, combined with a certain relaxation of totalitarian political controls. Still, it remained a very far cry from a pluralistic democracy, as aptly demonstrated by the 1989 Tienanmen massacre.

The death of Deng has not yet produced the disarray that some had predicted, but neither is the political direction of the CCP entirely clear. Neither the emergence of a 'Chinese Gorbachev' representing a new generation of technocrats, nor a greater political assertiveness of the PLA (People's Liberation Army), nor a devolution of political power to semi-autonomous provincial leaders can probably be entirely ruled out.[59]

Unattractive though the PRC's form of governance may be (especially when viewed through Western eyes), it does bear a certain resemblance to the other authoritarian political systems in East Asia—and the gap seems to be narrowing with the progressive decline of the ideological factor in the PRC. Indeed, one might even argue that the traditional confucian values have reasserted their primacy over the communist ones, i.e. that the PRC (including the CCP) has come to emphasize 'China' over 'People's Republic'.

Taiwan has, on the other hand, for most of its existence been an authoritarian dictatorship of a staunchly anti-communist persuasion. While upholding traditional confucian values, it developed into an economically remarkably successful capitalist economy with a growing, and increasingly assertive, middle class. In 1987, the KMT embarked on the road of democratization, reaching the end station in March 1996 with the first entirely democratic presidential elections.[60]

Still, confucian values remain predominant, with the possible implication that the gap may be narrowing between 'communist confucianism' on the mainland and 'capitalist confucianism' on Taiwan, perhaps almost to the point of becoming bridgeable.

CHINESE UNIFICATION (?)

As argued in the introductory parts of this chapter, it is not self-evident that any state claiming to be divided has a legitimate claim to be (re)united. Nevertheless, claims for unification have been raised and when they are so by a power with the stature of the PRC, they cannot simply be ignored. This raises the question how unification might be achieved with a minimum of negative repercussions for the two Chinas as well as for regional and global stability.

International norms (and partly law) have gradually delegitimized colonialism (*vide supra*), hence given China an uncontested right to reclaim her lost parts, i.e. Hong Kong and Macao. A gradual and peaceful re-unification thus took place with Hong Kong in 1997 and Macao is scheduled for the same fate in 1999, in both cases with the promise of a preservation of a 'special status'. Except for foreign and defence policy, Hong Kong is thus to remain largely autonomous, at liberty to preserve her free foreign trade and capitalist system.[61] If Beijing abides by these treaties there will be few problems, at least with regard to international law. If it does not, but either abrogates, disregards or simply violates the treaty, there will be a legal problem, but realistically not much anybody can do about it. It will, however, have serious negative repercussions in Taiwan, where it might even precipitate a unilateral declaration of independence.

International Law

Neither international law nor other sets of international norms have much to say about entities such as Taiwan. Even though Taiwan is treated as a *de facto* state by most other states (including, in many respects, by the PRC), it has no *de jure* status because of the PRC's 'One China' policy. However much one may disapprove of the PRC's reserving for itself the right of reunification by force, and even more of any actual attempt at such forceful reunification, such a venture would thus clearly be lawful. The provocative manoeuvres in March 1996 that were intended to dissuade a democratically elected Taiwanese government from a unilateral declaration of independence were thus, legally speaking, nobody else's business.

Matters would, of course, change if Taiwan were to declare itself independent and apply for UN membership. It is very unlikely that it would admitted (if only because of a likely veto by the PRC), but it is conceivable that a significant number of countries would extend diplomatic recognition to the new state as a tribute to its democratic legitimacy. Just how many would be required for a 'quorum' remains unsettled, but the entire diplomatic situation could certainly become 'messy', especially if the PRC were to retaliate by severing diplomatic relations with states that recognized 'the Republic of China'. This would undoubtedly be a very unstable and unsatisfactory solution, raising the question, what are the alternatives?

The PRC's Unification Policy

The CCP in mainland China has ever since 1949 seen itself as the only legitimate representative of China, a view that has been underpinned by a mythology of the CCP as having fought most decisively against the Japanese invasion—which is actually a fairly accurate representation of history. This self-image as the 'saviours of the nation' was reinforced by the US-Taiwan alliance that seemed to confirm the view of the KMT as traitors to the nation. Taiwan is thus seen in Beijing as a 'renegade province' governed by national traitors, and its eventual return to the PRC is regarded as merely the final step in the liberation of China commenced by Sun Yat-sen.

As a corollary, the PRC has been unwilling to renounce the use of force to reestablish control over Taiwan, also because Beijing regards it as an internal affair (*vide supra*). Generally, China has been very opposed to any infringement of its national sovereignty (say, on human rights issues, or the question of Tibet), even to the point of treating mere discussions about such 'internal affairs' as impermissible. Mainland China has on several occasions resorted to the (apparently carefully calibrated) use of force against Taiwan, e.g. in the 1954 and 1958 crisis over the islands Quemoy and Matsu,[62] as well as on the eve of the March 1996 presidential elections. In all three cases, however, the leaders in Beijing showed considerable restraint, implying that they wanted to 'send signals' rather than actually inflict significant harm.

Principles aside, there has been considerable pragmatism in the mainland Chinese policy vis-à-vis Taiwan. First of all, there has been a certain *de facto* normalization of relations, e.g. in the form of a growing trade between the two Chinas (albeit mostly channelled via Hong Kong), large Taiwanese investments on the mainland, and increasingly frequent Taiwanese visits. Also both countries have established semi-official departments and organizations to handle their interaction: the PRC established the Association for Relations across the Taiwan Straits (ARTS), while Taiwan created a Mainland Affairs Council (MAC) as well as a Straits Exchange Foundation (SEF).[63] The volume of these transactions notwithstanding, however, because of the asymmetrical nature of the relationship nothing approaching interdependence has yet developed that might be peace-furthering and perhaps point towards integration. Taiwan may well have become dependent on China, but the reverse is far from true—at least not on a national scale, even though the 'Taiwan factor' is important for the Fujian and Guangdong provinces.[64] There is, however, little doubt that the relationship is mutually beneficial.

Secondly, Chinese leaders have promised Taiwan a status similar to that of Hong Kong (*vide supra*), something that might be attractive (or at least satisfactory) to the Taiwanese, if only they believe that China will abide by the provisions of such a unification treaty. In that sense, what will happen to Hong Kong in the decade ahead will be an important determinant of Taiwanese unification policy.

Thirdly, China has allowed for certain *de facto* cross recognition, i.e. for the fact that some countries have maintained or established 'almost normal' relations with Taiwan—if only they have 'been discrete' about it, i.e. not behaved as if this were tantamount to diplomatic recognition. On other occasions, however, China has reacted ferociously to seemingly innocent signs of 'creeping recognition'—most recently, in the summer of 1995, to the US granting of a visa to the Taiwanese President, even though he was travelling in his capacity as a private citizen. This was probably due to the, by then impending, presidential elections in Taiwan, which the PRC feared might lead to a declaration of independence.

This ambivalence and vacillation between principles and pragmatism was also audible in PRC President Jiang Zemin's 30 January 1995 'Reunification Speech', where he also explained the PRC's unwillingness to renounce its right to use force:

> It remains the sacred mission and lofty goal of the entire Chinese nation to achieve the reunification of the motherland and promote the all-round revitalization of the Chinese nation ... We must firmly oppose any words or actions aimed at creating 'an independent Taiwan'.... We do not challenge the development of nongovernmental economic and cultural ties by Taiwan with other countries. Under the principle of one China and in accordance with the charters of the relevant international organizations, Taiwan has become a member of the Asian Development Bank, the Asia-Pacific Economic Cooperation forum, and other international economic organizations in the name of 'Chinese Taipei'.... We hold that political differences should not affect or interfere with the economic cooperation between the two sides ... Leaders of Taiwan are welcome to pay visits in appropriate capacities ... We should strive for the peaceful reunification of the motherland, since Chinese should not fight fellow Chinese. Our not undertaking to give up the use of force is not directed against our compatriots in Taiwan but against the schemes of foreign forces to interfere with China's reunification and to bring about the 'independence of Taiwan'.[65]

Taiwan's Unification Policy

Taiwan's views on Chinese unification are even more complex than those of the PRC, if only because of the new democracy. For all its merits, democracy tends to make matters messier, especially when intermingled with nationalism. In the Taiwanese case, there is even a historical dimension to the problem.

The KMT elite that sought refuge on Taiwan was predominantly of Han Chinese origins (and stemming mainly from Northern China), i.e. significantly different from both the indigenous Taiwanese and those Hans that had lived on the island for generations.[66] Both types of Taiwanese might thus view themselves as having been occupied by 'almost foreigners', especially as the KMT's rule over the island was far from democratic until the reforms of 1987 onwards. Secession from China might thus be attractive to some, especially if combined with a dethroning of the

KMT elite, whose main claim to power has been that it represented China as a whole. Conversely, for the KMT to abandon this myth might be tantamount to relinquishing power in Taiwan.[67]

The KMT thus remains committed to the one-China policy, while the Democratic Progressive Party (DPP) is in favour of independence, albeit to be achieved in a gradual and piecemeal fashion.[68] The introduction of democracy obviously entails the risk that the DPP may either win future elections and form the new government, or that a KMT government may become so dependent on their votes in parliament that it may have to give in on its one-China and pro-unification principles.

The present government on Taiwan envisions unification as a three-stage process: in the short term, 'a phase of exchanges and reciprocity', during which neither side should 'endanger each other's security and stability', while interaction should be intensified; in the medium term, 'a phase of mutual trust and cooperation', where direct links should be established in all issue areas; and, in the long term, 'a phase of consultation and unification'.[69] So far, alas, nothing has come out of this wonderful scheme.

WHETHER AND HOW TO UNIFY CHINA?

Whatever might be said (quite a lot in fact) in favour of abandoning unification for good, I shall disregard this otherwise attractive option, as it is very unlikely to be acceptable to the PRC. Accepting, however reluctantly, that unification is thus likely to occur at some stage raises the questions when and how this should take place. Let us recall the modes of unification identified *in abstracto* above in order to analyze their implications for the Chinese case. First, there were two modes of unification by military means:

- Unification by conquest is not yet an option for either China, but it will probably become so for the PRC a decade or so hence, depending on a range of contextual factors, above all on the continued presence or disengagement of the United States (*vide infra*).
- 'Unification by compellence' might seem more promising, since it requires no actual invasion capabilities, but might conceivably be undertaken by means of aircraft and/or surface-to-surface ballistic missiles that are already in the arsenal. Alternatively, China might seek to starve Taiwan into submission through a naval blockade imposed by means of its growing fleet of submarines, obsolete though they may be.[70]

Both of these military options, however, suffer from the drawback that victory would annihilate a good deal of the spoils. An actual war of conquest would inevitably destroy a significant part of Taiwan's accumulated wealth. More importantly, any involuntary reunification, and especially a brutally enforced one, would undoubtedly scare off foreign investors, hence deprive the new province of much of its present attraction. Finally, upon reunification China would assume control of an unruly population that would by then have grown accustomed to the democratic rules of the political game and have created a powerful civil society. Retaining control would thus call for quite harsh repressive measures, to which the rest of the world would undoubtedly react unfavourably—thereby further reducing the economic value of Taiwan.

Second, there were three modes of unification by political means:

- Unification by political fiat only seems conceivable in the voluntary mode on the precondition that the PRC first undergoes a rather profound democratization. While certainly conceivable, at present this does not seem likely at all. Enforced unification, on the other hand, will be practically indistinguishable from the aforementioned one by compellence, suffering from all the same drawbacks.
- Unification by absorbtion seems very unlikely to happen the way it did in Germany (or as it might in Korea) for the simple reason that life in Taiwan is more attractive than in most of the PRC, whereas in the German case it was the other way around. Except for the aforementioned unlikely eventuality of Chinese democratization, it thus strains the imagination to envision the citizens of Taiwan demanding a 'return to China'.
- Unification by gradual merger thus seems to be the most promising mode of unification, bringing us to an investigation of what its successive stages might mean for China, and especially for Taiwan.

The present stage being one of deliberate non-recognition, the preliminary stages would consist of the establishment of 'normal' relations between the two Chinas:

- Mutual *de facto* recognition would seem quite possible, based on a simple extrapolation from present trends. Direct travels might be permitted, entry visas granted freely, etc.
- Cross-recognition by other states, with the tacit consent of the PRC, would probably precede the formal normalization of relations between the two Chinas. It could involve UN membership for Taiwan and the establishment of bilateral diplomatic relations with a growing number of states.
- *De jure* recognition would be more problematic, especially if seen by the PRC as tantamount to 'losing face'. Still, in the present author's opinion, it is an indispensable ingredient of normality, hence a necessary prelude to embarking upon the path to unification. One might hope that a tampering with names might suffice for face-saving, say by Taiwan's abandoning the name 'Republic of China' in favour of the 'Chinese Taipei'.

The resultant establishment of normal state-to-state relations between the two Chinas might, in its turn, evolve through the aforementioned three stages of unmitigated hostility via a security regime to a security community. It does, however, seem quite conceivable that this would be a very short path, especially if there is agreement on eventual reunification as the goal. In fact, a PRC renunciation of the use of force might almost suffice.

The next stage might then be a confederation, in which Taiwan would retain its right to secede—a right that would become increasingly hypothetical as a reflection of growing interdependence. The next step might be a federation, in which Taiwan would retain considerable autonomy, but no sovereign powers or right of secession, i.e. a 'Hong Kong status'. Whether it would be advisable to ever proceed beyond this stage to the creation of a unitary state (whether consociated or centralized) seems debatable, simply because of China's immense size and diversity. A federal structure might be preferable, not only for mainland China-Taiwan relations but also for relations among the mainland provinces.

Chinese Unification and Defensive Restructuring

A defensive restructuring on both sides of the Taiwan Straits will be a valuable element in the above strategy for gradual unification, albeit more with regard to the process than to the product.

- It will be important during the 'normalization phase', if only because the general rules for international relations would then be applicable to PRC-Taiwan relations, including the unlawfulness of use, or threat of use, of force. A strictly defensive strategy and posture would be the logical corollary of this.
- It will remain important after normalization for the establishment of a security regime, pointing forward to a security community. The switch to defensive military postures on both sides would be a significant contribution to a regime intended to regulate behaviour so as to make is less conflict-prone and stable, as in a security regime; and they would be an indispensable ingredients of a security community.
- Defensiveness will be essential for the confederation phase, when political powers are to be gradually merged, including the military establishments. For the two parties to a confederation to continue to view each other as enemies is inconceivable.

Even after unification (albeit not so much *because of* unification) the maintenance of a defensive posture will be important with a view to preventing an arms race in East Asia that could be very unpleasant and detrimental to (the unified) China's security. This consideration, however, carries less weight for China than for Korea, simply because the addition of Taiwan's military strength to that of China would make less of a difference than would a merger of the armed forces of the two Koreas.

To argue in favour of defensive restructuring, however, begs the question of what this might entail, especially in light of the present, rather defensive, strategies and military postures of both Chinas. If one could freeze the present situation, it might well be sufficient, but this is hardly an option. What matters is to prevent things from getting any worse.

THE MILITARY SITUATION

Presently China does not have the military capabilities required for a full-scale invasion of Taiwan—nor is Taiwan, of course, capable of invading the mainland. To do so would require a much longer range of land-based aircraft and/or the acquisition of aircraft carriers, as well as a considerable expansion of amphibious capabilities.[71] This is a fairly stable situation, where neither side has anything to gain from starting a premeditated war of aggression and conquest. It almost corresponds to a situation of 'mutual defensive superiority', as described by proponents of non-offensive defence.[72] It is captured in the following 'pseudo-formula', where O stands for offensive and D for defensive strength, C for China and T for the Taiwan:

$$D^C > O^T \ \& \ D^T > O^C$$

The defensive strength of China is thus superior to the offensive strength of Taiwan, and vice versa. Factoring in the US military power only makes this stalemated situation even more stable, as the US would, at most, support Taiwan if it were to be attacked by the PRC, but under no circumstances assist in an attack against the mainland. In fact, the Taiwan Relations Act of 1979 stated as much in rather unequivocal terms:

> It is the policy of the United States ....
> (4) to consider any effort to determine the future of Taiwan by other than peaceful means .... a threat to the peace and security of the Western Pacific and of grave concern to the US.
> (5) To provide Taiwan with arms of a defensive character...[73]

The amended formula would be as follows (with U standing for the USA):

$$D^C > O^T \ \& \ D^{T+U} > O^C$$

The defensive strength of China is thus superior to the offensive strength of Taiwan (without US support), while the combined US-Taiwanese defensive strength would surpass China's offensive power. Since both Chinas are probably aware of this situation, neither Beijing nor Taipei probably has any incentives to launch a preventive war or a pre-emptive attack. There remains some asymmetry, however, since China would 'merely' lose such a war in the sense of not attaining its objective, whereas Taiwan would stand to 'lose in a big way', were the government in Taipei foolish enough to attack.

MILITARY TRENDS

Things may be changing, however. Even though Chinese defence expenditures are shrouded in secrecy, most observers agree that they have been growing steadily since 1989—after a similarly steady decline through the 1980s. The defence production potential is, likewise, considerable. It may, indeed, have been strengthened by the special Chinese form of 'conversion' implemented during the 1980s, which implied the maintenance of an undiminished mobilization base. For further details, see the paper by Yitzhak Shichor in the present volume.

At least part of this build-up could be seen as a grasp for long-range power projection capabilities. It thus includes longer-range aircraft, ballistic missiles and what may eventually become (but is not yet) a blue water navy.[74] Also, China has been steadily improving her nuclear capabilities that might be used for intimidation and compellence, albeit not really for invasion or other forms of attack.[75]

The Chinese defence doctrine is not entirely clear. Even though the old, quite defensive, 'people's war' doctrine has not been officially abandoned, it has been significantly amended. Under the new label of 'people's war under modern conditions' or 'active defence' it now envisages a greater role for the air force and navy, a partial professionalization of the PLA, a shift of emphasis from in-depth to forward defence, and from total war to limited warfare.[76]

Eventually, China might gain the actual capability of conquering Taiwan, without thereby even violating international law, unless the Taiwanese had declared their independence before the attack, and had received international recognition. Even in that case, however, China could simply exercise her veto powers in the Security Council in order to block international sanctions, or any (extremely unlikely) repetition of the Desert Storm enterprise by the United Nations. In the extremely unlikely situation that a coalition should be assembled (under UN auspices, or otherwise) to evict China from Taiwan, China would still hold the nuclear trump card, making it extremely unlikely that anybody would want to get involved. The Taiwanese people would have the sympathy of the world community, but very little else.

This hypothetical scenario illustrates the importance of some prophylactic steps, especially since the military balance between the two Chinas is very unfavourable for Taiwan—albeit not as unfavourable as a simple comparison of country or population size might lead one to expect. In view of the PRC's refusal to commit itself not to attack, Taiwan certainly has a defence problem. (For an elaboration see the paper by Chen-yi Lin). As far as possible remedies are concerned, three such measures immediately spring to mind to which Taiwan might resort.

Taiwan might, of course, go nuclear in order to be able to deter a Chinese attack. However, the nuclear option has very little to say for it, even though it was apparently contemplated during the 1970s. It would be expensive (although perhaps not prohibitively so); and to implement it might damage the new-born democracy, thereby also depriving Taiwan of international sympathy. Furthermore, Taiwan has foresworn the option (e.g. by pledging to abide by the NPT Treaty, even though as a non-state it cannot formally become a signatory);[77] and to renege on this obligation would further damage Taipei's international image—indeed, it might even bring about international sanctions or military interventions in the name of counter-proliferation.

Alternatively, Taiwan might seek powerful allies, whose combined strength could deter China. Most obviously, Taipei could seek to reforge its former relationship with the United States, but another option might be to forge new ties—say with other Asian countries fearful of the Chinese military build-up (e.g. the ASEAN states, Japan, and/or South Korea). The obvious attractiveness of this option is, unfortunately, not matched by any realistic prospects of being implemented. Other states might have to sacrifice a profitable and strategically important relationship with mainland China for the sake of a Taiwan that, in comparison, has little to offer. It strains the imagination to envision the US, Japan or European states doing so, and it is hard to imagine why the ASEAN states would want to. Even if they did, their combined strength would not suffice for a military deterrence of China.

Finally, Taiwan might try to dissuade (as opposed to deter) China by making the present 'division' more attractive (or at least acceptable) to the leaders in Beijing. A modified version of this strategy might be to combine elements of deterrence with 'appeasement' measures, thus making the status quo appear acceptable and its alternatives unappealing. Such 'appeasement' of the PRC should be achievable by means of a defensive military posture, in principle without any sacrifice of national security.

Ideally, this would be a bilateral process where both Chinas built down their offensive capabilities—or, even better, a regional one, where a 'defensive regime' would be established for East Asia as a whole. Realistically, however, the question may be how Taiwan is to solve its defence problem without provoking China into an attack. I shall, briefly and tentatively, sketch some ideas for these three scenarios, beginning with the unilateral option. In this respect, I shall completely disregard as irrelevant the unilateral option for the PRC. Not because China is inherently offensive (far from it, in fact), but because the present problem is the future attack capability of China vis-à-vis Taiwan, not vice versa.

THE UNILATERAL OPTION

Taiwan already spends a lot on her military defence—as small countries with much larger and partly hostile neighbours tend to do (viz. Israel, Pakistan). To simply spend more does not seem to be an option, also because it would tend to undermine Taiwan's greatest asset, namely its higher standard of living and the accompanying freer lifestyle.

Generally, the Taiwanese national defence doctrine seems quite in line with NOD recommendations. It is, for instance, based on an acknowledgement of the security dilemma, and actually uses the label 'defensive defence' as illustrated by the following formulation from the *1993-94 Defence Report*:

> The main objective of national defense is to protect the national security from being violated and threatened. In the process of pursuing, it is impossible for any given country to obtain absolute safety, because as soon as one country obtains absolute safety, other neighbouring countries around it would conversely have a feeling of absolute unsafety ... the concept of our armed forces buildup has been transformed from the strategy of 'offensive defensive' to 'defensive defense'.[78]

The missions of all four branches of the armed forces are, likewise, quite defensive, which is reflected in a predominantly defensive military posture:[79] a high percentage of reserves to active armed forces; a strictly conventional posture;a clear emphasis on anti-invasion and counter-mobility force elements such as fighter aircraft and ground-based air defence, coastal artillery, mine warfare vessels and anti-tank weapons; and a low priority given to (counter-)offensive force elements such as long-range strike aircraft (fighter-bombers, for instance), surface-to-surface ballistic missiles, and amphibious forces.

The implication seems to be that there is little Taiwan can do in material terms to allay (hypothetical) Chinese fears. However, what she can do is, first of all, to present this as a principled choice (as in the quote above). Secondly, Taiwan might invite the USA to promise (discretely) some reciprocation of Chinese military restraint, which brings us to the second option, to which I shall return shortly.

Defensiveness is no panacea. Because of the size difference, it would be foolish to expect even the most effective and strictly defensive defence on the part of Taiwan to suffice for thwarting a concerted Chinese attack a decade hence, for instance. On the other hand, offensive or counter-offensive capabilities would not really help remedy this deficiency. Even though the KMT has previously clung to the myth of the armed liberation of the mainland, the time has long since passed when this could be taken seriously. At most, Taiwanese forces (aircraft and missiles) might be able to retaliate (partially) to Chinese strikes, which would probably only lead to counter-retaliation.

More importantly, to desperately cling to the notion of (more than tactical or operational-scale) counter-offensives might give mainland China a pretext for attacking. To be strictly and unmistakably defensive, on the other hand, places the onus of aggression on the PRC—with all the possible implications of UN or (perhaps more realistically) unilaterally imposed US sanctions such as a withdrawal of MFN (Most Favoured Nation) status. Very hypothetically, an attack might even be met with a UN resort to 'article 42' counter-measures as means to restore the sovereignty and territorial integrity of Taiwan—something that would, of course, presuppose that Taiwan had been internationally recognized prior to the attack.

BILATERALISM OR TRILATERALISM

A bilateral defensive restructuring of the two Chinas would certainly be valuable. Realistically, however, there is not much Taiwan could offer that would make such a process attractive to the PRC. For this a third party is needed. Because of the size difference, an 'equalizer' would be extremely valuable. Not an unconditional ally of the weaker side, but a conditional and partial one, whose assistance could only be counted upon in the eventuality of an unprovoked attack. This is where the United States becomes important for the security of Taiwan.

The Taiwan Relations Act quoted above is a good point of departure, by stating (albeit somewhat equivocally) that an attack against Taiwan will meet with a US response, but also that the US will only provide Taiwan with means of defence. It would probably be counter-productive to clarify these commitments which appear to be as clear as may be required. Deterrence (or dissuasion) is, after all, 'in the eyes of the beholder', i.e. of the party to be deterred, hence may actually benefit from a certain amount of unpredictability.

What the United States might further do is to provide 'carrots' to go with the 'stick', i.e. some forms of rewards to the PRC for peaceful behaviour. The aforementioned MFN status is an important non-military 'carrot', but one could also think of military carrots, i.e. US measures to strengthen Chinese security. Conventional and nuclear 'detargeting' of China would help as would a deliberate abstention from coming within aircraft, cruise missile or gun range of the Chinese coast with major surface combatants (especially aircraft carriers) in peacetime. This would be tantamount to unilateral confidence-building measures just as it would actually limit US capabilities for offensive action against the PRC. Since the US has no intentions of attacking anyhow, the costs would be negligible.

The question immediately springs to mind what the US should then do in another situation like that of March 1996. To do nothing would obviously be tantamount to signalling disengagement, which might lead the PRC to believe that an actual attack would be unopposed. On the other hand, to deploy aircraft carriers in (or at the entry to) the Taiwan Strait (as a form of 'large-scale gunboat diplomacy') might be seen as provocative by Beijing, perhaps even as an offensive threat that would call for reciprocal steps. An ominous spiral of escalatory moves might conceivably result, which just might get out of control, i.e. lead to war, especially as the two giants have much less experience with each other's crisis behaviour than the USA and the Soviet Union gradually accumulated through the Cold War. Some have argued in favour of a 'routinisation' of what would be typical crisis behaviour,[80] which would speak in favour of a regular US presence in the Taiwan Strait—with all its negative implications for the establishment of peaceful relations. It may, however, be possible to combine peacetime with crisis stability by means of a regular (i.e. not permanent, but frequent) US presence in the Straits with such vessels as possess no (or very limited) offensive capabilities, but which nevertheless signal a continued engagement, e.g. cruisers, destroyers or even frigates, but without aircraft carriers.

Agreements such as the above might, of course, be formally negotiated and duly codified, but it may be more realistic to approach the problem in an 'informal arms control' mode,[81] i.e. via tacit understandings between the two Chinas, with the USA in the role of a silent partner.

THE MULTILATERAL SOLUTION

The best of all solutions would be to embed defensive restructuring-*cum*-Chinese unification in a wider, multilateral framework. This might, indeed, be the best way of averting the aforementioned region-wide arms race that might otherwise erupt. Relevant participants in such a multilateral scheme covering North-East Asia would be the PRC, Taiwan, the United States, Russia, Japan, the DPRK and the ROK—with the ASEAN states as well as India attending as associate members or observers. One might also want to include Australia (and perhaps New Zealand) who would probably be quite eager to join.

Formal, negotiated arms control is hampered by the multipolar setting, where 'parity' makes no sense and other numerical formulas are difficult to apply. Also the relevant area of application will be hard to define. This leaves us with informal arms control approach (also known as 'coordinated unilateralism') as the most promising avenue of implementation. It would imply a combination of information exchange and consultations with the exercise of deliberate restraint by all parties in anticipation of reciprocal behaviour by the others (for concrete suggestions, see the paper by Owen Greene). This would be tantamount to a security regime which might, in the fullness of time, be codified in formal agreements.

For all their attractions, informal understandings have their limitations. As a longer-term perspective, therefore, it will be valuable to formalize such agreements as well as to institutionalize the implied cooperation. Even though 'the Asian way' may imply an unfavourable attitude towards institutions, the latter do provide greater predictability and stability—which may be especially important as far as China is concerned. One way of institutionally 'tying China into the international system', as Gerald Segal puts it, might be to combine regional institutionalization with a more prominent regional representation (i.e. a 'higher profile') of the PRC in global fora, such as the UN, G-7, etc.[82]

CONCLUSION

We have thus seen that the issue of Chinese unification is theoretically challenging. Depending on the interpretation of the Chinese 'from division to reunification' discourse, one might see a future unification of Taiwan with mainland China as either the completion of a historical process of decolonization, or as one step in a long-term expansion.

The issue of Chinese unification is, furthermore, politically challenging, not only because of China's geographical, political and military size, but also because it is a question of uniting political entities belonging to different systems. It remains to be seen whether this can happen peacefully or whether it will take a war to do so. As a peaceful reunification would be much preferable to one by war, it is important to analyze the preconditions and modalities of such a hypothetical unification process. Even though political and economic measures will probably be the most important ones, they will have to be accompanied by appropriate military steps, for which purpose a defensive restructuring of the armed forces seems to hold some promise.

NOTES

1. On the military aspects of the crisis see, for instance, *Jane's Defence Weekly*, vol. 25, no. 10 (6 March 1996), p. 26; *ibid.*, no. 11 (13 March 1996), p. 11; *ibid.*, no. 12 (20 March 1996), pp. 17-18; *ibid.*, no. 14 (3 April 1996), p. 4.
2. On the North Korean movement of troops into the DMZ, see *Jane's Defence Weekly*, vol. 25, no. 16 (17 April 1996), p. 27. The allegations of attack preparations stem from a defected North Korean pilot (*The Guardian Weekly*, 2 June 1996, p. 15). What might support these allegations was the redeployment of aircraft closer to the DMZ, reported in *Jane's Defence Weekly*, vol. 25, no. 14 (3 April 1996), p. 3. For an alternative explanation of the pattern of North Korean military activities as mere harassment, see Kang, David C.: 'Preventive War and North Korea', *Security Studies*, vol. 4, no. 2 (Winter 1994-95), pp. 330-364.
3. Wendt, Alexander: 'Anarchy is What States Make of It: The Social Construction of Power Politics', *International Organization*, vol. 46, no. 2 (Spring 1982), pp. 391-425. See also Vasquez, John A.: 'The Post-positivist Debate: Reconstructing Scientific Enquiry and International Relations Theory After Enlightenment's Fall', in Ken Booth & Steve Smith (eds.): *International Relations Theory Today* (Cambridge: Polity Press, 1995), pp. 217-240; George, Jim: *Discourses of Global Politics: A Critical (Re)Introduction to International Relations* (Boulder, CO: Lynne Rienner, 1994). For a critique see Østerud, Øyvind: 'Antinomies of Postmodernism in International Studies', *Journal of Peace Research*, vol. 33, no. 4 (1996), pp. 385-

390.
4. The best example is probably Bull, Hedley: 'International Theory. The Case for a Classical Approach', *World Politics*, vol. 18, no. 3 (April 1966), pp. 361-377.
5. Murphy, Alexander B.: 'Territorial Ideology and International Conflict: The Legacy of Prior Political Formations', in Nurit Kliot & Stanley Waterman (eds.): *The Political Geography of Conflict and Peace* (London: Belhaven Press, 1991), pp. 126-141.
6. Gilpin, Robert: *War and Change in World Politics* (Cambridge: Cambridge University Press, 1981), pp. 106-155 & *passim*; Boulding, Kenneth: *Conflict and Defense* (New York: Harper & Bros. 1962), chapters 12-13.
7. Crawford, Neta: 'Decolonization as an International Norm; The Evolution of Practices, Arguments, and Beliefs', in Laura W. Reed & Carl Kaysen (eds.): *Emerging Norms of Justified Intervention* (Cambridge, MA: AAAS, 1993), pp. 37-62; Emerson Rupert: *From Empire to Nation. The Rise to Self-Assertion of Asian and African Peoples* (Boston: Beacon Press, 1960), pp. 295-359. See also Ofuatey-Kodjoe, W.: 'Self-Determination', in Oscar Schachter & Christopher C. Joyner (eds.): *United Nations Legal Order*, vol. 1 (Cambridge University Press, 1995) pp. 349-389.
8. Ayoob, Mohammed: *The Third World Security Predicament. State Making, Regional Conflict, and the International System* (Boulder: Lynne Rienner, 1995); Goor, Luc van de, Kumar Rupesinghe & Paul Sciarone (ed.): *Between Development and Destruction. An Enquiry into the Causes of Conflict in Post-Colonial States* (Houndmills, Basingstoke: Macmillan, 1996).
9. Gomes, Solomon: 'The OAU, State Sovereignty, and Regional Security', in Edmond J. Keller & Donald Rothchild (eds.): *Africa in the New World Order* (Boulder: Lynne Rienner, 1996), pp. 37-51.
10. Ramet, Sabrina P.: *Nationalism and Federalism in Yugoslavia, 1962-1991*, 2nd edition (Bloomington, Indiana University Press, 1992); Wiberg, Håkan: 'Divided States and Divided Nations as a Security Problem: The Case of Yugoslavia', *Working Papers*, no. 14 (Copenhagen: Centre for Peace and Conflict Research, 1992).
11. Halperin, Morton & David J. Scheffer: *Self-Determination in the New World Order* (Washington, D.C.: Carnegie Endowment, 1992); Müllerson, Rein: *International Law, Rights and Politics. Developments in Eastern Europe and the CIS* (London: Routledge, 1994).
12. Zartmann, William I. (ed.): *Collapsed States. The Disintegration and Restoration of Legitimate Authority* (Boulder: Lynne Rienner, 1995); Herbst, Jeffrey: 'Responding to State Failure in Africa', *International Security*, vol. 21, no. 3 (Winter 1996/97), pp. 120-144.
13. Kupchan, Charles: 'Introduction: Nationalism Resurgent', in idem (ed.): *Nationalism and Nationalities in the New Europe* (Ithaca: Cornell University Press, 1995), p. 2.
14. Hobsbawn, E.J.: *Nations and Nationalism Since 1780. Programme, Myth, Reality*. 2nd, revised edition (Cambridge: Cambridge University Press, 1992); Seaton-Watson, Hugh: *Nations and States. An Enquiry into the Origins of Nations and the Politics of Nationalism* (London: Methuen, 1977), pp. 89-192; Keating, Michael: *State and Regional Nationalism. Territorial Politics and the European State* (Hemel Hempstead: Harvester Wheatsheaf, 1988), pp. 25-120.

15. See, for instance, Gellner, Ernst: *Nations and Nationalism* (London: Basil Blackwell, 1983); Anderson, Benedict: *Imagined Communities. Reflections on the Origins and Spread of Nationalism* (London: Verso, 1991); Brass, Paul: *Nations and Nationalism. Theory and Comparison* (London: Sage, 1991); Kellas, James G.: *The Politics of Nationalism and Ethnicity* (Houndmills, Basingstoke: Macmillan, 1991); Wæver, Ole, Barry Buzan, Morten Kelstrup & Pierre Lemaitre: *Identity, Migration and the New Security Agenda in Europe* (London: Pinter Publishers, 1993); Iivonen, Jyrki (ed.): *The Future of the Nation State in Europe* (Aldershot: Edward Elgar, 1993); Griffiths, Stephen Iwan: *Nationalism and Ethnic Conflict. Threats to European Security* (Oxford: Oxford University Press, 1993).
16. Anderson: *op. cit.* (note 15).
17. Sandler, Shmuel: *The State of Israel, the Land of Israel. The Statist and Ethnonational Dimensions of Foreign Policy* (Westport, Connecticut: Greenwood Press, 1993); Evron, Boas: *Jewish State or Israeli Nation?* (Bloomington: Indiana University Press, 1995).
18. Ganguly, Sumit: *The Origins of War in South Asia. Indo-Pakistani Conflicts Since 1947* (Boulder, CO: Westview Press, 1994); Juergensmeyer, Mark: *Religious Nationalism Confronts the Secular State* (Delhi: Oxford University Press, 1993), pp. 78-109 & passim. On India's problems with managing diversity see Kohli, Atul: *Democracy and Discontent. India's Growing Crisis of Governability* (Cambridge: Cambridge University Press, 1990); Chatterjee, Partha: 'History and the Nationalization of Hinduism', in Vashuda Dalmia & Heinrich von Stietencron (eds.): *Representing Hinduism. The Construction of Religious Traditions and National Identity* (New Delhi: Sage, 1995), pp. 103-128; Chadda, Maya: *Ethnicity, Security and Separatism in India* (Delhi: Oxford University Press, 1997), pp. 49-77 & passim. For an overview see Rupesinghe, Kumar & Khawar Mumtaz (eds.): *Internal Conflicts in South Asia* (London: Sage, 1996).
19. The 1933 Montevideo Convention on the Rights and Duties of States thus laid down four criteria of statehood, including 'a defined territory' and governability. See Shaw, Malcolm N.: *International Law*, 3rd Edition (Cambridge: Cambridge University Press, 1991), pp. 138-142. See also Väyrynen, Raimo: 'Territory, Nation State and Nationalism', in Iivonen (ed.): *op. cit.* (note 15), pp. 159-179; Weiss, Thomas G. & Jarat Chopra: 'Sovereignty Under Siege: From Intervention to Humanitarian Space', in Gene M. Lyons & Michael Mastanduno (eds.): *Beyond Westphalia? State Sovereignty and International Intervention* (Baltimore: John Hopkins University Press, 1995), pp. 87-114; Walker, R.B.J.: *Inside/Outside: International Relations as Political Theory* (Cambridge: Cambridge University Press, 1993). In geopolitics see Tunander, Ola, Pavel Baev & Victoria Ingrid Einagel (eds.): *Geopolitics in Post-War Europe. Security, Territory and Identity* (London: Sage, 1997); Tuathail, Gearóid α.: *Critical Geopolitics* (London: Routledge, 1996).
20. Shaw: *op. cit.* (note 19), pp. 156-166.
21. Valencia, Mark J.: 'China and the South China Sea Disputes', *Adelphi Paper*, no. 298 (1995).

22. For the text of the Dayton Agreement, see *Review of International Affairs* (Belgrade), vol. 47, no. 1041 (15 February 1996), *passim*. On the 'territorial history' of ex-Yugoslavia see Carter, F.W. & H. T. Norris (eds.): *The Changing Shape of the Balkans* (London: UCL Press, 1996).
23. On Yemen see Braun, Ursula: 'Yemen: Another Case of Unification', *Aussenpolitik*, vol. 43, no. 2 (2nd Quarter 1992), pp. 174-184. On the UAE see Goldberg, Joseph E.: 'United Arab Republic (UAR)', in Bernard Reich (ed.): *An Historical Encyclopedia of the Arab-Israeli Conflict* (London: Aldwych Press, 1996), p. 523.
24. On the unification process see Glaeßner, Gert Joachim & Ian Wallace: *The German Revolution of 1989. Causes and Consequences* (Munich: Berg, 1992); Heisenberg, Wolfgang (ed.): *German Unification in European Perspective* (London: Brassey's, UK, 1991); Pond, Elizabeth: *Beyond the Wall. Germany's Road to Unification* (Washington, D.C.: The Brookings Institution, 1993); Møller, Bjørn: *Resolving the Security Dilemma in Europe. The German Debate on Non-Offensive Defence* (London: Brassey's, 1991), pp. 212-259.
25. See the chapters by Seongwhun Cheon, Hong Kwan-Hee, L. Gordon Flake and Alexander Z. Zhebin in *The Korean Journal of National Unification*, vol. 6 (Seoul: Korea Institute of National Unification, 1997), pp. 7-100.
26. On Ostpolitik see Griffith, William E.: *The Ostpolitik of the Federal Republic of Germany* (Cambridge, Mass.: MIT Press, 1978). On the North Policy of the ROC see Ok, Tae Hwan: 'The Process of South-North Dialogue and Perspectives for Unification of Korea', *The Korean Journal of National Unification* (Seoul: Research Institute for National Unification, RINU), vol. 1 (1992), pp. 85-106. On the similarities between the two cases see Schmidt, Helmut: 'Lessons of the German Reunification for Korea', *Security Dialogue*, vol. 24, no. 44 (December 1993), pp. 397-408; Yang, Sung-Chul: 'The Lessons of United Germany for Divided Korea', in Young Whan Kihl (ed.): *Korea and the World. Beyond the Cold War* (Boulder: Westview Press, 1994), pp. 261-278; Flassbeck, Heiner & Gustav A. Horn (eds.): *German Unification: an Example for Korea?* (Aldershot: Dartmouth, 1996).
27. A treaty to this effect was signed between the two Koreas in 1991: 'Agreement on Reconciliation, Nonaggression, and Exchanges and Cooperation Between the South and the North', in Kihl (ed.): *op. cit.* (note 26), pp. 343-346.
28. See the special section on cross-recognition in *The Korean Journal of National Unification*, vol. 3 (1994), especially Park, Young-Ho: 'Issues and Prospects for Cross-Recognition: A Korean Perspective', pp. 49-62.
29. On the security dilemma see Collins, Alan: 'The Security Dilemma', in Jane M. Davis (ed.): *Security Issues in the Post-Cold War World* (Cheltenham: Edward Elgar, 1996), pp. 181-195.
30. Jervis, Robert: 'Security Regimes', *International Organization*, vol. 36, no. 2 (Spring 1982), pp. 357-378. See also idem: 'Cooperation Under the Security Dilemma', *World Politics*, vol. 30, no. 2 (1978), pp. 167-214.
31. Independent Commission on Disarmament and Security Issues: *Common Security. A Blueprint for Survival* (New York: Simon & Schuster, 1982); Nolan, Janne E. *et al.*: 'The Concept of Cooperative Security', in idem (ed.): *Global Engagement. Cooperation and Security in the 21st Century* (Washington, D.C.: The Brookings

Institution, 1994), pp. 3-18.
32. Deutsch, Karl W. et al.: *Political Community and the North Atlantic Area. International Organization in the Light of Historical Experience* (Princeton, N.J.: Princeton University Press, 1957), pp. 3-9.
33. On (neo)functionalism see Haas, Ernst B.: *International Political Communities* (New York: Anchor Books, 1966). On federalism see Burgess, Michael: *Federalism and European Union. Political Ideas, Influences and Strategies in the European Community, 1972-1987* (London: Routledge, 1989).
34. Wilke, Marc & Helen Wallace: 'Subsidiarity: Approaches to Power-sharing in the European Community', *RIIA Discussion Papers*, no. 27 (London: Royal Institute of International Affairs, 1990).
35. For a comparative study see Ok, Tae Hwan: 'A Case Study of Confederations', *The Korean Journal of National Unification*, vol. 3 (Seoul: Research Institute for National Unification, 1994), pp. 275-292.
36. Lapidoth, Ruth: *Autonomy. Flexible Solutions to Intrastate Conflicts* (Washington, D.C.: United States Institute of Peace Press, 1996).
37. McRae, K. (ed.): *Consociational Democracy: Political Accommodation in Segmented Societies* (Toronto: McLelland and Stewart, 1974).
38. Møller, Bjørn: *op. cit.* 1991 (note 24); idem: *Common Security and Nonoffensive Defense. A Neorealist Perspective* (Boulder: Lynne Rienner, 1992); idem: *Dictionary of Alternative Defense* (Boulder: Lynne Rienner, 1995).
39. Kang: *loc. cit.* (note 2).
40. The agreements are reprinted in Kihl (ed.): *op. cit.* (note 26), pp. 341-348.
41. See the chapter by Yong-Sup Han in the present volume as well as his *Designing and Evaluating Conventional Arms Control Measures: The Case of the Korean Peninsula* (Santa Monica, CA: RAND Graduate Institute, 1993). See further Wiberg, Håkan: 'Nonoffensive Defence and the Korean Peninsula', in UNIDIR (ed.): *Nonoffensive Defense. A Global Perspective* (New York: Taylor & Francis, 1990), pp. 132-142; Møller, Bjørn: 'Non-Offensive Defence and the Korean Peninsula', *Working Papers*, no. 4 (Copenhagen: Centre for Peace and Conflict Research, 1995); idem: 'Common Security and Non-Offensive Defence: Are They Relevant for the Korean Peninsula?', in Hwang, Bypong-Moo & Yong-Sup Han (eds.): *Korean Security Policies Toward Peace and Unification*, KAIS International Conference Series, no. 4 (Seoul: Korean Association of International Studies, 1996), pp. 241-291.
42. Wettig, Gerhard: *Entmilitarisierung und Wiederbewaffnung in Deutschland 1943-1955. Internationale Auseinandersetzungen um die Rolle der Deutschen in Europa* (München: Oldenburg Verlag, 1967); Schubert, Klaus von: *Wiederbewaffnung und Westintegration. Die innere Auseinandersetzung um die militärische und außenpolitische Orientierung der Bundesrepublik 1950-1952* (Stuttgart: Deutsche Verlags-Anstalt, 1970).
43. Brill, Heinz: *Bogislaw von Bonin im Spannungsfeld zwischen Wiederbewaffnung, Westintegration, Wiedervereinigung. Ein Beitrag zur Entstehungsgeschichte der Bundeswehr 1952-1955* (Baden-Baden: Nomos Verlagsgesellschaft, 1987); idem (ed.): *Bogislaw von Bonin im Spannungsfeld zwischen Wiederbewaffnung, Westintegration, Wiedervereinigung. Band 2, Dokumente und Materialien* (Baden-Baden, Nomos

Verlagsgesellschaft, 1989). See also Møller: *op. cit.* 1991 (note 24), pp. 38-62.
44. See Møller: *op. cit.* 1991 (note 24), pp. 212-259.
45. On embedment, see Rotfeld, Adam Daniel & Walther Stützle (eds.): *Germany and Europe in Transition* (Oxford: Oxford University Press, 1991), which contains all the relevant documents.
46. Faust, John R. & Judith F. Kornberg: *China in World Politics* (Boulder, CO: Lynne Rienner, 1995), pp. 11-13, 31-33; Hsü, Immanuel C.Y.: *The Rise of Modern China*, second edition (New York: Oxford University Press, 1975), pp. 3-7, 129-168.
47. The following account is based mainly on Faust & Kornberg: *op. cit.* (note 46); Hsü: *op. cit.* (note 46); Lowell Dittmer & Samuel S. Kim (eds.): *China's Quest for National Identity* (Ithaca: Cornell University Press, 1993); Nathan, Andrew J. & Robert S. Ross: *The Great Wall and the Empty Fortress: China's Search for Security* (New York: W.W. Norton & Co., 1997). For a (semi)official account of the ROC's history see *The Republic of China Yearbook 1996* (Taipei: Government Information Office, 1996), pp. 43-64.
48. Isaacs, Harold R.: *The Tragedy of the Chinese Revolution* (1938, second revised edition Stanford: Stanford University Press, 1961); Guillermaz, Jacques: *A History of the Chinese Communist Party 1921-1949* (London: Methuen, 1972), pp. 3-147.
49. Snow, Edgar: *Red Star Over China* (Harmondsworth: Penguin Books, 1972); Wilson, Dick: *The Long March 1935. The Epic of Chinese Communism's Survival* (Harmondsworth: Penguin Books, 1977); Ch'ên, Jerome: *Mao and the Chinese Revolution* (Oxford: Oxford University Press, 1965), pp. 127-200; Schwartz, Benjamin I.: *Chinese Communism and the Rise of Mao* (New York: Harper Torchbooks, 1967), pp. 172-204.
50. Faust & Kornberg: *op. cit.* (note 46), pp. 38-40, 169. On Mongolia see Scalapino, Robert A.: 'China's Multiple Identities in East Asia: China as a Regional Force', in Dittmer & Kim (eds.): *op. cit.* (note 47), pp. 215-236, especially pp. 228-229.
51. Heberer, Thomas: 'The Tibet Question as a Problem of International Politics', *Aussenpolitik*, vol. 46, no. 3 (3rd Quarter 1995), pp. 299-309. See also Hughes, Christopher: *Taiwan and Chinese Nationalism. National Identity and Status in International Society* (London: Routledge, 1997).
52. White, Lynn & Li Cheng: 'China Coast Identities', in Dittmer & Kim (eds.): *op. cit.* (note 47), pp. 154-193; Segal, Gerald: 'China Changes Shape: Regionalism and Foreign Policy', *Adelphi Paper*, no. 287 (1994). See also Xueming Song: 'End of the Deng Era and China's Unity', *Aussenpolitik*, vol. 47, no. 1 (1st Quarter 1996), pp. 90-98.
53. Faust & Kornberg: *op. cit.* (note 46), pp. 78-80; Smith, Paul J.: 'The Strategic Implications of Chinese Emigration', *Survival*, vol. 36, no. 2 (Summer 1994), pp. 60-77; Kim, Samuel S. & Lowell Dittmer: 'Whither China's Quest for National identity?', in idem & idem (eds.): *op. cit.* (note 47), pp. 237-290, especially pp. 277-278.
54. See, for instance, Garver, John W.: *The Sino-American Alliance. Nationalist China and American Cold War Strategy in Asia* (Armonk, NY: M.E. Sharpe, 1997); Yahuda, Michael: *The International Politics of the Asia-Pacific, 1945-1995* (London: Routledge, 1996), pp. 43-76. See also Kim, Ilpyong J. (ed.): *The Strategic Triangle.*

China, the United States and the Soviet Union (New York: Paragon House, 1987), passim; and Mandelbaum, Michael (ed.): *The Strategic Quadrangle. Russia, China, Japan and the United States in East Asia* (New York: Council of Foreign Relations Press, 1995).
55. Faust & Kornberg: *op. cit.* (note 46), pp. 18-19. See also Ness, Peter Van: 'China as a Third World State: Foreign Policy and Official National Identity', in Dittmer & Kim (eds.): *op. cit.* (note 47), pp. 194-214.
56. See, for instance, Lin Piao (1965): 'Long Live the Victory in the People's War', in Walter Laqueur (ed.): *The Guerilla Reader. A Historical Anthology* (London: Wildwood House, 1978), pp. 197-202. On the background see Mao Zedong: 'Report on an Investigation of the Peasant Movement in Hunan', in *Selected Works of Mao Tse-Tung*, vol. 1 (Peking: Foreign Languages Press, 1975), pp. 23-62.
57. Geldenhuys, Deon: *Isolated States. A Comparative Analysis* (Johannesburg: Jonathan Ball Publishers, 1990).
58. Yang, Maysing H. (ed.): *Taiwan's Expanding Role in the International Arena* (Armonk, NY: M.E. Sharpe, 1997); Cheng, Tuan Y.: 'Foreign Aid in ROC Diplomacy', in Bih-Jaw Lin (ed.): *Contemporary China and the Changing International Community* (Taipei: Institute of International Relations, National Chenchi University, 1993), pp. 170-185; Henckaerts, Jean-Marie (ed.): *The International Status of Taiwan in the New World Order* (London: Kluwer Law International, 1996).
59. Baum, Richard: *Burying Mao. Chinese Politics in the Age of Deng Xiaoping* (Princeton, N.J.: Princeton University Press, 1994), *passim*.
60. Leng, Tse-Kang: *The Taiwan-China Connection. Democracy and Development across the Taiwan Straits* (Boulder: Westview Press, 1996); Bullard, Monte: *The Soldier and the Citizen. The Role of the Military in Taiwan's Development* (Armonk, NY: M.E. Sharpe, 1997).
61. See the feature article 'Hong Kong' in *The Economist*, 22 June 1996, pp. 23-25; Tsang, Steve: 'The Chinese Take-Over of Hong Kong: Implications for Britain', *The RUSI Journal*, vol. 141, no. 2 (April 1996), pp. 57-61. On the military implications see Dutton, Bryan: 'Hong Kong—The Transfer to China from a Military Viewpoint', *ibid.*, vol. 142, no. 5 (October 1997), pp. 17-26.
62. Halperin, Morton H. & Tang Tsou: 'The 1958 Quemoy Crisis', in Morton H. Halperin (ed.): *Sino-Soviet Relations and Arms Control* (Cambridge, MA: MIT Press, 1967), pp. 55-62; Chang, Gordon H.: 'To the Nuclear Brink. Eisenhower, Dulles, and the Quemoy-Matsu Crisis', in Sean M. Lynn-Jones, Steven E. Miller & Stephen Von Evera (eds.): *Nuclear Diplomacy and Crisis Management. An* International Security Reader (Cambridge, MA: MIT Press, 1990), pp. 200-227; Brands, H. W. Jr.: 'Testing Massive Retaliation. Credibility and Crisis Management in the Taiwan Strait', *ibid.*, pp. 228-255.
63. Chang, Parris: 'Beijing's Policy Toward Taiwan: An Elite Conflict Model', in Tun-jen Cheng, Chi Huang & Samuel S.G. Wu (eds.): *Inherited Rivalry. Conflict Across the Taiwan Straits* (Boulder, CO: Lynne Rienner, 1995), pp. 65-79; Wu-Shan Wu: 'Economic Reform, Cross-Straits Relations, and the Politics of Issue Linkage', *ibid.*, pp. 111-133, especially pp. 126-128; Leng: *op. cit.* (note 60), *passim*.

64. Goodman, David S.G. & Feng Chongui: 'Guandong. Greater Hong Kong and the New Regionalist Future', in David S.G. Goodman & Gerald Segal (eds.): *China Deconstructs. Politics, Trade and Regionalism* (London: Routledge, 1994), pp. 177-201; Long, Simon: 'Regionalism in Fujian', *ibid.*, pp. 202-223; Womack, Brantley & Guangzhi Zhao: 'The Many Worlds of China's Provinces. Foreign Trade and Diversification', *ibid.*, pp. 131-176; Chan, Steve & Cal Clark: 'The Mainland China-Taiwan Relationship: From Confrontation to Interdependence?', in Cheng et al. (eds.): *op. cit.* (note 63), pp. 47-62; Wu: *loc. cit.* (note 63).
65. Reprinted in *Orbis*, vol. 39, no. 3 (Fall 1995), pp. 591-594.
66. White & Cheng: *loc. cit.* (note 52), pp. 173-180.
67. See, for instance, Hsieh, John Fug-sheng: 'Chiefs, Staffers, Indians, and Others: How Was Taiwan's Mainland China Policy Made', in Cheng et al. (eds.): *op. cit.* (note 63), pp. 137-152.
68. *Republic of China Yearbook 1996* (note 47), pp. 94-105.
69. *Republic of China Yearbook* (note 47), pp. 109-115. See also Chien, Fredrick F.: 'A View from Taipei', in idem: *Opportunity and Challenge. A Collection of Statements, Interviews and Personal Profiles* (Tempe, Arizona: Arizona Historical Foundation, Hayden Library, Arizona State University, 1995), pp. 71-79; Chan, Lien: 'A Pragmatic Strategy for China's Peaceful Unification', Sponsored Statement inserted into (rather than published by) *Foreign Affairs*, vol. 75, no. 2 (March-April 1996).
70. Starr, Barbara: 'USA Fears Growth in Nuclear Chinese Navy', *Jane's Defence Weekly*, vol. 23, no. 1 (7 January 1995), p. 6. On the purchase of 'Kilo' diesel-powered attack submarines, see *ibid.*, vol. 22, no. 20 (19 November 1994), p. 1; and Starr, Barbara: 'China's SSK Aspirations Detailed by USN Chief', *ibid.*, vol. 23, no. 11 (18 March 1995), p. 3. On the possibility of a mainland Chinese blockade of Taiwan see Chao, John K.T.: 'Legal Aspects of a Pacific Blockade of Taiwan', in Jayant Lele & Kwasi Ofori-Yebotah (eds.): *Unravelling the Asian Miracle* (Aldershot: Dartmouth, 1996), pp. 141-167.
71. Starr, Barbara: 'USA Deploys Carriers, But Doubts Invasion Threat Against Taiwan', *Jane's Defence Weekly*, vol. 25, no. 12 (20 March 1996), pp. 17-18. That China does not have such capabilities is also acknowledged by the ROC authorities, who highlight the presumed Chinese intentions to invade. See *National Defence Report 1993-94* (Taipei: Ministry of National Defence, 1994), pp. 86-92.
72. Boserup, Anders: 'Non-offensive Defence in Europe', in Derek Paul (ed.): *Defending Europe. Options for Security* (London: Taylor & Francis, 1985), pp. 194-209; Møller: *op. cit.* 1992 (note 38), pp. 79-100.
73. Quoted from Kau, Michael Y.M.: 'The Implications of Triangular Relations for Taiwan: An Emerging Target of Opportunity', in Kim (ed.): *op. cit.* (note 54), pp. 188-189.
74. Zhan, Jun: 'China Goes to the Blue Waters: The Navy, Seapower Mentality and the South China Sea', *The Journal of Strategic Studies*, vol. 17, no. 3 (September 1994), pp. 180-208; Till, Geoffrey: 'China, Its Navy and the South China Sea', *The RUSI Journal*, vol. 141, no. 2 (April 1996), pp. 45-51.

75. Pollack, Jonathan D.: 'The Future of China's Nuclear Weapons Policy', in John C. Hopkins & Weixing Hu (eds.): *Strategic Views from the Second Tier. The Nuclear Weapons Policies of France, Britain and China* (New Brunswick: Transaction Publishers, 1996), pp. 157-166; Xue, Litai: 'Evolution of China's Nuclear Strategy', *ibid.*, pp. 167-189; Lewis, John Wilson & Xue Litai: *China's Strategic Seapower. The Politics of Force Modernization in the Nuclear Age* (Stanford: Stanford University Press, 1994).
76. Dellios, Rosita: *Modern Chinese Defence Strategy. Present Developments, Future Directions* (London: Macmillan, 1989); Joffe, Ellis: *The Chinese Army After Mao* (London: Weidenfeld & Nicholson, 1987); Shulong Chu: 'The PRC Girds for Limited, High-Tech War', *Orbis*, vol. 38, no. 2 (Spring 1994), pp. 177-191; Singh, Swaran: 'China's Post-Cold War National Security Doctrine', *Strategic Analysis*, vol. 18, no. 1 (April 1995), pp. 45-60.
77. Albright, David & Corey Gay: 'Taiwan: Nuclear Nightmare Averted', *Bulletin of the Atomic Scientists*, vol. 64, no. 1 (January 1998), pp. 54-60.
78. *National Defence Report* (note 71), pp. 83, 101.
79. *ibid.*, pp. 200-201 (on the army), 204-205 (navy), 208-209 (air force), 212 (coast guard). See also Yang, Andrew N.D.: 'Threats Across the Taiwan Strait: Reaching Out for the Unreachable', *The RUSI Journal*, vol. 141, no. 2 (April 1996), pp. 52-56.
80. Grove, Eric: 'Naval Cooperative Security', in Stan Windass & idem: *The Crucible of Peace. Common Security in Europe*. Common Security Studies, vol. 1 (London: Brassey's, 1988).
81. According to Gerald Segal 'flexible arms control based on unstated self-restraint seems to be the hallmark of the Pacific approach'. See his *Rethinking the Pacific* (Oxford: Clarendon Press, 1990), p. 276.
82. Segal, Gerald: 'Tying China into the International System', *Survival*, vol. 37, no. 2 (Summer 1995), pp. 60-73.

9 Taiwan's Defence Policy: Threat Assessment and Security Strategies

CHENG-YI LIN

INTRODUCTION

With the ROC-US Mutual Defense Treaty, the Republic of China (ROC) on Taiwan was under US protection from 1954 to 1978. In this period, President Chiang Kai-shek and his *Kuomintang* (KMT) followers deemed the recovery of sovereignty over mainland China to be the primary task of the ROC defence program. Therefore, a high proportion of the ROC government's expenditures were allocated to defence spending. Although the US protected Taiwan from invasion by the People's Republic of China (PRC), it also restrained the ROC from any offensive actions against the mainland. US involvement in the 1954-1955 and 1958 Taiwan Strait crises thwarted Beijing's strategy of 'liberating' the ROC-held offshore islands.

When the United States normalized relations with the PRC in 1979, Taipei faced the challenge of adapting Taiwan's military force to a transformed security setting. In the 1979 Taiwan Relations Act, the Carter administration pledged that the 'United States will make available to Taiwan such defence articles and defence services in such quantity as may be necessary to enable Taiwan to maintain a sufficient self-defence capability'. However, Taiwan's defence program suffered a significant setback with the US-PRC communique of August 17, 1982, in which the US indicated that 'it does not seek to carry out a long-term policy of arms sales to Taiwan', and 'it intends to reduce gradually its sales of arms to Taiwan, leading over a period of time to a final resolution'.[1] Thus, in the 1980s, Taiwan tried not only to diversify its arms procurement sources, but also to develop such defence capabilities as its indigenous fighter jets and missiles.

By the late 1980s, in tandem with the lifting of martial law and relaxation of regulations concerning contact with the mainland, Taiwan began to modify its national security policy to a strictly defensive posture. Therefore, the current objective of Taiwan's defence policy is to safeguard those territories actually under its control rather than to topple the Chinese Communist regime. As long as Beijing refuses to renounce the use of force to settle the Taiwan issue, Taiwan not only needs to raise the costs for the PRC of a military coercion of the island, it also has to make preparations for dealing with nonmilitary pressure, military shows of force, and other kinds of harassment.

THE PRC MILITARY THREAT TO TAIWAN

Taiwan's defence planning is based on the assumption that Beijing has no intention of relinquishing the option of a military solution of the Taiwan issue, although in 1979 the PRC replaced the phrase of 'liberation of Taiwan' with 'reunification of China.' In fact, the late PRC's paramount leader Deng Xiaoping explicitly pointed out that the decision not to renounce the use of force was a matter of principle (because the Taiwan question is regarded as China's internal affair) and of practical necessity—to keep the option open for the PRC.[2] PRC policy has an essential premise that, if it were to give up the right to use force, Taiwan would be less concerned about China's intentions, and therefore less inclined to consider Beijing's reunification proposal seriously. The PRC has more than refused to renounce the use of force; in fact, Beijing has clearly indicated that it would actively consider military means against a *de jure* independent Taiwan and any countries interfering in what it regards as an internal Chinese affair. Beijing military leaders even rank an independent Taiwan above the Korean peninsula in evaluating potential threats to PRC security.[3]

The fact that the PRC is increasing its military capabilities despite the end of the Cold War has a great impact on the security of Taiwan. For example, the PRC defence budget rose from US$5.86 billion in 1988 to US$8.4 billion in 1996.[4] In addition, it is widely believed that the true figure for PRC defence spending is much higher than the published amount. Ironically, in the post-Cold War era the PRC's traditional threat, Russia, has emerged as the PRC's primary arms supplier. The PRC's purchase of 50 Su-27 sophisticated fighters and their deployment at Wuhu, a city near Shanghai in southern China, and Beijing's deal with Moscow to produce Su-27s in China gave rise to grave concerns throughout East Asia, especially in Taiwan. Moreover, hundreds of Russian defence scientists and technicians are currently stationed in China helping to develop new defence technology.[5] Beijing's purchase of Russian *Kilo*-class submarines, *Sovremenny*-class destroyers, and its interest in acquiring the *Varyag* aircraft carrier from the Ukraine indicate the PRC navy's intention to become a viable blue-water force.[6]

As a result of this PRC build-up, the ROC's military leaders believe that at least 15 divisions of the People's Liberation Army (PLA) and two airborne brigades could be sea-lifted and air-lifted to invade Taiwan (see Table 8). However, one US military expert argues that Taiwan might have exaggerated the PLA's sea power projection capability. According to Lieutenant Colonel Larry M. Wortzel, the PLA can only conduct an amphibious landing away from China's territorial waters at the level of division strength (10,000 to 15,000 men) and a separate amphibious operation with a brigade of marines (about 2,000 men).[7] A PRC invasion of Taiwan might require a minimum of 300,000 troops, and this is clearly beyond the PLA's current capability.[8] Because the cost/benefit ratio to Beijing of a PRC invasion of Taiwan cannot be easily calculated, it is difficult, even controversial, to assert that the PRC has acquired the military capabilities to invade Taiwan. Nevertheless, the PRC does have the means to initiate a broad spectrum of coercive actions to intimidate Taiwan.

In October 1984, Deng Xiaoping disclosed to Japan's *Komeito* Party leader Yoshikatsu Takeiri that, while at that time the PRC did not have the capability to invade Taiwan, it had in fact acquired sufficient military strength to blockade the Taiwan Strait.[9] After this menacing statement by Deng Xiaoping, mainland Chinese military leaders took an increasingly hawkish stand against a *de jure* independent Taiwan. In March 1996, China fired three missiles into an area 52 km south-west of Taiwan and the other 35 km off the island's northeast coast with a clear warning that Beijing could blockade the two largest harbours of Taiwan. In the meantime, China started two rounds of military exercises to the west of the Taiwan Strait. These exercises code-named 'Strait 961' were regarded as Beijing's intention to test Taiwan invasion scenario.[10]

TABLE 8: ROC ASSESSMENT OF PRC CAPABILITIES OF AMPHIBIOUS INVASION OF TAIWAN	
Cheng Wei-yuan (Defence Minister) April 1989	20 to 30 divisions of PRC troops could be sea-lifted to Taiwan
Hau Pei-tsun (Defence Minister) December 1989	15 divisions of PRC troops could be sea-lifted to Taiwan
Fang-ping Shen (Deputy Chief of Planning, General Staff) October 1993	2 to 4 divisions of PRC paratroops could be air-lifted to Taiwan; 16 to 17 divisions of PRC troops could be sea-lifted to Taiwan
Sources: *Legislative Yuan Bulletin*, vol. 78, no. 58 (22 July 1989), p. 24; *ibid.*, vol. 79, no. 48 (16 June 1990), p. 319; Committee on National Defence of Legislative Yuan, *Proceedings of Defense Policy Seminar* (October 1993), p. 21.	

Many military and political analysts in Taiwan and the United States consider a naval blockade to be the most dangerous and likely action the PRC could take against Taiwan. For example, former ROC Minister of National Defence Chen Lian once predicted that before any PRC assault on Taiwan, Beijing would likely 'blockade Taiwan in order to suffocate its economy'.[11] The *1992 ROC National Defense Report* also revealed that one of Beijing's possible military actions is to 'besiege Taiwan by using naval and air forces to carry out [a] long-term blockade'.[12] US Navy expert David G. Muller, Jr., also confirms that there are many reasons for Beijing to choose a naval blockade over an invasion:

> A blockade would strike at Taiwan's weakness while negating its strengths. Taiwan's ground forces would be useless. Taiwan's fundamental vulnerability is economic, and a blockade would strike at the economy's heart. Though self-sufficient in food if necessary, Taiwan depends almost exclusively upon oil imported from the Persian Gulf to run an economy oriented largely toward the processing of imported raw materials and the export of finished goods. Free access to the sea-lanes is essential to Taiwan's survival as a modern economy. A blockade would be a powerful lever to bring about the island's capitulation. A blockade would cost the Chinese far less in lives, equipment, and operating funds than would an invasion. A blockade would occasion little civilian loss of life. Taiwan's industry would be brought to a standstill, but its infrastructure would be undamaged. As a result, any combat would occur at sea, far from the cameras of the world's newsmen.[13]

In the event of a naval blockade, most of Taiwan's harbours directly facing the Taiwan Strait would be seriously interdicted. The loading and unloading capacity of the ports Keelung, Taichung, and Kaohsiung has accounted for 95 percent of Taiwan's freight annually since 1985.[14] Hualien and Suao on the Pacific coast remain too small to provide an alternative to the port facilities on the Taiwan Strait. Furthermore, from 1985 to 1995 ROC-flag ships carried about 31 percent of Taiwan imports and 22.9 percent of the island's exports.[15] In the event of an embargo, Lloyd's of London could either suspend insurance on those foreign-flag vessels attempting to evade the blockade or charge exorbitant insurance fees. The ROC-flag vessels, escorted by the ROC Navy, could only transport a small portion of the imported raw materials and exported finished goods, not enough to maintain Taiwan's economic viability for long. This trade is vital to Taiwan's economic stability because of the overall importance of foreign trade to ROC GNP. For example, from 1983 to 1992, the amount of total foreign trade annually averaged 87.8 percent of the GNP of Taiwan.[16] If its exports and imports were severely reduced, Taiwan would find its economic development dramatically reduced and its survival seriously endangered.

ROC NATIONAL SECURITY STRATEGY

After several decades of confrontations with the PRC, Taipei has developed a new national security strategy.

- First, through military build-up, Taipei seeks to maintain a balance of power in the Taiwan Strait. Taipei closely monitors the PRC's military modernization program, and continually assesses any change in order to evaluate its potential impact on Taiwan's security. At the same time, Taipei hopes the US could play the role of a balancer and stabilizer in Taiwan-

China military relations.
- Second, Taipei is eager to put itself under the protection of the United Nations or a regional collective security system.
- Third, Taipei has adopted a functional approach to cultivate cooperative interactions with the PRC, and to help alleviate tensions in the Taiwan Strait.
- Fourth, Taipei has proposed certain kinds of confidence-building measures that might be adopted to lessen the tension in the Taiwan Strait.
- Finally, the ROC's current leadership believes that a *de jure* Taiwan independence would almost definitely result in a strong response from Beijing, most likely including the use of force against Taiwan. Therefore, it is necessary to restrain the movement for independence. Nevertheless, some members of the opposition Democratic Progressive Party (DPP) and the Taiwan Independence Party (TAIP) tend to regard Beijing's warnings as no more than bluff.

As the Cold War came to an end, a reduction in overall number of contracts for Western defence industries gave Taiwan an opportunity to negotiate many new contracts and implement a military modernization program. For example, Taiwan negotiated contracts for 150 F-16s from the United States and 60 Mirage 2000-5s from France in 1992. Under pressure from Beijing, France refused to sell frigates to Taiwan in 1990, however, Paris then reversed its decision in 1991, and agreed to sell six *La Fayette*-class frigates to Taiwan. In the short term, this series of major overseas arms purchases greatly aids Taiwan in its effort to maintain a balance of military forces across the Taiwan Strait. However, the immediate impact on the *Chung Shan* Institute of Science and Technology (CSIST) of fewer orders for locally-made fighter aircraft and missiles is worrisome, and will delay the process of upgrading Taiwan's indigenous defence technology.

It is impossible for Taiwan to compete with the PRC in every aspect of military capability, but Taiwan believes that only by prevailing in quality can it overcome its inferiority in numbers of fighters and warships. In the 1990 Legislative Yuan session, then ROC Premier Hau Pei-tsun publicly renounced the use of force in any offensive actions against the PRC.[17] Taiwan's contemporary military posture is for self-defence purposes only, but it aims at making the PRC's costs of any coercive actions against the island unacceptably high.[18] Therefore, Taipei emphasizes the importance of a combat-ready and quality force not only to repel a full-scale amphibious invasion but also to counter a series of limited attacks from China. If Taiwan does not provoke China by proclaiming independence, but it is the PRC that initiates an unprovoked military confrontation, Taipei urges the US government to intervene according to the spirit of the Taiwan Relations Act and the 17 August 1982 Communique. It is obvious that the US government prefers unspecified support rather than a specified defence commitment in the event of PRC coercion. However, President Clinton's decision to dispatch two aircraft carrier battle groups to the region near Taiwan quickly defused the 1996 Taiwan Strait crisis and allowed Taiwan's first direct presidential election to proceed smoothly.[19]

Although attempting to modernize and increase the size of its military, Taiwan still believes that its capability is insufficient for defence against a PRC attack. Therefore, the ROC is looking to collective security measures to supplement its military strength. Even though not a member of the UN, Taiwan supported the twelve UN Security Council resolutions condemning and imposing sanctions against Iraq for its invasion of Kuwait. In addition, in September 1990, Foreign Minister Fredrick Chien announced that Taipei would contribute a total of US$30 million to three frontline states (Jordan, Turkey, and Egypt) whose economies were directly affected by the Gulf crisis. It was also reported that the ROC offered US$100 million for assistance to the United States in the Desert Shield and Storm Operations. However, Washington refused this offer.[20] The KMT newspaper *Zhongyang ribao* (Central Daily News) suggested in an editorial that the ROC government make available nonmilitary and military assistance. Had it been implemented, this would supposedly have included a medical team, a minesweeping naval unit, and frigates for use in the Persian Gulf operation.[21]

Taipei's support for UN actions against Iraq was aimed at encouraging the development of a collective security system that could someday protect Taiwan from a coercion attempt by the PRC. Thus, ROC's recent bid to become a UN member should be regarded as part of its grand strategy to enhance Taiwan's security. In addition, President Lee Teng-hui initiated a proposal to enlist US support in establishing a collective security system first in South-East Asia, later to be expanded to include the entire Asia-Pacific area. After urging all concerned countries to participate in an Asian collective security system, President Lee proposed the establishment of a collective protection fund to enable concerned countries to contribute to regional collective security, general arms reduction in Asia, and joint exploration of natural resources in the South China Sea in order to avoid potential conflicts over territorial disputes.[22]

In South-East Asia, there has been movement toward a regional security system, the official (i.e. 'track-one') ASEAN regional Forum (ARF) and the unofficial ('track-two') Council for Security Cooperation in the Asia Pacific (CSCAP) on security issues. Under pressure from Beijing, Taiwan has been excluded from the ARF since 1994, and Taiwan's membership in the CSCAP has, likewise, been obstructed by Beijing. Taiwan's scholars in their private capacities have started to attend CSCAP Working Group meetings since April 1996, but with a tacit understanding that the issue of Taiwan should not be raised in the CSCAP. In light of the security issues of the Taiwan Strait and the South China Sea, Taipei's absence will necessarily diminish the effectiveness of the ARF.[23]

There is a Taiwan perspective in which it is argued that the development of economic and social cooperation between states is a prerequisite for the ultimate solution of political conflicts without resort to war. In other words, the social and economic effects of mutual cooperation are said to spill over to aid in the settlement of security issues. This form of 'functionalism' has been used by the ROC as an approach to the PRC. Functionalists in the ROC firmly believe that, as economic, social, and cultural differences between both sides of the Taiwan Strait diminish, the conditions for peaceful reunification will gradually improve.

In February 1991, the ROC government adopted the Guidelines for National Unification which envisage a three-phase process of reunification, beginning with exchanges and reciprocity, followed by increased mutual trust and cooperation, and ending with consultation and unification.[24] Rejecting Beijing's proposal for direct party-to-party talks regarding reunification, the ROC insists that cultural exchanges come first, followed by bilateral trade, and only then, by direct political contacts. It is clear from the Guidelines that the ROC's policy is not to have official contacts with the PRC unless and until Beijing renounces the use of force as a means for unification as well as other efforts to isolate the ROC in the international arena.

Despite their lack of official contacts, Taiwan and mainland China have developed a number of informal relations since 1987. Tourism, trade, investment, and cultural and sports exchanges are increasing rapidly. A private but government-endorsed Straits Exchanges Foundation (SEF) was established by the ROC to handle bilateral issues in conjunction with its PRC counterpart, the Association for Relations across the Taiwan Strait (ARATS). The first high-level, semi-official meeting between Koo Chen-fu, Chairman of ROC's SEF, and Wang Daohan, Chairman of the PRC's ARATS, was held in Singapore in April 1993. The Koo-Wang meeting was described by Taipei as 'non-governmental, administrative, economic, and functional in nature'. Altogether, four agreements were signed between SEF and ARATS. Three of the four agreements covered cross-strait delivery of registered mail, verification of official documents, and the establishment of regular communication channels between the two organizations. The fourth agreement was a joint statement listing topics to be addressed by both sides in the future, including crime, illegal immigrants, fishing disputes, copyright protection, and judicial cooperation, and cross-strait exploitation of natural resources.[25]

Since the historical Koo-Wang talks, at least seven rounds of negotiations have been conducted between the SEF and the ARATS. Two joint statements were issued by the vice chairman of the two respective organizations, Chiao Jen-ho of the SEF and Tang Shubei of the ARATS, in February and August 1994. In the August 1994 joint statement, the SEF and the ARATS announced a preliminary agreement regarding the return of air hijackers and illegal immigrants, and the resolution of fishing disputes.[26] However, no agreements on these issues were signed when the seventh round of cross-strait talks ended in Beijing in January 1995 because of disagreement on 'a provision which allows personnel on official vessels to carry out on-the-spot settlements' in fishing disputes.[27]

The prospect of cross-strait relations looked promising when the leaders of the two sides issued their blueprints for improvement of cross-strait relations in the first half of 1995.

Chinese President Jiang Zemin made his eight-point proposal on 30 January 1995, urging a cross-strait summit be held on Chinese soil and suggesting that 'talks be initiated and an agreement be reached on officially ending the state of hostility between the two sides of the Taiwan Straits under the principle of one China'.[28] President Lee Teng-hui responded on 8 April 1995, by issuing a six-point proposal to 'pave the way for peace talks on ending the state hostility'. President Lee also urged Beijing to consider that 'both sides should be assured of the ability to join international organizations on an equal footing', and leaders of both sides should be able to 'meet on international occasions'.[29] Even though President Jiang Zemin mentioned that 'Chinese should not fight their fellow Chinese', Beijing did not forswear the use of force against 'foreign forces attempting to interfere in China's reunification and advancing Taiwan independence'. Even so, President Lee Teng-hui pledged that 'Chinese should help their fellow Chinese to serve their mutual interests in trade and business', and that Taiwan was willing 'to provide agricultural expertise to help farmers on the mainland'.

Although the large gap in military capability between Taiwan and China makes it hard to establish confidence-building measures in the Taiwan Strait, Taipei is paying more attention to this aspect of its security. For example, Taipei has announced that its defence goal is to protect Taiwan, Penghu (Pescadores), Kinmen (Quemoy), and Matsu, rather than to retake the mainland. In May 1990, President Lee Teng-hui called for Beijing's leaders to roll-back the PLA's deployment to 300 kilometers from the Fujian Province, facing Quemoy and Matsu.[30] In May 1992, Cheyne Chiu, then President Lee's close aide and presidential spokesman, suggested that a non-aggression agreement be signed between Taiwan and China.[31] After Beijing shifted from its peaceful reunification policy to a militant strategy of combining 'media criticism campaigns with coercive military pressure', President Lee in a February 1996 press conference said he would pursue a peace accord with China if elected, and that this should have priority over the opening of direct links of postal service, transportation and trade between the two sides of the Taiwan Strait.[32] In addition, President Lee and Premier Lien Chan have persistently declared that Taiwan would not pursue a nuclear option for Taiwan's ultimate defence.[33]

In 1991, a group of Taiwan's scholars published a draft treaty aimed at alleviating the crisis across the Taiwan Strait. The clauses included an agreement to 'avoid dangerous military operations', the establishment of a hot-line between the top leaders on the two sides, a pledge not to use nuclear, biological, or chemical weapons against each other, and military budget reductions.[34] In the present circumstances, it would be difficult for Taipei and Beijing to adopt open confidence-building measures in the form of a treaty. Yet, regulations on military encounters that are tacitly agreed by the two sides should be encouraged.

ROC DEFENCE POLICY

From 1950 to the 1970s, the ROC maintained an offensive military policy not only to counter the threat of a PRC invasion threat, but also in preparation for toppling the Communist regime on mainland China. As already noted, in the 1980s, the ROC shifted to a more defensive policy that emphasized the importance of deterring a PRC invasion of Taiwan, and thus began to reduce its total armed forces.

Before the 1970s, ROC defence expenditures accounted for approximately 75 percent of annual governmental spending. Military expenditures dropped to 50 percent of the government budget in the 1970s. They fell below 40 percent in 1981 and below 30 percent of the government budget in 1992. In the 1990s, the ROC government has decreased military expenditures to approximately 25 percent of the budget, or about US$10 billion (see Table 9). As a result of the ongoing arms replacement program, the ROC defence budget has increased despite the end of the Cold War and the changed focus of Taiwan's military strategy and defence priorities. The proportion of military expenditure in the ROC government budget compared to the gross domestic product has nevertheless decreased.[35]

TABLE 9: DEFENCE SHARE OF TOTAL ROC GOVERNMENT BUDGET, 1987-1996							
1987	50.8%	1988	49.2%	1989	47.7%	1990	35.2%
1991	31.8%	1992	27.7%	1993	25.3%	1994	24.3%
1995	24.5%	1996	22.8%				
Source: The ROC's Ministry of National Defence, cited from *The Republic of China Yearbook 1997* (Taipei: Government Information Office, 1997), p. 124.							

The total number of ROC armed forces was reduced from 600,000 during the 1950-1970 period to 470,000 in the early 1990s. This reduction trend first became evident in the early 1980s. At least 35,000 troops were eliminated from the ROC armed forces between 1982 and 1986.[36] In 1996, Taiwan's total armed forces stood at 459,000.[37] Under the Plan of Restructuring of Defence Organizations and Armed Forces and the so-called 'elite troop' policy, the ROC's armed forces will be maintained at 400,000 by year 2003. Taipei currently believes that 400,000 is the minimum size force needed to support a defence strategy to deter the PRC attacking Taiwan. Because the ROC's military leaders still argue that 'decisive land battle remains the last resort to win the war', Taiwan's army is maintained at a level of 50 percent of total armed forces, while the navy and air force each comprise 25 percent.[38]

Responding to an interpellation by an opposition legislator, Huang Huang-hsiung, in the 1982 Legislative Yuan session, then Defence Minister Soong Chang-chih for the first time specified that the ROC's military policy was based upon the principle of strategic defence. The priority of the strategic defence is to prevent the spread of war with the PRC into Taiwan. The ROC needs first to maintain air and sea superiority over the Taiwan Strait, thereby keeping the PLA (People's Liberation Army) from crossing the 100-mile natural barrier.[39] Only after having ensured its survival and economic development would Taiwan be in a position to talk about the goal of national unification.

This principle as indicated in Minister Soong's remarks has become the ROC's contemporary military defence policy. For example the *1992 ROC National Defense Report* mentioned that 'the defence operations in the Taiwan Area should firstly lay stress on air domination and sea control'.[40] Then Premier Hau Pei-tsun also told the legislators in 1992 that:

> To guarantee the military security of Taiwan, the Pescadores, Quemoy, and Matsu, the government has adopted an overall strategy of balanced development of the armed forces with naval and air supremacy as first priority, based on a policy of high-calibre manpower and requiring a build-up of forces through thrift and hard work. Under the strategy, the armed forces will be re-structured, command levels streamlined, logistics systems renovated, and military school and upper-ranking staff units merged or streamlined.[41]

AIR DEFENCE

Taiwan's ability to secure its air space is essential for overall defence. If Taiwan cannot control its air space, the possibility of a successful PRC amphibious invasion will increase; supply routes to offshore islands could be interrupted; and ROC air traffic safety could be jeopardized. The maximum tactical warning time of a PRC air attack is only 15 minutes. As a result, the ROC has installed an automated command and control system to detect flying objects or aircraft approaching Taiwan at the earliest stage. To improve its air defence capability, the ROC has prescribed joint combat areas in which fighters, missiles, air-research radars, and anti-aircraft artillery are integrated into one enhanced 'Sky Net' system.[42] This strategy is aimed at keeping the air battle as far as possible from the Taiwan Strait. Given the proximity between the PRC air bases and Taiwan, the ROC's military analysts believe that the US F-16 could be used to develop the so-called roll-back strategy. This strategy is aimed at keeping the PRC as far away as possible from the Taiwan Strait.

Before the United States agreed in 1992 to sell F-16s to Taiwan, Taipei had tried every possible avenue to acquire advanced all-weather aircraft. More than a decade earlier, in 1978, Taipei had the opportunity to obtain 50 Israeli-made *Kfir* fighter aircraft. However, Taiwan eventually backed away from the deal partly to avoid damaging its close relationship with Saudi Arabia, and, more importantly, because the *Kfir* is only marginally superior to the F-5E.[43] Taipei also requested such sophisticated aircraft as F-4 fighter-bombers or F-16s and F-Xs (F-5G or F-16/J-79) from the United States, but the Carter and Reagan administrations rejected those requests.[44] Adding insult to injury, the Reagan administration in August 1982 yielded to Beijing's pressure by pledging to 'reduce gradually sales of arms to Taiwan' provided the PRC maintains its peaceful reunification policy toward Taiwan. Disappointed but not willing to give up, Taiwan decided to build its own high-performance fighter aircraft. The Aero Industry Development Center in central Taiwan developed the AT-3 advanced aircraft for fighter pilot training and ground attack, and the first production aircraft made its initial flight in February 1984. In 1985, ROC Defence Minister Soong Chang-chi further revealed that Taiwan was developing its own fighter aircraft to replace the obsolescent F-104s.[45] Later it was confirmed that three American corporations—General Dynamics, Garret Corporation, and Lear Siegler International—had contracted with Taipei to help refine the aircraft design, to develop a powerful twin-engine with afterburner capability, and to improve avionics integration.[46]

The PRC's purchase of Russian Su-27 aircraft, together with US election-year political considerations about defence-related jobs, led to President Bush's announcement in September 1992 of the sale of 150 F-16 A/B fighter jets to Taiwan. These aircraft were 'to sustain the confidence it [Taiwan] needs' and to reduce tensions in the Taiwan Strait.[47] Shortly afterward, France also decided to sell 60 *Mirage* 2000-5s to Taiwan. However, the *Mirage* sales turned out be the last major French arms sales to Taiwan. Yielding to pressure from Beijing, in January 1994 France declared that 'in view of the concerns of the Chinese side, the French government has undertaken not to authorize any French enterprises to participate in the arming of Taiwan'.[48] Before the delivery of F-16s and Mirage 2000-5s, the ROC air force still flew F-5E and F-104 jets, which were so outdated that at least 34 of them were involved in crashes during manoeuvres from May 1987 to October 1991.[49] In April 1996, Taiwan began to take delivery of the first batch of F-16s and its first wing of Ching-kuo Indigenous Defensive Fighters (IDF) was also commissioned. The first five Mirage 2000-5s arrived in May 1997 and they will replace the aging F-104 fighters as high altitude interceptors of invading aircraft. The ROC calculates that 430 fighter aircraft, including 150 F-16s, 60 Mirage 2000-5s, 130 IDFs, and 90 F-5E/Fs, would be sufficient to overcome its numerical inferiority to the PRC's 1,500 combat aircraft deployed within 250-500 nautical miles of Taiwan.[50]

In addition to maintaining superiority in the quality of combat fighters, the ROC believes that its air defence should be upgraded. Taipei seeks to obtain the newest air-to-air missiles such as AIM-120 AMRAAM to add to its Israeli-made Shafrir, US-made Sparrow and Falcon and Taiwan-made *Tien Chien* (Sky Sword) missiles. The ROC's land-based air defence is safeguarded by Patriot and ROC-made *Tien Kung-II* (Sky Bow) targeted against approaching high-altitude objects, and improved Hawk, Chaparral, Stinger, and *Tien Kung-I* missiles against low- and medium-range targets. The indigenous ground-to-air *Tien Kung* missile was first developed in 1982 and deployed in 1993. It is integrated with the Aegis-type system, known as *Chang Bai* (Long White), complementing the quantities of ROC Hawk missiles.[51]

In its development, production, and deployment of fighters, missiles, and anti-aircraft artillery, Taiwan has endeavoured to augment and improve its air defence weaponry. In the early 1980s, the ROC began constructing underground shelters (the *Chia Shan* project) in the east coast of Taiwan near Hualien in an effort to preserve the air force's combat strength under ground for decisive battles and to strive for 'operational depth in the rear'.[52] These efforts are intended to facilitate and preserve ROC air superiority over the Taiwan Strait to guarantee that its naval convoys will be uninterrupted in missions to supply the offshore islands and to ensure that the ROC's busy air traffic will be safe from the PRC interdiction.

MARITIME DEFENCE

Taiwan's economy depends upon secure sea lines of communication. In addition, the supply routes to the ROC's offshore islands could be easily disrupted by the PRC because of their proximity to mainland China. For example, in 1958 the PRC employed the tactics of artillery bombardment and torpedo patrol boat operations to cut off ROC resupply missions to Quemoy. In addition, Deng Xiaoping revealed in 1984 that the PRC had already obtained the capability to blockade Taiwan, as well as Quemoy and Matsu.

ROC leaders fully realize the pressing need to enhance Taiwan's counter-blockade capability. As a result, Taipei has attempted to acquire advanced weaponry while updating contingency plans annually. Admiral Yeh Chang-tung, former ROC Navy Commander-in-Chief, explained that 'the navy's main priorities were to develop anti-submarine warfare (ASW) and merchant escort capabilities'[53] According to US Vice Admiral and former head of the ROC Defence Command, Edwin K. Snyder, six defensive submarines would be adequate for Taiwan to break a PRC naval blockade. Nevertheless, the ROC navy announced a goal of acquiring ten submarines in its Military Strength Renovation Program (1993-2003).[54] In addition to two World War II vintage US *Guppy* II submarines, Taiwan purchased two *Zwaardvis*-class submarines from the Netherlands in 1981. However, in 1983, the Dutch government turned down Taiwan's request for four additional submarines. Taiwan also recently expressed interest in acquiring *Type-209* (Germany), *Agosta* (France), and *Walrus* (Dutch) submarines, but to no avail.[55]

If a threatening amphibious force were to present itself, the ROC would respond with operations based on anti-submarine warfare, coastal defence, and the mining of PRC harbours. According to the *Military Balance, 1996-1997*, the PRC has 63 strategic and tactical submarines (in addition to roughly 50 non-operational Romeo-class submarines). It is believed that a third of the PRC's submarines could be assigned to the Taiwan Strait if Beijing were to decide to mount an offensive against ROC. Moreover, the military balance could shift even further toward the

PRC after a military engagement with Taiwan, given the PRC's numerical superiority. Under these circumstances, to balance the defence of the PRC more effectively, Taiwan requires more submarines, early warning aircraft, P-3 ASW aircraft, and a Sound Surveillance System to track the passage of the PRC diesel-powered submarines.[56]

Recognizing the importance of Taiwan's ASW capability in deterring the PRC's blockade, the United States decided in 1986 to upgrade Taiwan's S-2A/E maritime reconnaissance and ASW aircraft to S-2T Turbo-Tracker with longer range and improved acoustic systems.[57] Subsequently, the Bush administration agreed to sell 4 E-2T (modified E-2C Hawkeye) early warning aircraft to Taiwan.[58] To strengthen the ASW capability of ROC destroyers and frigates, the United States additionally provided Taiwan with anti-submarine rockets and ASW helicopters such as the SH-2F, S70C, and *Hughes* MD-500.

Although the US-supplied airborne early warning system and ASW helicopters will improve Taiwan's capability to counter a PRC blockade, Taiwan must build more of its own national flag vessels in order to carry at least 50 percent of its exports and imports as part of an overall effort to maintain Taiwan's economic viability under a blockade. Taiwan must stockpile at least six months of raw materials to maintain current short-term production levels. In addition, the threat from mainland China has forced Taiwan's civil-military analysts to reconsider the long-forgotten development of Taiwan's east coast. It is imperative for Taiwan to deepen the defence structures and port facilities in the harbours at Hualien and Suao in order to prolong the economic viability of the island during a naval blockade. The longer Taiwan is able to resist a blockade, the better the chance for US intervention and sympathy from international public opinion.[59]

Other counter-blockade measures taken by the ROC include improvements in ship-launched missiles on destroyers, frigates and fast-attack craft. US-made Sea Chaparral and Standard-1 missiles have augmented the ROC navy by increasing its surface ship air-defence capability. Taiwan developed its own *Hsiung Feng* (Gallant Wind)-1, Gabriel-type ship-to-ship missiles, and deployed some of them as coast-based missiles on the offshore islands to acquire more operational depth through a more substantial presence close to the PRC. Taipei requested longer-range US *Harpoon* missiles (approximately 70-mile range) to supplement the shorter-range *Hsiung Feng*-1 (approximately 25 miles). However, this request was turned down by the Carter and Reagan administrations. In 1988, Taiwan first test-fired a longer-range *Hsiung Feng*-2 (approximately 50 miles), which approached the performance of the *Harpoon* missiles. In 1993, the Clinton administration agreed to sell 41 ship-launched *Harpoon* missiles to Taiwan, and in 1997 again agreed to sell 54 air-launched AGM-84 anti-submarine *Harpoon* missiles to Taiwan. It is also believed that the ROC developed an antimissile rocket system for its warships in order to deflect such missiles as the PRC *Styx*.[60]

As of 1996, the ROC has 18 destroyers, i.e. as many as the PLA Navy.

However, they are World War II-vintage US *Gearing*, *Sumner*, and *Fletcher*-class. According to the ROC's ten-year Military Strength Renovation Program (1993-2003), the navy will maintain approximately 40 principal surface combatants.[61] These destroyers will be maintained under the Fleet Rehabilitation and Modernization Program (*Wu Chin* conversion project) or phased out through one-for-one replacement by US *Perry*-class, *Knox*-class, and French *La Fayette*-class frigates. In addition, Taiwan plans to build 12,500-ton *China Chiang*-class fast-attack missile craft to be used on near-shore defence missions.[62]

In 1987, the United States agreed to provide technology to help Taiwan construct *Perry*-class (4,100 tons) frigates in Kaohsiung China Shipbuilding Corporation's shipyards. In 1991, France agreed to sell six unarmed *La Fayette*-class (3,200 tons) frigates to Taiwan and the first 'Kang Ting' frigate was commissioned in May 1996.[63] Through US Congress initiatives, the Bush administration leased three *Knox*-class (3,000 tons) to Taiwan in 1992. With these modern US and French frigates, Garry Klinworth argues that Taiwan's recent efforts constitute 'the biggest naval modernization program in East Asia and [these improvements and additions] will significantly upgrade Taiwan's naval capabilities, especially in the area of ASW'.[64]

While the ROC has been making an effort to strengthen its ASW capability, a gap may exist in the ROC's minesweeping capability. J.V.P. Goldrick and P.D. Jones, two experts on the navies of Far Eastern countries, write that the ROC has shown 'a curious lack of emphasis on mine warfare'.[65] Mines could be used to block the sea lines of communication to and from Taiwan, and could create additional dangers if the PRC were to invade the island. To upgrade its mine countermeasures capability, and possibly in an attempt to acquire the technology to build minesweepers, Taiwan in 1991 obtained four German minesweepers.[66] For defence purposes, the ROC also needs to acquire sea- and aerial-mine-laying capability that will allow it to disrupt the PRC's naval activities in southeastern China in case of a conflict.

GROUND DEFENCE

Counter-landing warfare is the primary task for the ROC army in the event of a PRC amphibious invasion. PRC air and sea superiority in the Taiwan Strait would be a likely precursor of an invasion from the mainland. Even without air and sea superiority in the Taiwan strait, the PRC could blockade Quemoy and Matsu. Although the ROC gradually reduced the numbers of ground troops on the offshore islands, a total of one fifth of the ROC's troops are still deployed on Quemoy (55,000) and Matsu (18,000).

Beijing regards the Quemoy and Matsu islands as a part of the mainland Fujian Province. Nevertheless, since the 1958 Quemoy crisis, the PRC has acknowledged that the offshore islands could serve as useful connections between the mainland

and Taiwan. The PRC would not likely capture the offshore islands to cut Taiwan's ties with mainland China. For the ROC, the Quemoy and Matsu islands are the first defence perimeter, the Pescadore Islands the second, and the island of Taiwan the last. To prevent a conflict from reaching Taiwan represents the overall priority of the ROC defence strategy.

After the US normalization of relations with the PRC, some pro-ROC US civil-military analysts doubted the wisdom of maintaining one fifth of the best ROC troops on the offshore islands. It was argued that, from a military perspective, the ROC would pay a high price for defending the offshore islands, because they are very exposed and vulnerable to attack. The troops garrisoned there would be sacrificed in any determined invasion, and their loss would significantly reduce the defence capabilities of the ROC in any subsequent invasion of Taiwan. Given such considerations, a reduction in force level on the offshore islands might even lessen the possibility of PRC attack, since such an attack, without the potential for reducing the military capabilities of the ROC, would net the PRC only small fragments of lands.[67]

Compared to Quemoy, Matsu is more vulnerable to PRC attacks and more difficult for the ROC to resupply should the island come under siege. The fortifications of the Quemoy and Matsu islands may be impressive, but a naval blockade would quickly dry up ROC firepower and force the garrison to become a PRC hostage. The PRC has not waged harassment tactics against the offshore islands or the ROC-occupied Spratly islands in South China Sea primarily because Beijing does not want to disrupt increasing interactions on both sides of the Taiwan Strait. Therefore, the offshore islands should be regarded by Taipei only as a small military outpost and additional troops should be redeployed to Taiwan.

In order to enhance mobile operation and reconnaissance capabilities, the ROC Army successfully negotiated an agreement with the United States to sell 42 AH-1W Cobra attack helicopters and 26 OH-58D Kiowa Scout helicopters to Taiwan.[68] The role of two ROC marine divisions, which had been trained to carry out amphibious warfare on mainland China, has gradually shifted to supporting counter-landing warfare and serving as a rapid deployment force. Concerning main battle tanks, the ROC Army purchased 160 M60A3 tanks from the United States to replace some of its M-48A5 and supplement 150 M-48Hs. However, opposition from lawmakers questioning the wisdom of purchasing medium-sized rather than light tanks for Taiwan's ground defence had stalled the plan in 1993.[69] The ROC anti-armour capability has been gradually improved through Taiwan's indigenous missiles and purchases of new advanced US missiles. The sophisticated antitank equipment in the ROC inventory includes US-made TOW and Taiwan's *Kun Wu* (Fire God, TOW-type) missiles.

To deter the PRC's possible invasion, Taipei could consider an option of developing medium-range surface-to-surface cruise missiles as an alternative to the development of nuclear weapons. The ROC has been able to produce *Ching Feng*

(Green Bee, Lance-type; approximately 75 miles) missiles and has developed technology for a surface-to-surface missile with a range of 1,000 kilometers able to strike targets in Guangzhou and Shanghai.[70] Such a missile could put mainland China's major south-eastern cities under attack if there were any signs of troops assembling in preparation to invade Taiwan. However, the latter program was discontinued by the early 1980s without leading to deployment.

CONCLUSION

By the year 2000, Taiwan will have a completely new fighter force and a modernized navy. Thus its power projection will be much greater than it is now. Before these fighter jets and frigates become operational, however, there will be a window of vulnerability in Taiwan's security because the ROC's obsolete F-5Es and destroyers could not effectively defend against an attack by the PRC. Military and political analysts argue that this window of vulnerability would be overcome by increasing cross-strait interactions. Also, the PRC will be preoccupied by consolidating its power base in the Hong Kong Special Administrative Region before and soon after 1997.

Taiwan has begun to transform its defence-oriented national security policy by balancing the dimensions of diplomacy, defence, trade, and cross-strait relations. In addition to its military build-up and replacement program, Taiwan also depends to a large extent on diplomacy as well as increasing nongovernmental contacts and negotiations with mainland China. In the meantime, Taiwan shifted its national security emphasis from being primarily offensive to an essentially defensive posture.

Facing increasing Legislative Yuan oversight in defence matters, the ROC's Ministry of National Defence committed itself to reduce personnel and raise efficiency in order to win support for the new defence budget. However, the opposition parties have continued to criticize government arms procurement scandals, and wants less secrecy in the management of defence programs. At the same time, they share the view of the KMT that Taiwan should maintain a strong conventional defence capability.

Last but not least, both government and opposition parties agree that only by acquiring a formidable and balanced self-defence capability can Taiwan continue to resist Beijing's pressure for a premature or forced reunification. Self-defence capability becomes the trump card which the island could play in assuring that Taiwan would not become another Hong Kong.

NOTES

1. For the text of the communique, see Gibert, Stephen P. & William M. Carpenter (eds.): *America and Island China* (Lanham, MD: University Press of America, 1989), p. 313.
2. 'Vice-Premier Deng Xiaoping Interviewed by U.S. Newsmen', *Beijing Review*, no. 2 (12 January 1979), p. 17; Hickey, Dennis Van Vranken: *United States-Taiwan Security Ties: From Cold War to Beyond Containment* (Westport, Connecticut: Praeger, 1994), pp. 95-116.
3. 'China Adopts a New Stance', *Jane's Defence Weekly*, vol. 21, no. 8 (26 February 1994), p. 21; see also remarks of PRC President Yang Shangkun to Taiwan delegates, in *Zhongguo shibao* [China Times] (Taipei), 25 September 1990, p. 2.
4. *The Military Balance, 1988-1989* (London: The International Institute for Strategic Studies, 1988), p. 178; *The Military Balance, 1996-1997* (London: The International Institute for Strategic Studies, 1996), p. 179.
5. Tai Ming Cheung: 'China's Buying Spree', *Far Eastern Economic Review*, vol. 156, no. 27 (8 July 1993), p. 24; 'China Is Poised to Buy Third Batch of Su-27s', *Jane's Defence Weekly*, vol. 25, no. 17 (24 April 1996), p.10; Wu Chia-chin, 'Ex-CIA Chief Says Taiwan Needs a Strong Military', *China News* (Taipei), 30 August 1996, p. 2.
6. 'China Expands Reach with Russian Destroyers', *Jane's Defence Weekly*, vol. 27, no. 2 (13 January 1997), p. 5.
7. Wortzel, Larry M.: 'China Pursues Traditional Great-power Status', *Orbis*, vol. 38, no. 2 (Spring 1994), p. 172.
8. Emerson, Tony: 'Mind Games', *Newsweek*, 19 February 1996, p. 8; 'Lee Emphasizes Quality Forces', *China Post* (Taipei), 10 July 1996, p. 15.
9. 'Deng Warns of "Eruption" in U.S.-China Ties over Taiwan', *The New York Times*, 12 October 1984, p. A8.
10. 'Chinese Army Exercise Tested Invasion Scenario, Says Report', *Jane's Defence Weekly*, vol. 26, no. 21 (20 November 1996), p. 4; Starr, Barbara, 'China Could "Overwhelm" Regional Missile Shield', *ibid.*, vol. 27, no. 16 (23 April 1997), p. 16; Shambaugh, David: 'Taiwan's Security: Maintaining Deterrence Amid Political Accountability', *China Quarterly*, no. 148 (March 1997), pp. 1311-1317; Binnendijk, Hans A. & Patrick L. Clawson: *Strategic Assessment 1997: Flashpoints and Force Structure* (Washington, D.C.: National Defense University, 1997), pp. 51-52.
11. Kien-hong Yu, Peter: 'The JDW Interview', *Jane's Defence Weekly*, vol. 15, no. 1 (5 January 1991), p. 32; Chang, Felix K.: 'Conventional War across the Taiwan Strait', *Orbis*, vol. 40, no. 4 (Fall 1996), pp. 599-604.
12. *1992 National Defense Report, Republic of China* (Taipei: Li Ming Cultural Enterprise Company, 1992), p. 57.
13. Muller, David G., Jr.: 'A Chinese Blockade of Taiwan', *U.S. Naval Institute Proceedings*, vol. 110, no. 9 (September 1984), p. 53. For details of a PRC blockade option, see also Lander, James B.: 'Taiwan's Troubled Security Outlook', *Strategic Review*, vol. 8, no. 4 (Fall 1980), p. 52; Chong-pin Lin, 'The Role of the People's Liberation Army in the Process of Reunification: Exploring the Possibilities', in

Richard Yang (ed.), *China's Military: The PLA in 1992/1993* (Taipei: Chinese Council of Advanced Policy Studies, 1993), pp. 170-171.
14. For details, consult *Taiwan Statistical Data Book, 1996* (Taipei: Council for Economic Planning and Development, 1996), pp. 114-115.
15. *Taiwan Statistical Data Book, 1996*, p. 116.
16. *1992 Foreign Affairs Statistical Yearbook, Republic of China* (Taipei: Ministry of Foreign Affairs, 1992), p. 130.
17. *Lianhebao* [United Daily News] (Taipei), 27 June 1990, p. 2.
18. *1993-1994 National Defense Report, Republic of China*, Chinese Edition (Taipei: Li Ming Cultural Enterprise Company, 1994), p. 73.
19. 'China Condemns USA as Taiwan Vote Nears', *Jane's Defence Weekly*, vol. 25, no. 13 (27 March 1996), p. 3; 'Taiwan Elections End China's Military Show', *ibid.*, vol. 25, no. 14 (3 April 1996), p. 4.
20. *Zhongyang ribao* [Central Daily News] (Taipei), 24 May 1991, p. 3; *The Asia 1992 Yearbook* (Hong Kong: Far Eastern Economic Review, 1992), p. 202.
21. *Zhongyang ribao*, 3 February 1991, p. 3.
22. *Zhongyang ribao*, 18 September 1992, p. 4; 9 November 1992, p. 2; 1 April 1993, p. 2.
23. Karniol, Robert: 'The JDW Interview', *Jane's Defence Weekly*, vol. 21, no. 3 (22 January 1994), p. 32.
24. For the text of the Guidelines for National Unification, see 'Peaceful Exchanges, Friendly Interaction, Democratic Unification Toward a New Era in Cross-Strait Relations', (Taipei: Mainland Affairs Council, The Executive Yuan, June 1996), pp. 25-29.
25. *A Resume of the Koo-Wang Talks* (Taipei: Straits Exchange Foundation, 1993), pp. 28-31.
26. Sheng, Virginia: 'Talks Break Deadlock on Hijacking, Other Issues', *The Free China Journal*, 12 August 1994, p. 1.
27. 'Cross-Strait Talks Near Accord, but Negotiators Come Upon a Snag', *The Free China Journal*, 27 January 1995, p. 1.
28. 'President Urges Cross-strait Summit', *Beijing Review*, 13-19 February 1995, p. 5; 'The Text of Jiang's Call for Reunification', *The China Daily* (Beijing), 2 February 1995, p. 2.
29. Su, Christie: 'Lee Maps 6-point Policy for Taiwan-Mainland Relations', *The Free China Journal*, 14 April 1995, p. 1.
30. *Lianhebao*, 23 May 1990, p. 2.
31. Taiepi Voice of Free China, 19 May 1992, in *FBIS-China*, 21 May 1992, p. 54.
32. Sheng, Virginia: 'Lee Says March 23 Victor Must Pursue a Peace Pact', *The Free China Journal*, 1 March 1996, p. 2.
33. *Ziyou shihbao* [Liberty Times] (Taipei), 29 July 1995, p. 3; *Zili zaobao* [Independence Morning Post] (Taipei), 14 October 1995, p. 2; 'Military Promises Not to Use Uranium for Nuclear Weapons', *China Post*, 18 August 1996, p. 11.
34. Kien-hong Yu, Peter *et al.*: 'Treaty for Alleviating the Crisis Across the Taiwan Strait', *Mao yu dun zazhi* [Spear and Shield] (Taipei), no. 54 (15 October 1991), pp. 3-4.

35. *ROC Government Budget Book*, cited from Yang Chih-heng: 'ROC's Defense Budget Lacks Global View', *Wealth Magazine* (Taipei), no. 133 (April 1993), p. 240; *Qingnian Ribao* [Youth Daily News] (Taipei), 4 April 1997, p. 3; *The Military Balance, 1993-1994*, p. 168; 'Chinese Threat Prompts Taiwan Budget Rise', *Jane's Defence Weekly*, vol. 25, no. 23 (12 June 1996), p. 19; 'Defence Gets Lion's Share in Taiwan's Budget Plan', *Straits Times* (Singapore), 8 March 1997, p. 17.
36. *The Military Balance, 1964-1965* (London: The International Institute for Strategic Studies, 1964), p. 30; *The Military Balance, 1988-1989* (London: The International Institute for Strategic Studies, 1988), p. 178; *Zhongyang ribao*, international edition, 25 February 1987, p. 2; *1992 National Defense Report, Republic of China*, p. 118.
37. *Lianhebao*, 25 September 1996, p. 4; cf. *The Military Balance, 1996-1997*, p. 196.
38. For details of the ten-year ROC Military Strength Renovation Program (1993-2003), see *Lianhebao*, 26 July 1993, p. 1; *1993-1994 National Defense Report, Republic of China*, pp. 74, 153; 'Taiwan Army Changes Focus', *Jane's Defence Weekly*, vol. 26, no. 15 (9 October 1996), p. 21; 'Taiwan Wants Lean, Combat-ready Army', *Straits Times*, 24 February 1997, p. 13; 'Military Set for Major Restructuring', *China News*, 8 April 1997, p. 2.
39. *Zhongguo shibao*, 17 March 1982, p. 1.
40. *1992 National Defense Report, Republic of China*, p. 52; Yang, Andrew: 'Taiwan's Defence Build-up in the 1990s: Remodelling the Fortress', in Gary Klintworth (ed.): *Taiwan in the Asia-Pacific in the 1990s* (Canberra: Australian National University, 1994), pp. 79-85.
41. *The Republic of China Yearbook 1993* (Taipei: Government Information Office, 1993), p. 735.
42. Karniol, Robert: 'Taiwan's Space and Missile Programs', *International Defense Review*, vol. 22, no. 8 (August 1989), p. 1078.
43. Liu, Melinda: 'Propping up a Fading Friendship' *Far Eastern Economic Review*, vol. 102, no. 43 (27 October 1978), p. 19.
44. Harding, Harry: *A Fragile Relationship: The United States and China since 1972* (Washington, D.C.: The Brookings Institution, 1992), p. 79.
45. *Zhongguo shibao*, 24 October 1984, p. 1.
46. *Aviation Week & Space Technology*, 31 March 1986, p. 31; 21 April 1986, p. 77; 'The Military Weans Itself from Dependency on US', *Far Eastern Economic Review*, vol. 132, no. 19 (8 May 1986), p. 27.
47. *Weekly Compilation of Presidential Documents*, vol. 28, no. 30 (7 September 1992), p. 5. See also Starr, Barbara: 'F-16 Sale Justified by "Discrepancy"', *Jane's Defence Weekly*, vol. 18, no. 11 (12 September 1992), p. 5.
48. 'France: No More New Arms to Taiwan', *China Post*, 13 January 1994, p. 1; 'Tension with France over Arms Sale Has Ended: Qian', *Straits Times*, 12 January 1997, p. 16.
49. *Zhongguo shibao*, 13 October 1991, p. 4; *Lianhebao*, 29 May 1991, p. 2; 'Taiwan to Phase out Aging F-104s', *China News*, 12 June 1996, p. 1.
50. *1993-1994 National Defense Report, Republic of China*, p. 47; *Lienhebao*, 26 July 1993, p. 1; Lasater, Martin L.: 'The PRC's Forced Modernization: Shadows over Taiwan and U.S. Policy', *Strategic Review*, vol. 12, no. 1 (Winter 1984), p. 61;

Sengupta, Prasun: 'Taiwan and Its Fighters', *Military Technology*, November 1992, pp. 14-18; 'Taiwan Takes Delivery of First Mirage 2000-5s', *Jane's Defence Weekly*, vol. 27, no. 19 (14 May 1997), p. 15.
51. 'Taiwan's Chiang Bai on Display', *Jane's Defence Weekly*, vol. 13, no. 9 (3 March 1990), p. 384; 'Taiwan to Come up with Extensive Air Defence System, Say Report', *Straits Times*, 5 December 1996, p. 3; 'Taiwan Test-fires Two New Hawk Missiles Successfully', *Straits Times*, 2 April 1997, p. 2; Chung, Lawrence: 'Taipei May Drop French Deal for U.S. Missiles', *China Post*, 17 April 1997, p. 16.
52. *1992 National Defense Report, Republic of China*, pp. 207-208. See also *Lianhebao*, 13 February 1991. p. 6.
53. Karniol, Robert: 'The JDW Interview', *Jane's Defence Weekly*, vol. 14, no. 3 (21 July 1990), p. 96.
54. *Lianhebao*, 26 July 1993, p. 1; U.S. Congress, Senate, Committee on Foreign Relations: *Taiwan*, Hearings before the Committee on Foreign relations, 96th Congress, 1st session (Washington, D.C.: Government Printing Office, 1979), p. 655.
55. *Zhongguo shibao*, 16 May 1993, p. 6; 'ROC Navy Chiefs Asks U.S. for New Submarine Policy', *China Post*, 20 August 1996, p. 16; 'Navy Mum on Reports of Submarine Deal', *China Post*, 8 April 1996, p. 1.
56. 'US Think Tank Suggests Arms Sales', *China News*, 20 February 1997, p. 2; Holloway, Nigel: 'On the Offensive', *Far Eastern Economic Review*, 23 May 1996, p. 34.
57. Taipei *CNA*, 9 August 1986, in *FBIS-China*, 11 August 1986, p. V1; Foxwell, David: 'Far East Navies Building Well-Balanced Fleets', *International Defense Review*, vol. 25, no. 2 (February 1992), p. 131.
58. *Qingnian Ribao*, 25 February 1994, p. 3.
59. *Zhongyang ribao*, 7 September 1993, p. 4; 'ROC May Buy New Missiles, Helicopters from U.S.', *China Post*, 2 April 1997, p. 19.
60. *Lianhebao*, 2 June 1986, p. 1.
61. *Lianhebao*, 26 July 1993, p. 1; *The Military Balance, 1996-1997*, pp. 180, 197.
62. Yeh, Benjamin: 'ROC Navy to Retire Old Destroyers', *China Post*, 15 June 1996, p. 16.
63. 'Taiwan Commissions New Frigates', *China Post*, 25 May 1996, p. 1.
64. Klintworth, Garry: 'Developments in Taiwan's Maritime Security', *Issues & Studies*, vol. 30, no. 1 (January 1994), p. 78; see also Baker, A.D., III: 'World Navies in Review', *U.S. Naval Institute Proceedings*, vol. 123, no. 3 (March 1997), p. 99.
65. Goldrick, J.V.P. & P.D. Jones, 'The Far Eastern Navies', *ibid.*, vol. 112, no. 3 (March 1986), p. 66.
66. Baum, Julian: 'Steel Walls', *Far Eastern Economic Review*, vol. 155, no. 27 (9 July 1992), p. 11; Goldrick & Jones: *loc. cit.* (note 65), p. 72.
67. Snyder, Edwin K., A. James Gregor & Maria Hsia Chang: *The Taiwan Relations Act and the Defense of the Republic of China* (Berkeley: University of California, 1980), p. 50.
68. 'Lee Inspects New Copters from U.S.', *China Post*, 16 November 1993, p. 1.

69. 'ROC Quest for Tanks Persists', *The China Post*, 1 February 1994, p. 15; Opall, Barbara: 'U.S. Government Finds Tough Customer in Taiwan', *Defense News*, 17-23 January 1994, p. 1; Chen, Kao: 'Taiwan's Military Is Learning to Play by New Rules of the Games', *Straits Times*, 15 June 1995, p. 38.
70. Liu: *loc. cit.* (note 43); Karp, Aaron: 'Ballistic Missile Proliferation in the Third World', *SIPRI Yearbook 1989: World Armaments and Disarmament* (Oxford: Oxford University Press, 1989), p. 307.

10 Russia's Security Policy in East Asia

ALEXANDER A. SERGOUNIN[*]

INTRODUCTION

East Asia is of vital and growing concern to Russia. According to official foreign policy doctrine, the region as a part of Asia-Pacific is quite important for Russia. In the Russian Foreign Ministry document of 1993 it ranked sixth on a list of fifteen priorities (Asia-Pacific follows the CIS, arms control and international security, economic reform, the United States and Europe).[1] In February 1996, the new Russian Foreign Minister Yevgeny Primakov elevated Asia-Pacific to the third position in his system of priorities (the region follows the CIS and East Europe). The Russian leadership has repeatedly emphasised that Russia has always been a Eurasian country, not only with regard to its territory but also its interests, policies, and even psychology.[2]

Russia is very interested in the development of the Russian Far East through cooperation with the neighbouring countries. East Asia is one of the largest Russian trading partners. The region represents an extremely important market for Russian civilian and military products. Russia's annual trade with China, Japan and South Korea amounts to $5-7 billion, $6 billion and $3 billion, respectively.[3] In the 1990s, Russia has been selling arms to the Far Eastern nations for as much as $1 billion a year.[4]

East Asia is also in the forefront of a global revolution in world power. With the end of the Cold War, the focus is shifting from power's military aspects to its economic dimensions. East Asia is the world's fastest growing economy, producing, together with other countries of the Asia-Pacific region (APR), more than one third of total world trade and, together with the United States, half of the world's gross national product (GNP).[5] East Asia is one of the world's largest consumer markets.

East Asia also holds enormous strategic significance for Russia. It remains an area of immense concentration of military power, including many of the largest armies in the world. There are a number of unsettled territorial and ethno-religious

---

[*] This article is prepared with a fellowship research grant from the United States Institute of Peace (Washington, DC).

conflicts which cause or may cause instability in the entire region. It should be noted that Russia itself is a party to some unresolved territorial disputes such as the disputed demarcation of the Sino-Russian border and the problem of the four Kuril Islands.

Four major powers interact in the region: China, Japan, Russia, and the United States. With the collapse of the USSR and growth of local economic powers, the Cold War regional balance has been dramatically changed. However, the outcome of this process initiated by both regional and global dynamics remains unclear. Given the power shifts both in the APR and Europe, Moscow tries to re-define its alliance strategy in a way to find counter-balances both to the local resurgent powers and to NATO and EU enlargement.

For these reasons, the Russian leadership regards the East Asian dimension of its foreign policy as critical to the success of Russian strategy in the post-Cold War era. Moscow needs an effective strategy toward the region to serve its economic, security, political, and cultural interests. The main problem for Moscow with regards to the region is to stay engaged and remain an important player in the future development of East Asia. This is hampered by two developments: First, Russian military power has been dramatically reduced in the area. Russia simply can no longer afford to maintain the same level of military presence in the region as was the case when the Soviet Union still existed. Second, because of the dire economic conditions that now prevail in Russia, it currently does not have much to offer other Far Eastern countries, at the very time that economic strength has become the manifestation of a country's power and significance.

Despite its economic and military weakness, and America's inclination to ignore Russia's role in the region, Moscow tries to conduct active policy in the area. To overcome its own weakness and to counter-balance American and Japanese influence in East Asia, Moscow has continued to support a multilateral security system for the region. The second part of the Russian strategy in the area is a much more intense effort to improve bilateral relations with Far Eastern countries, including defence ties.

The purpose of this study is to examine the main components of the Russian security strategy in East Asia such as threat perceptions, military posture, arms sales policy and defence cooperation with neighbouring countries, confidence-building and conflict resolution.

THREAT PERCEPTIONS

The Russian leadership believes that both the Chinese and American military threats have disappeared for the foreseeable future, and Moscow no longer plans for a general war to preserve its territorial integrity against potential Chinese or American attack. The post-Cold War international environment, however, appears chaotic and unpredictable to Russian leaders. Moscow remains vigilant with regard to threats to its security stemming from turbulent processes in East Asia.

RESURGENT REGIONAL POWERS

Russia is concerned about military threats originating from some of its neighbours, particularly Japan. Russian security elites see Japan's economic and technological capability as being easily transformed into a cutting-edge indigenous military production capacity that would provide Japan with the economic and military strength required for regional pre-eminence.

Following the US military draw-down in East Asia and the Western Pacific Moscow believes (as does Beijing) that an 'unbridled Japan... [might] seek to transform its enormous economic power into military strength'.[6] If the US military draw-down continues, Japan will have the largest number of major surface combatants in Asia, and with the most modern capabilities. It will also have the most effective anti-submarine warfare capability and most modern air force. Russian security specialists often express genuine concern about the future regional strategic balance in the 21st century.

Not only for Russia but also for leaders throughout the Asia-Pacific region, the most significant aspect of the Japan-US security alliance is that it serves to limit and constrain any Japanese sense of insecurity and to temper any inclination to play a more independent security role, with all of its undesirable regional consequences.[7] However, the Japan-US security cooperation sometimes does not fulfil its main function properly. For example, the new US-Japan military accord concluded in June 1997 has raised security concerns in Russia and many East Asian capitals, notwithstanding American and Japanese assurances that these arrangements were not aimed at any particular country. According to some accounts, the new security cooperation guidelines appear to promise the US Japanese assistance for a dispatch of troops in an emergency on the Korean Peninsula, the Taiwan Straits, the disputed Spratly Islands or elsewhere in areas surrounding Japan.[8] The new guidelines envisage no combat role for the Japanese, but they might lead to Japan deploying minesweepers outside combat areas or repairing US planes and ships. However, in its note the Russian Foreign Ministry asked Japan to provide more details on the document and to explain its new strategy.[9] China advised Japan to 'learn the lessons of history' and to avoid destabilizing the Asia-Pacific region. The South Korean Foreign Ministry said it would tolerate no Japanese troops on its soil and demanded to know the details of the new pact.[10] Japan sent diplomats to Beijing and Seoul to try to allay fears about the new agreement.

Moscow is also discontented with the fact that it is not a welcome guest in certain regional economic and security organizations. In recent years a Russian temptation to 'play the China card' against Tokyo and Washington could be explained in part by its isolation from the principal economic and security institutions that are gradually being developed in the Asia-Pacific region. Moscow believes that it could influence regional power balance through its defence ties with China. Given Russia's weakening economic, political and military position in East Asia, Moscow views a strong China as a counterweight to Japan and the United States.

It should be noted that in some Russian political quarters, it is China rather than Japan that is seen as a potential threat. For instance, some politicians and experts close to the *Yabloko* party perceive the PRC as a revisionist power. Arbatov suggests that China may represent the greatest external security threat to Russia in the long run.[11] He and other moderate liberals do not approve of too rapid a military rapprochement with the PRC and warn against the possibility of Russia's one-sided dependence on Beijing.[12]

They have three main concerns. First, they fear that in the distant future the Chinese military build-up could be directed not only against Taiwan, Japan and the United States but against Russia as well.[13] Second, they point out that a Sino-Russian military rapprochement makes the West nervous, hence might damage Moscow's relations with the latter.[14] They suggest more cautious and consistent arms sales policy in the region. Third, they stress that technology transfers will enable China to export Chinese versions of Russian weapon systems, thus undercutting Russia in the global arms bazaar.[15]

Along with moderate liberals right extremists (in particular, the Liberal Democratic Party of Russia led by Vladimir Zhirinovskiy) have raised concerns about Sino-Russian rapprochement. Zhirinovskiy considers China the main global threat to Russia in East Asia and opposes arming China with Russian weapons and, even more so, any transfers of technology and production rights. The Liberal Democrats insist on global China's 'containment' instead of its 'appeasement'.[16] The LDPR also fears Chinese 'ethnic aggression' against the Russian Far East and favours using tough economic, administrative, and military means to stop Beijing.[17]

However, anti-Chinese sentiments are rather marginal compared to general feelings among the Russian political elites. Despite the covert or overt opposition of certain foreign policy schools, the vast majority of the Russian political groups and experts are strongly in favour of military cooperation with China.

THREAT OF NUCLEAR PROLIFERATION

Moscow also views the proliferation of weapons of mass destruction as a major threat to its security as well as to that of other friendly nations.

North Korea's development of nuclear weapons was perceived by Russia as a serious challenge to the international nuclear non-proliferation regime and a threat to peace and stability on the Korean Peninsula. According to some accounts, North Korea's one existing (five megawatt) and two projected (50MW and 200MW) graphite reactors could have produced as many as thirty nuclear weapons per year.[18] In addition to the immediate security threat this posed, it created the potential for an even larger and more far-reaching threat: that of driving other regional powers to the development of their own weapons of mass destruction, thereby threatening to unravel the entire global non-proliferation framework. Pyongyang's resistance to IAEA inspections and intentions to withdraw from the NPT regime led to the crisis in American-Korean relations during 1993-94.[19]

Along with China, Russia played a major role in mediating this conflict. Fortunately, their international efforts contributed to the successful signing, 21 October 1994, of the US-North Korean framework agreement,[20] which stops the development of North Korea's nuclear weapons. However, as some experts suggest, Pyongyang could suddenly decide to regenerate its reactors and reprocess into weapons-grade material the approximately 8,000 spent fuel rods containing up to 30kg of plutonium extracted from the 5MW reactor. According to some experts, if the North Koreans should decide to renege on current agreements, they could rapidly produce a small stockpile of three to seven nuclear weapons.[21] While this would not constitute a region-wide nuclear threat, it might undermine the military balance on the peninsula.

Similar to the US, Russia is also deeply concerned about the prospects that countries which are advancing economically and technologically might engage in weapons and technology transfers to regimes in the Middle East and South Asia. China is a subject of primary concern. Although throughout the 1980s China professed opposition to the spread of nuclear weapons, its rejection of the NPT detracted from its credibility on proliferation issues among the members of the international community.[22]

Russia was particularly anxious about China-Pakistan nuclear cooperation. However, Moscow kept a low profile in this issue because it did not want to complicate its relations with Beijing. Russia carefully avoided making Sino-Russian disagreements public and tried to capitalize on Sino-American tensions stemming from US discontent with China's nuclear policies in South Asia.

Beijing acceded to the NPT as late as in March 1992 and, as mentioned, facilitated the US-North Korea dialogue on nuclear issues. However, in contrast to its position regarding North Korea, China's approach to proliferation in South Asia has been more ambiguous. Beijing favoured the establishment of a nuclear-free zone in South Asia. At the same time the PRC insisted that its provision of nuclear-power plants and technology to Iran and Pakistan was entirely for peaceful purposes and that such technology transfers came under IAEA supervision.[23] In 1992, China agreed to cancel the supply of some nuclear equipment to Iran in response to US lobbying. Nevertheless, the US maintained pressure on China to restrain its nuclear exports to Iran and Pakistan because of persistent reports that the China National Nuclear Corporation (CNNC) continued questionable technology transfers. Moscow tacitly supported the US efforts and was very happy when the PRC adopted nuclear export control regulations in 1997.[24]

ISLAMIC FUNDAMENTALISM

As mentioned, Russia shares with China a number of common security interests in the area, including the fear of Islamic fundamentalism. While Moscow is afraid of an Islamic threat to its southern borders, officials in Beijing suspect that Iran or the Central Asian republics might attempt to export Islamic fundamentalism to western China, where the Xinjiang province is considered to be particularly susceptible to such influences.[25]

Some reports suggest that China's April 1996 strategic accord with Russia, Kazakhstan, Kyrgyzstan, and Tajikistan was aimed at preventing military clashes along its frontiers, but it may also restrict the flow of arms from Afghanistan to Muslim separatist rebels in Xinjiang.[26] Separatist activities, combined with Tibetan unrest, force China to maintain sixteen divisions on alert in the neighbouring Lanzou region. Arms smugglers start from Talogan, the Mujahideen/ Tajik headquarters in Afghanistan, then slip past Russian guards on the Afghan-Tajik frontier. They then traverse the high Pamirs, cross the Chinese frontier and arrive at Kashgar in Xinjiang. China hopes that the treaty will bring about increased Russian and Tajik cooperation with its frontier guards in policing the border against unlawful elements.

LOCAL CONFLICTS

There are a number of historical and territorial disputes in East Asia which undermine the regional security system. Russia is involved in territorial disputes with China and Japan. If the Sino-Russian border demarcation problems are almost resolved, the Russian-Japanese conflict over four Kuril Islands still poisons the regional security environment.

The China-Taiwan conflict which engages the Russia's 'strategic partner' into dangerous confrontation is also the subject of particular security concerns for Moscow. On a number of occasions, such as the private visit of the Taiwanese President Lee Teng-hui to the United States (June 1995) and the presidential elections in Taiwan (March 1996), Beijing and Taipei have come very close to a military confrontation. This might also involve the United States which traditionally supports Taiwan militarily and politically.

Russia is, furthermore, interested in resolving conflicts between two Koreas. Given the uncertainties surrounding the ongoing political transition in Pyongyang after the death of Kim Il Sung, anything from internal collapse to desperate aggression is possible. Russia tries, on the one hand, to prevent an outbreak of military hostilities on the peninsula, on the other hand, to maintain good relations with both parties. Similar to the China-Taiwan conflict Moscow is worried about the US involvement in the conflict. Russia is not happy with the fact that Washington provides Seoul with significant military assistance and that 36,000 US troops are stationed in South Korea.

ECONOMIC SECURITY

Present-day Russian security thinking does not limit the notion of security to strategic-military issues ('hard security'), but acknowledges that in the contemporary world 'soft security' may matter more than security in the traditional sense. Moscow considers the protection of Russia's economic interests in East Asia as an important foreign policy objective.

Some of Russia's vital economic interests are at stake in the Far East. Despite economic, infrastructure, and logistic problems, and a perceived lack of entrepreneurial drive on the part of Russians, the Russian Far East has succeeded in establishing direct economic links with East Asia and the entire APR. By mid-1994, in Russia's Maritime Province alone, more than 800 joint ventures were registered, with over $300 million of foreign funds invested. These changes are occurring despite the fact that no special economic zones (which, so far, seem not to work in the Russian environment) have been set up, with the exception of Nakhodka.[27]

Exports from Russia's Far East are rising. In 1993, the area's estimated share of national exports doubled and the export volume exceeded $2 billion. The region's total trade volume was $2.7 billion in 1992 and $3.2 billion in 1993. The region's trade surplus in 1994 exceeded $1 billion. Asia-Pacific countries account for about 80 percent of this trade, with Japan being the leading market for traditional exports. As the transit role of Russia's Pacific coast expands, Russian ports are emerging as a base for re-export operations, particularly for trade with China and Korea. Four major sea ports (Vostochniy, Vladivostok, Nakhodka, and Vanino) handle the same volume of foreign cargo as the three largest ports in European Russia (St. Petersburg, Novorossiysk, and Murmansk). In 1992-1993, 46 percent of all foreign cargo and 54 percent of the high-value cargo in containers was channelled through Russia's Pacific coast ports.[28] As mentioned above, Russia's trade with the three Far Eastern nations (China, Japan and South Korea) accounts for $14-16 billion a year. A number of Russian and Chinese regions have developed very close economic relations. In fact, the southern part of the Russian Far East and China's Dongbei form an interdependent and complimentary economic organism.[29]

Hence, Russia seeks to create favourable conditions for developing its foreign economic relations with the countries of the region and eliminating any barriers to such a cooperation. For example, Moscow pushes ASEAN and the Asia-Pacific Economic Cooperation forum (APEC) to promote free trade principles in the APR and make Russia a full-fledged economic partner. At the third session of the ASEAN Regional Forum (ARF) in July 1996, Russian Foreign Minister Primakov suggested an ambitious programme of economic cooperation between Russia and the APR countries including joint projects on development of the Russian Far East and 'Greater Mekong', as well as establishment of a space research and monitoring centre and a Russia-ASEAN Business Council.[30] Russia also calls for international cooperation to fight piracy which endangers trade interests of many countries in the APR.

At the same time, Moscow is anxious about the prospects that the Russian Far East could eventually fall under the influence of foreign powers as a result of its active participation in international economic cooperation. Given the economic decline in Russia and the disruption of economic ties between different parts of Russia and the CIS member-states, economic cooperation with foreign countries is much more profitable for the Russian Far East than with partners at home. For instance, in 1994, the South Korean firm Yu Kong promised to provide Kamchatka with every kind of fuel at an acceptable price. Canada offered the Far Easterners wheat at half the price charged by the Stavropol Province. The same year, the Chukchee Peninsula for the first time bought food in the United States. Australia was ready to supply inexpensive high-quality coal, and Vietnam was positioned to sell oil to the Far East. In exchange, the Asia-Pacific countries were interested in timber, fish, ore, and other raw materials as well as some finished products.[31] In 1992 the Russian Far East could survive in a 'foodstuff crisis' only thanks to the barter trade with China.[32] To prevent this dangerous trend the Russian leadership tries to both encourage the region's foreign economic relations and keep them under its control. Moscow becomes especially nervous when the Far Eastern provinces exhibit any signs of separatism.[33] For instance, the federal centre several times tried to oust the governor of the Maritime Province, Yevgeny Nazdratenko, who followed a rather independent course in both domestic and foreign policies.

MIGRATION

Russia's Far East and Moscow are the two main regions facing the problem of migration from the APR driven by economic rationales. In 1993, the Russian Ministry of Interior registered thousands of illegal immigrants in Moscow: 50,000 Chinese, 23,000 Indians, 15,000 Afghans, 10,000 Iranians and Iraqis. The Ministry was unable to count the Vietnamese and the Mongols who outnumbered illegal migrants from the above countries.[34]

Chinese migrants are a matter of particular concern for the Russian Far Eastern provinces. According to some accounts, there are 2,000,000 Chinese in the Russian Federation (from 300,000 to 1,000,000 in the Far East).[35] The Chinese migrants were suspected of buying up real estate, vouchers and shares as well as charged with a spread of organized crime. Many Russian experts were afraid of further Chinese mass migration due to overpopulation in the northern provinces of the PRC. 'All of us here fear the Chinese', said one Russian expert from the Maritime Province, 'On one side of the border there is population of 2.5 million, and on the other there are 120 million who are beginning to feel they have too small an area to live in'.[36] However, other (and better informed) sources disagree about the existence of a 'Chinese threat'. According to official statistics, the daily number of Chinese visitors to the Maritime Province fluctuated from 40,000 to 150,000 in 1993. On 29 January 1994 the Russian authorities established a visa regime for the Chinese. Over the period of 1994-95, 6,003 illegal migrants were deported from the Maritime Province (this figure included not only Chinese citizens). The number of Chinese who became permanent residents in the Russian Far East is insignificant: 87 persons in the Amur Region and 170 in the Khabarovsk Province. The number of Chinese contracted for work in the Far Eastern provinces was quite modest as well: 10,000 workers in 1990 and 17,000-18,000 migrants in 1992-93. There were 10,000 Chinese workers in the Chita Region, 1,000-2,000 workers in Maritime Province and Amur Region, and 1,560 in Khabarovsk Province in 1993. Comparing to the period prior to the year 1937, when the Chinese and Koreans were deported from the Russian Far East, the level of the Chinese migration is insignificant: these two ethnic groups comprised twenty percent of the local population in the past and nobody was anxious about this.

Contrary to the 'alarmists', some Russian experts consider a limited immigration of Chinese and Koreans as a welcome factor that could contribute to the positive development of the Russian Far East.[37] Migrants can compensate for a decline in the labour force and bring investments to the troubled economy of the region.

NON-TRADITIONAL THREATS

Narcotics and ecological issues are essential for Russian security as well. Some of the Far Eastern countries are involved in international narcotics trade which could potentially spread to Russia. The lack of proper ecological standards in many Asian countries, industrial pollution, the burial of radioactive waste on the seas, Chinese land and air nuclear tests pose other kinds of threat to Russian national interest. Finally, the evidence steadily accumulates that the AIDS epidemic may run rampant, similarly to the bubonic plague in medieval Europe.

Despite the seeming number of threats, most Russian politicians, military and analysts assess the above-mentioned challenges optimistically rather than pessimistically. They view East Asia as a region largely without major security threats. Most threats have to do with 'soft' rather than 'hard security', and they could be successfully met by promoting economic and humanitarian cooperation and cultivating interdependency, whereas traditional means of security such as military preparations or alliance-building are ineffective or irrelevant.

RUSSIAN MILITARY PRESENCE

The Sino-Soviet confrontation of the 1960-80s led to a high level of militarization of the Russian Far East. However, with the beginning of the Sino-Russian détente and the reshaping of the military alliances in East Asia, the region has lost its former military-strategic significance for Moscow. Russia thus places the main emphasis on socio-economic rather than on military developments in the region. As Mr Primakov stressed, Moscow strongly supports economic cooperation between the Russian Far East and the above region.[38] The central authorities provided the local governments with greater powers to develop more or less independent economic and cultural ties with the Asia-Pacific countries. Sino-Russian relations have experienced the most dramatic changes. In addition to trade, Sino-Russian cooperation has been evolving in a number of delicate and sensitive fields, such as arms and technology transfers, conversion, military training and research, intelligence, etc., contributing to an atmosphere of trust and mutual confidence in relations between the two countries.

Along with international security dynamics some domestic factors such as economic decline and the virtual collapse of the Russian military have contributed to further force reductions in the region. Defence budget cuts, low salaries, lack of housing, draft evasion and Russia's defeat in the Chechen war have undermined morale and reduced readiness of the Russian military. The armed forces often have no fuel for exercises and training programmes. Modernization programmes have been cut. Acquisition of advanced weapon systems has almost been stopped. Since the Russian economy will hardly recover in the foreseeable future the poor state of the Russian military is likely to persist.

As a result of the above international and domestic processes, Russia's military presence in the region has been significantly diminished and its force configuration has become more defensive. In 1992, Moscow completed the withdrawal of troops from Mongolia initiated by Gorbachev in 1987. In 1986-96 the number of Russian divisions in the Far Eastern Strategic Theatre decreased from 57 to 23, the number of tanks fell from 14,900 to 10,068, that of surface-to surface missiles from 363 to 102, that of attack helicopters from 1,000 to 310, and that of combat aircraft from 1,125 to 425. The number of submarines in the Pacific Fleet fell from 109 (32 strategic and 77 tactical) to 45 (14 strategic and 31 tactical), and the number of principal surface combatants from 82 to 45.[39] For all of the above reasons, Russia no longer constitutes any serious military threat to the neighbouring countries.

MILITARY-TECHNICAL COOPERATION

The arms sales policy is the most dynamic dimension of Russian security strategy in the region. With arms exports Moscow hopes to compensate for the degradation of its armed forces and the lack of economic and diplomatic instruments as well as to support Russian defence industry. Three East Asian countries are the Russian partners in this area: China, North and South Koreas.

CHINA

Military contacts between the PRC and the former Soviet Union were resumed, after a thirty-year period of enmity, within the framework of the Gorbachev policy of rapprochement which was established at the Sino-Soviet summit meeting in May 1989. It was Russian President Boris Yeltsin, however, who concluded the most extensive military agreements with the PRC since the 1950s. After travelling to Beijing in December 1992 President Yeltsin promised to sell to China 'the most sophisticated armaments and weapons'.[40] In May 1995, during his visit to China, Russian Defence Minister Pavel Grachev confirmed that arms transfers would remain an essential element in bilateral relations. However, in contrast with the Sino-Soviet military cooperation in the 1950s (when Moscow generously shared weapons and military technology with Beijing) current Russian policy is more heavily influenced by economic rather than strategic or ideological considerations.[41]

At the same time, Moscow regards Beijing (alongside India and Kazakhstan) as an important pillar of the Eurasian security system in the post-Cold War era. Moreover, when tensions with the West appeared in 1994, Russia began to view China as a counter-weight to NATO eastward extension and other Western moves pointing towards a 'new containment' of Russia. Beijing made it clear that it supported Moscow in its resistance to NATO enlargement, and the two countries declared that their common aim was to build a 'strategic partnership'.[42] It was not, however, by accident that both Moscow and Beijing carefully avoided the term 'strategic alliance'. As they emphasised in their joint declaration (24 April 1997), both states opposed military bloc politics and favoured a 'multipolar world order'.[43]

Since the resumption of Sino-Russian military cooperation Moscow has become China's largest arms supplier. Russian arms sales to China reportedly totalled from $1 to nearly $2 billion in 1992.[44] There was a certain decline in 1993, but since then Russian-Chinese arms trade has been re-activated. Arms sales contracts reached a figure of $1 billion up to the end of 1994.[45] The total cost of China's purchase of Russian weapons and equipment in 1991-94 has been estimated as $4.5-6 billion.[46] In 1995, Beijing received arms worth $626 million from Moscow. The year 1996 began with the $2 billion contract to co-produce the Su-27 in China, and in the same year Russia also delivered to China arms and ammunition worth $728 million.[47]

Russia is assisting with the modernization of the Chinese ground forces, air force and navy as well as transferring some military technologies. China is estimated to have 10,000 tanks in its inventory, mostly consisting of Chinese versions of Soviet-designed main battle tanks (MBTs).[48] However, most of these designs are outdated, having been developed from the T-54/55 series that were designed in the early 1950s. Moreover, many Chinese tanks are believed to be non-operational and the need to modernize the tank fleet became obvious by the end of 1980s. According to Russian military sources, in 1992 Beijing agreed to purchase roughly fifty T-72 MBTs and seventy BMP armoured infantry fighting vehicles (AIFVs) at a cost of approximately US $250 million.[49] According to some reports, Russia delivered these tanks by the end of 1993.[50] The transfer involved the latest model of the heavily-armed and relatively modern T-72 family—an improved version of the T-72M1. If the T-72 was to replace the immense inventory of older tanks used by China this would represent a major increase in capability.[51]

During President Yeltsin's April 1996 visit other purchases were discussed, such as tanks, tank fire control systems and BTR-80 armoured personnel carriers (APCs).[52] Some reports suggest that Beijing is going to order about 200 BMP-3s from Russia.[53] In October 1992, the People's Liberation Army (PLA) became the first export customer to receive the Russian S-300 surface-to-air missile (NATO designation SA-10B Grumble).[54] China has bought a handful of launchers and approximately 60 S-300 air defence missiles for testing purposes. According to other sources, four S-300 launchers with 100 missiles have been ordered by Beijing.[55] The Chinese PLA has no system with a performance similar to the S-300, which would represent a significant boost in its air defence capabilities.

Until the resumption of military cooperation with Russia China had a fleet of 5,000 obsolete combat aircraft, most of them based on old Soviet designs such as the MiG-21 and MiG-19 fighter aircraft and the Tu-4 bomber. Chinese helicopters are also mostly based on Soviet designs, the Mi-4 and Mi-8/17 series.[56] The PLA Air Force (PLAAF) has made a significant investment in trying to modernize its equipment by indigenous means, but with limited success. This failure forced the PLAAF to seek aircraft from alternative sources, and the dramatic reduction in tension between Russia and China made Moscow an obvious choice. In 1992, China received 26 Su-27 Flanker fighter aircraft (Russia's most advanced air superiority fighter) including two trainer versions.[57] The Su-27s are currently based at Wuhu in Anhui province near China's east coast and will primarily be used as interceptors. However, if deployed in Southern China (probably on Hainan Island), the aircraft could operate over the South China Seas.[58] Taiwanese military sources suggest that Beijing has deployed its Su-27s not only in Anhui but also in Guangdong province and that both Taiwan and Japan are within range of these aircraft.[59]

Procurement of a further batch of 24 Su-27s (plus two twin-seat trainers) was reported in early 1995. Deliveries were expected to begin in 1995 and to end within 6-12 months of the first arrival. Some Su-27 aircraft (as a part of the second batch) arrived in China to coincide with President Yeltsin's visit to Beijing on 25 April 1996, when Mr. Yeltsin agreed to transfer a third batch of Su-27 fighters. China expects to have 72 Su-27s (plus six trainers) by the end of 1997.[60] The third batch of Su-27s is almost certainly linked directly to the licensing agreement, perhaps serving as a further inducement to Moscow to transfer the required technology. It may also reflect more immediate Chinese operational requirements, as the locally-built aircraft will not be available for several years with the initial production rate likely to be limited to just 10-20 platforms annually.[61]

The Su-27 deal was followed in 1992 by a contract for 100 Klimov RD-33 aircraft engines, which Russia uses to power its MiG-29 fighter and which China will employ to upgrade its export-oriented Super F-7 fighter.[62] There are also reports that China is prepared to buy 24-36 MiG-31 and 40 MiG-29 fighter aircraft as well as 12 Su-24 fighter bombers.[63] According to some accounts, in July 1994 China's State Council approved an additional $5 billion worth of armament imports from Russia including an unspecified number of Su-30 MK and Su-35 fighters.[64] Russia, however, apparently refused to sell the advanced Su-35, but offered the Su-27 and Su-30 aircraft as an alternative.[65] In addition to these fighter aircraft, Moscow has apparently offered the supersonic Tu-22M Backfire bomber (4,000 km unrefuelled range) to replace China's obsolete H-6 bomber force.[66] Although spare parts may become a problem, the mere possession of this system, let alone any production capability, will worry China's neighbours. Following President Yeltsin's April 1996 visit China reportedly ordered 118 sets of missile systems and four Tu-26 long-range bombers.[67] The PLAAF has taken delivery of at least ten Ilyushin Il-76 heavy transport aircraft.[68] The Il-76 should prove a particularly important addition, since up until now the PLAAF transport fleet has only included light cargo aircraft. A further 7 Il-76 transports are said to be on order.[69]

According to some reports the PRC has apparently also agreed to buy an unspecified number of A-50 airborne warning and control aircraft and long-range early warning radar systems.[70] According to sources in Beijing and Moscow, China has finalized arrangements to acquire its airborne early warning capability (AEW). The AEW programme involves four main suppliers, including Russia. Ilyushin Il-76 four-turbofan long-range transports are to obtained from Turkmenistan and refurbished in Russia, while Israeli IAI Elta Electronics is a principal contractor for system installation, and some UK components are reportedly included in the package. The first Il-76 is expected to arrive in Israel for refitting in 1997. The programme is said to involve eight AEW aircraft.[71] As mentioned above, China has at least ten Il-76MD transports, the militarized version of the Il-76M, together with facilities to service them. These may be supplemented in the current inventory by an additional 15 Il-76Ms obtained from Uzbekistan.

Another Russian weapon that is a supposed candidate for procurement by China is the AS-15 air-launched cruise missile, which has a 3,000-km range and is capable of being launched by the PLAAF's B-6D bomber.[72] The status of a proposed transaction remains uncertain.

In October 1990 the first significant Chinese post-détente military purchase was made from the then Soviet Union and consisted of 24 Mi-17 HIP-H transport helicopters.[73]

If these programmes are all completed, the addition of sophisticated Russian equipment such as that discussed above would represent a spectacular improvement over current PLAAF hardware. Aircraft such as the Flanker and the Backfire would give the Chinese a credible tool for military intervention beyond its borders. In lieu of actual combat, such aircraft would stand as a symbol of Chinese power and prestige and offer an effective deterrent. Modern military aircraft will also add to PLAAF efforts to develop an effective combined armed capability.[74]

Russia has also contributed greatly to the development of the PLA Navy (PLAN). The Chinese Navy includes seven ex-Soviet and Chinese Romeo Class submarines (though these are probably no longer operational), twenty ex-Soviet Kronstadt Class patrol craft and 23 Soviet T-43 class ocean minesweepers.[75]

The PRC has in recent years been rapidly strengthening its military preparedness because of heightened concern over perceived pro-independence tendencies in Taiwan. The PLAN's lack of suitable long-range offensive capabilities was highlighted when the USA deployed two aircraft carrier battle groups close to the Taiwan Strait in the spring of 1996. The dispute over the Spratly Islands as well as the growth of Japanese sea power has also given China an immediate incentive to modernize its naval forces. According to some assessments, China is moving from a 'brown-water' coastal navy to a 'green-water' navy which is capable of projecting power into the Pacific and Indian Oceans.[76]

Sino-Russian military-technical cooperation in the naval field started in 1991 with the Chinese purchase of two Russian Ka-27 Helix A anti-submarine warfare helicopters.[77] In February 1994 the Nizhny Novgorod Mashzavod plant signed a contract with the PLAN to supply three shipborne 77 millimetre automatic artillery systems. In March 1995 the Chinese specialists were trained at the 'Mashzavod' to use these guns which were to be delivered by the end of the year.[78] The PLAN is also working to modernize its submarine fleet. China has purchased four Varshavyanka (Kilo) Class submarines from Russia and apparently intends to obtain the rights to manufacture additional vessels in China.[79] The first submarine produced in Nizhny Novgorod was already delivered to China in February 1995 and the second was reportedly sent to St. Petersburg for sea trials in June 1995.[80] Delivery of the second ship was expected in the summer of 1995, with the third and fourth due late 1995 or early 1996.[81] Some reports contend that China may ultimately obtain up to 22 Kilos, but sources in Beijing with a closer knowledge of the programme dismiss this.[82] It was reported in March 1995 that Beijing struck a new deal with Moscow for the purchase of six more submarines.[83]

There were also numerous reports that Beijing might purchase from Russia several Sovremenny Class destroyers. These ships have formidable air defence and anti-ship capabilities and can accommodate anti-submarine helicopters.[84] However, Moscow has persistently denied that Sovremenny Class destroyers were on offer.[85] Beijing first asked Moscow to sell two Russian Sovremenny class destroyers in 1994. The Sovremenny sale took more than three years of tough negotiations, especially over pricing and terms of payment. When Moscow and Beijing reportedly agreed in November 1996 that all future arms transfers would be fully paid for in hard currency, this facilitated the signing of the contract. The growing sense of urgency on the part of the PLAN about the expansion of its operational capabilities may also have helped speed agreement on the destroyer deal. The deal for two Sovremenny class destroyers worth $800 million was finalised during the late December 1996 visit to Moscow by Chinese Premier Li Peng,[86] even though no mention of the agreement was made in the official communiqué issued at the conclusion of his three-day stay. The two destroyers will substantially enhance the PLAN's surface strike capabilities and its ability to deploy over long distances.

According to Tai Ming Cheung, the clearest sign of China's blue water aspirations is its aircraft carrier plans.[87] According to some reports, the Chinese leadership has decided that it will acquire an aircraft carrier.[88] Since the late 1980s, China has been examining an off-shelf purchase of an aircraft carrier hull and has sent teams to inspect Spanish, Italian, French, Russian, Ukrainian and Indian aircraft carriers. There have been frequent reports that China was interested in the Ukrainian ship Varyag—a large unfinished carrier that is part of the disputed Soviet Black Sea Fleet. It now appears that China will not purchase the Varyag but will either acquire a smaller Russian carrier or build a 30-48,000 ton vessel domestically.[89]

Although there is no confirmation of China's intentions, initial training of naval officers began almost a decade ago and a dummy deck was constructed at Beijing North military airfield for deck landing and deck handling trials with the J-8-III naval fighter.[90] Another indicator of genuine interest in an aircraft carrier is the attention paid to the Yak-41 Vertical/Short Take-Off Landing naval fighter aircraft. Bin Yu also argues that it is no coincidence that China purchased the Su-27 for the PLAAF as it can be modified for use on board an aircraft carrier.[91] Numerous sources have suggested that after the completion of the existing Su-27 Flanker deal, a follow-on purchase may include the Su-27K, the naval variant specially designated for aircraft carrier-based operations.[92] Some military sources say that China is at an advanced stage of negotiations for the proposed purchase of up to fifty Su-30MK multi-role fighters. Agreement could be reached by the end of 1997.[93] According to other accounts, other Russian equipment, including the Su-25 strike aircraft and MiG-29K naval fighter, could be sought. MiG-MAPO has recently begun demonstrating the MiG-29 naval version to India and China, perhaps indicating that the larger, more complex naval version of the Su-27 is not the only maritime fighter on offer.[94] Eventual deployment of any aircraft by the air force in a maritime strike role would further boost PLAN's offensive capabilities. Moreover, if the PLAN was also to purchase the naval variant of the S-300 (NATO designation SA-N-6), it would possess the foundation for building an adequate defensive and escort force for an aircraft carrier.

Although Chinese officials can cogently argue that the Taiwan problem and Spratly Islands dispute demand that China modernize its naval capabilities, these disputes are probably not the underlying or fundamental reasons for Chinese aspirations for a blue-water navy. The cost of an aircraft carrier and its associated escort vessels and air wing make it a prohibitively expensive tool for use against countries with extremely weak navies. Chinese military interests in the Spratlys would probably be better served by warships covered by long-range and aerial-refuelled aircraft from the Paracel Islands. An aircraft carrier, as well as China's nuclear submarines, would be much better suited for use on the open seas than in the relatively shallow and constricted waters of the South China Sea.[95]

Another area of Sino-Russian defence cooperation is Russian military technology transfer to the PRC. Chinese military technology is as much as twenty years behind the West. Past efforts to resolve this problem through reverse engineering (often Soviet-made) have not overcome this gap. China's military industry has a well-documented history of problems with reverse engineered systems, and some Chinese copies of foreign-designed weapons never reached production—for example, the Chinese copies of the Soviet T-62 tank and MiG-23 fighter-bomber.

In its pursuit of defence industrial cooperation, China has found Russia a more willing partner than Western countries. Russia has been prepared to consider transfers of advanced technology even at the risk of a long-term adverse impact on the regional balance of power. This willingness stemmed from the desperate economic straits of the Russian defence industry and pressure from the defence industry and defence ministry officials to overrule the objections foreign-ministry counterparts. The military-industrial complexes (MICs) of the two countries develop about 100 joint projects. Of these about thirty projects are targeted at adapting Russian basic models to Chinese standards; the remainder should result in creation of new weapon systems and ammunition.[96]

As mentioned above, in 1995 Russia agreed to produce the Su-27 aircraft in China. The deal, revealed in Moscow in February 1996, is worth a conservative $2 billion, but it will likely take the form of a complex cash and barter arrangement. The licence production deal was covered by a letter of intent that should be finalized once the second batch of the Su-27s is delivered and paid for. A two-stage programme was proposed, the first being assembly in China from kits produced in Russia, and the second, full production in China (probably at Shenyang Aircraft Factory). The eventual aim is thought to cover around 90-100 aircraft annually, but observers say production will likely be half that number, beginning at a rate of 10-20 aircraft per year.[97] The Sukhoi bureau officials also reportedly proposed co-production of the Su-35 in China on condition that the PRC purchase close to 120 of the aircraft produced.[98]

It has been suggested that Beijing is negotiating with Russian officials for a technology exchange that could include joint development of an advanced fighter aircraft 'with capabilities falling midway between the MiG-29 fighter and the MiG-31 high-altitude interceptor'.[99] According to other accounts, Russia will move some production of the MiG-31 to the PRC. It has been suggested that 150-300

MiG-31 Foxhounds could be made in the PRC over an eight-year period.[100] This warplane is a high-altitude interceptor with superior extended-range radar and multiple target-engagement capabilities.[101]

Another recent report suggests that Russia offered to develop a brand new fighter for the PLAAF for as little as $500 million. Senior Russian Defence Ministry officials have said that there have been negotiations over a deal which could see Russian aerospace firms provide up to two-thirds of the required technical and design work, as well as providing avionics and an engine, for a new fighter based on the Xinjian J-10 airframe. China is supposedly planning to produce the new aircraft at the rate of 100 per year according to Russian statements.[102] The Chengdu-built aircraft, due to fly in 1996, will be fitted with the Russian radar system and engines of the Su-27. First flight test of the Phazotron radar system on board the F-10 was due in 1997, Russian industry officials said. The radar is similar to the Zhuk system being installed in the F-8II M fighter upgrade programme in China. A Russian radar system may have been preferred because of Chinese insistence on licensed indigenous production.[103]

In addition to advanced fighter technology, the PRC has been trying to acquire in-flight refuelling capabilities from Russia. This will enable the PLA air force to extend its reach. According to SIPRI experts, the technical assistance most needed by China would be aircraft engines and stealth technology. China is developing its next-generation fighter (the F-10) and such technology transfers at relatively concessional prices would be of considerable help.[104] The PRC is also attempting to purchase Kilo class submarine and anti-submarine warfare technology, and technical data on the design and construction of airframes.

China has shown keen interest in acquiring missile technologies from systems known to be MIRV-capable, i.e. which could be equipped with multiple independently targetable re-entry vehicles. According to a leaked US Defense Intelligence Agency (DIA) report, the PRC has been attempting to acquire SS-18 'Satan' intercontinental ballistic missile (ICBM) technology, possibly including engine and guidance technology, from Russia and/or Ukraine. China has made no secret of its attempts to acquire SS-18 technology, claiming that it would be used to improve Beijing's commercial space launch capabilities. However, some experts suggest that with Russia's assistance the Chinese will be able to create an ICBM with a range up to 12,000 km (instead of current range of 8,000) by 2005.[105] With such a missile Beijing can threaten not only Asia-Pacific but also the United States and Europe.

China has reportedly also received information on the SS-24 'Scalpel' and SS-25 'Sickle' ICBMs, designed at Russia's Nadiradze Design Bureau and Ukraine's Southern Machine Building Plant. Such information might also prove useful since both missiles are MIRV-capable. The SS-24 (Russian designation RS-22 or RT-23U) is a rail-mobile and silo-based solid-fuel ICBM that can carry up to 10 MIRVed warheads. The SS-25 (Russian designation RS-12M Topol) is a road-mobile solid-fuel ICBM that can be armed with single or multiple warheads.[106] In June 1996, the Tokyo-based Nihon Keizai Shimbun reported that China had purchased computer simulation technology from Russia to simulate the testing of multiple nuclear explosions and/or to design multiple-warhead missiles. However, a spokesman for Russia's Ministry of Atomic Industry (Minatom) subsequently denied this report.[107]

Military technology transfers were combined with exchanges of personnel and expertise. According to Russian Defence Ministry sources, 'more than 1,000 Russian defence scientists and technicians have travelled to China since 1991 on defence-industrial exchanges [and]... there are around 300-400 Chinese defence specialists in Russia'.[108] It was reported that of this group, 300 Russian experts remained with long-term commitments.[109] Some of the Russian scientists now believed to be based permanently in China are apparently experts 'in the fields of cruise missiles, anti-submarine warfare, missile launching experiments and nuclear explosions'.[110] Chinese defence scientists and technicians are working at Russian aerospace institutes, including some in Moscow, Ryazan, Samara and Saratov. Some are studying at organizations such as the Central Institute of Aircraft Dynamics in Moscow.[111] Moreover, thanks to the electronic revolution, scientists no longer have to travel abroad to assist a foreign partner. In 1993, Russian defence laboratories and their Chinese counterparts were linked by an e-mail system.[112]

China and Russia have also agreed to strengthen their cooperation in military conversion programmes. A Sino-Russian document has been signed similar to that signed by China and the United States during the visit of US Secretary of Defence William Perry to Beijing in October 1994.[113] A number of Sino-Russian joint ventures were set up to develop conversion programmes. The companies involved in the first Sino-Russian venture are Xing-Yui-Ju (Beijing), Yuilang Trading (Hong Kong) and the Nizhny Novgorod-based Impex and Institute of Applied Physics at the Russian Academy of Sciences.[114] The joint venture will take electro-optical defence items and re-configure the designs to create the commercial laser, electro-optic and optical device for sale in the Middle East. Russia will provide research personnel and expertise, leaving the manufacturing and marketing to the Chinese. The Sino-Russian joint venture 'Sungari', set up by the Ural Device-Building Plant (Ekaterinburg) and Kharbin Commercial Trade Company, has started production of car tape recorders at the former defence plant 'Lazur' in Nizhny Novgorod.[115]

There has been a plan to convert a Russian tank repair plant near Chita on the border with China into a passenger car factory with the help of Chinese engineers. China was building a VCR plant in Zelenogorsk near Moscow and modernizing a Russian tractor factory near Krasnoyarsk. Russian technicians meanwhile were renovating Soviet-built industrial plants like the Baotou steel plant, the fifth biggest in China.[116]

In fact, Sino-Russian arms deals and defence-industrial cooperation became the focal point of the PRC's efforts to engage Russia in a substantive military relationship, obtain advanced military equipment and technology to modernize the PLA inventory, enhance air force and naval capabilities, and to advance PRC power projection in East and South-East Asia.[117]

To summarize, the scope and results of Sino-Russian military cooperation are quite impressive (especially taking into account the former enmity between the two countries and the tempo of their rapprochement). However, this cooperation should not be overestimated. It is far from a relationship between the two real allies in terms of its depth and openness. Despite the seriousness of the partners their motives are fairly pragmatic and sometimes selfish. There is no real cordiality or frankness in their relations. The two parties are quite cautious and even suspicious as regards each other's intentions and motives, and both Moscow and Beijing worry about their national interests. Russia does not permit export of its most advanced weapon systems and technologies, and it is not completely satisfied with the financial conditions of its arms deals with the PRC. In turn, China is concerned about overdependence on Russian arms supplies and tries to diversify its sources of arms acquisitions. It is hardly possible that the two countries will abandon all their concerns and suspicions and radically change the very nature of their relationship in the foreseeable future. Regardless of their common interests, Moscow and Beijing will definitely keep some distance between them as concerns military and security matters.

NORTH KOREA

Along with China the former Soviet Union was instrumental in installing the Communist regime in North Korea following World War II, and it provided Pyongyang with military support during the Korean War. The two countries included formal provisions for automatic military intervention in the event of attack by a third country under their 1961 Treaty of Friendship, Cooperation and Mutual Assistance. Since the mid-60s the USSR has delivered arms worth 3.3 billion roubles to North Korea, including MiG-23 and MiG-29 fighters, T-72 MBTs, various SAMs, helicopters and small arms. More than half of the combat equipment of the North Korean army was thus Soviet-made.[118]

At the end of the 1980s, North Korea concluded a contract with the former Soviet Union to buy 100 MiG-29s, after having received about 30 MiG-29s in the mid-1980s. Although none of the 100 planes was delivered, North Korea succeeded in assembling two MiG-29s in 1992.[119]

With the Russia-South Korea rapprochement, military-technical cooperation between Moscow and Pyongyang was put on hold. However, very soon the DPRK expressed its interest in re-opening defence cooperation with Russia. North Korea's ageing armaments is one of the likely reasons why Pyongyang would like to resume its military ties with Russia. Five North Korean military aircraft crashed in 1996, according to a South Korean Defence Ministry official. An Mi-2 helicopter crashed in March, a MiG-19 fighter in September, a MiG-21 in October and two MiG-21 in December.[120] Some reports suggest that in the future North Korea may be able to produce MiG-29s indigenously, possibly under Russian licence. North Korea could conceivably purchase or produce under licence up to 25 MiG-29s by 2000 in an effort to begin replacing the obsolete J-5s, J-6s, MiG-21s and MiG-23s which make up a major part of its combat aircraft.[121]

Many Western and Asia-Pacific nations were concerned with the so-called 'brain drain' of some of the former Soviet scientists with expertise in the research and development and production of weapons of mass destruction. Economic reform, hyperinflation, and cuts in scientific spending have contributed to economic and social hardship, resulting in an exodus of scientific knowledge. The relaxation of travelling restrictions imposed during the Soviet era has allowed many of these specialists to leave the country. Moreover, the opening of the former Soviet borders has enabled foreign governments and private companies to establish trade offices in the Russian cities.

However, Russian experts note that most of such specialists are under tough control of the Russian security services. For example, a recent Russian press report suggested that the Russian Federal Security Service (FSB) had identified and were monitoring a 'core group' of such specialists. On one occasion, a group of 36 Russian scientists from the Makeev design bureau (which designs submarine-launched ballistic missiles) was stopped at Moscow's Sheremetyevo Airport en route to North Korea in late 1992.[122] Two North Korean officials were deported.[123] On another occasion, North Korea tried unsuccessfully to entice 100 Russian rocket engineers to Pyongyang under the guise of official scientific exchanges. Russian intelligence officials claimed that the real purpose was to modernise 'Scud-C' missiles.[124]

It should be noted that long before its collapse, the Soviet Union had developed co-operative training, and nuclear- and weapons-related trade relations with some Third World countries, including North Korea. Soviet relations with the DPRK in the nuclear field date from the 1950s, when training was provided for North Korean scientists at the Joint Institute for Nuclear Research in Dubna, Russia. This cooperation was crucial for the development of North Korea's first test nuclear reactor in 1963. The country maintains a cadre of about ten scientists in Dubna. Russian specialists, some of whom have changed their names to disguise their identity, have been reported to be working in North Korean laboratories.[125]

SOUTH KOREA

The Russo-Korean rapprochement in the political and military spheres started under Gorbachev in 1991. Moscow regarded Seoul as a profitable trade and economic partner as well as an additional counter-weight to Japan.[126]

Military issues were at the heart of Russian-South Korean relations from the very beginning. In April 1991, it was revealed that Moscow offered both the MiG-29 and MiG-31 to the RoK, the former at lower than usual prices, in return for Korean consumer goods. In August 1992, Seoul announced its intention to ask Russia for permission to supply facilities related to commercializing Russian defence industry, and stated that it was considering buying some Russian defence industries in order to operate them as joint ventures. Later it was reported that those ventures were in aerospace, advanced materials, electronics, lasers, and genetic engineering. Russian and Korean defence industries established some scientific and discussion links to review joint projects. South Koreans have made visits to secret defence plants and were optimistic about joint projects. Korean firms were particularly interested in acquiring aerospace technology, including composite materials for aircraft. It was also reported that Seoul was considering buying MiG-29s, mines, torpedoes, tank ammunition, and SA-6, SA-8, and SA-16 surface-to-air missiles. Moscow was also willing to sell space technology and even nuclear technology in line with South Korean interest in reproducing fissionable materials. Soon after, it was announced that a Korean consortium would build the Almaz S-300 anti-tactical ballistic missile system and its associated radars under licence.[127] This production should fulfil RoK's aim of countering the DPRK's Scud ballistic missile.

Finally, the two countries signed a military cooperation agreement in 1993. However, at that stage cooperation between the two countries did not make any essential progress. Defence ties between Russia and South Korea have been stimulated by a rather unusual factor. In 1991, Seoul loaned the former Soviet Union $1.47 billion in an effort to develop relations with its former adversary. Being unable to repay its debt Russia offered to trade weapons for debt forgiveness. According to South Korea's semi-official *Yonhap* News Agency, the Government (over the objections of its senior defence officials) concluded that they had 'no choice but to accept the offer' with Russia's foreign debt steadily rising.[128]

In April 1995, a barter repayment deal was forged to cover the first $450.7 million in principal and interest. Nearly half the initial sum, or $208.81 million, was in military hardware obtained by Seoul largely for intelligence evaluation and training purposes, with delivery from 1995 until 1998. This included unknown numbers of T-80U MBTs, BMP-3 AIFVs, AT-7 'Saxhorn' anti-tank guided missiles and SA-16 'Gimlet' SAMs. Some sources suggest that the deal covered MiG-29 and S-300 SAMs as well.[129] In 1995, an undisclosed number of South Korean army personnel began a training course in Russia to prepare for the change-over, which was to start at the end of 1996.[130] According to Russian sources, there were thirty Koreans in the Russian training centres in 1996,[131] and Russian military specialists were sent to South Korea as consultants.

Seoul has asked Moscow to provide a battalion of thirty T-80U MBTs, thirty BMP-3 AIFVs, several hundreds of AT-7 'Saxhorn' anti-tank guided missiles 'Metis-M' and SA-18 'Igla' portable anti-aircraft missiles, ammunition, and spare parts. Delivery was due in the autumn of 1996.[132] A number of BTR-80 8x8 wheeled APCs have also been ordered. The South Korean army activated its first unit with Russian AIFVs, a mechanised infantry battalion with 30 BMP-3s, on 1 October 1996, and Seoul formed its first armoured battalion equipped with Russian MBTs on 1 November.[133] According to *Jane's Defence Weekly* sources, in early 1997 South Korea received a third shipment of Russian military equipment including 26 T-80Us.[134] Russia delivered equipment worth $150 million by the end of 1996. It was announced that Seoul will receive a further shipment of BMP-3 infantry combat vehicles, spares and ammunition worth $31.25 million from Russia during 1997.[135]

Seoul was also interested in Russian advanced fighters. According to some accounts, Russia's Su-35 is one of four aircraft which Seoul has said is in contention for its F-X requirement for a new fighter.[136]

Given that Thailand has acquired a Spanish-built aircraft carrier and China's intentions to do the same, many countries of the region (including South Korea) are contemplating the same possibility. It is being suggested that the RoK could be competing with India for acquisition of the 70,000-tonne Russian aircraft carrier Admiral Kuznetsov. Other possibilities are the Admiral Gorshkov which is under repair, or payment by another nation for resumption of work on the Admiral Kuznetsov sister ship Varyag which is said to be 70 percent complete in the Ukrainian Nikolayev shipyard.[137]

To conclude, Russian arms sale policies on the Korean Peninsula in the 1990s have a mixed record. On the one hand, Moscow succeeded in establishing military-technical cooperation with South Korea, and its security relations with North Korea were also redefined in a more pragmatic way. At the same time, notwithstanding Russian promises to conduct 'even-handed' strategy and not violate a military balance in the area, Moscow's actual arms transfer policy was more favourable to Seoul than Pyongyang. Moreover, Moscow's arms sale policy was sometimes a 'hostage' to technical or economic problems rather than an instrument of security strategy. For instance, military-technical cooperation with Seoul was subordinated to economic and financial issues. It thus remains unclear how Moscow is going to use arms transfers to promote security and stability on the peninsula or to encourage dialogue between two Koreas with the final aim of their unification. It appears that Russia's short-term and purely pragmatic needs (such as repaying debts or acquiring currency) can sometimes undermine or distort the long-term objectives of Moscow's security policy in the region.

ARMS CONTROL AND CONFIDENCE AND SECURITY-BUILDING MEASURES

Another crucial element of Russian security policy in East Asia is confidence-building among the nations of the region. As many analysts emphasise, a confidence-building process contributes to changing perceptions of security, and information is critical in this regard. Transparency or access to accurate information can provide reliable evidence that certain behaviour and actions do not constitute a threat and thereby help reduce mistrust and misperceptions. Another positive implication of such a process is that debating, developing, negotiating and implementing CSBMs involve the parties in dialogue and interaction. This enables the parties involved to present and explain their views, discuss their positions, expose their goals and motives, and uncover each other's perceptions and interpretations. The result of these activities is a transformation not only in thinking and perceptions but also in behaviour and policies. CSBM implementation results in the establishment of principles, rules, norms or standard of conduct that regulate states' behaviour.[138] Moreover, CSBMs strengthen existing, or encourage the creation of new multilateral mechanisms and institutions which serve a solid basis for security and stability in a region.

Compared to Europe arms control process and confidence and security building measures (CSBMs) remain in embryo in East Asia, but some undertakings have been initiated by Moscow and Beijing in their bilateral relations. Russia, Japan and South Korea inaugurated some modest CSBMs as well. Russian confidence-building strategy in the region focuses on the following issues:

DEFENSIVE NUCLEAR STRATEGY

Moscow tries to persuade the regional actors that it has no intention to use its nuclear potential against them. For instance, the September 1994 Yeltsin-Jiang communiqué mentioned several CSBMs, including no-first-use of nuclear weapons and a retargeting of nuclear missiles away from each other's territory.

REDUCTION OF ARMED FORCES AND ARMAMENTS IN BORDER AREAS

To appease Japan Russia has embarked on a programme of gradual demilitarization of the four disputed Kuril Islands. Furthermore, as mentioned above, Russia and China have significantly reduced their forces in the border areas, and in 1992 Russia completed the withdrawal of troops from Mongolia initiated by Gorbachev in 1987. While visiting China in December 1992 Mr Yeltsin signed a declaration calling for a reduction of troops along the border to 'a minimal level'. In May 1996, then Defence Minister Grachev said that Russia had cut 150,000 troops from its Far Eastern deployment since 1995, adding that the Pacific Fleet had been reduced by 50 percent since 1985.[139]

In March 1996, on the eve of his visit to Beijing, Yeltsin suggested that an agreement be reached with China on moving troops 100 km away from the frontier.[140] Hardly noticed in Moscow, this evoked a clamorous response in the Maritime and Khabarovsk Provinces. The main industrial centres and communication lines of the Far East are close to the border, while those of China are deep in the country. The Trans-Siberian Railway Line, which is of strategic importance to Russia, in some places runs a mere five kilometres from the border rivers of Ussuriisk and Amur. The distance between Khabarovsk, a big industrial centre, and the frontier is only seven km. Vladivostok, a major base for the Pacific Fleet, is only 70 km away. During Yeltsin's visit to China the Chinese delegation proposed moving its troops 200 km from the border, but the Russian visitors claimed that this would pose them 'technical' difficulties.[141]

On 24 April 1997 China and four neighbouring CIS member-states concluded a path-breaking border treaty aimed at reducing tensions along their common frontiers. The pact was signed in Moscow by the presidents of China, Kazakhstan, Kyrgyzstan, Russia, and Tajikistan. The treaty, which will run until 2020 (following parliamentary notification by each of the signatory states), is primarily intended to control troop levels within a 100 km band on either side of an affected border. According to some accounts, some quotas were established for the four CIS countries: 130,000 servicemen (of these are 120,000 Russian troops), 3,900 tanks, 5,800 APCs and AIFVs, 4,500 artillery pieces, 290 aircraft and 434 helicopters.[142] The treaty envisages reductions of conventional land forces, tactical aviation and air defence aircraft only. Strategic forces, navies, strategic aviation and air defence missiles are not subject to the agreement. The treaty also sets up limitations for the border guard troops.[143] Commenting to his counterparts at the signing ceremony, Chinese President Jiang Zemin said: 'As the first treaty in the Asia/Pacific region on reducing military forces, this agreement has major political and military significance'.[144] It should be noted that the above agreement among other implications also leads to a disengagement of armed forces in the areas of their direct confrontation and thus limits the risks of surprise attack.

PREVENTION OF DANGEROUS MILITARY ACTIVITIES

In July 1994, the Russian and Chinese defence ministers signed an agreement to prevent incidents between the two countries' armies, such as combat aircraft crossing into the other country's airspace. It will also regulate unsanctioned missile launches, the use of lasers which could harm the other side, and jamming of communication equipment.[145] The agreement, which entered into force immediately and set out mechanisms for mutual security, will be reviewed at an annual meeting between the two sides. Russia has signed similar agreements with Canada, Greece and the USA.[146]

In April 1996, at a summit meeting in Shanghai, the PRC signed an agreement on preventing border incidents with Russia and a number of the CIS countries (Kazakhstan, Kyrgyzstan, and Tajikistan).[147] Russia and China had been negotiating a border agreement since at least 1992, and this was extended to include the three Central Asian republics. Russia's land border with China totals 3,645 km. Moscow and Beijing have agreed on 90 percent of their common border.[148]

Russia and Japan conduct annual consultations on preventing incidents at sea beyond the territorial waters and the air-space above them.[149]

CONSTRAINTS ON MILITARY ACTIVITIES, EXERCISES AND MANOEUVRES

During his visit to China in May 1995, then Russian Defence Minister Grachev suggested that Russian observers should attend Chinese military exercises. The provisions (which include a pledge of prior notification of military exercises, limits on the number and types of exercises permitted within 100km of the border, and the attendance of exercises by observers) were incorporated in an agreement signed by the four CIS states and the PRC during President Yeltsin's April 1996 visit to China. CSBMs have also been initiated between the border-security forces of the two countries. In 1996, Russian and Chinese border guards exchanged delegations which attended command-staff exercises.[150]

In April 1996, Russia and Japan also agreed on enhancing transparency and mutual notification of large-scale exercises.

MILITARY-TO-MILITARY CONTACTS, JOINT EXERCISES, EXCHANGES, AND VISITS

In 1994 intensive exchanges began with port visits made by the North China Fleet and Russian Pacific Fleet units. Some Russian and Chinese local commanders visited each other's military districts. In late 1994 Admiral Feliks Gromov, commander of the Russian Navy, signed agreements on military cooperation, including joint naval exercises. By the year of 1997 about 200 Chinese officers were trained in the Russian military academies.[151] Also significant is the fact that China and Russia have resumed intelligence ties. Although details of the intelligence liaison pact remain unknown, US officials confirm that ties were restored in September 1992.[152] The two governments will probably share information and/or opinions about mutual security concerns in the region, including the volatile situation in Central Asia and the military posture of Japan.[153]

Military-to-military contacts are also developing between Moscow and Tokyo. During his visit to Moscow in March 1996, Japanese Foreign Minister Ikeda and his Russian counterpart Primakov agreed that Japan's Defence Agency and Russia's Defence Ministry should begin ministerial-level exchanges. Following this agreement, Japan's then Minister of State and Director-General of the Defence Agency, Hideo Usui, visited Russia in April 1996. This was the first time in the history of the two countries' bilateral relations that a Japanese Defence Minister had visited Russia. The two countries signed a document on various CSBMs, including exchange visits by naval vessels. On 26 July 1996, the 5,200 ton destroyer Kurama arrived in Vladivostok, the home of the Russian Pacific Fleet. This was the first port call made by a Japanese military vessel to Russia since 1925,[154] and in June 1997, the Russian destroyer Admiral Vinogradov visited Tokyo.[155] In May 1997, former Russian Defence Minister Igor Rodionov visited Tokyo and the two sides agreed to intensify the Russian-Japanese security dialogue and further exchanges.[156]

In November 1992, Russian and South Korean presidents signed a memorandum providing for military exchanges and naval visits between Vladivostok and Pusan. When Mr Grachev visited South Korea in May 1995, the two countries signed a memorandum on technological cooperation between their defence industries. In December 1995, during his visit to Seoul the Russian Prime Minister Viktor Chernomyrdin initialled the Declaration on the Development and Promotion of Trade, Economic, Science and Technology Cooperation, which indicated military technology as one of the major fields of cooperation to be developed.[157]

REGIONAL SECURITY DIALOGUE WITHIN MULTILATERAL INSTITUTIONS

Another fundamental mechanism for confidence-building is the active engagement of regional governments and certain global actors in institutionalized dialogue and consultation on regional security issues. Such fora enhance mutual understanding and trust and prevent the misinterpretations and suspicions that often cause tensions and even armed conflict. They also provide confidence-building processes with proper organizational support.

ASEAN, the main regional organization, has yet to establish a tight-fit cooperative unity between its member-states. However, there have been some very significant developments, both with regard to broadening the regional security agenda and to an institutionalisation of regional security fora in the past few years. Security issues have been introduced to the agenda of the ASEAN-Post Ministerial Conference (ASEAN-PMC), and a formal multilateral forum, called the ASEAN Regional Forum (ARF), for discussion of political and security issues, was established in July 1993.

In late 1995, the ASEAN member-states signed the South-East Asian Nuclear Weapons-Free Zone Treaty. It was, however, criticized by the US which was worried that the treaty could constrain the operation of its nuclear-powered or nuclear-armed ships and aircraft, as well as by China which was discontented with the agreement's geographical scope that included parts of the South China Sea in dispute between Beijing and some ASEAN nations.[158] Despite this disagreement the treaty, in general, has promoted the confidence-building process in the area. A number of other important security issues are under consideration in the ARF: CSBMs, the establishment of a Zone of Peace, Freedom and Neutrality (ZOPFAN), nuclear non-proliferation, peace-keeping cooperation, the exchange of non-classified military information, maritime security issues, preventive diplomacy, the participation of ARF countries in the UN Conventional Arms Register, etc.[159] However, to be an effective instrument of a regional security community, the ARF must overcome uncertainties and limitations as well as provide for more institutional support. Indeed, as a multilateral security institution, the ARF has a long way to go before it can affect the regional states' continuing preference for bilateral mechanisms. At present, the ARF remains a consultative institution which still lacks a proper administrative and implementation mechanism.

It should be noted that regional security institution-building in Asia-Pacific is no longer an exclusively inter-governmental affair. A number of non-governmental actors are increasingly active in promoting dialogues and suggesting policy options on regional security. Such organizations as the ASEAN Institute for Strategic and International Studies and the Council for Security Cooperation in Asia-Pacific (CSCAP), in which fourteen countries are represented (including Russia) played a key role in pushing ASEAN in the direction of a formal process of security dialogue including arms sales issues.[160]

Some Russian diplomats and analysts also suggest that Moscow could contribute to the development of regional CSBMs by initiating negotiations between the major suppliers of arms and military technologies to the region; by its participation in drawing-up a regional 'code of conduct' and in creation of a system of regional conflict resolution, peace-keeping forces, and of a regional centre for conflict prevention and resolution.[161]

CONFLICT RESOLUTION

There are a number of disputes (territorial claims and local conflicts) which undermine the security in the region. Russia's policy towards these conflicts differentiates depending on their type. Moscow has been rather active in conflict to which it is a party, but has kept a relatively low profile compared to the USSR with regard to mediation of other regional conflicts (e.g. China-Taiwan or ROK-DPRK).

THE KURIL ISLANDS

The Northern Territories dispute between Russia and Japan is a source of long-term instability in East Asia. Tokyo lost the four islands off the northern tip of Japan to the Soviet Union at the end of the Second World War (Kunashiri, Shikotan, Etorofu and Habomai). Khrushchev promised to return two of the lesser Kuril Islands in exchange for a peace treaty in 1956,[162] but Soviet Foreign Minister Andrey Gromyko nixed the deal in 1960 as East-West tensions soured. The Soviet Union almost agreed to return at least two of the four disputed islands again in 1973, with hints that the other two islands could follow. But after bellicose demands from Japan's prime minister Kakuei Tanaka for the return of all four islands an angry Leonid Brezhnev put the offer back into cold storage. All subsequent attempts to conclude a peace treaty, putting an official end to hostilities between the two countries, have been thwarted by this territorial dispute. Moscow officially denied the existence of the problem throughout the 1970s and 1980s.

The Japanese claim to the islands became more forceful upon the dissolution of the Soviet Union. Tokyo promised large-scale assistance to Russia in exchange for the contested territories but refused to provide Moscow with aid until progress was made on the return of the Northern Territories. Since his coming into power Russian President Yeltsin has appeared to recognize the problem and to attempt to work out some framework for a future agreement. He even went so far as to suggest alignment with Japan in his letter to then Japanese prime minister Kiichi Miyazawa.[163] According to some accounts, he intended to sign a peace treaty with Japan during 1993,[164] and in May 1992 Mr. Yeltsin announced that all Russian troops, except for border guards, would be withdrawn from the disputed islands. In Tokyo in October 1993, he told Japanese prime minister Hosokawa that half the troops had been withdrawn and that the other half would definitely leave.

During his visit to Japan in 1993 Mr Yeltsin recognized the validity of a 1956 joint declaration promising a return of two of the islands to Japan. The Tokyo Declaration that emerged after the 1993 summit agreed to seek a solution to the territorial dispute 'on the basis of historical and legal facts'. The Russian and Japanese leaders also confirmed the importance of political dialogue, and agreed to broaden talks between their two governments on a wide range of issues, including security. Tokyo agreed to assist Moscow in constructing facilities in Russia to store nuclear material retrieved from dismantled warheads, as well as facilities to process liquid radioactive waste in Vladivostok, and to treat liquid missile fuel.[165] By signing the Economic Declaration, the two countries agreed to develop trade and economic relations on the basis of the 'principle of expanded equilibrium'. Potential areas for cooperation included energy, transport, telecommunications, defence industry conversion, the safety of nuclear-power plants and environmental conservation.

Contrary to expectations that Russian-Japanese negotiations on the Kuril Islands would start promptly, after the Tokyo summit Moscow backed off sharply on a promise of talks because of nationalist pressure at home. President Yeltsin called for joint economic development of the region while setting aside sovereignty issues, and hinted at some concessions in the future if Russian internal situation would permit it. In January 1996, the Russian foreign minister Yevgeny Primakov even suggested that resolving the territorial dispute should be left to the next generation. He proposed that Japan and Russia should adopt a policy over the islands similar to that taken by Japan and China over the Senkaku Islands—namely to postpone the issue of sovereignty and in the meantime to develop cordial relations.[166]

The two countries have managed to resolve a number of bilateral problems. For example, they defined safe fishing zones and ways of arbitrating disputes that did not compromise either side's claim to the islands. In March 1996 Mr Primakov announced that Russia was proceeding with its demilitarisation of the islands, and that the number of Russian military troops currently stationed there was around 3,500, with none on Shikotan island. Both governments are encouraging mutual visits by the Russian inhabitants of the four islands and Japanese citizens without passport or visa, in accordance with the framework established in 1991. By mid-1997 the two countries decided to freeze discussion of sovereignty issues and start intensive economic cooperation covering not only the Kuril Islands but also other areas of the Russian Far East. Russian-Japanese trade is expected to top $6 billion in 1997. Japan has also invested heavily in a monumental $25 billion project to extract oil and natural gas from Russia's Sakhalin Island.[167] The Japanese prime minister Ryutaro Hashimoto approved a joint $10 billion project to develop a natural-gas field in Irkutsk in Russia and build a pipe-line to Japan via Mongolia, China, and South Korea.[168]

SINO-RUSSIAN TERRITORIAL DISPUTES

Compared to Russian-Japanese relations, the resolution of the Sino-Russian territorial disputes has been more successful. Under the 1991 Sino-Soviet Treaty, confirmed in 1994 and ratified by the Parliaments of both countries, the demarcation of 33 disputed border sections in Russia's Amur Region and the Khabarovsk and Maritime Provinces should be resolved. Except for some small segments, the entire Sino-Russian border has now been delimited.

However, the demarcation of the border has had some unexpected domestic implications for Moscow and led to the conflict between the Russian federal authorities and some local political leaders. Under the treaty, 70 hectares of ploughland near Lake Khanka, a newly built road and a power transmission line, have already been placed under Russia's jurisdiction. In return, the Chinese are to get 968 hectares in the Ussuriisk District and another 300 hectares on the Tuman River in the Khasan District. The latter is the key issue in the dispute between the Maritime administration and the Russian Foreign Ministry. Historically, the land was Chinese, but under the 1860 Peking Agreement, the land was given to Russia. Until 1913 it belonged to the Russian Zarechensko-Podgornensky land community, after which it was leased to people living in China and Korea. In 1926 the lease expired, but the Chinese continued to cross the border and use the land. They still considered it Chinese land. The Japanese followed suit when they occupied the northern part of China in 1931, and this set off an armed conflict in October 1936. Big battles also erupted at Lake Khasan in 1938. This land contains the graves of Russian soldiers who died 60 years ago. The dispute along the Tuman River broke out again in the 1960s, when the Chinese tried to gradually infiltrate the area.[169]

The disputed area is at the junction of the Chinese, Russian and North Korean borders. The Tuman River is 150 metres wide and runs into the Bay of Peter the Great. Its western bank belongs to China and its eastern bank to Russia. The bank line on the Chinese territory starts about 5 km from the seashore. If the territory is ceded to China, a channel could be dug and an ocean port could be built to rival the Russian ports of Vladivostok and Nakhodka. There are also some reports that

China intends to build a naval base there. According to some Russian experts, the Chinese project on the Tuman River will be detrimental to the interests of the Maritime Province and Russia, not only because of the planned sea port and naval base but also because this project will inevitably cause the area to become yet another Free Trade Zone. Competition there will make Vladivostok and Nakhodka the biggest losers.[170] In turn, Russian officials, including Yeltsin, have disputed each point and told the local leaders that the Chinese assured Moscow that Beijing has no plans to build a port on the Tuman River.

Maritime Province Governor Yevgeny Nazdratenko was the first to protest against the ratification of the 1991 Sino-Soviet Treaty. In 1994 he threatened to resign if the Chinese received the disputed lands. However, after the President ordered the demarcation to proceed as quickly as possible, the rebellious Governor changed his mind and announced he would not resign. He was backed by the local Duma, which issued an appeal to the Council of the Russian Federation, saying that demarcation was inadmissible unless a national referendum was held.

In Khabarovsk, the local authorities have requested President Yeltsin not to cede fifteen islets on the Amur River to the Chinese, and the population has held small rallies and written appeals. Vitaly Poluyanov, chieftain of the Ussuriisk Cossack Force (allegedly with the support of all Cossack leaders in Russia) declared that Moscow risked tensions in the area and that the border should remain unchanged. If not, the cossacks would reserve the right to take any actions, including extreme ones. Major-General Valery Rozov, head of the Russian demarcation group, also resigned from his post in a protest against 'selling out Russia'.[171] President Yeltsin, however, ignored the protests and ordered Russian officials to proceed with demarcation of the Sino-Russian border.

THE CHINA-TAIWAN CONFLICT

China-Taiwan animosity is another factor which destabilizes the regional security system. Russia faces a dilemma how to increase economic and cultural ties with Taipei without irritating Beijing. In 1992-95, Russian-Taiwanese trade increased from $213 mln to $551 mln.[172] However, it was significantly less than Russian trade with mainland China. In September 1992, President Yeltsin issued a decree reassuring the PRC that Russia would avoid formal political relations with Taiwan.

The Russian leadership also managed to resist the temptation to begin arms sales to Taipei. According to Sergey Glaziev, then Deputy Minister for Foreign Economic Relations, the ministry was ready to issue a licence for arms merchants to sell Taiwan ships, missiles and light arms if the Russian leadership should decide that arms transfers to Taipei would not harm relations with mainland China.[173] Former Minister for Foreign Economic Relations, Pyotr Aven, noted that Russian defence plants put formidable pressure upon the government to permit arms deals with Taiwan.[174] However, the Kremlin blocked the proposed deal.

In the mid-1990s the PRC became increasingly bellicose in its actions towards Taiwan and in its statements on issues relating to reunification. According to the Chinese government, Taiwan remains part of China, its future must be resolved by Beijing alone, and the PRC reserves the right to use force to take Taiwan. Moreover, the Taiwan issue again became an area of controversy in Sino-American relations following the private visit of the Taiwanese President Lee Teng-hui to his US Alma Mater, Cornell University, in early June 1995. Chinese President Jiang Zemin alleged that China had been deceived by US Secretary of State Warren Christopher, who had given assurances that Lee would not be allowed into the US.[175] China responded to Lee's visit by recalling its ambassador from Washington; postponing a visit by its defence minister to the US; calling off talks with the United States relating to the Missile Technology Control Regime (MTCR); suspending a scheduled round of cross-Strait negotiation; and intensifying PLA military exercises off the Zhejiang coast north of Taiwan. The PLA fired guided missiles into an area of the East China Sea just 145 km north of Taiwan.[176] These developments brought relations between Taiwan and mainland China back to a state of Cold War-style military confrontation.

The Taiwanese presidential elections of 1996 intensified the public debate over 'Taiwanisation' and put pressure on the Chinese leadership to use force to reassimilate the island into the Chinese mainland. On the eve of the presidential elections the PRC started the exercise in the Taiwan Strait. In response to this move the United States sent two carrier battle-groups to the Strait to deter Beijing from aggressive action.[177]

Given this US military pressure on China and NATO eastward expansion Beijing and Moscow shared a common interest in demonstrating their united position on a number of important domestic and international issues. In the Sino-Russian Joint Statement signed by the Russian and Chinese presidents on 25 April 1996, the two countries expressed their support for each other on delicate domestic issues such as Chechnya, Taiwan and Tibet. Beijing supported Russia in its resistance to NATO enlargement. On Taiwan, the two leaders asserted that the Russian Federation reiterates that the PRC is the sole legal government representing the whole of China, that Taiwan is an inalienable part of Chinese territory, and that Russia will neither establish official relations nor enter into official contacts with Taiwan.[178]

THE KOREAN PENINSULA

Since perestroika Russia faces a serious challenge to its diplomacy on the Korean Peninsula. On the one hand, North Korea was a traditional ally of the Soviet Union since the late 1940s. Contrary to Russia itself, however, Pyongyang did not want to reform its socialist regime or ease its tensions with South Korea. On the other hand, Moscow was eager to establish diplomatic and economic relations with Seoul to attract South Korean investments to the troubled Russian economy. Generally,

Moscow wants to be a key player on the peninsula, an area that affects Russia's economic, political and security positions in North-east Asia.

Russia attempted to define the principles of the so-called 'even-handed' policy towards the two Koreas. As Russian diplomats and academics emphasize, Russian national interests are best served by détente and fruitful inter-Korean dialogue, constructive mutually complementary partnership with the ROK and good-neighbourly, mutually advantageous relations with the DPRK. They also comment that Moscow's interests are stability on the peninsula, co-ordinated reductions of weapons supplies, a curtailment of third country military activities around the peninsula, and US withdrawal to foster inter-Korean dialogue and confidence building. They underline that Moscow proceeds from these premises in its Korean policy rather than from traditional balance-of-power principles. Russia does not develop its ties with one Korean state at the expense of the other.[179] However, in reality Russia has not always been able to implement the declared principles. Its 'even-handed' policy has met with numerous difficulties.

The early Yeltsin administration, hoping for South Korean investments, initially tried to continue the Gorbachevian course on rapprochement with Seoul (Gorbachev established the diplomatic relationship with South Korea in September 1990). In March 1992, then Russian Foreign Minister Andrei Kozyrev visited South Korea and assured Seoul that Moscow would not cooperate with Pyongyang in developing its nuclear programme, and that Moscow has stopped arms sales to North Korea.

In November 1992, President Yeltsin visited Seoul where he signed a treaty on the principles of Russia-RoK bilateral relations which should be based on common ideals of freedom, democracy and commitment to a market economy. Mr Yeltsin also supported peaceful reunification through North-South dialogue. He further proposed multilateral consultations among the North-east Asian countries as a preliminary step towards establishing a consultative regional security body to mediate international disputes, and creating a centre for regional strategic research.

However, the first results of the Russia-RoK economic and political cooperation have been discouraging. Because of the unfavourable investment climate in Russia, South Korean investment in its economy has been quite small (only $25 mln in 1995).[180] Moscow has been irritated by the March 1995 agreement on the creation of the Korean Peninsula Energy Development Organisation (KEDO) signed by the US, South Korea and Japan. In accordance with this document, KEDO was to provide South Korean light-water nuclear reactors to North Korea. Since the Soviet Union had dominated the North Korean nuclear industry market, and the two countries had some plans to develop Pyongyang's nuclear programme, Russia regarded the supply of South Korean reactors to North Korea as the loss of the lucrative market.

Russia also has been discontented with South Korean and US tactics of ignoring Russia in the discussions of major security problems on the peninsula. Russia has also been angered by the fact that it had not been invited to participate in the four-party talks (the two Koreas, the US and China) aimed at establishing a lasting peace on the peninsula and has emphasized that a comprehensive solution to the peninsula's problems should be sought by an international conference attended by all parties concerned, including Russia.[181]

Russia's rapprochement with the RoK has been accompanied by deteriorating relations with the DPRK, in particular by a severance of the defence ties between the two countries. By mid-1992, Russian officials were openly claiming that they would not supply Pyongyang with weapons systems or technical assistance for military purposes and that Moscow opposed a nuclearization of the peninsula. When Yeltsin came to Seoul in November 1992, he denounced the 1961 treaty with the North. Yeltsin strongly suggested that Russia would no longer honour the pledge to defend the North in a war, would cut off military aid to it, and would 'impose political pressure' on the DPRK to stop its nuclear weapons programme.[182] In 1996, the treaty officially expired and no new treaty has been concluded so far.

However, as a result of some difficulties in Russian-South Korean relations, Moscow has modified its South Korean-oriented foreign policy and tried to improve relations with Pyongyang. The two countries declared their intention to conclude a new agreement, and in August 1995 (i.e. before the expiry of the old treaty), the Russian Foreign Ministry proposed a draft of a new treaty. In September 1996, Pyongyang proposed a counter-draft. According to some reports, renewed military cooperation, excluding a military intervention clause, is expected to feature in a new basic agreement on relations between Russia and North Korea, which is likely to be concluded in the near future.

The first round of talks aimed at forging a new agreement, held in Pyongyang between 21 and 24 January 1997, represented 'considerable progress' by Russian accounts.[183] Russian Deputy Foreign Minister Grigoriy Karasin said that the new agreement will include provisions for 'establishing absolutely normal military and technical cooperation with North Korea'. Karasin, who headed the Moscow delegation at the January talks, said in an interview on Russian television that such cooperation would include supply of weapons and spare parts, training and military exchanges. The only constraints are that cooperation should not contravene Russia's international commitments or upset the military balance on the Korean Peninsula, he added.[184]

It appears that the Russian leadership eventually adopted a more balanced approach to its relations with both Koreas. However, as Harada underlines, the main problem for Russia is its marginalization in the sub-region. The real reason for Russia's marginalization is its weakened political, military and economic power.[185] It should be noted, however, that, as especially Moscow's active arms sales policy shows, Russia will try to remain an important regional player, even though some other countries favoured its limited role in the area.

CONCLUSIONS

Eight conclusions emerge from the above. First, East Asia remains an important foreign policy priority for Russia. Moscow has significant economic, political and security interests in the area. Second, Russian threat perceptions have gradually shifted from 'hard security' to 'soft security' issues. Since there is no immediate military threat to Russia its attention has turned to economic, societal, environmental problems, territorial disputes, illegal migration, drug trafficking and so on. These challenges can be successfully met by the progress of the Russian domestic reforms and Moscow's active cooperation with the Far Eastern nations in various areas from trade to CSBMs.

Third, the end of the military confrontation with China and the US as well as degradation of the Russian military have led to dramatic force reduction, a certain defensive restructuring and a decline in combat readiness. Generally, the Russian military presence in East Asia has decreased, and major regional players have acknowledged that Russia no longer poses a military threat to its neighbours.

Fourth, Moscow tries to compensate for its current economic and military weakness by an aggressive arms sale policy in the region. The immediate background for such a policy has basically been the need for Russia to support its defence industry, but other domestic factors have also driven the Russian arms export policy, such as the need for hard currency to finance economic reforms (conversion among them) and ease social constraints, attempts to develop the Russian Far East, domestic political struggles and interest group competition.

At the same time, some important strategic and security considerations push Moscow to continue its active arms sale policy in the APR. Russia tries to remain an influential player in a region which might determine the future of the world. Moscow also hopes that military ties with the countries of the region will provide Russia with a strategic counterweight to a number of threats and challenges in the post-Cold War era. These might include US hegemonism, the rise of Japanese and Chinese powers, or a militant Islam.

Fifth, China is Russia's most important strategic partner in the region. Moscow resumed its defence ties with Beijing which became Russia's principal recipient in the region. Moscow has been able to build a fully-fledged military-technical cooperation with the PRC which includes arms and military technology transfers, defence industry and conversion programmes, joint military R&D projects, exchange and training programmes. Arms imports from Russia became an important part of the PLA's modernisation programme which may result in substantial increase in China's military capabilities. Although Beijing tries to diversify its sources of arms acquisition, Sino-Russian military-technical cooperation has proven to be a long-term enterprise rather than short-term arrangement. Such cooperation is both an important element in Sino-Russian bilateral relations and a powerful incentive for their further development.

Sixth, along with an active arms sale policy Russia endeavours to develop a regional system of CSBMs, including a redefinition of nuclear strategy, reduction of armed forces and armaments in the border areas, prevention of dangerous military activities, limitation of military activities and exercises, military-to-military contacts, joint exercises, exchanges, visits and promotion of a regional security dialogue within multilateral institutions. Although it remains unclear how Moscow is going to combine the aggressive arms trade policy with the development of CSBMs, if implemented the above measures could contribute to the amelioration of the regional security environment.

Seventh, for a number of reasons, such as national security considerations and the desire to remain (or become, once again) an influential regional actor, Russia is eager to resolve residual territorial disputes and local conflicts in East Asia. Such policy has, however, a mixed record. While the Sino-Russian border disputes have been almost settled, Russia and Japan are only at the very beginning of a long way to resolution of the so-called problem of the Northern Territories. Russia backs China in the Taiwan dispute but this hardly facilitates the search for an adequate solution. Russia is nearly isolated from discussions on settling down the Korean conflict. Because of increasing marginalisation the Russian strategy of balancing the two Koreas has not been really efficient.

Eighth, Russia's security policies in East Asia should be considered not only in the international context but, first of all, as a reflection of the domestic processes. A country in a period of dramatic transition is unlikely to have a sound and coherent security strategy. Positive changes in Russian policy will mainly depend on the success or failure with Russian domestic reforms. It should be noted, however, that it is also important to provide Russia with a favourable international environment. Russia's shift towards democratic and co-operative policies will be facilitated if Moscow gets access to the existing multilateral organizations and arrangements and thus becomes a full-fledged participant in the regional security process.

NOTES

1. Ministry of Foreign Affairs of the Russian Federation, 'Konzeptsia vneshney politiki Rossiyskoi Federatsii' (Foreign policy concept of the Russian Federation), Special Issue of *Diplomaticheskiy Vestnik* (January 1993), pp. 3-23 (in Russian).
2. Bogaturov, A.D., M.M. Kozhokin, & K.V. Pleshakov: 'Vneshnyaa politika Rossii' ['Russia's foreign policy'], in *USA: Economics, Politics, Ideology, 1992*, no. 10, p. 31 (in Russian); *International Affairs* (Moscow) (January 1993), p. 48; Singh, Anita Inder: 'India's Relations with Russia and Central Asia', *International Affairs*, vol. 71, no. 1 (1995), p. 71.
3. Menon, Rajan: 'The Strategic Convergence Between Russia and China', *Survival*, vol. 39, no. 2 (Summer 1997), p. 104; Jordan, Mary: 'Russia Signals A New Status With Japan', *International Herald Tribune*, 2 June 1997, p. 4; *Literaturnaya Gazeta*, no.

45 (6 November 1996), p. 14 (in Russian).
4. *Izvestia*, 22 September 1994; and 15 March 1997 (in Russian).
5. Lasater, M.: *The New Pacific Community: U.S. Strategic Options in Asia* (Boulder: Westview Press, 1996), p. IX.
6. Brick, A.: 'The Asian Giants: Neighbourly Ambivalence', *Global Affairs*, Fall 1991, p. 84.
7. Godwin, P. & J. Schulz: 'China and Arms Control: Transition in East Asia', *Arms Control Today*, November 1994, p. 8.
8. Richardson, M.: 'A "Critical Moment" for Security', *International Herald Tribune*, 10 June 1997, p. 7.
9. *Rossiyskaya Gazeta*, 2 October 1997, p. 7.
10. *International Herald Tribune*, 11 June 1997, pp. 5, 10.
11. Arbatov, Alexei: 'Russian national interests', in Robert D. Blackwill & Sergei A. Karaganov (eds.): *Damage Limitation or Crisis? Russia and the Outide World* (Washington, D.C: Brassey's, 1994), p. 72.
12. *ibid.*, p. 72; and Trush, S.: 'Prodazha rossiyskogo oruzhiya Pekinu: rezony i opaseniya' ['Russian arms sales to Beijing: pro and contra'], *Nezavisimaya Gazeta*, 25 April 1996 (in Russian).
13. Trenin, Dmitry: 'Kak prikryt vostochniy geostrategicheskiy "fasad" Rossii?' [How to protect the eastern geostrategic facade of Russia?], *Nezavisimoye Voennoe Obozreniye*, no. 17, 1997, p. 4 (in Russian).
14. Trush: *loc. cit.* (note 12). See also: Larin, V.: 'Rossiya i Kitay na poroge tretyego tysyacheletiya: kto zhe budet otstaivat nashy natsionalnye interesy' [Russia and China on the threshold of the Third Millennium: who will protect Russia's national interests?], *Problemy Dalnego Vostoka*, no. 1, 1997, pp. 15-26 (in Russian).
15. Menon: *loc. cit.* (note 3), p. 112.
16. Zhirinovskiy, Vladimir: *Poslednyi Brosok na Yug* [Last Dash to South] (Moscow: LDPR, 1993) (in Russian); and 'Election 1995: Parties' Foreign Policy Views', *International Affairs* (Moscow), vol. 41, nos. 11-12 (1995), pp. 15-16.
17. *ibid.*, p. 13.
18. Stuart, Douglas T. & William T. Tow: 'A US Strategy for the Asia-Pacific', *Adelphi Paper* no. 299 (1995), pp. 16-17; *Jane's Defence Weekly*, vol. 23, no. 6 (11 February 1995), p. 32.
19. See in detail 'North Korea's Nuclear Program: Challenge and Opportunity for American Policy. A Report of the North Korea Working Group of the United States Institute of Peace' (Washington, DC: The United States Institute of Peace, 1994).
20. For the text of agreement see *Arms Control Today*, December 1994, p. 19.
21. Stuart & Tow: *op. cit.* (note 18), p. 31; Niksch, Larry A.: 'Opportunities and Challenges in Clinton's Confidence-Building Strategy Towards North Korea', *The Korean Journal of Defence Analysis*, vol. 6, no. 2 (Winter 1994), p. 151.
22. Sutter, Robert G. & Shirley Kan: 'China as a Security Concern in Asia: Perceptions, Assessment, and US Options', *CRS Report for Congress*, January 5, 1994 (Washington, DC: Congressional Research Service, 1994), p. 5.
23. Medeiros, Evan S.: 'China, Russia Plan to Go Ahead with Nuclear Reactor Sales to Iran', *Arms Control Today*, May 1995, p. 23.

24. See the Russian Foreign Ministry's statement in *Rossiyskaya Gazeta*, 2 October 1997, p. 7.
25. Rumer, B.: 'The Gathering Storm in Central Asia', *Orbis*, vol. 37, no. 1 (Winter 1993), p. 90.
26. *Jane's International Defence Review*, vol. 29, no. 8 (August 1996), p. 13.
27. Ivanov, Vladimir I.: 'Russia and the United States: Still Cold in Northeast Asia?', *Asia-Pacific Review*, vol. 2, no. 2 (Autumn/Winter 1995), p. 107.
28. *Ibid.*
29. Kerr, David: 'Opening and Closing the Sino-Russian Border: Trade, Regional Development and Political Interest in North-East Asia', *Europe-Asia Studies*, vol. 48, no. 6 (1996), pp. 934-939.
30. *Diplomaticheskiy Vestnik*, August 1996, pp. 38-40 (in Russian).
31. Matveyeva, Yelena: 'Russia's Far East: Tired, Cold and Ready for Independence', *Moscow News*, 30 Sept-6 Oct 1994, p. 13.
32. Portyakov, Vladimir: 'Kitaytzy Idut? Migratzionnaya Situatziya na Dalnem Vostoke Rossii' ['The Chinese Are Coming? The Migration Processes in Russia's Far East'], *Mezhdunarodnaya Zhizn*, vol. 42, no. 2 (February 1996), p. 80 (in Russian).
33. On international factors of Russia's regionalization see Sergounin, Alexander A.: *Russia's Regionalization: The External Dimension* (Nizhny Novgorod: University of Nizhny Novgorod Press, 1997).
34. Kutepova, Natalya: '"Gruppy Riska" i Problemy Zastoynoi Bezrabotitzy' ['"Risk groups" and the Problem of Stagnant Unemployment'], *Chelovek i Trud*, no. 10, 1993, p. 7 (in Russian).
35. Portyakov: *loc. cit.* (note 32), p. 83.
36. Balburov, Dmitry: 'Maritime Population Wants No "Fair Frontier" With China', *Moscow News*, no. 15 (18-24 April 1996), p. 4.
37. Portyakov: *loc. cit.* (note 32), p. 83.
38. *Diplomaticheskiy Vestnik*, August 1996, pp. 35-39 (in Russian).
39. *The Military Balance 1986-1987* (London: The International Institute for Strategic Studies, 1986), pp. 45-46; and *The Military Balance 1996-1997* (London: The International Institute for Strategic Studies, 1996), pp. 115, 118.
40. *The Washington Post*, 19 December 1992.
41. Trenin: *loc. cit.* (note 13), p. 4.
42. Fanlin, Li: 'Strategicheskoye partnerstvo' [Strategic partnership], *Rossiyskaya Gazeta*, 22 April 1997, p. 7 (in Russian).
43. See the text of declaration in *Rossiyskaya Gazeta*, 25 April 1997, p. 3 (in Russian).
44. Sismanidis, Roxane: 'China and the Post-Soviet Security Structure', *Asian Affairs. An American Review*, vol. 21, no. 1, (Spring 1994), p. 51.
45. *Izvestia*, 22 September 1994 (in Russian).
46. Gill, Bates & Taeho Kim: *China's Arms Acquisitions From Abroad: A Quest For 'Superb And Secret Weapons'*. SIPRI Research Report No. 11 (New York: Oxford University Press, 1995), p. 55.
47. Platkovsky, A. 'Oruzheynyi biznes na grani myasnoi voiny' (Weapon business on the brink of the pork war], *Izvestiya*, 15 March 1997 (in Russian).

48. *World Defence Almanac 1993-94 (The balance of military power)*, vol. 18, no. 1 (1994), p. 222.
49. *Far Eastern Economic Review*, 8 July 1993, p. 26; *The Washington Post*, 31 March 1993.
50. *Izvestia*, 30 March 1994 (in Russian).
51. Bain, William: 'Sino-Indian Military Modernization: the Potential for Destabilization', *Asian Affairs. An American Review*, vol. 21, no. 3 (Fall 1994), pp. 133-134.
52. *Jane's Defence Weekly*, vol. 25, no. 17 (24 April 1996), p. 10.
53. Baliev, A.: 'Obshiye interesy velikikhih sosedey' [Common interests of the great neighbours], *Nezavisimoye Voennoye Obozreniye*, no.10, 1997 (in Russian).
54. Dantes, Edmond: 'Changing Air Power Doctrines of Regional Military Powers', *Asian Defence Journal*, March 1993, p. 43.
55. *World Defence Almanac 1993-94*, p. 222; *Izvestia*, 5 March 1993 (in Russian); Gill, Bates: 'Trade, Production, and Control of Conventional Weapons in East Asia' (unpublished manuscript, 1995), p. 21.
56. *World Defence Almanac 1993-1994*, p. 222.
57. *The Military Balance 1993-1994* (London: The International Institute for Strategic Studies, 1993), p. 154; Cheung, T.M.: 'Sukois, Sams, Subs', *Far Eastern Economic Review*, 8 April 1993, p. 23.
58. Fulghum, D. & P. Proctor: 'Chinese Coveting Offensive Triad', *Aviation Week and Space Technology*, 21 September 1992, p. 21.
59. *Nizhegorodskiye Novosti*, 16 November 1996 (in Russian).
60. Mufson, S.: 'Muscle Flexing in Pacific', *International Herald Tribune*, 12 June 1997, p. 5.
61. *Jane's Defence Weekly*, vol. 25, no. 17 (24 April 1996), p.10.
62. Gill: *loc. cit.* (note 55), p. 21; *Jane's Defence Weekly*, vol. 21, no. 3 (22 January 1994), p. 3; *ibid.*, no. 7 (19 February 1994), p. 26.
63. Dantes: *loc. cit.* (note 54), p. 43; *SIPRI Yearbook 1993*, p. 501; *The Military Balance 1993-94*, p. 148; Bin Yu: 'Sino-Russian Military Relations', *Asian Survey*, vol. 33, no. 3 (1993), pp. 308-310; *Asian Security 1994-95* (Washington: Brassey's, 1994), p. 15; *Military and Arms Transfers News*, 17 June 1994, p. 5.
64. *Asian Recorder*, 27 Aug-2 September 1994, p. 24192.
65. *Military and Arms Transfers News*, 26 August 1994, p. 5.
66. Bain: *loc. cit.* (note 51), p. 135; Blank, Stephen J.: *Challenging the New World Order: the Arms Transfers Policies of the Russian Republic* (Carlisle Barracks, Pa.: Strategic Studies Institute, U.S. Army War College, 1993), pp. 53-60; idem: 'Russian Arms Exports and Asia', *Asian Defence Journal*, March 1994, p. 78; Davis, M.: 'Russia's Big Arms Sales Drive', *Asia-Pacific Defence Reporter*, Aug-Sept. 1994, p. 12.
67. *Jane's Intelligence Review*, July 1996, p. 330.
68. *The Military Balance 1996-97*, p. 181.
69. *World Defence Almanac 1993-94*, p. 222.
70. *Far Eastern Economic Review*, 8 July 1993, p. 26; *The Washington Post*, 31 March 1993.

71. *Jane's Defence Weekly*, vol. 27, no. 22 (4 June 1997), p. 12.
72. Allen, K., G. Krumel, J.D. Pollack: *China's Air Force Enters the 21st Century* (Santa Monica, Ca.: RAND, 1995), p. 159.
73. Jencks, H.: *Some Political and Military Implications of Soviet Warplane Sales to the PRC* (Kaohsiung: Sun Yat-Sen Center for Policy Studies, 1991), p. 15.
74. Bellows, Michael D. (ed.): *Asia in the 21st Century: Evolving Strategic Priorities* (Washington, DC: National Defense University Press, 1994), p. 95; Sismanidis: *loc. cit.* (note 44), p. 51; Hickey, Dennis van Vranken & Christopher C. Harmel: 'United States and China's Military Ties With the Russian Republics', *Asian Affairs*, vol. 20, no. 4 (Winter 1994), pp. 241-253; Bain: *loc. cit.* (note 51), p. 131-147; Afanasiev, Evgeny: 'Russia-China Relations: from Normalization to Partnership', *Far Eastern Affairs* (Moscow), no. 1 (1994), pp. 3-8; Taylor, R.I.D.: 'Chinese Policy towards the Asia-Pacific Region: Contemporary Perspectives', *Asian Affairs*, vol. 25, part 3 (October 1994), pp. 259-269; Shambaugh, David: 'The Insecurity of Security: the PLA's Evolving Doctrine and Threat Perceptions towards 2000', *Journal of Northeast Asian Studies*, vol. 13, no. 1 (Spring 1994), pp. 3-25; Munro, Ross: 'China's Waxing Spheres of Influence', *Orbis*, vol. 38, no. 4 (Fall 1994), pp. 585-605.
75. *World Defence Almanac 1993-94*, p. 221.
76. Bain: *loc. cit.* (note 51), p. 136.
77. *SIPRI database 1995*.
78. *Birzha*, 14 April 1994, p. 3 (in Russian).
79. Cheung: *loc. cit.* (note 57), p. 23; idem: 'China's Buying Spree', *Far Eastern Economic Review*, 8 July 1993, p. 26; Bain: *loc. cit.* (note 51), p. 137.
80. *Delo*, 7-13 April 1995 (in Russian).
81. Some accounts suggest that third and fourth boats are still under construction. See Markov, D.: 'More Details Surface of Rubin's "Kilo" Plans', *Jane's Intelligence Review*, May 1997, p. 215.
82. *Jane's Defence Weekly*, vol. 23, no. 19 (13 May 1995), p. 18.
83. *Asian Recorder*, 26 March-1 April 1995, p. 24672; *Jane's Defence Weekly*, vol. 23, no. 11 (18 March 1995), p. 3.
84. Preston, A.: 'Russian Weapons and Ships in the Asia-Pacific Region', *Asian Defence Journal*, December 1992, p. 60.
85. *Jane's International Defense Review*, September 1996, p. 9.
86. *Jane's Defence Weekly*, vol. 27, no. 2 (15 January 1997), p. 5.
87. Cheung, T.M.: *Growth of Chinese Naval Power* (Singapore: Institute of Southeast Asian Studies, 1990), p. 27.
88. *The New York Times*, 11 January 1993; Ball, Desmond: 'A New Era in Confidence Building: the Second-Track Process in the Asia/Pacific Region', *Security Dialogue*, no. 2, vol. 25 (June 1994), pp. 159-160; Chong-Pin Lin, 'Chinese Military Modernization: Perceptions, Progress, and Prospects', *Security Studies*, vol. 3, no. 4 (Summer 1994), p. 731.
89. *The New York Times*, 11 January 1993; Cheung: *op. cit.* (note 87), p. 27; Ryan, S.: 'The PLA Navy's Search for a Blue Water Capability', *Asian Defence Journal*, no. 5 (1994), p. 30. With Sovremenny class destroyer and Kilo class submarine programmes costing upwards of $2 billion, some analysts contend this means there

is little likelihood that the PLAN can find sufficient funds before the turn of the century to finance its proposed acquisition of an aircraft carrier. See *Jane's Defence Weekly*, vol. 27, no. 2 (15 January 1997), p. 5.
90. Beaver, Paul: 'China Looks to Europe for Carrier', *Jane's Intelligence & Jane's Sentinel Pointer*, December 1996, p. 1.
91. Yu: *loc. cit.* (note 63), pp. 302, 308.
92. Dantes: *loc. cit.* (note 54), p. 43; Ackerman, J. & M. Dunn: 'Chinese Airpower Revs Up', *Air Force Magazine*, July 1993, p. 59; *Military and Arms Transfers News*, 7 October 1994, p. 4.
93. *Jane's Defence Weekly*, vol. 27, no. 2 (15 January 1997), p. 5.
94. Beaver: *loc. cit.* (note 90), p. 1.
95. Bain: *loc. cit.* (note 51), p. 137.
96. Baliev: *loc. cit.* (note 53).
97. *Jane's Defence Weekly*, vol. 23, no. 18 (6 May 1995), p. 3.
98. Taeho Kim: *The Dynamics of Sino-Russian Military Relations: an Asian Perspective* (Taipei: Chinese Council of Advanced Policy Studies, 1994), p. 19.
99. Cheung: *loc. cit.* (note 79), p. 24.
100. Dantes: *loc. cit.* (note 54), p. 43; *World Defence Almanac 1993-94*, p. 222; *The Military Balance 1993-1994*, p. 148; Yu: *loc. cit.* (note 63), pp. 308-310.
101. Taylor, John W.R.: 'Gallery of Soviet Aerospace Weapons', *Air Force Magazine*, March 1990, p. 75.
102. Gallaher, Michael: 'China's Illusory Threat to the South China Sea', *International Security*, vol. 19, no. 1 (Summer 1994), p. 175; *Jane's Defence Weekly*, vol. 21, no. 7 (19 February 1994), p. 28.
103. *Jane's Defence Weekly*, vol. 24, no. 21 (25 November 1995), p. 4.
104. *SIPRI Yearbook 1993*, p. 389.
105. Kovalenko, Y.: 'V Kitaye Moskva stolknyetsya s interesami Frantsii' [Moscow will confront French interests in China], *Izvestiya*, 7 May 1997 (in Russian).
106. Lamson, J. & W. Bowen: 'One Arrow, Three Stars: China's MIRV Programme', *Jane's Intelligence Review*, June 1997, p. 267.
107. *Ibid.*
108. Cheung: *loc. cit.* (note 79), p. 24.
109. Hull, A. & D. Markov: 'Trends in the Arms Market', *Jane's Intelligence Review*, May 1997, p. 233.
110. 'Peking Recruits Russian Weapons Experts: Report', Central News Agency (Taipei), 29 December 1992; Hickey & Harmel: *op. cit.* (note 74), p. 243; *Wall Street Journal*, 14 October 1993; Shulong Chu: 'The Russian-US Military Balance in the Post-Cold War Asia-Pacific Region and the "China Threat"', *Journal of Northeast Asian Studies*, Spring 1994, pp. 89-90.
111. *Jane's Defence Weekly*, vol. 21, no. 7 (19 February 1994), p. 28.
112. Hull & Markov: *loc. cit.* (note 109), p. 234.
113. *Izvestia*, 19 October 1994 (in Russian).
114. Beaver, Paul: 'Russian Industry Feels the Cold', *Jane's Defence Weekly*, vol. 21, no. 18 (7 May 1994), p. 30.
115. *Nizhegorodskie Novosti*, 14 April 1995 (in Russian).

116. Klintworth, Gary: 'China and East Asia', in Ramesh Thakur & C. A. Thayer (eds.): *Reshaping Regional Relations: Asia-Pacific and the Former Soviet Union* (Boulder: Westview Press, 1993), p. 133.
117. Sismanidis, Op. cit., pp. 51-52.
118. Sergei Strokan: 'Moscow Balancing Two Koreas', *Moscow News*, no. 36 (9-15 September 1994), p. 5.
119. Cohen, J. & A. Peach: 'The Spread of Advanced Aircraft', in Randall W. Forsberg (eds.): *The Arms Production Dilemma* (Cambridge, MA: The MIT Press, 1994), p. 251.
120. *Jane's Defence Weekly*, vol. 27, no. 3 (22 January 1997), p. 12.
121. Cohen & Peach: *loc. cit.* (note 119), p. 251.
122. Hull & Markov: *loc. cit.* (note 109), p. 233.
123. Moody, R. A.: 'Armageddon for Hire', *Jane's International Defense Review*, February 1997, p. 22.
124. Hull & Markov: *loc. cit.* (note 109), p. 233.
125. Moody: *loc. cit.* (note 123), p. 22.
126. *Rossiyskaya Gazeta*, 26 April 1997, p. 3 (in Russian).
127. Blank: *op. cit.* (note 66), p. 64.
128. Hull & Markov: *loc. cit.* (note 109), p. 234.
129. *Ibid.*
130. *Jane's Defence Weekly*, vol. 25, no. 8 (21 February 1996), p. 15; *The Arms Control Reporter*, 1996 (Cambridge, MA: IDDS, 1996), p. B63.
131. *Literaturnaya Gazeta*, no. 45 (6 November 1996), p. 14 (in Russian).
132. *Rossiyskaya Gazeta*, 13 August 1996, p. 1 (in Russian).
133. *Jane's Defence Weekly*, vol. 26, no. 19 (6 November 1996), p. 17.
134. *Jane's Defence Weekly*, vol. 27, no. 2 (15 January 1997), p. 13.
135. *Jane's Defence Weekly*, vol. 26, no. 25 (18 December 1996), p. 11.
136. *Jane's Defence Weekly*, vol. 26, no. 19 (6 November 1996), p. 17.
137. *Asian Defence Journal*, January 1996, p. 75.
138. Desjardins, Marie-France: 'Rethinking Confidence-Building Measures', *Adelphi Papers*, no. 307 (1996), p. 18.
139. Menon: *loc. cit.* (note 3), p. 107.
140. Balburov: *loc. cit.* (note 36), p. 4.
141. *Jane's Intelligence Review*, June 1996, p. 280.
142. *Izvestia*, 15 April 1997 (in Russian).
143. *Rossiyskaya Gazeta*, 25 April 1997, p. 3 (in Russian).
144. Cited in *Jane's Defence Weekly*, vol. 27, no. 17 (30 April 1997), p. 13.
145. *Asian Recorder*, 6-12 August 1994, p. 24144.
146. *Kyodo News Service*, 12 July 1994; *NOD & Conversion*, no. 30 (September 1994), p. 42; *Military and Arms Transfers News*, 15 July 1994, p. 8.
147. *Jane's International Defence Review*, August 1996, p. 13.
148. Fanlin: *loc. cit.* (note 42), p. 7.
149. Harada, Chikahito: 'Russia and North-East Asia', *Adelphi Papers*, no. 310 (1997), p. 57.
150. Menon: *loc. cit.* (note 3), pp. 108-109.

151. Litovkin, V.: 'Kitayskaya armiya krepchaet russkim oruzhiem' [The Chinese army is getting stronger due to Russian arms], *Izvestiya*, Moscow, 25 April 1997 (in Russian).
152. *The Washington Times*, 21 October 1992.
153. Cheung, T.M.: 'Arm in arm', *Far Eastern Economic Review*, 12 November 1992, p. 28.
154. Blanche, Bruce: 'Progress on the Kurils Dispute', *Jane's Intelligence Review & Jane's Sentinel Pointer*, November 1996, p. 8.
155. Jordan: *loc. cit.* (note 3), p. 4.
156. Harada: *loc. cit.* (note 149), pp. 57-58.
157. *Ibid.*, pp. 66-67.
158. Desjardins: *loc. cit.* (note 138), p. 32; and Lasater: *op. cit.* (note 5), p. 141.
159. Odgaard, Liselotte: *The Reconstruction Process of the East Asian Regional Order: The Spratly Dispute* (Aarhus: Aarhus University Press, 1997), p. 9; Lasater: *op. cit.* (note 5), p. 140; and Acharya, Amitav: 'A New Regional Order in South-East Asia: ASEAN in the Post-Cold War Era', *Adelphi Paper*, no. 279 (1993).
160. Acharya, Amitav: 'A Regional Security Community in Southeast Asia?', in Desmond Ball (ed.): *The Transformation of Security in the Asia/Pacific Region* (London: Frank Cass, 1995), p. 187.
161. *Diplomaticheskiy Vestnik*, August 1996, pp. 36-40 (in Russian); and Zhiliaev, Boris: 'Partnership with ASEAN', *International Affairs* (Moscow), vol. 42, no. 4 (1996), pp. 39-42.
162. *Khrushchev Remembers: The Glasnost Tapes* (Boston: Little, Brown & Co., 1990), p. 89.
163. Harada: *loc. cit.* (note 149), p. 50.
164. *Komsomolskaya Pravda*, 27 May 1992 (in Russian).
165. Harada: *loc. cit.* (note 149), p. 52.
166. Blanche: *loc. cit.* (note 154), p. 8.
167. Jordan: *loc. cit.* (note 3), p. 4.
168. *The Economist*, 9 August 1997, p. 56.
169. Balburov: *loc. cit.* (note 36), p. 4.
170. Balburov: *loc. cit.* (note 36), pp. 4; and Menon: *loc. cit.* (note 3), p. 103.
171. Balburov: *loc. cit.* (note 36), p. 4.
172. Harada: *loc. cit.* (note 149), p. 41.
173. *Rossiyskaya Gazeta*, 4 March 1992 (in Russian).
174. *Izvestia*, 14 March 1992 (in Russian).
175. *Far Eastern Economic Review*, October 26, 1995, p. 16.
176. Yeh, Milton D.: 'Beijing's War of Words Causes Downturn in Cross-Strait Relations', *Issues and Studies*, vol. 31, no. 8 (August 1995), p. 122; *IBRU Boundary and Security Bulletin*, Autumn 1995, p. 16.
177. *The Independent*, 7 February 1996.
178. *Beijing Review*, no. 39 (13-19 May 1996), pp. 6-8.
179. Moiseyev, V.: 'Russia and the Korean Peninsula', *International Affairs*, vol. 42, no. 1 (Jan-Febr 1996), pp. 106-107.
180. Harada: *loc. cit.* (note 149), p. 66.

181. *Ibid.*, p. 64.
182. Reid, T.R.: 'Moscow, Seoul Forge New Relationship', *Washington Post*, 21 November 1992, p. A6.
183. *Jane's Defence Weekly*, vol. 27, no. 4 (29 January 1997), p. 14.
184. *Jane's Defence Weekly*, vol. 27, no. 7 (19 February 1997), p. 12.
185. Harada: *loc. cit.* (note 149), p. 69.

11 The US Role in East Asia

JONATHAN DEAN

The current US role and current US policy in East Asia are consistent with the United States' hopes for long-term developments in East Asia. Some Americans are today recommending that the United States seek to avoid ultimate direct military confrontation with a China determined to be the sole, dominant power in East Asia through a policy of containment, emphasizing a large US military presence in the area and a powerful Japan ranged at America's side.[1] However, majority US opinion today visualizes the chief US role in East Asia as assisting and urging the People's Republic of China to develop in the direction of becoming a world power willing to assume an equitable share of responsibility for maintaining world peace and world trade, and dealing with transnational problems like the environment. At the same time, if, as is probably, it seeks to follow this course, the US must seek to limit the numerous frictions, some of them quite dangerous, that will unavoidably attend this policy over the ten- or twenty-year period it would need to come to fruition.

COMPREHENSIVE ENGAGEMENT

Jeff Bader, Assistant US Secretary of State for East Asia, in an authoritative statement of US policy to China on 23 April 1997 before the House Committee on International Relations, described the overall aim in this way, 'We keep our eye on the long term goal of bringing China firmly into the international system as a responsible participant.' Bader's statement[2] contains a comprehensive statement of the current status of the US policy of 'comprehensive engagement' toward China. In distinction to Bader's description of current US policy, this chapter seeks to evaluate the dimensions of the long-term task of bringing China into the international system as a responsible partner, what the task might look like if it were carried out, and what the very real obstacles are to success.

Bringing China (and also Russia, because the same hopes apply here too) into the international system as responsible partners is clearly an extremely ambitious objective of daunting difficulty, an objective that has never been tried before in these dimensions. Is this objective another example of American Wilsonian idealism on an immense scale? Is it, as many foreign critics have complained, a hypocritical cover for old-fashioned hegemonialism, or is it a realistic course which conforms to the long-term interests both of China and the United States—and ultimately, of world peace? Perhaps American policy and the American role in East Asia is a combination of all three versions. In actuality, the US has carried out a policy of this kind before with considerable success, with Germany and Japan, but this was on a much smaller scale and both countries were defeated and occupied. Now, the US is trying it simultaneously with Russia and China, without a fraction of the control it was able to exercise over the defeated and occupied axis allies. In the case of China, the object of the policy is the world's most populous country, one with nearly unshakable conviction of the superiority of its own culture. Experience in the parallel goals with Russia thus far has been mixed. The US has invested too little in the relationship, and Russian leaders have often stated that the current relationship falls far short of partnership.

Moreover, the relationship with China that US policy would like to have requires on the part of America the self-discipline not to become overbearing and didactic, a self-restraint practised with only mixed success vis-à-vis Japan and Germany. By definition, the relationship will require from the United States the willingness at some point to relinquish dominant power and the leadership role. This is something the United States has not been able to do in Europe, with its consistent policy of maintaining and now expanding NATO as the chosen vehicle for US influence in Europe, while systematically repressing potential rival organizations like the Organization for Security and Cooperation in Europe and the Western European Union.

The projected relationship also requires from the junior partner very clear understanding of the objectives of the relationship, enormous self-discipline and self-restraint, and the capacity to digest repeated humiliations without choking on them or permitting domestic political forces to react violently. Germany and Japan have been able to do this, each in their own way. It is hard to visualize modern China in this role.

Just how ambitious the US objective is will become more clear as we seek here to break down the overall aim into subordinate objectives. It is also obvious that attempts to fulfil these objectives will encounter serious obstacles. Given the nature of the overall policy aim and of the obstacles to their fulfilment, the chance that this approach will be successful is less than one in two.

The China project fits into the pattern of earlier American efforts, not only those with Germany and Japan. During the past half century, the United States has been engaged in a restless search for global partners to confirm its own involvement in world affairs. In this search, Franklin Roosevelt placed his initial short-lived trust in China and Russia, then in the UN, then in the UK and France. President George Bush named Germany as a global partner of the US.

The US currently has only two such prospective partners, the European Union and Japan. Ironically, with its efforts to move into a partnership relationship with China and Russia, the US is back to Franklin Roosevelt's model for world order There are alternatives to this ambitious vision of partnership. Instead of the partnership relationship described above, the US could seek one of military containment as described at the outset, but such an approach directed at China would probably result in armed conflict at some point. A less ambitious policy confined to damage limitation and dealing with issues when and as they occur would probably encounter the same dangers over a still longer period.

THE OBJECTIVE BROKEN DOWN INTO COMPONENT ELEMENTS

SECURITY ISSUES

Cooperation in seeking solutions to regional security issues while avoiding direct military confrontation is a major part of the US objective. This means US and Chinese cooperation together with Russia, Japan and South Korea in urging North Korea into a long term peaceful transition that will avoid political implosion, anarchy, swarms of refugees or even bloody suicide by the North Korean regime. It also means Chinese restraint in pursuing territorial claims in the South China Sea and a measured tempo in developing Chinese capacity for force projection.

It means cooperation with the People's Republic of China and Taiwan to obtain for Taiwan the greatest possible degree of autonomy within the borders of China. A confederation structure, where both Chinese entities would have to agree for an action to take place in their joint name, and where both Taiwan and of course the People's Republic of China would have complete internal autonomy, is probably the best possible achievable solution. However, the obstacles here are formidable: neither side would now accept confederation as an official goal. Secessionist trends in Taiwan are gaining in strength, as are People's Republic of China's threats to use force to unify Taiwan with the mainland.

At the same time, no US president could stand by while the People's Republic of China reincorporated Taiwan by force without his administration and US status in Asia being very seriously discredited. Consequently, the reciprocal use of force by the United States in these circumstances is probable. On this issue, great restraint will be called for on both sides for an extended period.

It seems possible that the People's Republic of China will, in the long run, restrict political freedoms and representative democracy in Hong Kong and unlikely that it will be moved by external protests from doing so. If this takes place, it is likely to be a very sore point in the US-Chinese relationship because of heavy US economic and political involvement with Hong Kong. Annual US exports to Hong Kong are large, as are US investments there (they amount to about $14 billion in both cases). The 1992 Hong Kong Policy Act passed by the US Congress and signed by President Bush requires the administration to monitor Hong Kong's transition to rule by the People's Republic of China, including civil liberties, fundamental freedoms and the rule of law.

Another important area of potential cooperation and potential friction between the Chinese and US governments is disarmament and the operation of supplier controls in the sale of arms, including missiles and nuclear components. It is unlikely that China will meet American expectations in this area, whether because of resentment over American pressures, concerns over sovereignty, lack of understanding of the objectives of the program or ineffective domestic controls. China is suspected of avoiding controls in the sale to Pakistan of ballistic missiles and to Iran of chemical, biological and missile components and insists on continuing to produce anti-personnel landmines.

It will be a long time before the United States and Russia reduce their nuclear forces to the level well below 1,000 warheads each which could bring Chinese consent to negotiate its entry into a common regime of controls over nuclear weapons. China will pose other stiff conditions for participation in such a regime, such as a no-first-use commitment and restrictions on defence against long-range missiles that the US may find it very difficult to accept. However, despite the difficulties of this entire subject, the United States will continue to attempt to gain Chinese agreement to participation in an effective arms control regime. The next ten years may not bring much success in this area, which is likely to be another area of friction between the two governments.

In another important arena, the UN Security Council, the US will increasingly seek cooperation from China for peacekeeping efforts, many of which will involve infringement of or at least bending traditional concepts of sovereignty, an issue of particular sensitivity to China with its history of frequent foreign intervention in the nineteenth and early twentieth centuries. Agreement here will be incomplete. But because the US has become far more cautious as regards involvement in peacekeeping, it may be possible to avoid major frictions.

TRADE AND INVESTMENT

Trade is a further area of cooperation and tension between the Chinese and US governments. The United States is China's largest market by far with $60 billion imports annually by the US and with a lot of US investment in China, two facts which create considerable influence for the US. At the same time, trade is a source of considerable friction as the United States seeks to bring China, in a process similar to that with Japan over the last twenty years, to reduce the trade imbalance through opening China to American products. Because China is larger and more undisciplined than Japan, US success will only be partial. Energy and environment, especially China's huge consumption of polluting fossil fuel, are two related areas where the US is asking for cooperation from China with little material benefit in return.

HUMAN RIGHTS

The US administration will continue to press for improvement in China's performance on human rights. The Taiwan issue and human rights in Tibet play a major role here. The US will persevere in this area not only because of pressures to do so inside the American polity and because of a built-in desire to project national values, but because it correctly believes development of China toward a democracy would be of great assistance in achieving the American objective of encouraging China to become a responsible world power—and also in achieving the sub-goals described here: peaceful solution of regional disputes, disarmament, trade and cooperation in the UN Security Council. If China were a functioning democracy, for example, many peaceful solutions of the Taiwan problem would be possible that are not thinkable now, including peaceful secession like that of Slovakia from Czechoslovakia.

DIFFICULTIES

This point brings us directly to discussion of the specific difficulties and obstacles to achievement of the goals of this US policy toward China. Not only the human rights policy, but the requirements for transparency in trade, defence and disarmament probably are seen by Chinese political leaders as calling for the Chinese Communist Party to become the author of its own demise, giving up its monopoly on political power. This might happen if the Chinese party gradually made possible the emergence of pluralistic political groups and were willing to risk its own defeat in free elections, as the Polish and Hungarian communist parties did in the late 1980s and early 1990s. The Chinese Communist Party is very far from a decision to risk its hold on power. Instead, the most probable evolution in China away from one party rule by authoritarian communists is toward a nationalistic military-dominated authoritarianism, not popular democracy.

Movement here will be very slow and the human rights issue a source of continuing serious friction between the US and China. Yet some evolution is possible. The individual Chinese today has more personal latitude than has perhaps ever been the case in China. In the 1970s and 1980s, the introduction of economists and lawyers into the management structure of most state-owned industries in the Soviet Union expanded the group of scientists and technicians who wanted more scope for their own professional decisions and more protection against arbitrary interference. This process finally produced a civil society whose values were expressed by Mikhail Gorbachev. In China, this social role may be played by local government officials and enterprise managers.

Other obvious obstacles to the achievement of US policy aims toward China are lack of unity between the United States and the European Union countries and between the United States and Japan, where powerful social and political change is under way.

But the most important obstacle to achievement of a policy of bringing China to assume a role as a responsible world power is domestic political divisions inside the United States and inside China. Tough political infighting between Republicans and Democrats in the United States over China policy has taken place since the 1940s and is continuing. Any American president will come under immediate pressure from Republican conservatives to react decisively, probably with force, to any difficulty over Taiwan even if Taiwan's own actions have been its cause.

Speaker of the House Newt Gingrich's mischievous suggestion in April 1997 that the US administration extend most favoured nation treatment to China only for three or six month periods depending on Chinese actions in Hong Kong carries an inference that otherwise, Republicans will oppose extension of Most-Favoured-Nation status to China. Partisan shots by Congressional Republicans who do not now have responsibility for American foreign policy include uncharacteristic solicitude for human rights in China as well as historically founded concerns for Taiwan's independence of action. This is typical of the political minefield that any US president will have to traverse in deciding on policy toward China.

In China, participation in this policy will require great unity and coherence of policy from a polity, whether authoritarian or incipiently democratic, which is seeking to guide a very large country through a difficult transition to modernity. Moreover, achievement of the policy goals described here would require seven or eight successive US administrations over a thirty year period to maintain the same long-term policy and consistently to move toward it. This consistency of policy was possible for the American political system during the cold war, but only under the assumption that survival of the US was at stake throughout the period. The inescapable conclusion is that the domestic political process in the United States will not sustain such a policy in a disciplined and consistent way and that the same is also likely to be the case for China.

Conclusion

The most favourable conclusion possible from this list of formidable difficulties is that, if the US role and the US policy described at the outset of this paper is to have any measure of success, it will be partial, in fits and starts, and that success, if it ever comes, will take a great deal more time than the decade or two we arbitrarily assigned to it at the beginning of this article.

The huge dimensions of the US objective—no other country would have the power, the audacity, and the hubris to attempt it—will make the US role in East Asia an important one for the next generation. Perhaps—but this can only be a hope—the Chinese political leadership will at some point grasp and understand the concept of a global concert of major powers that the US is at least by implication proposing and will respond with its own policy of comprehensive engagement.

NOTES

1. See Bernstein, Richard & Ross Munro: 'China I: The Coming Conflict with America', *Foreign Affairs,* vol. 76, no. 2 (March/April 1997), pp. 18-32.
2. Available through USIS Washington file on the Internet.

About the Contributors

Jonathan Dean is Adviser for International Security Issues of the Union of Concerned Scientists, a large public interest organization. In over 35 years in the US foreign service, he worked mainly on East-West relations, disarmament, and peacekeeping. He has written several books on security and disarmament issues, most recently *Ending Europe's Wars. The Continuing Search for Peace and Security* (1994).

Owen Greene is Senior Lecturer in International Relations and Security Studies at the Department of Peace Studies, University of Bradford UK. He was trained in mathematics and physics, and worked for several years as a theoretical physicist at London Univeristy, Open University, and the Indian Institute of Science, Bangalore, India. For the last decade he has specialized in international security issues, including arms control, regional security, confidence-building measures and transparency arrangments, on which he has authored or co-authored or edited some ten books and over 100 research reports and articles.

Yong-Sup Han is a professor at the Korea National Defense University. He received BA and MA in political science from Seoul National University, MA from Harvard University and Ph.D in Public Policy from RAND Graduate School in 1991. Dr. Han worked for nuclear negotiation with North Korea as a staff member to the South-North Joint Nuclear Control Commission and had been the Special Advisor for the Korean Minister of National Defense in 1993. His publications include *Nuclear Disarmament and Non-Proliferation in Northeast Asia* (UNIDIR, 1995) and *Designing and Evaluating Conventional Arms Control Measures* (RAND, 1993).

Mitsuru Kurosawa is a professor of international law and international relations at Osaka School of International Public Policy, Osaka University, Japan. He has written some books and many articles on nuclear disarmament, nuclear non-proliferation, peace-keeping and security issues in Northeast Asia.

Cheng-yi Lin is Research Fellow and Deputy Director of the Institute of European and American Studies, Academia Sinica. He has published in the area of American policy towards Taiwan and China. One of his latest papers appeared in the *Asian Survey*.

Joon Num Mak is currently Director of Research at the Maritime Institute of Malaysia (MIMA) in Kuala Lumpur and heads the institute's Centre for Maritime Security and Diplomacy. His research interests centre around regional security issues, with special emphases on defence and naval strategies of Asian countries.

Bjørn Møller holds an MA in History and a Ph.D. in Political Science, both from the University of Copenhagen. He is senior research fellow at the Copenhagen Peace Research Institute (COPRI) and lecturer at the Institute of Political Science, University of Copenhagen, and Secretary General of the International Peace Research Association (IPRA). He is the author of the following books: *Resolving the Security Dilemma in Europe* (1991), *Common Security and Nonoffensive Defense* (1992) and *Dictionary of Alternative Defense* (1995).

Alexander A. Sergounin, Ph.D., is Professor of Political Science at the Institute of History, University of Nizhny Novgorod, Russia, and has been guest researcher at the Copenhagen Peace Research Institute (COPRI) 1996-98. He is the author of several books and articles in professional journals on international relations history and theory, including (with Vinay Kumar Malhotra) *Theories and Approaches to International Relations* (1997).

Yitzhak Shichor (Ph.D. the London School of Economics and Political Science) is Michael William Lipson Associate Professor of Chinese Studies and Political Science at the Hebrew University of Jerusalem, and Academic Head, Tel-Hai College, Israel. Formerly Executive Director of the Truman Institute for the Advancement of Peace, Dean of Students, and Chairman of the Departments of East Asian Studies and Political Science, he has written extensively on China's Middle Eastern policy and its defence reforms. In addition to studying the impact of post-Mao reforms on Xinjiang he is currently engaged in a book-length research of China's military-to-civilian conversion.

Jasjit Singh (AVSM, VrC, VM), Air Commodore (ret.) is former Director of Operations of the Indian Air Force and, since 1987, Director of the Institute for Defence Studies and Analyses, New Delhi. He is the author of *Air Power in Modern Warfare* and has published extensively on strategic and security issues. He is a visiting lecturer at defence and war colleges in India and abroad, and consultant to the Standing Committee of Defence of the Indian parliament.

Recent Books on Asia

BJØRN MØLLER

Acharya, Amitav: *An Arms Race in Post-Cold War South-East Asia: Prospects for Control* (Singapore: Institute of Southeast Asian Studies, 1994).
Akaha, Tsuneo (ed.): *Politics and Economics in the Russian Far East. Changing Ties with Asia-Pacific* (London: Routledge, 1997).
Akaha, Tsuneo & Frank Langdon (eds.): *Japan in the Posthegemonic World* (Boulder, CO: Lynne Rienner, 1993).
Bajpai, Kanti P. & Stephen P. Cohen (eds.): *South Asia After the Cold War. International Perspectives* (Boulder: Westview Press, 1993).
Ball, Desmond (ed.): *The Transformation of Security in the Asia-Pacific Region* (London: Frank Cass, 1996).
Ball, Desmond and Cathy Downes (eds.): *Security and Defence. Pacific and Global Perspectives* (Sydney: Allen & Unwin, 1990).
Ball, Desmond & Pauline Kerr: *Presumptive Engagement. Australia's Asia-Pacific Security Policy in the 1990s* (London: Allan & Unwin, 1996).
Barnett, Robert W.: *Beyond War. Japan's Concept of Comprehensive National Security* (Washington: Brassey's, 1984).
Baum, Richard: *Burying Mao. Chinese Politics in the Age of Deng Xiaoping* (Princeton, N.J.: Princeton University Press, 1994).
Bienen, Henry (ed.): *Power, Economics, and Security. The United States and Japan in Focus* (Boulder: Westview Press, 1992).
Bodansky, Yossef: *Crisis in: Korea* (New York: SPI Books, 1994).
Bose, Sumantra: *The Challenge in Kashmir. Democracy, Self-Determination and a Just Peace* (New Delhi: Sage Publications, 1997).
Bridges, Brian: *Japan and Korea in the 1990s. From Antagonism to Adjustment* (Aldershot: Edward Elgar, 1993).
Brönnelhörster, Jörn & John Frankenstein (eds.): *Mixed Motives, Uncertain Outcomes. Defense Conversion in China* (Boulder: Lynne Rienner, 1997).
Brown, Michael E. & Sumit Ganguly (eds.): *Government Policies and Ethnic Relations in Asia and the Pacific* (Cambridge, MA: MIT Press, 1997).
Brown, Michael E., Sean M. Lynn-Jones & Steven E. Miller (eds.): *East Asian Security. An International Security Reader* (Cambridge, MA: MIT Press, 1996).
Bullard, Monte: *The Soldier and the Citizen. The Role of the Military in Taiwan's Development* (Armonk, NY: M.E. Sharpe, 1997).
Campos, Jose Edgardo & Hilton L. Root: *The Key to the Asian Miracle. Making Shared Growth Credible* (Washington, D.C.: Brookings, 1996).
Carpenter, William M. & David G. Wiencek: *Asian Security Handbook. An Assessment of Political-Security Issues in the Asia-Pacific Region* (Armonk, NY: M.E. Sharpe, 1997).

Chalmers, Malcolm: *Confidence Building in South-East Asia* (Boulder: Westview Press, 1996).

Chalmers, Malcolm, Owen Greene & Xie Zhiqiong (eds.): *Asia Pacific Security and the UN* (Bradford: University of Bradford, Dep. of Peace Studies, 1995).

Changing U.S.-Japan Relations. Reports of the Carnegie Endowment and GISPRI Study Groups (Washington, D.C.: Carnegie Endowment for International Peace, 1995).

Chee, Chan Heng (ed.): *The New Asia-Pacific Order* (Singapore: Institute of Southeast Asian Studies, 1997).

Cheng, Tun-jen, Chi Huang & Samuel S.G. Wu (eds.): *Inherited Rivalry. Conflict Across the Taiwan Straits* (Boulder, CO: Lynne Rienner Publishers, 1995).

Chinworth, Michael W.: *Inside Japan's Defense. Technology, Economics and Strategy* (Washington, D.C.: Brassey's, 1992).

Coulmy, Daniel: 'Le Japon et sa défense', *Dossiers*, no. 43 (Paris: Fondation pour les études de défense nationale, 1991).

Cunha, Derek da (ed.): *The Evolving Pacific Power Structure* (Singapore: Institute of Southeast Asian Studies, 1996).

Curtis, Gerald L. (ed.): *The United States, Japan, and Asia. Challenges for U.S. Policy* (New York: W.W. Norton & Co., 1994).

Defence Agency: *Defence of Japan* (Tokyo: The Japan Times, 1990).

Dellios, Rosita: *Modern Chinese Defence Strategy. Present Developments, Future Directions* (Houndmills: Macmillan, 1989).

Dittmer, Lowell & Samuel S. Kim (eds.): *China's Quest for National Identity* (Ithaca: Cornell University Press, 1993).

Domange, J.M.: *Le Réarmement du Japon* (Paris: Fondations pour les études de défense nationale, 1985).

Dore, Ronald: *Japan, Internationalism and the UN* (London: Routledge, 1997).

Drifte, Reinhard: *Japan's Rise to International Responsibilities. The Case of Arms Control* (London: Athlone, 1990).

Faust, John R. & Judith F. Kornberg: *China in World Politics* (Boulder, CO: Lynne Rienner Publishers, 1995).

Flassbeck, Heiner & Gustav A. Horn (eds.): *German Unification: an Example for Korea?* (Aldershot: Dartmouth, 1996).

Friedman, George & Meredith Lebard: *The Coming War With Japan* (New York: St. Martin's Press, 1991).

Funabashi, Yoichi (ed.): *Japan's International Agenda* (New York: New York University Press, 1994).

Ganguly, Sumit & Ted Greenwood (eds.): *Mending Fences. Confidence- and Security-Building Measures in South Asia* (Boulder: Westview Press, 1996).

Ganguly, Sumit: *The Origins of War in South Asia. Indo-Pakistani Conflicts Since 1947* (Boulder, CO: Westview Press, 1994).

Garby, Craig C. & Mary Brown Bullock (eds.): *Japan. A New Kind of Superpower*

(Baltimore: John Hopkins University Press, 1994).
Garver, John W.: *The Sino-American Alliance. Nationalist China and American Cold War Strategy in Asia* (Armonk, NY: M.E. Sharpe, 1997).
Garver, John W.: *The Sino-American Alliance. Nationalist China and American Cold War Strategy in Asia* (Armonk, NY: M.E. Sharpe, 1997).
Gill, Bates & Taeho Kim: *China's Arms Acquisitions from Abroad: A Quest for 'Superb and Secret Weapons'*. SIPRI Research Report, no. 11 (Oxford: Oxford University Press, 1995).
Godement, François: *The New Asian Renaissance. From Colonialism to the Post-Cold War* (London: Routledge, 1997).
Gong, Gerrit W.: *Remembering and Forgetting: The Legacy of War and Peace in East Asia* (Washington, DC: Center for Strategic and International Studies, 1996).
Goodman, David S.G. & Gerald Segal (eds.): *China Deconstructs. Politics, Trade and Regionalism* (London: Routledge, 1994).
Hänggi, Heiner: *Neutralität in Südostasien. Das Projekt einer Zone des Friedens, der Freiheit und der Neutralität* (Bern: Verlag Paul Haupt, 1993).
Harris, Stuart & Gary Klintworth (eds.): *China as a Great Power. Myths, Realities and Challenges in the Asia-Pacific Region* (New York: St. Martin's Press, 1995).
Harrison, Selig S. (ed.): *Japan's Nuclear Future. The Plutonium Debate and East Asian Security* (Washington, D.C.: The Carnegie Endowment, 1996).
Henckaerts, Jean-Marie (ed.): *The International Status of Taiwan in the New World Order* (London: Kluwer Law International, 1996).
Hook, Glenn D.: *Militarisation and Demilitarisation in Contemporary Japan* (London: Routledge, 1996).
Hopkins, John C. & Weixing Hu (eds.): *Strategic Views from the Second Tier. The Nuclear Weapons Policies of France, Britain and China* (New Brunswick: Transaction Publishers, 1996).
Hsiung, James C. (ed.): *Asia Pacific in the New World Politics* (Boulder: Lynne Rienner Publishers, 1993).
Huber, Thomas M.: *Strategic Economy in Japan* (Boulder: Westview Press, 1994).
Hughes, Christopher: *Taiwan and Chinese Nationalism. National Identity and Status in International Society* (London: Routledge, 1997).
Hwang, Bypong-Moo & Yong-Sup Han (eds.): *Korean Security Policies Toward Peace and Unification*, KAIS International Conference Series, no. 4 (Seoul: Korean Association of International Studies, 1996).
IDSA (Institute for Defence Studies and Analyses): *Asian Strategic Review 1996-97* (New Delhi: Institute for Defence Studies and Analyses, 1997).
Inoguchi, Takashi: *Japan's International Relations* (London: Pinter, 1991).
Inoguchi, Takashi & Grant B. Stillman (eds): *North-East Asian Regional Security. The Role of International Institutions* (Tokyo: United Nations University Press,

1996).

Jordan, Amos A. (ed.): *Korean Unification. Implications for Northeast Asia* (Boulder, CO: Westview Press, 1993).

Katzenstein, Peter J.: *Cultural Norms and National Security. Police and Military in Postwar Japan* (Ithaca: Cornell University Press, 1996).

Kihl, Young Whan & Peter Hayes (eds.): *Peace and Security in Northeast Asia. The Nuclear Issue and the Korean Peninsula* (Armonk, NY: M.E. Sharpe, 1997).

Kihl, Young Whan (ed.): *Korea and the World. Beyond the Cold War* (Boulder: Westview Press, 1994).

Kim, Ilpyong J. (ed.): *The Strategic Triangle. China, the United States and the Soviet Union* (New York: Paragon House, 1987).

King, Peter & Yoichi Kibata (eds.): *Peace Building in the Asia Pacific Region: Perspectives from Japan and Australia* (St. Leonards: Allen & Unwin, 1996).

Krepon, Michael & Amit Sevak (eds.): *Crisis Prevention, Confidence Building, and Reconciliation in South Asia* (New York: St. Martin's Press, 1996).

Kwak, Tae-Hwan & Edward A. Olsen (eds.): *The Major Powers of Northeast Asia: Seeking Peace and Security* (Boulder: Lynne Rienner, 1996).

Larkin, Bruce: *Nuclear Designs. Great Britain, France and China in the Global Governance of Nuclear Arms* (New Brunswick: Transaction Publishers, 1995).

Lasater, Martin L.: *The New Pacific Community: U.S Strategic Options in Asia* (Boulder, CO: Westview Press, 1996).

Lee, Suk Jung: *Ending the Last Cold War. Korean Arms Control and Security in Northeast Asia* (Aldershot: Ashgate, 1997).

Lele, Jayant & Kwasi Ofori-Yebotah (eds.): *Unravelling the Asian Miracle* (Aldershot: Dartmouth, 1996).

Leng, Tse-Kang: *The Taiwan-China Connection. Democracy and Development across the Taiwan Straits* (Boulder: Westview Press, 1996).

Lewis, John Wilson & Xue Litai: *China's Strategic Seapower. The Politics of Force Modernization in the Nuclear Age* (Stanford: Stanford University Press, 1994).

Lincoln, Edward J.: *Japan's New Global Role* (Washington, D.C.: The Brookings Institution, 1993).

Little, David: *Sri Lanka. The Invention of Enmity* (Washington, D.C.: United States Institute of Peace Press, 1994).

Looney, Robert E. & David Winterford: *Economic Causes and Consequences of Defense Expenditures in the Middle East and South Asia* (Boulder: Westview Press, 1995).

Lorell, Mark: *Troubled Partnership. A History of US-Japan Collaboration on the FS-X Fighter* (New Brunswick: Transaction Publishers, 1996).

Lowry, Robert: *The Armed Forces of Indonesia* (London: Allan & Unwin, 1996).

Mack, Andrew & John Ravenhill (eds.): *Pacific Cooperation: Building Economic and Security Regimes in the Asia-Pacific Region Asia* (Boulder, CO: Westview

Press, 1995).
Mack, Andrew & Paul Keal (eds.): *Security and Arms Control in the North Pacific* (Sydney: Allen & Unwin, 1988).
MacLear, Michael: *Vietnam: The Ten Thousand Day War*, (London: Thames Methuen, 1981).
Mandelbaum, Michael (ed.): *The Strategic Quadrangle: Japan, China, Russia and the United States in East Asia* (New York: Council on Foreign Relations Press, 1995).
Matthews, Ron & Keisuke Matsuyama (eds.): *Japan's Military Renaissance?* (New York: St. Martin's Press, 1993).
Mazarr, Michael J.: *North Korea and the Bomb. A Case Study in Nonproliferation* (New York: St. Martin's Press, 1994).
McCann, David (ed.): *Korea Briefing. Toward Unification* (Armonk, NY: M.E. Sharpe, 1997).
McInnes, Colin & Mark C. Rolls (eds.): *Post-Cold War Security Issues in the Asia-Pacific Region* (London: Frank Cass, 1994).
Mendl, Wolf: *Japan's Asia Policy. Regional Security and Global Interests* (London: Routledge, 1995).
Millar, T.B. & James Walter (ed.): *Asian-Pacific Security after the Cold War* (St. Leonards, Australia: Allen & Unwin and London: UCL Press, 1993).
Miyoshi, Masao: *Off Center. Power and Culture Relations between Japan and the United States* (Cambridge, MA: Harvard University Press, 1991).
Nathan, Andrew J. & Robert S. Ross: *The Great Wall and the Empty Fortress: China's Search for Security* (New York: W.W. Norton & Co., 1997).
Ok, Tae Wan & Gerrit W. Gong (eds.) *Change and Challenge on the Korean Peninsula: Past, Present and Future* (Seoul: RINU, 1996).
Olcott, Martha Brill: *Central Asia's New States. Independence, Foreign Policy, and Regional Security* (Washington, DC: United States Institute for Peace, 1996).
Park, Han S.: *North Korea. Ideology, Politics, Economy* (Englewood Cliffs, NJ: Prentice Hall, 1996).
Pollack, Jonathan & Young Koo Cha: *A New Alliance for the Next Century. The Future of U.S.-Korean Security Cooperation* (Santa Monica, CA: RAND, 1995).
Regional Outlook: Southeast Asia 1997-98 (Singapore: Institute of Southeast Asian Studies, 1997).
Renwick, Neil: *Japan's Alliance Politics and Defence Production* (New York: St. Martin's Press, 1995).
Robinson, Thomas W. & David Shambaugh (eds.): *Chinese Foreign Policy. Theory and Practice* (Oxford: Clarendon Press, 1995).
Rosen, Stephen Peter: *Societies and Military Power: India and Its Armies* (Ithaca: Cornell University Press, 1996).
Ross, Robert S. (ed.): *East Asia in Transition: Toward a New Regional Order* (London: M.E. Sharpe and Singapore: Institute of Southeast Asian Studies,

1995).

Roy-Chaudury, Rahul: *Sea Power and Indian Security* (London: Brassey's, 1995).

Rupesinghe, Kumar & Khawar Mumtaz (eds.): *Internal Conflicts in South Asia* (London: Sage, 1996).

Samuels, Richard J.: *'Rich Nation, Strong Army'. National Security and the Technological Transformation of Japan* (Ithaca, NY: Cornell University Press, 1994).

Sasae, Kenichiro: 'Rethinking Japan-US Relations', *Adelphi Paper*, no. 292 (1994).

Sato, Ryuzo: *The Crysanthemum and the Eagle. The Future of US-Japan Relations* (New York: New York University Press, 1994).

Segal, Gerald: *Rethinking the Pacific* (Oxford: Clarendon Paperbacks, 1991).

Shafquat, Saeed: *Civil-Military Relations in Pakistan* (Boulder: Westview Press, 1997).

Simons, Geoff: *Korea. The Search for Sovereignty* (Houndmills, Basingstoke: Macmillan, 1995).

Smith, Hugh & Anthony Bergin (eds.): *Naval Power in the Pacific Toward the Year 2000* (Boulder & London: Lynne Rienner Publishers, 1993).

Smith, Chris: *India's Ad Hoc Arsenal. Directions or Drift in Defence Policy?* (Oxford: Oxford University Press, 1994).

Southeast Asian Affairs 1994 (Singapore: Institute of Southeast Asian Studies, 1994).

Sridharan, Kripa: *The ASEAN Region in India's Foreign Policy* (Aldershot: Dartmouth, 1996).

Stueck, William: *The Korean War. An International History* (Princeton, NJ: Princeton University Press, 1995).

Tang, James T.H. (ed.): *Human Rights and International Relations in Asia* (London: Pinter, 1995).

Thakur, Ramesh & Carlyle A. Thayer (eds.): *Reshaping Regional Relations. Asia-Pacific and the Former Soviet Union* (Boulder: Westview Press, 1993).

Thayer, Carlyle A.: *The Vietnam People's Army Under Doi Moi* (Singapore: Institute of Southeast Asian Studies, 1994).

The United States, Japan, and the Future of Nuclear Weapons. Report of the U.S.-Japan Study Group on Arms Control and Non-Proliferation After the Cold War (Washington, D.C.: Carnegie Endowment for International Peace, 1995).

Unger, Danny & Paul Blackburn (eds.): *Japan's Emerging Global Role* (Boulder and London: Lynne Rienner, 1993).

Weinbaum, Marvin G. & Chetan Kumar (eds.): *South Asia Approaches the Millenium. Reexaming National Security* (Boulder, CO: Westview Press, 1995).

Winrow, Gareth: *Turkey in Post-Soviet Central Asia* (London: Royal Institute of International Affairs, 1995).

Wurfel, David & Bruce Burton (eds.): *Southeast Asia in the New World Order. The Political Economy of a Dynamic Region* (New York: St. Martin's Press, 1996).

Yahuda, Michael: *The International Politics of Asia-Pacific 1945-1995* (London: Routledge, 1996).

Yang, Maysing H. (ed.): *Taiwan's Expanding Role in the International Arena* (Armonk, NY: M.E. Sharpe, 1997).

Yasutomo, Dennis: *The New Multilateralism in Japan's Foreign Policy* (Houndmills: Macmillan, 1995).

Zhang, Ming: *Major Powers at a Crossroads. Economic Interdependence and an Asia Pacific Security Community* (Boulder, CO: Lynne Rienner Publishers, 1995).

Zhao, Suisheng: *Power Competition in East Asia. From the Old Chinese World Order to the Post-Cold War Regional Multipolarity* (New York: St. Martin's Press, 1997).

Acronyms

ABM	Anti-Ballistic Missile Treaty
AEW	Airborne Early Warning
AFTA	ASEAN Free Trade Area
AIFV	Armoured Infantry Fighting Vehicle
APC	Armoured Personnel Carrier
APEC	Asia-Pacific Economic Cooperation
ARATS	Association for Relations Across the Taiwan Strait
ARF	ASEAN Regional Forum
ARF-SOM	ASEAN Regional Forum, Senior Officials Meetings
ASEAN	Association of South-East Asian Nations
ASEAN-PMC	ASEAN Post-Ministerial Conference
ASIATOM	Asia Atomic Energy Community
ASW	Anti-Submarine Warfare
BMD	Ballistic Missile Defence
C^4I	Command, Control, Communications, Computer and Intelligence
CAPUMIT	China Association for the Peaceful Use of Military Industrial Technology
CBM	Confidence-Building Measure
CCP	Chinese Communist Party
CIS	Commonwealth of Independent States
CNNC	China National Nuclear Corporation
COSTIND	Commission of Science, Technology, and Industry for National Defence
CSBM	Confidence and Security-Building Measure
CSCA	Conference on Security and Cooperation in Asia
CSCAP	Council for Security Cooperation in the Asia-Pacific
CSCE	Conference on Security and Cooperation in Europe
CTBT	Comprehensive Test Ban Treaty
DMZ	Demilitarized Zone
DPP	Democratic Progressive Party
DPRK	Democratic People's Republic of Korea
EEZ	Exclusive Economic Zone
ETBT	Explosive Test Ban Treaty
EURATOM	European Atomic Energy Community
GDP	Gross Domestic Product
GDR	German Democratic Republic
GNP	Gross National Product
IAEA	International Atomic Energy Agency
ICBM	Inter-Continental Ballistic Missile

INF	Intermediate-Range Nuclear Forces
KEDO	Korean Peninsula Energy Development Organization
KMT	Kuomintang
LDPR	Liberal Democratic Party of Russia
MBT	Main Battle Tank
MILEX	Military Expenditure
MIRV	Multiple Independently-Targetted Reentry Vehicle
MTCR	Missile Technology Control Regime
NATO	North Atlantic Treaty Organization
NEAATOM	North-East Asian Atomic Energy Community
NPT	Non-Proliferation Treaty
NWFZ	Nuclear Weapons-Free Zone
OSCE	Organization for Security and Cooperation in Europe
PACATOM	Pacific Atomic Energy Community
PLA	People's Liberation Army
PLAAF	PLA Air Force
PLAN	PLA Navy
PNE	Peaceful Nuclear Explosion
PRC	People's Republic of China
RMA	Revolution in Military Affairs
ROC	Republic of China
ROK	Republic of Korea
SAARC	South Asian Association for Regional Cooperation
SDF	Self-Defence Forces
SEANWFZ	South-East Asian Nuclear Weapons-Free Zone
SEF	Straits Exchange Foundation
SLOC	Sea Lines of Communication
START	Strategic Arms Limitation Treaty
WMD	Weapons of Mass Destruction
WWI	World War One
ZOPFAN	Zone of Peace, Freedom and Neutrality

Index

APEC 3, 46-47, 227
ARF 3, 10, 16, 38-40, 43-48, 77, 80, 84, 88, 97, 113, 131, 204, 227, 246, 247
ASEAN iv, 3, 5, 8, 9, 13-16, 19, 38, 41-43, 47-48, 77-81, 83-90, 97, 100, 113, 131, 185, 188, 204, 227-228, 246-247
ASEAN Regional Forum 3, 16, 38, 42, 47, 77, 88, 97, 113, 131, 204, 227, 246
Australia 41, 54, 99-100, 104, 188, 228
Brunei 13, 54, 79
Cambodia 4, 14-16, 41, 43, 54, 79, 84, 100
China iv, 2-4, 4-11, 13-16, 18, 38, 40-48, 50, 51, 54, 59, 61, 64, 66-70, 72-73, 79, 80, 82-84, 87, 90, 97-101, 103, 105, 109, 113, 117-121, 131-132, 137-140, 141-152, 157, 162, 164-165, 170-185, 187-189, 203-207, 210-214, 221-228, 230-239, 242-251, 253-255, 263-268
CIS 221, 228, 244, 245
DPRK 7, 11-12, 54, 102, 122-124, 126-127, 129, 132, 164, 168, 174, 188, 239-241, 247, 252, 253
Germany 51, 58, 117, 164-165, 167, 169, 170, 181, 210
Hong Kong 146, 164, 171-172, 177-178, 182, 214, 238, 265, 268
India iv, 3-6, 8, 15-18, 38, 42, 57, 59-62, 64-66, 68-73, 161, 188, 231, 235

Indonesia 2, 4, 13, 54, 79, 83-85, 87, 99, 173
Japan 4-11, 16, 18, 41, 46, 54, 79-80, 84, 93-99, 103-105, 109, 131, 170-172, 185, 188, 201, 222-224, 226-227, 232, 240, 243, 245, 247-249, 252, 255, 263-267
Laos 4, 14-16, 41, 43, 54
Macao 9, 164, 171-172, 177
Malaysia 2, 4, 13, 54, 77, 79, 85-88, 90, 99, 162, 173, 271
Mongolia 7, 41, 49, 54, 103, 173, 230, 243, 249
Myanmar 8, 14-16, 41, 43, 54, 84, 173
NATO 13-14, 16, 47, 71, 94, 170, 222, 231-232, 235, 251, 264
North Korea 2, 6, 11-12, 41, 43, 45-46, 80, 95, 96, 99, 101-102, 105, 109-110, 112-130, 132, 164, 168, 173, 224-225, 239-240, 242, 251-253, 265
Nuclear-Weapons-Free zone 13, 16, 168
Pakistan 3-6, 16-18, 42, 54, 59, 64-65, 67-69, 72-73, 161, 163, 186, 225, 266
PRC 8, 47, 139, 145, 149, 152, 164, 166, 170, 172-185, 187-189, 199-205, 207-214, 224-225, 228, 231, 233-234, 236-239, 244-245, 250-251, 254
ROC 164, 199-205, 207-214
ROK 7, 11-12, 114, 117, 122-124, 126, 129-130, 132, 164, 166, 168, 174, 188, 241-242, 247, 252-253

Russia v, vii, 3-4, 6-9, 13, 37-38, 41, 46, 49, 50, 61-62, 66, 97-99, 103, 105, 117-118, 128, 131, 149, 170, 188, 200, 221-234, 236-245, 247-252, 252-255, 263-266

South Korea 11, 18, 41, 45-46, 96, 99, 101-102, 104, 109-110, 112, 114-130, 132, 164, 185, 221, 227, 239-243, 246, 249, 251-252, 265

Taiwan iv, vii, 2-5, 9, 11, 14, 18, 41, 43, 45, 47-48, 80, 95, 97, 99, 103, 157, 162, 164, 166, 171-189, 199-214, 223-224, 226, 232, 234-235, 247, 250-251, 255, 265, 267-268

Thailand 4, 13, 54, 79, 84-85, 87, 99, 173, 242

UK 50, 51, 64, 71, 162, 233, 264, 271

United Nations vii, 3, 7, 10, 11, 15, 39-43, 47, 51, 55, 60, 62-63, 65, 72, 83, 90, 94, 104, 114, 119, 126-127, 171, 173-175, 177, 181, 184, 187, 189, 203-204, 246, 264, 266-267

United States 2, 4-6, 8, 10, 16, 18, 37, 41, 44-47, 49-51, 55, 58, 62, 65-67, 70, 84, 88, 93-96, 99-102, 105, 109-110, 112, 115-117, 119-121, 124-132, 138, 152, 165, 167, 172, 174-175, 180, 183, 185-188, 199, 201, 203-204, 208-209, 211-213, 221-222, 224, 226, 228, 234, 237-238, 244, 251, 263-268

Vietnam 3-5, 14-16, 54, 79, 84, 99, 145, 148, 164, 173-174, 228

ZOPFAN 16, 100, 246, 282